THE ISLAMIC CONQUESTS IN ASIA

GEW SOCIAL SCIENCES
GROUP

THE ISLAMIC CONQUESTS IN ASIA

Hichem Karoui (Ed.)

Global East-West (London)

Copyright © 2024 by GEW Social Sciences Group
Hichem Karoui (Research Director and Editor)
GEW Reports and Analyses (The Voice of the Mediterranean)
Global East-West
All rights reserved.

All rights reserved. No part of this book may be reproduced in any manner whatsoever without written permission except in the case of brief quotations embodied in critical articles and reviews.

First Printing, 2024

CONTENTS

I
Introduction to the Islamic conquests in Asia

— Overview of the Islamic conquests in Asia
13

— Importance of examining these conquests in the broader context of Islamic history
25

— The historical significance of Islamic conquests
38

Notes and References
51

II
The Conquest of Persia

— Geopolitical conditions in Persia
73

— Sassanian Empire's response
85

— Role of religion, economics, and politics
98

CONTENTS

- Main routes of Islamic expansion
  110

- Reaction of Nomadic Societies
  122

- Notable Military Commanders
  134

Notes and References
144

III

The Conquest of the Indian Subcontinent

- Religious and cultural dynamics in India
  163

- Response of Indian Rulers and Societies
  175

- Key military figures
  188

- Long-term consequences of Islamic rule
  200

Notes and References
211

IV

The Campaigns in Southeast Asia

- Interaction of diverse societies with Islam
  230

CONTENTS

– Objectives of Islamic expansion
241

Notes and References
254

V
The Challenges of Conquering China

– Diplomatic and military challenges
278

– Prominent military leaders
303

Notes and references
314

vi – The Legacy of the Islamic Conquests in Asia
320

– Shaping of the political landscape
347

– Lessons for understanding contemporary geopolitical dynamics
361

– Conclusion
374

– Post-Scriptum : Suggestions for further research
385

Bibliography
395

CONTENTS

Notes and References
407

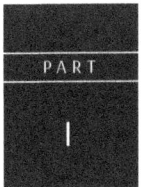

PART
I

INTRODUCTION TO THE ISLAMIC CONQUESTS IN ASIA

The Islamic conquests in Asia mark a crucial period in world history, shaping the political, social, and cultural landscape of the region for centuries to come. At the heart of these conquests lies the expansion of the Islamic empire, a process that unfolded with remarkable speed and determination. The historical backdrop of the Islamic expansion provides insight into the complex web of factors that propelled this transformative era forward. The rise of Islam in the Arabian Peninsula in the 7th century set the stage for a series of conquests that would extend the reach of the new faith across vast swathes of Asia. The unification of the Arabian tribes under the banner of Islam not only created a formidable military force but also imbued them with a sense of divine mission and ideological fervor. As the nascent Islamic state expanded beyond its borders, it encountered diverse civilizations and empires, each with its own unique characteristics and challenges. The political fragmentation of the Byzantine and Sassanian empires, as well as the weakened state of the Central Asian and Indian polities, provided fertile ground for Islamic expansion. The strategic location of the Arabian Peninsula at the crossroads of major trade routes facilitated the rapid spread of Islam beyond the Arabian Peninsula. The close proximity to key centers of power and commerce in Asia allowed Islamic forces to project their influence and establish footholds in strategic regions. The military successes of early Islamic commanders such as Khalid ibn al-Walid and Amr ibn al-As demonstrated the skill and ingenuity of Islamic armies in adapting to diverse terrains and tactics. Their use of cavalry, combined arms, and siege warfare proved decisive in defeating formidable opponents and securing key territories. The religious motivation driving the Islamic conquests cannot be overstated. The belief in the divine mandate to spread Islam and establish a just and righteous order energized Muslim warriors and inspired converts to join their ranks. The promise of material rewards and social mobility further incentivized soldiers to participate in the expansion. In conclusion, the historical background of the Islamic expansion lays the foundation for understanding the monumental shifts that occurred in Asia during this period. The convergence of military prowess, religious zeal, and strategic foresight propelled the Islamic empire to new heights of power and influence, leaving an indelible mark on the region's history.

HISTORICAL BACKGROUND OF THE ISLAMIC EXPANSION

The rise of Islam in the 7th century marked a pivotal moment in world history, setting the stage for a series of conquests that would significantly alter the geopolitical landscape of Asia. Emerging from the Arabian Peninsula, the early Muslims faced persecution and opposition, eventually leading to the establishment of a powerful Islamic state under the leadership of the Prophet Muhammad. With the death of the Prophet and the subsequent Caliphate of Abu Bakr, the Islamic expansion began in earnest. The rapid spread of Islam was fueled by a combination of religious zeal, military prowess, and strategic alliances. Arab armies, united by a common faith and sense of destiny, embarked on campaigns to extend the boundaries of the Islamic realm. The conquest of the Sassanian Empire in Persia marked a turning point in the Islamic expansion, bringing the rich lands of Mesopotamia and Persia under Muslim rule. The defeat of the Byzantine Empire in the Battle of Yarmouk solidified Islamic control over the Levant, paving the way for further advances into Anatolia and North Africa. As Muslim forces pushed eastward into Central Asia, they encountered diverse cultures and civilizations, blending elements of Persian, Indian, and Central Asian traditions into the expanding Islamic polity. The conquest of the Indian subcontinent, with its complex social and religious landscape, posed unique challenges and opportunities for the Islamic Caliphate. The strategic objectives of the Islamic expansion were multifaceted, encompassing political, economic, and religious considerations. The desire to spread the message of Islam, establish political dominion, and harness the resources of conquered territories drove the Islamic conquests in Asia. In the coming chapters, we will explore in detail the key regions targeted by Islamic forces, delving into the military tactics, economic implications, and socio-cultural exchanges that shaped the course of history in the wake of the Islamic expansion.

KEY REGIONS TARGETED BY ISLAMIC FORCES

The Islamic expansion in Asia saw the targeting of key regions strategically important for the spread of Islam and the consolidation of political power. Among these regions were the rich lands of Persia, the fertile plains of the Indian subcontinent, the trading hubs of Southeast Asia, and the ancient civilization of China. Each region presented unique opportunities and challenges for the Islamic forces, shaping the course of history in significant ways. The conquests in these key regions not only expanded the borders of the Islamic Caliphate but also facilitated the exchange of cultural, economic, and intellectual ideas across diverse civilizations. These conquests left a lasting impact on the political, social, and religious landscapes of Asia, laying the foundation for the emergence of new power structures and shaping the future trajectory of the continent.

IMPACT OF THE CONQUESTS ON EXISTING EMPIRES AND CIVILIZATIONS

The Islamic conquests in Asia had a profound impact on existing empires and civilizations of the time. The regions targeted by Islamic forces, including Persia, Central Asia, the Indian Subcontinent, Southeast Asia, and China, saw significant changes in their sociopolitical and cultural landscapes. The mighty empires that had long held sway in these regions were not immune to the transformative power of the Islamic conquests. The Sassanian Empire in Persia, with its rich history and deep cultural heritage, succumbed to the military might of the Islamic forces. The fall of Ctesiphon, the Sassanian capital, marked the end of an era for the Persian Empire and paved the way for the spread of Islam in the region. The conquest of Persia led to the rapid Islamization of the populace and the establishment of new Islamic dynasties in the region. In Central Asia, the Islamic conquests brought about a blending of cultures and traditions as Turkic and Persian influences intertwined with Islamic practices. The nomadic societies of Central Asia faced both resistance and assimilation as Islamic armies asserted their dominance in the region. The conquests transformed the political landscape of Central Asia, leading to the establishment of new Islamic states and the spread of

Islamic culture across the region. The Indian Subcontinent, with its diverse religious and cultural tapestry, saw a complex interplay of forces during the Islamic conquests. Islamic armies faced staunch resistance from Indian rulers and societies, leading to prolonged conflicts and power struggles. The impact of Islamic rule on Indian civilizations was profound, with the introduction of new architectural styles, administrative practices, and religious influences shaping the future course of Indian history. In Southeast Asia, the maritime routes to the region became avenues for the spread of Islam and the establishment of Islamic states. The interaction of diverse societies with Islamic culture led to the emergence of new trade networks and cultural exchanges. The conquests in Southeast Asia laid the foundation for the growth of Islamic civilization in the region and the integration of Islamic practices into local traditions. In China, the Islamic conquests posed a formidable challenge to the ruling dynasties, leading to diplomatic and military confrontations. The encounters between Islamic forces and Chinese armies shaped the geopolitical dynamics of the region and influenced the course of Chinese history. The legacy of the Islamic conquests in China left a lasting impact on the region's cultural and religious landscape, with the establishment of new Islamic communities and trade networks. Overall, the Islamic conquests in Asia left an indelible mark on existing empires and civilizations, paving the way for the spread of Islam and the integration of diverse cultures into the Islamic world. These conquests shaped the course of Asian history and contributed to the growth and development of Islamic civilization in the region.

MILITARY TACTICS AND STRATEGIES EMPLOYED BY ISLAMIC ARMIES

The Islamic conquests in Asia witnessed the implementation of sophisticated military tactics and strategies by the Islamic armies. These strategic maneuvers played a pivotal role in securing victories and expanding the boundaries of the Caliphate. One of the key aspects of the Islamic military approach was the integration of various military disciplines, including infantry, cavalry, and siege warfare. Islamic armies were known for their mobility and adaptability on the battlefield. Utilizing swift cavalry units, such as the famed Arab horsemen, they were able to outmaneuver their opponents and launch surprise attacks. The use of camel-mounted troops also provided the Islamic forces with a strategic advantage in navigating harsh terrains and maintaining supply lines during campaigns. In siege warfare, Islamic armies displayed ingenuity by utilizing innovative tactics to breach fortified positions. They employed siege engines, such as catapults and trebuchets, to weaken enemy defenses before launching assaults. Islamic commanders also understood the importance of psychological warfare, using intimidation tactics to demoralize besieged garrisons and prompt surrenders. Strategic alliances with local tribes and factions were another key element of Islamic military strategy. By leveraging existing rivalries and alliances within targeted regions, Islamic armies were able to bolster their forces and weaken opposition. Diplomatic maneuvers were often employed to secure advantageous positions and avoid protracted conflicts. Furthermore, the incorporation of religious ideology in warfare served to motivate and inspire Islamic soldiers. Believing in the righteousness of their cause, Muslim fighters fought with zeal and determination, fueled by the promise of heavenly rewards.

The concept of jihad, or holy war, provided a powerful ideological framework for justifying military actions and rallying the faithful to battle. Overall, the military tactics and strategies employed by Islamic armies during the conquests in Asia exemplified a combination of military prowess, strategic acumen, and ideological fervor. These multifaceted approaches contributed to the success of the Islamic expansion and left a lasting impact on the regions they conquered.

ROLE OF RELIGION IN MOTIVATING AND JUSTIFYING CONQUESTS

Religion played a central role in motivating and justifying the Islamic conquests in Asia. The rapid expansion of the Islamic Caliphate was fueled by a fervent belief in the spread of Islam as a divine mandate. Islamic armies were often inspired by religious fervor, seeing themselves as agents of God's will on earth. The concept of jihad, or holy war, served as a powerful motivator for soldiers, instilling a sense of duty and righteousness in their military campaigns. Islamic leaders and scholars often framed the conquests as a means of spreading the message of Islam to new territories and populations. This religious justification served to unite diverse tribal and ethnic groups under a common cause, strengthening the unity and resolve of the Islamic armies. The promise of spiritual rewards in the afterlife for those who fought in the name of Islam further incentivized soldiers to engage in conquests with zeal and determination. Furthermore, religion provided a moral framework for the conduct of warfare. Islamic teachings emphasized the importance of protecting non-combatants, preserving property, and treating prisoners of war with dignity. This ethical code, rooted in Islamic principles, guided the behavior of Islamic armies and differentiated them from other conquerors of the time. The religious dimension of the Islamic conquests also extended to the treatment of conquered populations. While non-Muslims were generally allowed to practice their own faith under Islamic rule, there were incentives for conversion to Islam, such as tax exemptions or social privileges. This approach facilitated the integration of diverse populations into the expanding Islamic empire, creating a sense of unity and common purpose among conquered peoples. In summary, the role of religion in motivating and justifying the Islamic conquests in Asia was multifaceted. It served as a driving force for soldiers, providing them with a sense of divine purpose and moral guidance in their military endeavors. Moreover, religion played a crucial role in unifying diverse societies under the banner of Islam, shaping the cultural and social landscape of the regions conquered by the Islamic Caliphate.

ECONOMIC IMPLICATIONS OF ISLAMIC CONQUESTS IN ASIA

The Islamic conquests in Asia had significant economic implications that shaped the region for centuries to come. The conquests facilitated the spread of trade networks, connecting distant regions and fostering economic growth. Islamic rulers established stable governance structures that promoted commerce, leading to increased prosperity and wealth accumulation. One of the key economic impacts of the Islamic conquests was the integration of diverse regions into a unified economic system. The establishment of Islamic caliphates and empires created a vast territorial expanse where goods, resources, and ideas could flow freely. This integration promoted economic interdependence and facilitated the exchange of goods and services across borders. Furthermore, the Islamic conquests brought about the introduction of new agricultural techniques, irrigation systems, and technologies that improved productivity and agricultural output. This led to increased surplus production and trade, stimulating economic development and urbanization in conquered territories. The Islamic rulers also implemented innovative financial systems such as the waqf (charitable endowment) and the development of a sophisticated banking system. These financial instruments helped mobilize capital, promote investment, and support economic activities, contributing to the overall prosperity of the Islamic lands. Moreover, the Islamic conquests facilitated the transfer of knowledge and expertise in various fields such as science, medicine, and architecture. This intellectual exchange not only enriched the local economies but also laid the foundation for future advancements and innovations. Overall, the economic implications of the Islamic conquests in Asia were profound, shaping the economic landscape of the region and fostering economic growth, trade, and innovation. The legacy of these economic transformations can still be seen in the commercial networks, architectural achievements, and cultural exchanges that characterize the Islamic world today.

SOCIO-CULTURAL EXCHANGES AND TRANSFORMATIONS BROUGHT ABOUT BY THE CONQUESTS

The Islamic conquests in Asia brought about significant socio-cultural exchanges and transformations across the region. The interactions between Islamic forces and the existing societies resulted in the blending of diverse cultural traditions, languages, and knowledge systems. One notable aspect of these exchanges was the spread of Arabic as a language of administration, trade, and culture. Arabic script and literature became widely adopted, leading to the enrichment of local languages and literary traditions. Moreover, the Islamic conquests facilitated the exchange of ideas and technology between different civilizations. Islamic scholars preserved and translated classical Greek, Persian, and Indian texts, contributing to the advancement of knowledge in fields such as mathematics, astronomy, medicine, and philosophy. This intellectual exchange laid the foundation for the flourishing of the Islamic Golden Age, where centers of learning like Baghdad, Damascus, and Cordoba became hubs of knowledge and innovation. Furthermore, the spread of Islam during the conquests had a profound impact on the religious and social fabric of Asian societies. While some regions embraced Islam willingly, others saw a combination of peaceful conversion and syncretism with existing belief systems. The Islamic faith introduced new ethical and legal frameworks, shaping the moral values and social norms of the conquered territories. As a result of these socio-cultural exchanges, artistic and architectural styles also underwent significant transformations. Islamic art and architecture blended local motifs and techniques with Islamic aesthetics, leading to the creation of unique and vibrant cultural expressions. The construction of mosques, madrasas, and palaces showcased the fusion of different artistic traditions, creating a visual legacy that continues to inspire awe and admiration. Overall, the socio-cultural exchanges and transformations brought about by the Islamic conquests in Asia played a crucial role in shaping the diverse and interconnected societies of the region. The legacy of these exchanges can be seen in the rich tapestry of cultural heritage, intellectual achievements, and religious pluralism that characterize contemporary Asian societies.

LEGACY OF THE ISLAMIC CONQUESTS IN SHAPING CONTEMPORARY ASIAN SOCIETIES

The Islamic conquests in Asia have left a profound and lasting legacy on contemporary Asian societies. The cultural exchanges and transformations brought about by these conquests continue to shape the region in significant ways. One of the key legacies of the Islamic conquests is the fusion of diverse cultural and religious influences, leading to the development of unique and vibrant societies. The spread of Islam across Asia facilitated the exchange of ideas, knowledge, and technology among different civilizations. This cultural interchange not only enriched the social fabric of the region but also fostered a sense of shared heritage among diverse communities. The Islamic conquests also played a crucial role in shaping the linguistic landscape of Asia, with Arabic becoming a prominent language of trade, administration, and scholarship. Furthermore, the Islamic conquests introduced new architectural styles, artistic techniques, and culinary traditions to Asia, leaving a lasting imprint on the region's cultural heritage. The assimilation of Islamic art and architecture into local traditions gave rise to distinctive cultural expressions that reflect the synthesis of different influences. In addition, the establishment of Islamic rule in various parts of Asia led to the spread of Islamic values, norms, and practices among local populations. This influence can be seen in the legal systems, social customs, and religious practices of many Asian societies today. The legacy of the Islamic conquests in shaping contemporary Asian societies underscores the enduring impact of historical events on the cultural identity and social dynamics of the region.

SIGNIFICANCE OF STUDYING THE ISLAMIC CONQUESTS IN UNDERSTANDING GLOBAL HISTORY

Studying the Islamic conquests in Asia is essential for gaining a comprehensive understanding of global history. These conquests not only shaped the development of Asian societies but also had far-reaching impacts that reverberated across borders and centuries. By examining the military campaigns, cultural exchanges, and lasting legacies of the Islamic conquests, we can gain insights into the interconnectedness of world history and the complex dynamics of power, religion, and civilization. The Islamic conquests in Asia were instrumental in spreading Islamic civilization and shaping the cultural landscape of the region. Through the establishment of new political structures, trade networks, and intellectual centers, the conquests facilitated the exchange of ideas, technologies, and artistic traditions among diverse societies. This cultural fusion not only enriched the heritage of Asian civilizations but also contributed to the global diffusion of knowledge and innovation. Moreover, the Islamic conquests had profound socio-political implications that continue to influence contemporary Asian societies. The legacy of these conquests can be observed in the religious diversity, legal systems, and social norms of many Asian countries. Understanding how these conquests transformed the socio-economic and political structures of the region is crucial for comprehending the complexities of present-day international relations and conflicts. By delving into the historical context, motivations, and consequences of the Islamic conquests in Asia, scholars and students can develop a nuanced perspective on the inherent power dynamics and cultural interactions that have shaped global history. This deeper understanding of the interplay between empires, religions, and civilizations is essential for navigating the complexities of our interconnected world and appreciating the enduring legacies of past conquests on contemporary societies.

OVERVIEW OF THE ISLAMIC CONQUESTS IN ASIA

The Early Expansion of Islam: The rapid spread of Islam in the Arabian Peninsula and its impact on neighboring regions

The rise and spread of Islam in the Arabian Peninsula marked a significant turning point in world history. Emerging in the early 7th century, Islam quickly gained traction under the leadership of the Prophet Muhammad. His teachings of monotheism, social justice, and spiritual equality resonated with many in Arabia, leading to a growing number of followers. The city of Mecca, a prominent trading hub in the region, became a center for early Islamic activity. Despite facing opposition from local tribes and the Quraysh elite, Muhammad's message continued to attract believers. The migration to Medina, known as the Hijra, marked a crucial moment in the consolidation of the Muslim community and the establishment of the first Islamic state. The military campaigns led by Muhammad and his successors played a crucial role in expanding Islamic influence beyond the Arabian Peninsula. Through a combination of diplomacy, warfare, and religious zeal, Islamic forces were able to conquer territories in the neighboring regions of the Levant, Egypt, and Persia. These conquests not only brought new lands under Islamic rule but also facilitated the spread of the Islamic faith. The rapid expansion of Islam in the

7th and 8th centuries transformed the political and cultural landscape of the Middle East and beyond. The Umayyad and Abbasid dynasties emerged as key players in this transformative process, establishing powerful caliphates that spanned vast territories. The administrative and military infrastructure of these dynasties facilitated the consolidation of Islamic rule and the integration of diverse populations. Overall, the early expansion of Islam in the Arabian Peninsula laid the foundation for the broader Islamic conquests in Asia. The military successes and religious fervor of the early Muslims set the stage for the establishment of a vast Islamic empire that would shape the course of history for centuries to come.

Key Players and Dynasties: The major Islamic dynasties involved in the conquests and their roles in shaping Asian history

The major Islamic dynasties that played crucial roles in the conquests of Asia included the Umayyad Caliphate, the Abbasid Caliphate, and the Ghaznavid Empire. The Umayyad Caliphate, under the leadership of Caliph Umar and his successors, expanded rapidly from its capital in Damascus, conquering significant territories in the Middle East, North Africa, and parts of Central Asia. The Abbasid Caliphate, which rose to power in Baghdad after overthrowing the Umayyads, continued the expansion of Islamic rule into new regions and established a vibrant cultural and intellectual center in the Arab world. The Ghaznavid Empire, based in present-day Afghanistan and ruled by the Turkic Ghaznavid dynasty, expanded further eastward into the Indian subcontinent, becoming a dominant power in the region. These dynasties not only expanded the Islamic faith but also facilitated the exchange of knowledge, technologies, and cultural practices across diverse regions, shaping the history and development of Asia in profound ways.

Military Tactics and Strategies: The military tactics employed by Islamic forces during their conquests in Asia

The Islamic conquests in Asia were characterized by a combination of strategic military tactics and effective planning. Islamic forces employed a variety of methods to achieve their victories, adapting to the diverse terrains and challenges they encountered. One of the key tactics utilized by Islamic armies was their mobility and speed, allowing them to surprise and outmaneuver their opponents. This was particularly evident in the use of swift cavalry units, which provided the flexibility needed to respond quickly to changing situations on the battlefield. In addition to their mobility, Islamic forces also utilized superior knowledge of the local terrain to their advantage. By leveraging their understanding of the geography and climate of the regions they sought to conquer, Islamic commanders were able to plan their campaigns more effectively and exploit any weaknesses in their enemies' defenses. Furthermore, Islamic armies made strategic use of siege warfare, employing various techniques to breach fortified cities and strongholds. This included the use of siege engines, such as catapults and battering rams, as well as mining and sapping to undermine enemy defenses. These tactics were instrumental in securing key strategic locations and breaking the resistance of fortified opponents. Islamic military commanders also demonstrated a high level of tactical flexibility, adapting their strategies to the specific challenges they faced in different regions. This included adjusting their formations and tactics to counter the tactics of their adversaries, as well as making use of local recruits and allies to bolster their forces. Overall, the military tactics and strategies employed by Islamic forces during their conquests in Asia were characterized by a combination of speed, mobility, strategic planning, and tactical flexibility. These factors were crucial in enabling Islamic armies to achieve their military objectives and establish their dominance in the region.

Social and Cultural Interactions: The interactions between Islamic conquerors and diverse Asian societies, including the assimilation of local customs and traditions

The interactions between Islamic conquerors and diverse Asian societies during the conquests were marked by a complex interplay of social and cultural exchanges. The assimilation of local customs and traditions played a significant role in shaping the dynamic relationships between the conquerors and the conquered. Islamic forces often encountered diverse ethnic groups, languages, and religions in the territories they conquered. Through interactions with these societies, the conquerors were exposed to new cultural practices and belief systems. This exposure led to a process of cultural exchange, where both parties influenced each other's customs and traditions. One notable aspect of these interactions was the tolerance shown by Islamic rulers towards existing social structures and religious practices in conquered territories. In many cases, Islamic rulers allowed local rulers to retain their positions of authority and respected the religious practices of the local population. This approach helped to foster a sense of cooperation and mutual respect between the conquerors and the conquered. At the same time, the spread of Islam in these regions also had a profound impact on local cultures and societies. The introduction of Islamic beliefs and practices led to the gradual adoption of new customs and traditions among the local population. Over time, Islam became an integral part of the cultural identity of many Asian societies, influencing everything from art and architecture to language and literature. The assimilation of local customs and traditions by Islamic conquerors also paved the way for the development of a rich and diverse cultural landscape in the conquered territories. This cultural fusion gave rise to new forms of art, music, and literature that reflected the blending of Islamic and local influences. These cultural exchanges not only enriched the social fabric of these regions but also laid the foundation for future artistic and intellectual developments. Overall, the social and cultural interactions between Islamic conquerors and diverse Asian societies during the conquests were characterized by a give-and-take relationship that led to the creation of a vibrant and dynamic cultural milieu. The assimilation of local customs and traditions played a crucial role in shaping the unique cultural identity of these regions, highlighting the enduring legacy of these interactions in the history of Islamic conquests in Asia.

Economic Impacts: The economic effects of the Islamic conquests on Asian economies and trade networks

The Islamic conquests in Asia had significant economic implications for the region. The integration of newly conquered territories into the Islamic Caliphate facilitated the exchange of goods, technologies, and ideas, leading to the expansion of trade networks and economic growth. The conquests created opportunities for increased commerce and cultural exchange between the Islamic empire and the diverse Asian societies under its rule. One of the key economic impacts of the Islamic conquests was the establishment of stable and efficient trade routes connecting different regions. The Islamic Caliphate's control over strategic trade routes, such as the Silk Road and Indian Ocean trade routes, enabled the flow of goods, commodities, and luxury items between Asia, Africa, and Europe. This facilitated the exchange of valuable goods such as silk, spices, textiles, and precious metals, stimulating economic activity and fostering prosperity in the newly conquered territories. The Islamic conquests also introduced new agricultural techniques, irrigation systems, and technologies to improve productivity and increase agricultural output in conquered territories. Islamic rulers invested in infrastructure development, including the construction of roads, bridges, and marketplaces, which facilitated trade and commerce and contributed to the overall economic development of the region. Furthermore, the Islamic economic system, based on principles of fairness, equity, and social welfare, influenced economic practices in the conquered territories. Islamic rulers implemented policies to regulate trade, standardize weights and measures, and ensure the fair treatment of merchants and traders. This created a conducive environment for economic growth and encouraged entrepreneurship and innovation in various sectors of the economy. The Islamic conquests also fostered cultural exchanges and the transfer of knowledge and technology across different regions. The translation of Greek, Persian, Indian, and Chinese texts into Arabic by scholars in the Islamic empire promoted the exchange of scientific, philosophical, and technological ideas, spurring advancements in various fields such as mathematics, astronomy, medicine, and architecture. Overall, the economic impacts of the Islamic conquests on Asian economies and trade networks were profound. The integration of diverse societies into the Islamic Caliphate created a dynamic and interconnected economic system that promoted trade, innovation, and prosperity, laying the foundation for the cultural and economic flourishing of the region.

THE ISLAMIC CONQUESTS IN ASIA

Religious Transformations: The spread of Islam and the conversion of local populations in conquered territories

The Islamic conquests in Asia not only had a significant impact on the political and economic landscapes of the conquered territories but also brought about profound religious transformations. As Islamic rulers expanded their domains across Asia, they encountered diverse populations with varying religious beliefs. The spread of Islam and the conversion of local populations played a crucial role in shaping the religious landscape of the regions under Islamic rule. Islamic conquerors often employed a combination of military might, diplomacy, and religious appeal to facilitate the conversion of local populations to Islam. The tolerance and respect shown towards existing religious practices and beliefs by Islamic rulers played a key role in facilitating the peaceful conversion of many individuals to Islam. This approach contributed to the gradual but steady spread of Islam in the conquered territories. One of the significant factors that contributed to the success of Islam's spread was the appeal of its monotheistic doctrine and the simplicity of its religious practices. The message of one God and the emphasis on individual piety resonated with many people in the newly conquered regions, leading to a gradual but widespread acceptance of Islam. Islamic scholars and missionaries also played a vital role in disseminating the teachings of Islam and facilitating the conversion of local populations. The conversion to Islam not only brought about changes in religious beliefs but also influenced various aspects of social and cultural life in the conquered territories. Islamic values, ethical principles, and legal norms became integral parts of the societies under Islamic rule, contributing to the formation of a distinct Islamic identity among the populace. The construction of mosques, the establishment of Islamic educational institutions, and the adoption of Arabic as the language of administration further solidified the influence of Islam in the conquered territories. Overall, the religious transformations brought about by the spread of Islam during the Islamic conquests in Asia were instrumental in shaping the cultural and social fabric of the conquered regions. The interaction between Islamic beliefs and local traditions resulted in a dynamic blend of religious practices and cultural expressions, creating a rich tapestry of diverse influences that continues to define the religious landscape of Asia.

Administrative Policies: The governance policies implemented by Islamic rulers in the conquered territories and their impact on local governance structures

The Islamic rulers implemented a series of administrative policies in the conquered territories aimed at consolidating their control and fostering stability. One key aspect of their governance approach was the establishment of a hierarchical administrative system that mirrored the structure of the Islamic Caliphate. Local governors, appointed by the caliph or his representatives, were tasked with overseeing the day-to-day affairs of the provinces and ensuring compliance with Islamic law. To facilitate the collection of taxes and maintenance of public order, Islamic rulers introduced standardized administrative practices across their territories. They established bureaucracies to manage finances, legal matters, and social welfare, with a focus on efficient governance and revenue generation. This centralized system helped streamline governance and promote uniformity in the application of Islamic law. Islamic rulers also promoted the use of Islamic law, or Sharia, as the basis for legal proceedings and governance in the conquered territories. Sharia courts were established to adjudicate disputes and administer justice according to Islamic principles. This legal system played a crucial role in maintaining social order and resolving conflicts within the diverse populations under Islamic rule. Furthermore, the Islamic rulers adopted a policy of religious tolerance towards non-Muslims in the conquered territories. While Muslims enjoyed certain privileges, such as exemption from certain taxes, non-Muslims were allowed to practice their own religions and maintain their cultural traditions. This policy of religious pluralism contributed to the peaceful coexistence of different religious communities and mitigated potential sources of conflict. The impact of these administrative policies on local governance structures was profound. The centralized administration introduced by Islamic rulers fostered stability and social order in the conquered territories. It provided a framework for governance that endured long after the initial conquests, shaping the political landscape of Asia for centuries to come. The legacy of these administrative policies continues to influence the governance structures of many countries in the region today, highlighting the enduring impact of the Islamic conquests on Asian history.

Resistance and Revolts: Instances of resistance and revolts against Islamic rule in Asia and their consequences

Resistance and revolts against Islamic rule in Asia were not uncommon during the period of the Islamic conquests. Local populations often resisted the imposition of Islamic governance and attempted to overthrow their new rulers. One notable example is the Kharijite rebellion in Persia, where dissenting groups rebelled against the Umayyad Caliphate's rule and sought to establish their own form of government. In India, the Hindu kingdoms put up fierce resistance against the Islamic invaders, most notably during the reign of Mahmud of Ghazni. The Rajputs in particular were known for their fierce resistance to Islamic conquests, often engaging in guerrilla warfare tactics to defend their territories. Similarly, in Central Asia, the nomadic tribes frequently rebelled against the Islamic Caliphate's attempts to subjugate them. The Khazars, for instance, resisted Islamic expansion into their territories and mounted several revolts to maintain their independence. These instances of resistance and revolts against Islamic rule often led to violent conflicts and bloodshed as both sides fought for control. The consequences of such resistance were varied, ranging from the imposition of harsher measures by the Islamic rulers to the eventual incorporation of local customs and practices into the governance structures. Overall, the resistance and revolts against Islamic rule in Asia highlight the complexities and tensions that arose from the process of conquest and colonization. The legacy of these conflicts continues to shape the historical narratives of the region and underscores the enduring impact of these events on subsequent historical developments.

Legacy and Long-Term Effects: The lasting legacy of the Islamic conquests in Asia and their influence on subsequent historical developments

The Islamic conquests in Asia left a profound and enduring legacy that continues to shape historical developments to this day. One of the most significant long-term effects of these conquests was the cultural and intellectual exchange that took place between Islamic and Asian civilizations. This exchange led to the transmission of knowledge, ideas, and technologies, fostering a rich and diverse cultural landscape in the region. Furthermore, the establishment of Islamic institutions and governance structures in conquered territories laid the foundation for the development of new political systems and administrative practices. The blending of Islamic principles with existing local traditions resulted in the emergence of hybrid cultural identities and sociopolitical frameworks that have persisted over the centuries. The influence of Islamic art, architecture, and literature on Asian societies is also a testament to the lasting impact of the conquests. The vibrant artistic traditions and architectural marvels that emerged during this period continue to be celebrated and preserved as part of the shared heritage of the region. Moreover, the spread of Islam through the conquests led to the religious and social transformation of many Asian communities. The syncretic nature of Islamic belief systems allowed for the integration of diverse religious practices and cultural values, creating a unique tapestry of religious expression in the region. Looking beyond the historical context, the legacy of the Islamic conquests in Asia offers valuable insights for understanding contemporary geopolitical dynamics. The interplay of religion, politics, and culture that defined the conquests continues to shape relations between different civilizations and informs current debates on identity, nationalism, and global governance. In conclusion, the lasting legacy of the Islamic conquests in Asia underscores the complex and multifaceted impact of historical events on the trajectory of human civilization. By reflecting on these legacies and their implications, we gain a deeper appreciation for the interconnectedness of world history and the enduring influence of past conquests on present-day societies.

Comparative Perspectives: The Islamic conquests in Asia with other imperial expansions in world history and draw parallels to contemporary geopolitical dynamics

The Islamic conquests in Asia present a fascinating case study when compared to other imperial expansions in world history. While each imperial expansion had its unique characteristics and motivations, there are notable parallels that can be drawn among them. One common theme is the use of military force to expand territorial control and influence over diverse populations. The Islamic conquests, like the Roman Empire, sought to integrate conquered territories into a larger political and cultural framework, promoting unity under a central authority. Similar to the Mongol Empire, the Islamic conquests in Asia led to the establishment of vast territorial holdings that facilitated the diffusion of ideas, technologies, and cultures across previously distinct regions. The Silk Road, for example, became a critical conduit for trade and cultural exchange, connecting the Islamic world with East Asia and Europe. This interconnectivity fostered economic growth and stimulated innovation in various fields, reflecting the dynamic nature of imperial expansions throughout history. Moreover, the Spanish conquest of the Americas shares parallels with the Islamic conquests in Asia in terms of the fusion of different cultures and the spread of new religious beliefs. Just as the Spanish colonization brought Christianity to the indigenous peoples of the Americas, Islamic conquests introduced Islam to diverse Asian societies, shaping religious practices and societal norms in the process. The enduring legacies of these religious transformations continue to influence contemporary cultural identities and political dynamics in the regions affected by these imperial expansions. In today's globalized world, the legacy of the Islamic conquests in Asia serves as a reminder of the interconnected nature of historical processes and the enduring impact of past imperial endeavors on contemporary geopolitical dynamics. By examining these conquests in comparative perspective with other imperial expansions, we gain insights into the complex interactions between power, culture, and identity that continue to shape our understanding of the world today.

IMPORTANCE OF EXAMINING THESE CONQUESTS IN THE BROADER CONTEXT OF ISLAMIC HISTORY

Historical Context: An overview of the Islamic conquests in Asia and their significance in shaping the course of Islamic history

The Islamic conquests in Asia were a pivotal series of military campaigns that reshaped the course of Islamic history. These conquests, driven by religious motivations, expanded the reach of Islam across vast territories, leaving a lasting impact on the socio-political landscape of the region. Beginning in the 7th century with the rapid expansion of the Islamic Caliphate, the conquests extended from the Arabian Peninsula into regions such as Persia, Central Asia, the Indian subcontinent, Southeast Asia, and even posed challenges to the Chinese dynasties. The conquests were not merely about territorial expansion but were deeply intertwined with religious imperatives. Islamic teachings emphasized the spread of the faith to all corners of the world, and the conquests served as a means to achieve this goal. The military campaigns were often justified on religious grounds, portraying the conquests as a divine mandate to bring Islam to new lands and establish Islamic rule. This religious influence played a crucial role in motivating both the leadership and the soldiers who participated in these campaigns. The Islamic conquests in Asia were significant in shaping the course of Islamic history. They facilitated the spread of Islamic influence, leading to the establishment of new political entities and the introduction of Islamic governance systems. The conquests also paved the way for the assimilation of diverse cultural practices and traditions, resulting in a rich tapestry of intercultural exchange. Moreover, the conquests served as a catalyst for economic growth and trade expansion, as the newly conquered territories became integral hubs for commerce and exchange. Overall, the historical context of the Islamic conquests in Asia highlights their paramount importance in shaping the trajectory of Islamic civilization. These conquests not only expanded the boundaries of the Islamic world but also left a profound impact on the religious, cultural, economic, and political dimensions of the regions they touched. By examining these conquests within their historical context, we gain a deeper understanding of the transformative power of Islam and its enduring legacy in the annals of world history.

Religious Influence: How religious motivations played a crucial role in driving the conquests and spreading Islam in the region

The Islamic conquests in Asia were deeply influenced by religious fervor and a sense of divine mandate. The expansion of Islam was not only a territorial conquest but also a spiritual mission to spread the teachings of the Prophet Muhammad. The early Muslim armies were imbued with a strong sense of religious duty, believing that their conquests were a means of fulfilling the commandments of their faith. The concept of jihad, or holy war, was central in motivating Muslim warriors to participate in the conquests. Jihad was not just about military conquest but also about spreading the message of Islam and bringing non-believers into the fold of the Islamic community. This religious zeal fueled the expansion of the Islamic Caliphate across Asia, as armies marched into new territories with the dual purpose of political conquest and religious propagation. Furthermore, Islamic rulers and commanders often invoked religious rhetoric to inspire and unite their troops. They portrayed the conquests as a divine mission sanctioned by God, drawing upon Islamic scriptures and traditions to justify their military campaigns. This religious influence not only motivated the soldiers on the battlefield but also served to legitimize the conquests in the eyes of the conquered peoples. As Islam spread through Asia, it encountered diverse cultures, beliefs, and practices. The interactions between Muslim conquerors and local populations led to a dynamic cultural exchange where traditions were shared, adapted, and blended. This cultural fusion was facilitated by the religious tolerance promoted in Islamic teachings, allowing for the coexistence of diverse faiths and customs within the expanding Caliphate. The religious influence on the Islamic conquests in Asia was profound and multifaceted. It provided the ideological framework for military expansion, inspired and mobilized the armies, and facilitated a process of cultural exchange that reshaped the region's social and intellectual landscapes. Through the lens of religious motivation, the conquests emerge not just as historical events but as transformative moments in the history of Islam and Asia.

Cultural Exchange: The cultural exchange that took place as a result of these conquests, leading to the blending of different traditions and practices

The Islamic conquests in Asia facilitated significant cultural exchanges that transformed the region. These conquests led to the blending of diverse traditions and practices, creating a rich tapestry of cultural interactions. One of the key factors in this cultural exchange was the dissemination of Islamic beliefs and practices among the conquered populations. Islam, as a monotheistic religion, brought a new spiritual and ethical framework to the regions it conquered. The spread of Islamic beliefs led to the adoption of Arabic as a language of religion and culture, influencing various aspects of daily life, from governance to literature. The construction of mosques and religious schools further solidified the presence of Islamic culture in the conquered territories. Moreover, the interaction between Islamic and local traditions resulted in the fusion of different architectural styles, artistic expressions, and culinary practices. This cultural syncretism gave rise to new forms of art, music, and literature that reflected the diverse influences at play. Islamic scholars and artisans also contributed to the preservation and dissemination of knowledge in fields such as mathematics, astronomy, and medicine, enriching the cultural landscape of the conquered regions. The cultural exchange that occurred as a result of the Islamic conquests was not unidirectional. Local traditions and practices also influenced Islamic societies, leading to the adaptation and incorporation of indigenous customs and beliefs. This reciprocal exchange of ideas and practices fostered a dynamic cultural environment that transcended religious boundaries and created a sense of shared heritage among diverse communities. Overall, the cultural exchange that took place during the Islamic conquests in Asia was a testament to the transformative power of cross-cultural interactions. It laid the foundation for the development of vibrant and inclusive societies that celebrated diversity and enriched the collective heritage of the region.

Political Impact: The political ramifications of the conquests, including the establishment of new rulers and governance systems

The conquests of Asia had far-reaching political implications, reshaping the governance systems and establishing new rulers in the conquered territories. As Islamic forces expanded their influence, they encountered existing power structures and administration, necessitating the establishment of new political entities to govern these regions. The incorporation of diverse cultures and populations under Islamic rule led to the formation of hybrid political systems that blended existing traditions with Islamic principles. The conquests resulted in the appointment of new governors and officials who oversaw the administration of the conquered territories on behalf of the Islamic Caliphate. These local administrators played a crucial role in maintaining law and order, collecting taxes, and implementing policies that aligned with the Caliphate's interests. The political landscape of the conquered regions underwent significant transformations, with the introduction of Islamic legal systems and governance practices that were distinct from the pre-existing structures. The establishment of Islamic rule also led to the integration of local elites and ruling classes into the new political framework. Some indigenous rulers chose to collaborate with the Islamic forces, aligning themselves with the Caliphate and retaining positions of power in exchange for their loyalty. This collaboration often resulted in a symbiotic relationship wherein local rulers retained a degree of autonomy while recognizing the authority of the Islamic Caliphate. Furthermore, the conquests facilitated the spread of Islamic political ideologies and principles, influencing the development of governance systems in the conquered territories. The implementation of Islamic law, known as Sharia, served as a guiding framework for political decisions and governance practices, emphasizing justice, equality, and adherence to religious principles. This infusion of Islamic governance principles into the political systems of the conquered territories shaped the administration and governance structures for centuries to come. Overall, the political impact of the Islamic conquests in Asia was profound, leading to the establishment of new rulers and political structures that reflected a blend of Islamic and local traditions. The legacy of these conquests is evident in the enduring influence of Islamic governance principles and the shaping of political institutions in the conquered territories.

Economic Consequences: The economic implications of the conquests on trade routes, industries, and commerce within the conquered territories

The Islamic conquests in Asia had profound economic consequences that reshaped trade routes, industries, and commerce in the conquered territories. The establishment of new rulers and governance systems brought about significant changes in the economic landscape of the region. With the expansion of the Islamic Caliphate came a restructuring of commercial networks, as trade routes were reconfigured to connect the newly conquered territories with the heartlands of the Islamic empire. One of the key economic implications of the conquests was the integration of diverse economic systems under a unified imperial administration. This led to a standardization of trade practices, currency, and taxation across the conquered territories, facilitating economic exchanges and fostering a more stable economic environment. The imposition of Islamic law, which regulated economic activities and transactions, also played a crucial role in promoting economic growth and stability in the newly acquired territories. The conquests also spurred the development of new industries and economic activities in the conquered lands. The influx of Islamic administrators, merchants, and settlers brought with them new technologies, agricultural practices, and economic opportunities that contributed to the economic development of the region. Trade networks flourished, connecting distant regions and facilitating the exchange of goods, ideas, and technologies across the Islamic world. Furthermore, the conquests had a profound impact on urbanization and the growth of cities in the conquered territories. As new administrative centers were established and existing cities expanded to accommodate the influx of people, urban centers became hubs of economic activity, trade, and innovation. Urbanization brought about changes in social structures as diverse populations intermingled in urban settings, leading to the exchange of ideas, cultures, and traditions. Overall, the economic consequences of the Islamic conquests in Asia were far-reaching, revolutionizing trade, industries, and commerce in the conquered territories. The integration of diverse economic systems under a unified imperial administration, the promotion of trade and economic exchange, and the development of new industries and urban centers all contributed to the economic prosperity and growth of the Islamic Caliphate.

Social Dynamics: The social changes brought about by the conquests, such as shifts in demographics, urbanization, and social structures

The Islamic conquests in Asia brought about significant social changes in the conquered territories. One of the key impacts was the demographic shifts that occurred as a result of the conquests. With the influx of new rulers, administrators, and settlers, the demographic composition of these regions underwent a transformation. This often led to the coexistence of diverse ethnic and religious groups within the same territories, fostering a sense of multiculturalism and social diversity. Urbanization was another notable aspect of the social dynamics resulting from the conquests. As Islamic rule expanded, new urban centers emerged as administrative, commercial, and cultural hubs. These cities became focal points for trade, education, and governance, attracting a diverse population and contributing to the growth of urban societies. The conquests also brought about changes in social structures within the conquered territories. The introduction of Islamic law and governance systems led to the reorganization of social institutions, including the redistribution of wealth, the establishment of new administrative hierarchies, and the integration of local traditions with Islamic principles. This restructuring of social norms and practices contributed to the formation of a distinctive social order within the Islamic Caliphate. Furthermore, the conquests facilitated the spread of knowledge, ideas, and technologies across different regions, promoting intellectual and cultural exchange. This exchange fostered a vibrant intellectual climate, where scholars, artists, and thinkers from diverse backgrounds converged to create a rich tapestry of intellectual and artistic achievements. Overall, the social dynamics resulting from the Islamic conquests in Asia had a lasting impact on the demographic, urban, and social fabric of the conquered territories. These changes not only shaped the social structures and identities of these regions but also laid the foundation for the cultural and intellectual flourishing that characterized the Islamic Caliphate during this period.

Military Strategy: The military strategies employed during the conquests and their effectiveness in achieving the expansion of the Islamic Caliphate

THE ISLAMIC CONQUESTS IN ASIA

The military strategies employed during the Islamic conquests in Asia were marked by a combination of tactical innovation, strategic adaptability, and organizational prowess. Islamic armies utilized a diverse array of military tactics, drawing on a mix of traditional Arab warfare methods and innovative approaches gleaned from conquered civilizations. One of the key strengths of the Islamic military was its ability to incorporate military knowledge and expertise from diverse cultural sources, allowing for a flexible and dynamic approach to warfare. The Islamic Caliphate's military success can be attributed to its robust organizational structure, which enabled effective command and control of large armies across vast territories. The rapid mobility of Islamic forces, facilitated by the use of light cavalry and camel-mounted troops, allowed for swift responses to changing battlefield conditions and strategic opportunities. Strategic coordination between different army units and commanders was a cornerstone of Islamic military campaigns, ensuring that forces could operate cohesively and exploit enemy weaknesses. Islamic leaders also demonstrated a willingness to adapt their tactics to suit the specific terrain, climate, and logistical challenges encountered in different regions, showcasing a pragmatic and resourceful approach to warfare. Moreover, the integration of siege warfare techniques, such as the use of siege engines and fortification techniques, played a crucial role in capturing fortified cities and strongholds. Islamic armies combined both conventional and unconventional tactics to besiege enemy positions, showcasing their ability to utilize a range of tools and methods to achieve their military objectives. Overall, the military strategies employed by the Islamic Caliphate during the conquests in Asia exemplified a blend of innovation, adaptability, and strategic acumen. By leveraging a diverse range of military assets and tactics, Islamic armies were able to achieve remarkable success in expanding the boundaries of the Caliphate and shaping the geopolitical landscape of the region for centuries to come.

Historiographical Significance: The importance of studying these conquests within the broader historiographical framework of Islamic history

The conquests of Asia by the Islamic Caliphate hold significant historiographical importance within the broader framework of Islamic history. By examining the military strategies employed during these conquests, historians can gain valuable insights into the expansion of the Islamic Caliphate and its lasting impact on subsequent developments in Islamic societies and political landscapes. The study of military strategies during the Islamic conquests allows historians to analyze the effectiveness of various tactics and approaches used by Islamic armies to achieve territorial expansion. Through a detailed examination of battles, sieges, and campaigns, researchers can uncover the key factors that contributed to the success of the Islamic Caliphate in capturing and consolidating power in diverse regions across Asia. Furthermore, a historiographical perspective highlights the interconnected nature of military conquests with broader socio-political transformations in Islamic societies. The legacy of these conquests, in terms of governance structures, legal systems, cultural exchange, and religious institutions, continues to shape the contemporary landscape of Islamic history and scholarship. By situating the Islamic conquests within a historiographical context, scholars can better understand the complexities of empire-building, statecraft, and the transmission of knowledge and ideas across different regions. This analysis sheds light on the dynamic interactions between conquerors and conquered peoples, as well as the enduring legacies of these encounters on historical narratives and collective memories within Islamic traditions. In conclusion, the historiographical significance of studying the Islamic conquests in Asia lies in its ability to provide a nuanced understanding of the interplay between military strategies, cultural exchanges, political developments, and socio-religious dynamics in shaping the course of Islamic history. Such a perspective enriches our comprehension of the diverse factors that have influenced the evolution of Islamic societies and the enduring legacies of conquest and empire in the Islamic world.

Legacy and Continuity: How the legacies of these conquests have influenced subsequent developments in Islamic societies and political landscapes

The Islamic conquests in Asia have left a profound legacy that continues to shape the development of Islamic societies and political landscapes to this day. The impact of these conquests can be seen in various aspects of Muslim civilization, ranging from religious practices and cultural traditions to political structures and social norms. One of the most significant legacies of the Islamic conquests is the spread and establishment of Islam as a dominant religion in the conquered territories. As Islam took root in these regions, it not only transformed the religious landscape but also influenced the cultural and social fabric of the societies. Moreover, the establishment of new political entities and governance systems following the conquests led to a restructuring of power dynamics in the conquered territories. This restructuring had lasting effects on the political structures and institutions of these regions, shaping their governance practices and administrative systems for centuries to come. Additionally, the economic impact of the conquests can be seen in the integration of trade routes, the development of new industries, and the exchange of goods and ideas across different regions. Furthermore, the social changes brought about by the Islamic conquests, such as shifts in demographics, urbanization, and the spread of Islamic education, have had a lasting impact on the social dynamics of the conquered territories. These changes have influenced the cultural practices, social norms, and familial structures of these societies, contributing to the rich tapestry of Islamic civilization. Overall, the legacies of the Islamic conquests in Asia are intertwined with the continuity of Islamic history and the evolution of Muslim societies over time. By examining these legacies, we gain a deeper understanding of the enduring impact of the conquests on the development of Islamic civilization and the shaping of contemporary political landscapes in the Muslim world.

Global Implications: The global impact of the Islamic conquests in Asia and their broader implications for world history, politics, and intercultural relations

The Islamic conquests in Asia left a profound impact on global history, politics, and intercultural relations. The expansion of the Islamic Caliphate into diverse regions such as Persia, Central Asia, the Indian Subcontinent, Southeast Asia, and China had far-reaching implications that reverberated beyond the borders of these conquered lands. One of the key global implications of the Islamic conquests in Asia was the spread of Islamic civilization and culture to new territories. The blending of local traditions with Islamic practices created a rich tapestry of artistic, architectural, and intellectual achievements that influenced the development of world civilizations. The Islamic conquests also played a significant role in shaping the geopolitical landscape of the time. The establishment of Islamic rule in strategic regions facilitated trade, communication, and cultural exchange between different parts of the world, paving the way for the interconnectedness of diverse societies and economies. Furthermore, the legacy of the Islamic conquests in Asia continues to impact contemporary political dynamics in the region and beyond. The establishment of Islamic empires and states during this period laid the foundation for the emergence of new political systems and governance structures that influenced subsequent developments in world politics. Moreover, the intercultural interactions that occurred as a result of the Islamic conquests fostered a spirit of multiculturalism and tolerance that contributed to the enrichment of global dialogue and mutual understanding between different civilizations. In conclusion, the global implications of the Islamic conquests in Asia transcend the boundaries of time and space, leaving an enduring legacy that continues to shape the world we live in today.

THE HISTORICAL SIGNIFICANCE OF ISLAMIC CONQUESTS

The Islamic conquests in Persia marked a pivotal moment in history, reshaping the political, cultural, and religious landscape of the region. These conquests were not just military campaigns but were driven by a complex interplay of factors that underscored the strategic importance of Persia and the motivations behind the expansion of the Islamic Caliphate. The conquest of Persia represented a significant turning point in the spread of Islam beyond the Arabian Peninsula. It marked the beginning of a series of conquests that would extend the reach of the Islamic Empire across vast territories, ultimately shaping the course of history in the region. Persia, with its rich history, advanced civilization, and strategic significance, presented an enticing target for the expanding Islamic forces. The motivations behind the Islamic expansion in Persia were multifaceted, encompassing religious, political, economic, and strategic factors. From a religious perspective, the spread of Islam was a central driving force behind the conquest of Persia. The early Islamic leaders saw the conversion of Persians to Islam as a means of expanding the faith and consolidating their political power. The message of Islam resonated with many Persians, leading to voluntary conversions and the gradual spread of the new faith. The political considerations behind the conquest were equally crucial. The Islamic Caliphate sought to assert its dominance in the region and establish its authority over key territories. By conquering Persia, the Caliphate could control vital trade routes, access valuable resources, and extend its influence over neighboring regions. Economically, the conquest of Persia presented opportunities for the Islamic forces to tap into the wealth and resources of the region. Persia's agricultural productivity, skilled artisans, and strategic location made it an attractive target for plunder and exploitation. The spoils of war from the conquest would enrich the Islamic Empire and help sustain its military campaigns. Strategically, the conquest of Persia was a means of securing the Caliphate's borders, expanding its sphere of influence, and countering rival powers in the region. By subjugating Persia, the Islamic forces could project their strength and establish a prominent foothold in a key geopolitical theater. The motivations behind the Islamic expansion in Persia were influenced by a combination of religious zeal, political ambitions, economic interests, and strategic imperatives. The conquest of Persia was a pivotal chapter in the history of the Islamic Empire, setting the stage for further conquests and shaping the trajectory of Islamic civilization in the centuries to come.

Exploration of the motivations behind Islamic expansion in Persia

The Islamic conquest of Persia was a pivotal moment in history, marking the expansion of the nascent Islamic empire into one of the greatest civilizations of its time. The motivations behind this expansion were multifaceted, intertwining religious, political, and economic factors. At the core of the Islamic expansion into Persia lay the religious zeal of the early Muslim armies. Driven by a fervent belief in the supremacy of Islam, they saw the conquest of Persia as a means to spread the message of the Prophet Muhammad and establish Islamic rule over new territories. This religious motivation provided a powerful impetus for the conquest, inspiring soldiers to fight with unwavering dedication and determination. Beyond religious zeal, the Islamic expansion into Persia also had strategic and political dimensions. The Sassanian Empire, weakened by internal strife and external threats, presented an attractive target for the expanding Islamic Caliphate. The conquest of Persia offered the Caliphate access to valuable resources, trade routes, and strategic military positions, enhancing its power and influence in the region. Moreover, the incorporation of Persian territories into the Islamic empire bolstered the Caliphate's political legitimacy and territorial control. Economic considerations also played a significant role in the motivations behind the Islamic expansion into Persia. The prosperous economy of Persia, fueled by its agricultural wealth, skilled artisans, and strategic location along key trade routes, presented lucrative opportunities for the Islamic Caliphate. The conquest of Persia allowed the Caliphate to tap into these economic resources, enriching its coffers and strengthening its economic position in the wider Islamic world. In sum, the motivations behind the Islamic expansion into Persia were deeply rooted in religious fervor, strategic calculations, and economic interests. The conquest of Persia represented a pivotal moment in the history of the Islamic empire, shaping its trajectory and leaving a lasting impact on the region for centuries to come.

Analysis of the tactics and strategies employed during the conquest

The Islamic conquest of Persia was a complex and multifaceted military campaign that required careful planning and strategic execution. The tactics and strategies employed by the Islamic forces played a crucial role in the success of the conquest. One key tactic was the effective use of diplomacy and alliances to weaken the Sassanian Empire from within. By exploiting internal divisions and forging alliances with local dissident factions, the Islamic forces were able to destabilize the Sassanian regime and create opportunities for conquest. In addition to diplomatic maneuvers, the Islamic forces also utilized a combination of siege warfare and swift, mobile cavalry units to strike at key strategic targets. Fielding highly trained and disciplined cavalry units, the Islamic forces were able to move rapidly across the rugged terrain of Persia, bypassing enemy defenses and launching surprise attacks on vulnerable positions. This mobility and speed allowed the Islamic forces to outmaneuver larger Sassanian armies and keep them off balance. Furthermore, the Islamic forces employed psychological warfare tactics to sow fear and confusion among their enemies. By spreading rumors of their invincibility and divine favor, the Islamic forces were able to intimidate and demoralize Sassanian troops, causing many to surrender without a fight. This psychological warfare played a significant role in undermining the morale of the Sassanian forces and hastening their defeat. Strategic coordination and communication were also key elements of the Islamic conquest strategy. Commanders made effective use of messenger networks and signal systems to coordinate movements and relay crucial information across vast distances. This enabled the Islamic forces to maintain unity of command and respond swiftly to changing battlefield conditions. Overall, the tactics and strategies employed during the Islamic conquest of Persia were characterized by a combination of diplomatic cunning, military prowess, and psychological warfare. By leveraging these factors effectively, the Islamic forces were able to overcome formidable obstacles and achieve a stunning victory that reverberated throughout the region for centuries to come.

Examination of the impact of the conquest on Persia's political landscape

The Islamic conquest of Persia had a profound impact on the political landscape of the region. The Sassanian Empire, which had ruled Persia for centuries, was overthrown, leading to significant changes in the governance and power structure of the region. The Islamic Caliphate's conquest resulted in the establishment of new administrative systems and the introduction of Islamic law, or Sharia, as the basis for governance. Many local rulers and nobles in Persia were either defeated or assimilated into the new Islamic administration, leading to a restructuring of political authority. The appointment of governors and local administrators by the Caliphate helped to centralize power and maintain control over the conquered territories. This centralized authority facilitated the collection of taxes and ensured the smooth functioning of the administrative machinery. The Islamic conquest also brought about changes in the social hierarchy of Persia. The Persian aristocracy, which had ruled the region under the Sassanian Empire, saw a decline in influence as new Islamic administrators were appointed to key positions of power. This shift in political power had a lasting impact on the social dynamics of Persia, reshaping traditional power structures and establishing new norms of governance. Furthermore, the Islamic conquest led to the spread of Arabic as the language of administration and education in Persia. This linguistic shift not only facilitated communication within the newly established Islamic administration but also promoted the cultural assimilation of Persian and Arab traditions. The fusion of Persian and Islamic cultural elements resulted in a unique blend of traditions that defined the cultural identity of the region for centuries to come. Overall, the Islamic conquest of Persia fundamentally altered the political landscape of the region, ushering in a new era of governance and cultural exchange.

The legacy of the conquest continues to shape modern-day Iran, reflecting the enduring influence of Islamic rule on Persia's political and cultural development.

Discussion of the cultural and religious implications of Islamic rule in Persia

The Islamic conquest of Persia marked a significant turning point in the region's cultural and religious landscape. As Islamic rule took hold, profound changes began to unfold, shaping the fabric of Persian society in ways that would endure for centuries. The fusion of Arab and Persian traditions gave rise to a unique blend of cultural identity reflected in art, architecture, literature, and daily life. Islamic principles, deeply rooted in the Quran and Hadith, began to influence every aspect of Persian society, from governance to social norms. The concept of sharia law became integral to the legal system, while Arabic script and language gained prominence in official documents and scholarly works. Mosques and madrasas sprang up across the land, becoming centers of learning and spiritual guidance. The Persian people, known for their rich history and intellectual legacy, embraced Islam with a fervor that transformed their religious practices and cultural expressions. The arts flourished under Islamic patronage, creating a vibrant artistic tradition that blended Persian aesthetic sensibilities with Islamic motifs. Calligraphy, miniature painting, and intricate tilework adorned mosques and palaces, embodying the fusion of Islamic and Persian artistic traditions. Sufism, a mystical branch of Islam, gained a strong foothold in Persian society, appealing to those seeking a deeper spiritual connection. The teachings of Sufi masters resonated with the Persian people, offering a path to inner enlightenment and divine love. Despite the challenges of adapting to a new cultural and religious order, the Persian people embraced Islam as a unifying force that transcended tribal and regional divides. The legacy of Islamic rule in Persia continues to shape the country's identity, with echoes of the past reverberating in the present-day cultural landscape. As Persian society evolved under Islamic influence, a rich tapestry of traditions emerged, blending the old with the new to create a vibrant and resilient cultural heritage.

Comparison of Persian society before and after the conquest

Persian society before the Islamic conquest was characterized by a rich cultural heritage, a well-established administrative system, and a thriving economy. Zoroastrianism was the dominant religion, influencing various aspects of daily life and shaping societal norms. The Sassanian Empire had created a sense of national identity among the people, fostering a strong sense of pride and unity. The Islamic conquest brought significant changes to Persian society. The introduction of Islam as the new religion led to a gradual decline of Zoroastrianism and the adoption of new religious practices. Arabic became the official language, replacing Persian in administrative and bureaucratic functions. The administrative structure was also reformed to align with Islamic principles, resulting in changes to governance and legal systems. Economically, the conquest opened up new trade routes and markets, facilitating cultural exchange and economic growth. Persian artisans and craftsmen continued to thrive under Islamic rule, contributing to the creation of a unique blend of Persian and Islamic artistic styles. Islamic architecture, influenced by Persian styles, flourished in cities like Baghdad and Isfahan, leaving a lasting impact on the region's cultural landscape. Socially, the Islamic conquest brought about a shift in societal norms and practices. The hierarchical structures of Sassanian society were altered, with Islamic principles of equality and justice influencing social interactions. Women's rights also underwent changes, with Islamic attitudes towards gender roles shaping norms and expectations within Persian society. Overall, the Islamic conquest fundamentally transformed Persian society, blending existing traditions with new Islamic practices to create a distinct cultural identity. The legacy of this period continues to resonate in modern-day Iran, with elements of Persian culture, art, and architecture reflecting the enduring impact of the Islamic conquest on the region.

Evaluation of the long-term legacy of the Islamic conquest on Persia

The Islamic conquest of Persia left a lasting legacy that reshaped the social, cultural, and political landscape of the region for centuries to come. The profound impact of the conquest can be observed through the transformation of Persia's society, economy, and religious practices. One of the most significant long-term effects of the Islamic conquest was the introduction of Islam as the dominant religion in Persia. This shift not only transformed the spiritual beliefs of the population but also influenced the legal, political, and social structures of Persian society. The fusion of Islamic and Persian cultural elements created a vibrant and diverse civilization that thrived for centuries. Furthermore, the Islamic conquest brought about economic changes in Persia, as trade routes expanded, commerce flourished, and new industries emerged. The integration of Persian and Islamic economic systems stimulated growth and development, leading to prosperity in various sectors of the economy. Key historical figures played pivotal roles in shaping the legacy of the Islamic conquest on

Persia. Military commanders such as Khalid ibn al-Walid and Saad ibn Abi Waqqas demonstrated exceptional leadership skills and strategic acumen, laying the foundation for the establishment of Islamic rule in Persia. Their contributions to the conquest helped solidify the Caliphate's authority in the region and facilitated the assimilation of Persian culture into the Islamic empire. Overall, the long-term legacy of the Islamic conquest on Persia was multifaceted and enduring. It not only transformed the religious and cultural fabric of the region but also had far-reaching consequences for its political and economic institutions. The fusion of Islamic and Persian traditions created a rich tapestry of civilization that continues to shape the identity of modern-day Iran.

Consideration of the role of key historical figures in the conquest

Under the rule of the Islamic Caliphate, the conquest of Persia was facilitated by the strategic brilliance and military prowess of key historical figures. Among these figures, Khalid ibn al-Walid emerged as a legendary commander whose tactical acumen and leadership skills were instrumental in securing decisive victories on the battlefield. His innovative strategies, such as the effective use of mobile cavalry units, enabled the Islamic forces to outmaneuver and outwit the larger Sassanian armies. Another notable figure in the Persian conquest was Sa'd ibn Abi Waqqas, whose diplomatic skills and ability to forge alliances with local tribes played a crucial role in expanding Muslim control in Persia. Sa'd's expertise in navigating complex political landscapes and winning the support of disparate groups further solidified the Caliphate's hold over the region. Additionally, the military genius of Qutaybah ibn Muslim contributed significantly to the success of the Islamic conquest in Persia. Qutaybah's strategic vision and bold tactics helped to overcome formidable resistance from Sassanian forces and secure key territories for the expanding Islamic empire. Furthermore, the administrative prowess of Umar ibn al-Khattab, the second Caliph of the Rashidun Caliphate, cannot be understated in the context of the Persian conquest. Umar's efficient governance and establishment of a centralized administrative system laid the groundwork for long-term stability and prosperity in the newly conquered territories. These key historical figures not only played instrumental roles in the military campaigns that led to the conquest of Persia but also shaped the socio-political landscape of the region in profound ways. Their leadership, strategic vision, and administrative abilities were pivotal in establishing Islamic rule in Persia and setting the stage for further expansion into new territories, ultimately leaving a lasting legacy on the history of the Islamic world.

Reflection on the broader implications of the Persian conquest within the context of Islamic history

The Islamic conquest of Persia marked a significant turning point in the expansion of the Islamic Caliphate and its broader implications within the context of Islamic history cannot be understated. The conquest of Persia not only altered the geopolitical landscape of the region but also had profound cultural, religious, and societal impacts that reverberated throughout the Muslim world. One of the key implications of the Persian conquest was the assimilation of Persian administrative practices and cultural elements into the Islamic Caliphate. The Persians had a rich tradition of governance, art, literature, and science, which greatly influenced the development of Islamic civilization. The fusion of Persian and Islamic traditions resulted in a unique and vibrant cultural synthesis that shaped the identity of the

Muslim world for centuries to come. Furthermore, the conquest of Persia facilitated the spread of Islam across the region and beyond. The conversion of the Persian population to Islam not only increased the size of the Muslim community but also contributed to the development of Islamic scholarship and jurisprudence. Persian scholars played a crucial role in translating and preserving ancient Greek and Roman texts, which laid the foundation for the flowering of Islamic intellectual and scientific achievements during the Golden Age of Islam. Additionally, the conquest of Persia had significant implications for the political structure of the Islamic Caliphate. The incorporation of the Persian administrative system into the Caliphate's governance helped centralize and streamline the administration of the vast empire. The establishment of a stable and efficient bureaucratic apparatus enabled the Caliphate to maintain control over its territories and facilitate the spread of Islam to new regions. Moreover, the Persian conquest reinforced the idea of Islamic universalism and the concept of a global Muslim community (Ummah). The successful expansion into Persia demonstrated the power and appeal of Islam as a unifying force that transcended ethnic, cultural, and linguistic boundaries. It underscored the Caliphate's mission to establish a just and egalitarian society based on Islamic principles and values. In conclusion, the Persian conquest holds a pivotal place in Islamic history as a watershed moment that shaped the trajectory of the Muslim world. Its implications, spanning cultural, religious, political, and social dimensions, continue to resonate in contemporary Islamic societies and underscore the complex interplay between conquest, assimilation, and innovation in the evolution of Islamic civilization.

THE ISLAMIC CONQUESTS IN ASIA

Conclusion highlighting the key takeaways from the chapter and setting the stage for subsequent discussions

The conquest of Persia marked a pivotal moment in the expansion of the Islamic Caliphate, shaping the course of history in the region and beyond. As we reflect on the broader implications of this conquest within the context of Islamic history, several key takeaways emerge. Firstly, the conquest of Persia demonstrated the military prowess and strategic acumen of the early Muslim armies, showcasing their ability to overcome formidable adversaries and establish a new political order. Furthermore, the conquest highlighted the complex interplay of religious, cultural, and political factors that underpinned Islamic expansion in the region. The assimilation of Persian traditions and administrative practices into the Islamic state underscored the dynamic nature of cultural exchange during this period. Additionally, the conversion of Persian subjects to Islam exemplified the transformative impact of religion on societal norms and identities. Moreover, the conquest of Persia laid the foundation for the emergence of a new Islamic civilization that drew on the diverse cultural legacies of the conquered territories. The fusion of Persian, Arab, and other regional influences shaped the development of art, architecture, literature, and scholarship in the Islamic world, laying the groundwork for a rich and vibrant cultural heritage that endured for centuries. As we look ahead to further explorations of Islamic conquests in Asia, the conquest of Persia serves as a compelling case study that illuminates the complex dynamics of power, identity, and cultural exchange in the medieval world. By delving into the nuances of this conquest, we gain a deeper understanding of the multifaceted interactions that shaped the course of history in the region and beyond. Building on the insights gleaned from the conquest of Persia, our subsequent discussions will delve into the expansion of the Islamic Caliphate into Central Asia, India,

Southeast Asia, and China, exploring the diverse trajectories of conquest and their enduring legacies. By examining these conquests through a holistic lens that integrates military, political, economic, religious, and cultural dimensions, we aim to elucidate the far-reaching impacts of Islamic expansion on the diverse societies and cultures of Asia.

NOTES AND REFERENCES

Here are some of the most important Arabic and Islamic sources covering the Islamic conquests in Asia:

1. Primary Arabic Sources:
- "The History of al-Tabari" (Tarikh al-Tabari) by Muhammad ibn Jarir al-Tabari - This is one of the most comprehensive early Islamic historical chronicles, covering the early Islamic conquests in great detail.
- "The Book of Conquests" (Kitab al-Futuh) by Ahmad ibn A'tham al-Kufi - An early 9th century work focusing specifically on the Islamic conquests.
- "The Book of Countries" (Kitab al-Buldan) by al-Baladhuri - A 9th century work providing detailed accounts of the conquests of various regions.
- "The Complete History" (Al-Kamil fi al-Tarikh) by Ibn al-Athir - A comprehensive historical work from the 13th century that covers the early Islamic conquests.

2. Modern Academic Works:
- "The Great Arab Conquests: How the Spread of Islam Changed the World We Live In" by Hugh Kennedy - A comprehensive modern academic treatment of the subject.
- "In God's Path: The Arab Conquests and the Creation of an Islamic Empire" by Robert G. Hoyland - A recent scholarly work examining the conquests.
- "The New Cambridge History of Islam, Volume 1: The Formation of the Islamic World, Sixth to Eleventh Centuries" - Contains chapters by leading scholars on the early Islamic conquests.

3. Primary Sources in Translation:
- "The History of al-Tabari" translated by various scholars and published by SUNY Press - This multi-volume English translation makes Tabari's work accessible to non-Arabic readers.
- "The Origins of the Islamic State" by al-Baladhuri, translated by Philip Khuri Hitti - An English translation of parts of al-Baladhuri's work.

4. Specialized Studies:

- "The Arab Conquest of Iran and its Aftermath" by D.G. Tor - Focuses specifically on the conquest of Iran.
- "The Muslim Conquest of Persia" by A.I. Akram - Another work examining the conquest of Iran in detail.
- "The Early Islamic Conquests" by Fred McGraw Donner - A scholarly examination of the early conquests.

These sources provide a mix of primary Arabic texts, modern academic treatments, and specialized studies that should give you a comprehensive understanding of the Islamic conquests in Asia from both historical and contemporary scholarly perspectives. The primary Arabic sources are particularly valuable for their early accounts, while the modern works provide critical analysis and incorporate a wider range of sources and perspectives.

Online:
[1] https://en.wikipedia.org/wiki/Early_Muslim_conquests
[2] https://library.gordon.edu/his344/primary-sources
[3] https://www.jstor.org/stable/j.ctt16gzmxj
[4] https://africame.factsanddetails.com/article/entry-841.html
[5] https://guides.library.cornell.edu/MideastIslamStudies/PrimarySources
[6] https://www.bibliomed.org/fulltextpdf.php?mno=144290
[7] https://openstax.org/books/world-history-volume-1/pages/11-2-the-arab-islamic-conquests-and-the-first-islamic-states
[8] https://libguides.library.nd.edu/arabic-islamic-studies/primary-sources
[9] https://www.researchgate.net/publication/340377397_Islam_in_Central_Asia_A_Study_from_Historical_Perspective
[10] https://en.unesco.org/silkroad/knowledge-bank/arab-conquest
[11] https://en.unesco.org/silkroad/content/did-you-know-spread-islam-southeast-asia-through-trade-routes
[12] https://www.oxfordbibliographies.com/abstract/document/obo-9780195390155/obo-9780195390155-0015.xml
[13] http://www.zekeriyakitapci.com/tr/bd/the-conquest-of-central-asia-by-the-muslim-arabs.html?I=5
[14] https://libraryguides.griffith.edu.au/islamic-studies/primary-sources
[15] https://www.degruyter.com/document/doi/10.1525/9780520957862-004/pdf?licenseType=restricted
[16] https://en.wikipedia.org/wiki/Muslim_conquest_of_Transoxiana
[17] https://guides.library.cornell.edu/c.php?g=141521&p=959026
[18] https://www.jstor.org/stable/45242351
[19] https://africame.factsanddetails.com/article/entry-256.html
[20] https://cnu.libguides.com/c.php?g=23214&p=136635

THE ISLAMIC CONQUESTS IN ASIA

Here are references from the available research papers that cover various aspects of the Islamic Conquests in Asia:

1. **Islamic Conquests in Central Asia**:
    - The paper by M. Sharon discusses the decisive battles in the Arab conquest of Syria, highlighting the strategic military engagements that were crucial in establishing Islamic rule in the region(Denaro, 2019).

2. **Islamic Expansion in Southeast Asia**:
    - The paper by I. Lapidus explores the spread of Islam from the Middle East to Southeast Asia, detailing how Islam reached the Malay Peninsula and the Indonesian archipelago through trade and Sufi missionaries(Habib, 2018).

3. **Islamic Rule in the Persianate World**:
    - The paper by George Lane discusses the Ilkhanate period, where Mongol rule extended over medieval Western Asia, including the integration of Islamic administration and culture(MacLean, 2013).

4. **Islamic Influence in the Mediterranean**:
    - The paper by R. Denaro examines the historiographical patterns recounting the end of Muslim rule in Sicily and al-Andalus, showing the cultural and political impacts of Islamic rule in these regions(Baba, 2013).

5. **Islamic Juridical Influence in Central Asia**:
    - The paper discusses the role of Islamic religious figures in the context of the Turkestan campaigns of the Russian Empire, highlighting the influence of Islamic jurisprudence in the region(Franzke et al., 2022).

These references provide a comprehensive overview of the Islamic conquests and their impacts across various regions in Asia, from military conquests and cultural assimilations to the integration of Islamic jurisprudence.

Bibliography:
Abdullah, M., Nasir, D. A., & Abdul, H. (2021). Nature And Scale Of Conversion From Conventional Banking To Islamic Banking In Selected ASEAN

Countries: Recent Conversion Models & Major Challenges. iEco | Islamic Economics Journal.

Alam, N., Duygun, M., & Ariss, R. T. (2016). Green Sukuk: An Innovation in Islamic Capital Markets. 167–185.

Altaweel, M., & Squitieri, A. (2018). Revolutionizing a World: From Small States to Universalism in the Pre-Islamic Near East.

Azzi, M. A. –. (2019). The Position of Population of Biladelsham (The Levant) on the Islamic Conquests. International Journal of Humanities and Social Sciences.

Baba, S. (2013). Origin and History of Volga Bulghars: A Study of the Journey from Central Asia to Volga-Ural Region and the Formation of Volga Bulgharia. 36, 189.

Bichi, A. A., & Embong, R. (2018). EVALUATING THE QUALITY OF ISLAMIC CIVILIZATION AND ASIAN CIVILIZATIONS EXAMINATION QUESTIONS. 1, 93–109.

Burhanudin, J. (2022). Two Islamic Writing Traditions in Southeast Asia: Kitab Jawi and Kitab Kuning with Reference to the Works of Da'ud al-Fatani dan Nawawi al-Bantani. Al-Jami'ah: Journal of Islamic Studies.

Burstein, S. (2022). When Greek Was an African Language: The Role of Greek Culture in Ancient and Medieval Nubia. Transition, 132, 170–187.

Bustamam-Ahmad, K. (2008). The History of Jama'ah Tabligh in Southeast Asia: The Role of Islamic Sufism in Islamic Revival. Al-Jami'ah: Journal of Islamic Studies, 46, 353–400.

Carballo, D. (2020). Invasion of the Mesoamerican Coast. 137–168.

Chaudhary, P., & Rathore, S. (2021). Chachnama Discourse: The Dichotomy of Islamic Origins in South Asia. Rupkatha Journal on Interdisciplinary Studies in Humanities.

Cornell, S. (2005). Narcotics, Radicalism, and Armed Conflict in Central Asia: The Islamic Movement of Uzbekistan. Terrorism and Political Violence, 17, 619–639.

Denaro, R. (2019). "And God Dispersed Their Unity": Historiographical Patterns in Recounting the End of Muslim Rule in Sicily and al-Andalus. Medieval Sicily, al-Andalus, and the Maghrib, 5, 105–126.

Din Yousefi, N. (2019). Confusion and Consent: Land Tax (Kharāj) and the Construction of Judicial Authority in the Early Islamic Empire (ca. 12–183 A.H./634–800 C.E.). Sociology of Islam.

Dunn, A. (1997). Byzantium and the early Islamic conquests. Byzantine and Modern Greek Studies, 21, 270–273.

Durand-Guédy, D. (2018). Book Review: A.C.S. Peacock and Deborah Tor, Medieval Central Asia and the Persianate World: Iranian Tradition and Islamic Civilisation. The Medieval History Journal, 21, 173–180.

Frank, A. J. (2013). Ron Sela: The Legendary Biographies of Tamerlane: Islam and Heroic Apocrypha in Central Asia. (Cambridge Studies in Islamic Civilization.) xviii, 164 pp. New York: Cambridge University Press, 2011. £55. ISBN 978 0521 51706 5. Bulletin of the School of Oriental and African Studies, 76, 154–156.

Franzke, S., Wu, J., Froese, F., & Chan, Z. (2022). Female entrepreneurship in Asia: a critical review and future directions. Asian Business & Management, 21, 343–372.

Fuchs, S. (2021). Major turning points for Shiʻi Islam in modern South Asia. Routledge Handbook on Islam in Asia.

Gani, I. M., & Bahari, Z. (2021). Islamic banking's contribution to the Malaysian real economy.

Gedacht, J. (2019). Port Cities and Islamic Insurgency across Southeast Asia, 1850–1913. Oxford Research Encyclopedia of Asian History.

Gradmann, R., Berthold, C., & Schüssler, U. (2015). Composition and colouring agents of historical Islamic glazes measured with EPMA and μ-XRD2. European Journal of Mineralogy, 27, 325–335.

Habib, S. (2018). Fundamentals of Islamic Finance and Banking.

Hall, K. R. (2015). European Southeast Asia Encounters with Islamic Expansionism, circa 1500–1700: Comparative Case Studies of Banten, Ayutthaya, and Banjarmasin in the Wider Indian Ocean Context. Journal of World History, 25, 229–262.

Hassan, M. K., Alshater, M. M., Rashid, M., & Hidayat, S. (2021). Ten years of the Journal of Islamic Marketing: a bibliometric analysis. Journal of Islamic Marketing.

Hawkley, E. P. (2015). Reviving the Reconquista in Southeast Asia: Moros and the Making of the Philippines, 1565–1662. Journal of World History, 25, 285–310.

Heidemann, S. (2020). Introduction: Transregional and Regional Elites – Connecting the Early Islamic Empire. Transregional and Regional Elites – Connecting the Early Islamic Empire.

Helmi, I., & Mulyany, R. (2020). Does Islamic Corporate Governance Contribute to the Performance of Islamic Banks? Evidence from Indonesia and Malaysia.

Hogan, H. (2009). Course Objectives, Expectations, and Requirements.

Islam, A. I., & Amin, M. N. (2023). Reflection on the Contributions of Ghaznavid Dynasty to the Islamic Civilization of Central Asia and Afghanistan (963-1187). Perspectives in Social Science.

Islam, M., & Islam, M. S. (2018). Politics and Islamic Revivalism in Bangladesh: The Role of the State and Non-State/Non-Political Actors. Politics, Religion & Ideology, 19, 326–353.

Jarmy, A. (2021). Dating the Emergence of the Warrior-Prophet in Maghāzī Literature. The Presence of the Prophet in Early Modern and Contemporary Islam.

Kamil, Dr. N. M., Sulaiman, M., Osman-Gani, A., & Ahmad, K. (2014). Investigating the Dimensionality of Organisational Citizenship Behaviour from Islamic Perspective (OCBIP): Empirical Analysis of Business Organisations in South-East Asia. Journal of Character & Leadership Integration (JCLI).

Kaul, V., & Vajpeyi, A. (2020). Minorities and Populism: Critical Perspectives from South Asia and Europe.

Khan, M. T., Rashid, A., Khan, M. H., Zaman, A., & Ali, S. (2023). Effects of oil price uncertainty on corporate investment of Islamic stocks: evidence from the extreme event of Covid-19 pandemic. Journal of Islamic Accounting and Business Research.

Khoso, Dr. A. A., Hammad, M., & Ahmed, Dr. M. (2022). Arabic 1. Islamic History of District Mardan in the Indian Subcontinent. Al Khadim Research Journal of Islamic Culture and Civilization.

Kim, K. (2012). Profit and Protection: Emin Khwaja and the Qing Conquest of Central Asia, 1759–1777. Journal of Asian Studies, 71, 603–626.

Kochnev, A. (2023). ON THE QUESTION OF THE ROLE OF ISLAMIC RELIGIOUS FIGURES IN THE CONTEXT OF THE TURKESTAN CAMPAIGNS OF THE RUSSIAN EMPIRE. ON THE EXAMPLE OF THE CORRESPONDENCE OF THE ORENBURG BORDER COMMISSION WITH MULLAH SHAGIMARDANOV. RSUH/RGGU Bulletin. Series Political Sciences. History. International Relations.

Lane, G. (2019). The Ilkhanate: Mongol Rule in Medieval Western Asia, 1256–1335. Oxford Research Encyclopedia of Asian History.

Lapidus, I. (2012). Islamic Societies to the Nineteenth Century: The Turkish Migrations and the Ottoman Empire. 427–467.

Laskin, E. (2022). Central Asia: A New History from the Imperial Conquests to the Present By Adeeb Khalid. Princeton, N.J.: Princeton University Press, 2021. 556 pp. ISBN: 9780691161396 (cloth). Journal of Asian Studies.

Ledhem, M. A., & Mekidiche., Mohammed. (2021). Islamic finance and economic growth nexus: an empirical evidence from Southeast Asia using dynamic panel one-step system GMM analysis. Journal of Islamic Accounting and Business Research.

Lyonnet, B., & Fontugne, M. (2021). Back to the Iron Age Chronology in Southern Central Asia. Ancient Civilizations from Scythia to Siberia.

MacLean, G. (2013). Ottomania: The Romantics and the Myth of the Islamic Orient. The International Journal of Turkish Studies, 19, 161.

Malik, A. (2024). Analysis of The Progress and Setback of Islamic Civilization of The Mughal, Safawi and Ottoman Türkiye. Tajdid.

Mcchesney, R. (2014). Waqf in Central Asia: Four Hundred Years in the History of a Muslim Shrine, 1480-1889.

Mir-Makhamad, B., & Spengler, R. (2023). Testing the applicability of Watson's Green Revolution concept in first millennium ce Central Asia. Vegetation History and Archaeobotany, 1–13.

Mīrzā, O., Khvāndamīr, G., Dīn, R., & Thackston, W. (2012). Classical writings of the medieval Islamic world: Persian histories of the Mongol dynasties.

Ng, S. (2019). Islamic Alexanders in Southeast Asia. Alexander the Great from Britain to Southeast Asia.

Nuraisah, N., Permata, Y., Tabroni, I., Kathryn, M., & Cale, W. (2023). Modern Islamic Civilization in South and Southeast Asia. International Journal of Educational Narratives.

Nurdiansyah, A. (2018). Halal Certification and Its Impact on Tourism in Southeast Asia: A Case Study Halal Tourism in Thailand. KnE Social Sciences, 3, 26–43.

Ottewill-Soulsby, S. (2023). Arab Conquests and Early Islamic Historiography: The Futuh al-buldan of al-Baladhuri. Al-Masaq, 35, 241–243.

Pasha, M. (2016). 15 Islam in the early modern world nile green.

Polymaths of Islam: Power and Networks of Knowledge in Central Asia. James Pickett (Ithaca, NY: Cornell University Press, 2020). Pp. 301. $54.95 hardcover. ISBN: 9781501750243. (n.d.).

Rehman, S., Wani, I., Khanam, M., & Almonifi, Y. S. A. (2021). A Brief Review of Growth and Development in Islamic Banking. Banking & Insurance eJournal.

Rock-Singer, A. (2020). Islamic Print Media. Islamic Studies.

SACRALIZATION OF BURIAL PLACES OF EARLY ISLAMIC AND SUBSEQUENT HISTORICAL FIGURES OF FERGANA AND MODERNITY. (n.d.).

Saiti, B., & Masih, M. (2014). The Co-movement of Selective Conventional and Islamic Stock Markets in East Asia: Is there any Impact on Shariah Compliant Equity Investment in China?

Sharon, M. (2007). The Decisive Battles in the Arab Conquest of Syria. 101, 297–358.

Siméon, P. (2020). Central Asia. The Oxford Handbook of Islamic Archaeology.

Staëvel, J.-P. V. (2023). Ribât in Early Islamic Ifrîqiya: Another Islam from the Edge. Religions.

The Islamic Juridical Field in Central Asia, ca. 1785–1918. (2016).

Tierney, B. (2012). Christianity in Afghanistan. 8.

Ulrich, B. (2019). The Azd and the Early Islamic State. Arabs in the Early Islamic Empire.

Wolters, A. (2013). Islamic finance in the states of Central Asia: Strategies, institutions, first experiences.

Yoon, D.-E., Choudhury, T., Saha, A., & Rashid, M. (2021). Contagion risk: cases of Islamic and emerging market banks. International Journal of Islamic and Middle Eastern Finance and Management.

Yuda, T. K. (2019). The development of "Islamic welfare regime" in South East Asia. International Journal of Sociology and Social Policy.

Дербисали, А. (2020). The Thinker of Otrar Province. 92, 14–25.

Хумидович, А. В., & Равильевич, К. Ш. (2023). Islamic education in Chechnya: historical, political, spiritual and cultural factors of formation. STATE AND MUNICIPAL MANAGEMENT SCHOLAR NOTES.

Online:

Here are more key scholarly sources and aspects of the Islamic conquests in Asia:

1. Key Sources:

- "Islamic Central Asia: An Anthology of Historical Sources" edited by Scott C. Levi and Ron Sela - This anthology provides primary documents for studying Central Asian history [1].

- "The New Cambridge History of Islam" edited by Anthony Reid, David Morgan, and R. Michael Feener - Contains chapters on the spread of Islam in Southeast Asia [3].

- "A History of Islamic Societies" by Ira M. Lapidus - Covers the history of Muslim rule in India [not in results, but a standard reference].

- "The History of India, as Told by Its Own Historians" edited by H.M. Elliot and John Dowson - Compiles translations of medieval Persian chronicles about Muslim rule in India [not in results, but an important source].

2. Key Aspects:

- The conquests began in the 7th century under Muhammad and expanded rapidly under the Rashidun and Umayyad Caliphates [6].

- Major areas conquered included Persia, Central Asia, parts of South Asia, and Southeast Asia [6][3].

- The conquests facilitated the spread of Islam, though conversion was generally not forced [8].

- Trade routes played an important role in the spread of Islam, especially in Southeast Asia [3][5].

- The process of Islamization was often gradual, with local cultures and traditions being incorporated [3][5].
- In Central Asia, the conquests faced resistance from local Buddhist and Zoroastrian populations [6][9].
- The Battle of Talas in 751 CE was a significant event in the Muslim conquest of Central Asia [9].
- In South Asia, the conquests led to the establishment of Muslim rule in parts of the subcontinent, though complete Islamization did not occur [11].
- The conquests had significant cultural, social, and political impacts on the conquered regions [10].

These sources and aspects provide a scholarly overview of the Islamic conquests in various parts of Asia, highlighting the complex processes of military expansion, cultural interaction, and religious change that characterized this historical period.

Citations:
[1] https://www.jstor.org/stable/j.ctt16gzmxj
[2] https://dergipark.org.tr/en/download/article-file/2284872
[3] https://oxfordre.com/asianhistory/display/10.1093/acrefore/9780190277727.001.0001/acrefore-9780190277727-e-40
[4] https://www.bibliomed.org/fulltextpdf.php?mno=144290
[5] http://repository.uin-malang.ac.id/11992/2/11992.pdf
[6] https://en.wikipedia.org/wiki/Early_Muslim_conquests
[7] https://www.degruyter.com/document/doi/10.31826/9781463232566-003/html?lang=en
[8] https://content.ucpress.edu/chapters/10213001.ch01.pdf
[9] https://en.wikipedia.org/wiki/Muslim_conquest_of_Transoxiana
[10] https://en.unesco.org/silkroad/sites/default/files/knowledge-bank-article/vol_III%20silk%20road_the%20arab%20conquest.pdf
[11] https://www.oxfordbibliographies.com/display/document/obo-9780195390155/obo-9780195390155-0079.xml

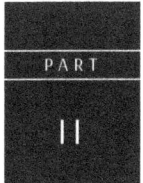

THE CONQUEST OF PERSIA

OVERVIEW OF THE PERSIAN EMPIRE'S GEOPOLITICAL LANDSCAPE

The Persian Empire, also known as the Sassanian Empire, encompassed a vast and diverse geopolitical landscape that held strategic importance in the ancient world. Stretching from the borders of the Byzantine Empire to the Indus River in the east, Persia was a formidable power with a rich history of imperial conquests and cultural achievements. At its height, the Sassanian Empire controlled key trade routes that connected the East and West, including the famed Silk Road that brought goods and ideas from distant lands. Its geographical position at the crossroads of Eurasia made it a coveted prize for neighboring empires seeking to expand their influence and wealth. The mountainous terrain of Persia provided natural defenses that shielded its heartland from invasions, while its vast plains and fertile valleys supported a thriving agricultural economy. Major cities like Ctesiphon and Persepolis served as centers of political power and cultural sophistication, showcasing the empire's grandeur and sophistication. The Persian Empire's strategic positioning along important trade routes, coupled with its strong centralized government and military prowess, made it a formidable force in the ancient world. Its armies were renowned for their discipline, organization, and skill in both siege warfare and open combat, making them a formidable adversary for would-be conquerors. Despite facing challenges from rival powers and internal strife, the Sassanian Empire's geopolitical landscape was a testament to the enduring legacy of Persian civilization. Its influence would shape the course of history in the region for centuries to come, leaving a lasting imprint on the world stage.

SASSANIAN EMPIRE'S MILITARY STRENGTH AND DEFENSES

The Sassanian Empire boasted a formidable military force, underpinned by a strong centralized command structure and a robust system of defense. The Sassanian army was known for its use of heavy cavalry, elite infantry units, and sophisticated siege tactics. The empire's strategic location, with natural barriers such as mountains and deserts, provided additional advantages in terms of defense. Additionally, the Sassanian Empire maintained a network of fortified cities and garrisons along its borders to protect against external threats. The Sassanian military was also highly disciplined and well-trained, with soldiers undergoing rigorous physical and mental conditioning. Furthermore, the empire's leaders invested heavily in military infrastructure, including the construction of arsenals, barracks, and military roads to ensure the rapid mobilization of troops. Overall, the Sassanian Empire's military strength and defenses played a crucial role in shaping the outcomes of conflicts with neighboring powers.

INITIAL ISLAMIC INCURSIONS INTO PERSIA

The Islamic incursions into Persia marked a significant turning point in the history of the region. The Sassanian Empire, known for its military strength and robust defenses, faced the initial wave of Islamic conquests with varying degrees of preparedness. As the Islamic forces advanced into Persian territories, they encountered a formidable opponent in the Sassanian army. Led by skilled military commanders, the Islamic incursions began with strategic raids on border regions, testing the Sassanian Empire's defenses and response capabilities. These early encounters set the stage for larger-scale campaigns that would shape the course of history in the region. The Sassanian Empire, with its centralized military structure and well-trained army, initially repelled the Islamic incursions with ferocity. However, the decentralized nature of the Islamic forces allowed them to adapt quickly to changing circumstances and employ innovative tactics in warfare. The Islamic incursions into Persia were not merely military conquests but also ideological struggles, as the spread of Islam played a significant role in shaping the conflict. The allure of a new religious and political order attracted many Persians to the Islamic cause, further destabilizing the Sassanian Empire's grip on its territories. As the Islamic forces gained momentum and secured key victories in battle, the Sassanian Empire's defenses began to crumble. The fall of major cities and strongholds to the Islamic armies signaled the beginning of a new chapter in the history of Persia, as the Islamic Caliphate established its presence in the region. The initial Islamic incursions into Persia laid the foundation for a prolonged and complex conflict that would reshape the political, cultural, and religious landscapes of the region. The interplay of military strategy, religious ideology, and cultural dynamics set the stage for the emergence of a new order in Persia, one that would leave a lasting impact on the course of history.

KEY BATTLES AND CAMPAIGNS IN THE CONQUEST

The Islamic conquest of Persia witnessed a series of key battles and campaigns that shaped the course of history in the region. One of the pivotal encounters was the Battle of Qadisiyyah in 636, where the Islamic forces, led by Saad ibn Abi Waqqas, faced the Sassanian army. This battle marked a turning point in the conflict, as the Islamic forces emerged victorious, paving the way for the subsequent conquest of Persia. Following the Battle of Qadisiyyah, the Islamic forces advanced further into Persian territory, engaging in a series of campaigns to consolidate their control. The Siege of Ctesiphon in 637 stands out as a significant military operation, resulting in the capture of the Sassanian capital and the defeat of the Persian forces. This marked a significant blow to the Sassanian Empire and further solidified the Islamic Caliphate's dominance in the region. Another notable campaign was the conquest of Persia's strategic cities, including Isfahan, Nishapur, and Rey. These urban centers played a crucial role in the economic and political landscape of Persia, and their capture symbolized the extent of Islamic control over the region. The successful campaigns in these cities not only demonstrated the military prowess of the Islamic forces but also highlighted their strategic acumen in expanding their influence. The Battle of Nahavand in 642 was another critical engagement that sealed the fate of the Sassanian Empire. Led by General Al-Nu'man ibn Muqarrin, the Islamic forces decisively defeated the Persian army, leading to the fall of many key Persian strongholds. The outcome of this battle further weakened the Sassanian resistance and accelerated the collapse of their empire. Overall, the key battles and campaigns in the conquest of Persia showcased the strategic planning, military skill, and determination of the Islamic forces in overcoming formidable resistance and establishing their dominance in the region. These military engagements not only shaped the course of history in Persia but also laid the foundation for the integration of Persian culture and society into the Islamic Caliphate.

ROLE OF RELIGIOUS AND CULTURAL FACTORS IN THE CONFLICT

The religious and cultural factors played a crucial role in shaping the conflict between the Islamic Caliphate and the Sassanian Empire during the conquest of Persia. The clash of religious ideologies, as well as the cultural differences between the two civilizations, significantly influenced the course of warfare and the subsequent outcomes. Islamic expansion into Persia was propelled by a sense of religious duty among the Arab Muslim armies. The concept of jihad, or holy war, motivated them to spread Islam and establish political authority over non-Muslim territories. This religious fervor not only provided a unifying force for the Arab forces but also instilled a sense of purpose and determination in their military campaigns. On the other hand, the Sassanian Empire's Zoroastrian religion played a central role in shaping their identity and motivating their resistance against the Islamic conquest. For the Sassanians, their religious beliefs were intertwined with their cultural heritage and national identity, leading them to view the Arab invaders as a threat to their way of life. Cultural differences between the two civilizations also exacerbated tensions during the conflict. The Arab armies, with their nomadic warrior culture and tribal alliances, clashed with the more centralized and hierarchical structure of the Sassanian Empire. These cultural differences not only affected the conduct of warfare but also influenced the strategies and tactics employed by both sides in battle. Furthermore, the cultural practices and social norms of Persia, such as its rich literary and artistic traditions, were impacted by the conquest. The Islamic Caliphate's administration and governance brought about changes in language, customs, and societal structures, leading to a gradual assimilation of Persian culture into the broader Islamic civilization. Overall, the role of religious and cultural factors in the conflict between the Islamic Caliphate and the Sassanian Empire was instrumental in shaping the course of the conquest of Persia. These factors not only influenced the motivations and strategies of the warring factions but also had lasting implications for the cultural and social landscape of the region in the centuries to come.

ECONOMIC SIGNIFICANCE OF PERSIA TO THE ISLAMIC CALIPHATE

Persia held immense economic significance for the Islamic Caliphate, serving as a vital hub for trade, agriculture, and industry. The region's fertile agricultural lands produced abundant crops such as wheat, barley, and rice, which not only sustained the local population but also supplied food to neighboring territories. Persia's strategic location along the Silk Road enabled the Caliphate to control key trade routes linking East and West, facilitating the exchange of goods and ideas across different regions. Persia's rich mineral resources, including gold, silver, copper, and precious gems, fueled the Islamic economy and financed military campaigns. The region's skilled artisans and craftsmen excelled in various industries, such as textile production, metalworking, and pottery, contributing to the Caliphate's prosperity and cultural development. The bustling markets of cities like Baghdad and Basra attracted merchants from far and wide, creating a vibrant commercial network that extended to distant lands. The Islamic Caliphate's administration of Persia's economic affairs was characterized by a sophisticated system of taxation, trade regulations, and infrastructure development. The establishment of bazaars, caravanserais, and currency mints enhanced economic growth and facilitated commerce within the empire. The construction of irrigation systems and agricultural projects boosted productivity and ensured food security for the population. Furthermore, Persia's intellectual and scientific achievements in fields such as medicine, astronomy, and mathematics greatly influenced Islamic scholarship and contributed to the Caliphate's cultural prestige. The translation of Persian texts into Arabic broadened the knowledge base of Muslim scholars and facilitated the exchange of ideas between different civilizations. In conclusion, Persia's economic significance to the Islamic Caliphate was multifaceted, encompassing agriculture, trade, industry, and intellectual pursuits. The region's wealth, resources, and skilled workforce played a crucial role in sustaining the empire's prosperity and influence, shaping its economic policies and cultural development for centuries to come.

INFLUENCE OF PERSIAN SOCIETY ON ISLAMIC GOVERNANCE

Persian society's rich history, bureaucratic structures, and administrative systems significantly influenced the governance practices of the Islamic Caliphate. The Sassanian Empire's sophisticated administrative framework, with its emphasis on centralized rule, taxation systems, and provincial governance, left a lasting impact on how the Islamic rulers managed their vast territories. Islamic administrators borrowed extensively from Persian models, adopting practices such as the diwan (royal court) and divan (financial administration), which helped streamline governance and ensure efficient management of resources. Persian officials and bureaucrats were often integrated into the new ruling structures, bringing their expertise and knowledge to the Islamic administration. The Persian influence extended to cultural and social aspects of governance as well. The Islamic Caliphate embraced Persian art, architecture, and intellectual traditions, incorporating them into the fabric of Islamic civilization. Persian poets, scholars, and philosophers played a crucial role in shaping the intellectual landscape of the Islamic world, contributing to the flourishing of scholarship and learning during this period. Furthermore, Persian concepts of rulership, justice, and governance influenced Islamic political thought and administration. The idea of the ruler as a just and benevolent figure, responsible for upholding the law and ensuring the welfare of his subjects, was a core tenet of Persian political philosophy that resonated with Islamic rulers. In essence, the influence of Persian society on Islamic governance was profound and far-reaching. It not only shaped the administrative structures and practices of the Islamic Caliphate but also enriched its cultural and intellectual heritage. The fusion of Persian and Islamic traditions laid the foundation for a diverse and dynamic civilization that thrived for centuries to come.

TREATY NEGOTIATIONS AND DIPLOMATIC RELATIONS

During the treaty negotiations between the Islamic Caliphate and the remaining Persian authorities, both sides faced the challenge of reconciling their differing political systems and cultural norms. The Persians, accustomed to a centralized, hierarchical governance structure under the Sassanian Empire, found themselves negotiating with a more decentralized Islamic administration that relied heavily on tribal alliances and religious leadership. Despite these differences, both parties recognized the mutual benefits of establishing diplomatic relations. The Islamic Caliphate sought to integrate Persia's wealth, resources, and administrative expertise into its growing empire, while the Persians sought to secure favorable terms that would guarantee the preservation of their cultural identity and religious practices. Through a series of negotiations, mediated by respected religious and political figures from both sides, a treaty was eventually reached. This treaty outlined the terms of governance, taxation, and religious freedoms for Persians living under Islamic rule. It also established protocols for diplomatic communication and trade relations between the two powers. The treaty negotiations marked a significant turning point in the relationship between the Islamic Caliphate and Persia, laying the foundation for a more stable and harmonious coexistence. While both sides had to make concessions and compromises, the resulting agreement set the stage for a period of cultural exchange, economic cooperation, and mutual respect that would shape the legacy of the conquest on Persian culture and identity.

LEGACY OF THE CONQUEST ON PERSIAN CULTURE AND IDENTITY

The Islamic conquest of Persia left a profound and lasting impact on the culture and identity of the region. The assimilation of Persian customs, traditions, and administrative practices by the Islamic Caliphate resulted in a unique blending of Arab and Persian influences. This cultural fusion not only enriched the Islamic civilization but also preserved and transmitted many aspects of Persian heritage to future generations. The legacy of the conquest on Persian culture and identity can be seen in various spheres of life, including art, literature, language, and governance. One of the most significant legacies of the conquest is the preservation and promotion of Persian literature and poetry. Persian poets and scholars played a crucial role in translating and disseminating Greek, Indian, and Persian works into Arabic, thereby enriching the Islamic intellectual tradition. The famous Persian epic, the Shahnameh, continued to be revered and studied, fostering a sense of pride and cultural continuity among the Persian people. Furthermore, the Islamic Caliphate's administrative reforms in Persia introduced new systems of governance that drew upon both Arab and Persian administrative practices. The adoption of Persian administrative techniques, such as the use of diwans (administrative councils) and the maintenance of a bureaucratic hierarchy, streamlined the administration of the vast territories under Islamic rule. This synthesis of Arab and Persian administrative systems laid the foundation for a more efficient and stable governance structure in the region. The conquest also had a profound impact on Persian art and architecture. The fusion of Islamic and Persian artistic styles gave rise to a distinctive aesthetic that is evident in the design of mosques, palaces, and other monumental structures. The intricate patterns, geometric motifs, and ornate calligraphy that characterize Persian art were incorporated into Islamic architectural masterpieces, creating a visual language that reflected the cultural synthesis of the two civilizations. In conclusion, the legacy of the Islamic conquest on Persian culture and identity is a testament to the enduring influence of the Persian civilization on the Islamic world. The blending of Persian and Islamic traditions in literature, governance, and art created a rich and diverse cultural tapestry that continues to shape the identity of the Persian people today.

COMPARISON OF PRE-AND POST-CONQUEST PERSIA

The Islamic conquest of Persia marked a significant turning point in the history of the region, with far-reaching implications for Persian culture and identity. Before the conquest, Persia was a powerful empire with a rich history, strong cultural traditions, and a well-established social hierarchy. The Sassanian Empire, which ruled over Persia at the time, had a centralized government, a sophisticated bureaucracy, and a thriving economy. The arrival of the Islamic forces led to a period of upheaval and transformation in Persia. The conquest brought about changes in religion, language, and customs, as Islam gradually became the dominant faith in the region. Persian society adapted to new Islamic norms and practices, leading to a blending of Persian and Arab cultures. The Arabic language also gained prominence in the administration and communication of the conquered territories, alongside the native Persian language. The conquest of Persia also had a profound impact on the political landscape of the region. The centralized Sassanian Empire was replaced by a more decentralized system under Islamic rule, with power dispersed among various local rulers and governors. This shift in governance had long-term implications for the structure of Persian society and the relationship between the ruling elite and the general population. Economically, the conquest of Persia brought about changes in trade and commerce, as the Islamic Caliphate integrated Persian territories into its vast network of markets and trade routes. Persian artisans and craftsmen continued to produce goods of high quality, which were in demand both within the empire and beyond its borders. The exchange of goods and ideas between Persian and Islamic cultures enriched both societies and contributed to the development of new artistic and intellectual achievements. Overall, the comparison of pre-and post-conquest Persia highlights the complex interplay of culture, religion, and politics in shaping the history of the region. The legacy of the conquest continues to influence modern-day Iran, as the country reflects on its dual heritage of Persian and Islamic traditions.

GEOPOLITICAL CONDITIONS IN PERSIA

ESTABLISHMENT OF THE SASSANIAN EMPIRE

The Sassanian Empire rose to power in Persia during the 3rd century CE, establishing itself as a formidable force in the region. Building upon the foundations laid by the Parthian Empire, the Sassanians consolidated their rule and expanded their territories through strategic military campaigns and diplomatic maneuvering. Under the leadership of Ardeshir I, the founder of the Sassanian dynasty, Persia experienced a resurgence of centralized power and cultural revival. Ardeshir I's conquest of the Parthian Empire marked the beginning of Sassanian rule and set the stage for the empire's growth and consolidation over the centuries. The Sassanian Empire's territorial extent spanned from modern-day Iran to parts of Iraq, Armenia, and the Caucasus region. Its capital city, Ctesiphon, became a hub of political and cultural activity, attracting scholars, artisans, and traders from across the empire and beyond. The Sassanian rulers presented themselves as divine monarchs, fostering a sense of religious legitimacy through their adherence to Zoroastrianism, the dominant faith in Persia. They patronized the Zoroastrian clergy and promoted the worship of Ahura Mazda, the supreme deity in Zoroastrian cosmology. Military conquests, administrative reforms, and economic prosperity characterized the early years of the Sassanian Empire. The centralization of power and the creation of a professional army enabled the Sassanians to assert their dominance over rival empires and maintain control over diverse territories. The establishment of the Sassanian Empire marked a significant turning point in the history of Persia, shaping its cultural identity, political institutions, and social structures for centuries to come. Through a combination of military prowess, diplomatic finesse, and cultural vibrancy, the Sassanians left a lasting legacy that continues to resonate in the present day.

RELATIONSHIP WITH NEIGHBORING EMPIRES

The Sassanian Empire, with its strategic location and formidable military strength, maintained complex relationships with neighboring empires, particularly the Byzantine Empire and the Roman Empire. Trade routes crisscrossed the region, facilitating economic exchanges and cultural interactions that shaped the political landscape. The Sassanian rulers navigated alliances and rivalries, seeking to bolster their own power while contending with external pressures. The dynamic interactions with neighboring empires influenced not only the empire's economic well-being but also its diplomatic and military strategies. This chapter delves into the multifaceted relationships that defined the Sassanian Empire's position in the broader geopolitical context of the ancient world.

INTERNAL DIVISIONS AND POLITICAL DYNAMICS

The Sassanian Empire was not without its internal divisions and political complexities. Power struggles among noble families and court factions were common, leading to periods of instability and uncertainty within the empire. The intricate web of competing interests often hindered cohesive governance and decision-making, with different factions vying for control and influence over the throne. Religion played a pivotal role in Sassanian politics, shaping both domestic policies and external relations. The Zoroastrian clergy wielded significant power and influence, often acting as kingmakers and advisors to the ruling monarch. The intertwining of religious authority with political power created a unique dynamic in which the spiritual and temporal realms were inextricably linked. Furthermore, the decentralized nature of Sassanian governance allowed provincial governors and local magnates to amass power and resources, sometimes challenging the central authority of the Shah. Ambitious nobles and aristocrats frequently engaged in intrigue and power struggles, seeking to advance their own interests at the expense of stability and unity within the empire. The succession of the throne was a constant source of contention and conflict, as rival claimants vied for legitimacy and support from powerful factions. Succession crises often led to civil unrest and military confrontations, further fragmenting an already fragile political landscape. The lack of a clear and orderly succession process exacerbated internal divisions and hindered effective governance. Despite these internal challenges, the Sassanian Empire managed to maintain a degree of stability and resilience, navigating through periods of turmoil and upheaval. The intricate balance of power among competing factions, combined with the enduring influence of religious institutions, provided a semblance of order amidst the chaos of court politics and rivalries.

MILITARY STRENGTH AND DEFENSE CAPABILITIES

The Sassanian Empire maintained a formidable military force that played a crucial role in safeguarding its borders and asserting its power in the region. The army was a complex institution comprising of various units with specialized functions and training. Infantry troops formed the backbone of the military, equipped with advanced weapons such as swords, spears, and bows. Cavalry units were highly valued for their mobility and efficiency in combat, often deploying heavy armored cavalry known as cataphracts. Strategic planning and military tactics were integral to Sassanian warfare, with commanders relying on a combination of conventional formations and innovative strategies. The use of siege engines and advanced fortifications demonstrated the empire's commitment to military advancement. Additionally, the Sassanian army benefitted from a sophisticated logistics system that ensured the timely provision of supplies and reinforcements during campaigns. The defense capabilities of the Sassanian Empire extended beyond its land forces to encompass naval strength in the Persian Gulf and the Mediterranean Sea. The navy played a crucial role in protecting maritime trade routes and projecting power along coastal regions. Naval warfare tactics evolved to counter threats from rival powers and ensure the security of Sassanian territories. Despite the military prowess of the Sassanian Empire, internal divisions and political rivalries occasionally undermined its ability to project unified strength. Competition among noble families and court factions sometimes led to weakened leadership and disjointed military command. However, the empire's military resilience and adaptability enabled it to withstand external pressures and maintain a formidable defense posture in the face of diverse challenges. Overall, the military strength and defense capabilities of the Sassanian Empire were central to its geopolitical influence and sustained power in the region. The legacy of its military traditions and strategic innovations continued to shape the dynamics of warfare and governance in the centuries that followed.

ECONOMIC RESOURCES AND AGRICULTURAL PRODUCTIVITY

The Sassanian Empire boasted a thriving economy supported by rich agricultural resources and vibrant trade networks. The fertile lands of Persia yielded abundant crops, such as grains, fruits, and vegetables, which formed the backbone of the empire's agrarian economy. Sophisticated irrigation systems and agricultural techniques ensured high productivity and sustained the empire's population. Furthermore, Persia's strategic location at the crossroads of major trade routes facilitated extensive commerce with neighboring regions. The Silk Road, connecting the East and West, brought valuable goods and cultural exchanges to Persia, enhancing its economic prosperity. The empire's control over key trade routes enabled it to levy taxes on goods passing through its territories, contributing to its wealth and influence. In addition to agriculture and trade, the Sassanian Empire thrived on various industries, including textiles, ceramics, and metallurgy. Skilled artisans produced high-quality goods sought after in both domestic and international markets. The empire's craftsmen were renowned for their exquisite craftsmanship and artistic innovations, attracting buyers from distant lands. The Sassanian Empire's economic strength was also bolstered by its currency system and fiscal policies. The empire minted its own coins, which were widely accepted in trade transactions and served as a symbol of its economic power. Efficient tax collection and administration further supported the empire's financial stability and enabled the funding of large-scale infrastructure projects and military endeavors. Overall, the Sassanian Empire's economic resources and agricultural productivity played a crucial role in sustaining its prosperity and influencing its relations with neighboring powers. The empire's ability to harness its natural resources, promote commerce, and foster a culture of innovation contributed to its status as a flourishing economic hub in the ancient world.

CULTURAL AND RELIGIOUS DIVERSITY

Zoroastrianism was the dominant religion in the Sassanian Empire, deeply influencing its cultural and religious landscape. However, the empire also exhibited a remarkable degree of tolerance towards minority religions and ethnic groups. This religious diversity enriched the social fabric of the empire, fostering a sense of coexistence and respect among different belief systems. The Sassanian Empire was home to various ethnic and religious communities, including Christians, Jews, Buddhists, and Manicheans. These diverse groups coexisted within the empire, practicing their faiths and contributing to the cultural tapestry of Sassanian society. Religious tolerance was not only a matter of policy but also a reflection of the empire's cosmopolitan nature. The Zoroastrian clergy held significant influence in Sassanian society, presiding over religious rituals and shaping moral values. Zoroastrian temples, known as fire temples, were centers of religious activity and served as important community gathering places. The teachings of Zoroastrianism emphasized the dualistic nature of existence, with a focus on cosmic balance and ethical living. Despite the prominence of Zoroastrianism, the Sassanian Empire demonstrated a remarkable degree of religious pluralism. Different faiths were able to practice freely, and religious syncretism was not uncommon. This diversity enriched the cultural landscape of the empire, fostering a spirit of tolerance and mutual respect among its inhabitants. The Sassanian Empire's commitment to religious diversity was a defining feature of its society. By embracing different faiths and traditions, the empire showcased a level of acceptance and inclusivity that set it apart from many other contemporary empires. This cultural and religious diversity contributed to the resilience and vibrancy of Sassanian civilization, leaving a lasting legacy that transcended the boundaries of its time.

SOCIAL HIERARCHY AND CLASS STRUCTURE

Sassanian society was intricately structured, with a distinct social hierarchy that governed the lives of its inhabitants. At the top of the hierarchy were the nobility, comprising the king, the royal family, and the aristocracy. These elite individuals wielded immense power and influence, holding key positions in the government and military. They enjoyed lavish lifestyles, with access to luxury goods and lavish palaces that showcased their wealth and status. Beneath the nobility were the clergy, who played a crucial role in propagating and upholding Zoroastrianism, the dominant religion of the Sassanian Empire. The clergy held significant sway over religious matters and often had close ties to the ruling elite. They oversaw religious rituals, maintained temples, and exerted moral authority over the populace. The majority of Sassanian society comprised commoners, who engaged in various professions such as farming, crafts, and trade. While some commoners lived modest lives, others accumulated wealth and influence through their skills and entrepreneurship. Social mobility was possible for ambitious commoners who sought education or excelled in their chosen field. Women in Sassanian society occupied a subordinate position, with limited rights and freedoms compared to men. They were primarily expected to fulfill domestic roles and maintain the household, although some women from noble families wielded influence behind the scenes through their connections and relationships. Slavery was also prevalent in the Sassanian Empire, with slaves serving in households, agricultural estates, and various industries. Slaves had no legal rights and were considered property that could be bought, sold, or inherited. Despite their marginalized status, some slaves managed to gain freedom through manumission or exceptional service to their masters. The social hierarchy in Sassanian society reinforced a rigid system of power and privilege, with opportunities for advancement largely determined by birth and social status. While the elite enjoyed luxury and prestige, commoners, women, and slaves faced various forms of marginalization and oppression. The social structure of the Sassanian Empire reflected the complexities of power, status, and hierarchy that defined life in ancient Persia.

TECHNOLOGICAL ADVANCEMENTS AND INFRASTRUCTURAL DEVELOPMENTS

The Sassanian Empire was marked by impressive technological advancements and infrastructural developments that contributed to its grandeur and efficiency. One of the most notable achievements was in architectural prowess, evident in the construction of majestic palaces, elaborate cities, and intricate irrigation systems. Urban planning was a key focus, with cities designed to accommodate growing populations and facilitate trade and commerce. Several engineering feats highlighted the Empire's technological prowess, such as the advanced water management systems that enabled efficient irrigation of farmlands. The construction of aqueducts, dams, and underground water channels served to sustain agricultural productivity and support urban centers. These innovations not only improved the quality of life for the populace but also showcased the Empire's sophistication in engineering and infrastructure development. Transportation networks played a crucial role in facilitating communication and trade across the vast territories of the Sassanian Empire. Well-maintained roads and bridges connected major cities, allowing for the swift movement of goods and people. The Empire's strategic location at the crossroads of trade routes further necessitated the development of efficient transportation systems, which bolstered economic prosperity and cultural exchange. Architectural excellence extended beyond urban centers to religious structures and royal palaces, reflecting the Empire's commitment to artistic expression and grandeur. Elaborate frescoes, intricate mosaics, and ornate sculptures adorned monumental buildings, illustrating the Empire's cultural sophistication and aesthetic sensibilities. Additionally, advancements in engineering enabled the construction of massive fortifications to safeguard strategic locations and defend against external threats. Technological innovations in communication, such as the development of postal systems and courier networks, facilitated efficient administration and coordination of military campaigns. The establishment of formalized communication channels enhanced the Empire's capacity for governance and military operations, enabling rapid dissemination of orders and intelligence across vast distances. Overall, the Sassanian Empire's investment in technological advancements and infrastructural developments underscored its commitment to progress and efficiency. These achievements not only enhanced the Empire's economic prosperity and military capabilities but also left a lasting legacy of architectural magnificence and engineering ingenuity in the annals of history.

RELATIONS WITH NOMADIC TRIBES AND FRONTIER REGIONS

Relations with nomadic tribes and frontier regions in the Sassanian Empire were characterized by a complex interplay of diplomacy, trade, and military engagements. The nomadic tribes inhabiting the frontier regions held significant influence over the empire's security and territorial integrity. Sassanian rulers recognized the strategic importance of maintaining stable relations with these tribes to safeguard their borders and ensure uninterrupted trade routes. Nomadic tribes often posed a challenge to the centralized authority of the empire, as their mobile lifestyle and decentralized leadership structure made them difficult to control. However, the Sassanian Empire adopted a pragmatic approach towards these tribes, incorporating diplomatic strategies alongside military campaigns to manage their potential threats. Trade played a crucial role in fostering relations with nomadic tribes, as the empire sought to leverage the economic benefits of engaging with these mobile communities. Nomads provided access to valuable resources such as livestock, furs, and skilled labor, which enriched the empire's economy and enhanced its cultural exchange with frontier regions. At the same time, the Sassanian Empire faced periodic conflicts with nomadic tribes who sought to assert their autonomy or expand their territorial holdings. Military engagements were often necessary to deter incursions and maintain control over strategic borderlands. The empire deployed its well-trained army and utilized frontier fortifications to guard against external threats posed by nomadic raids. Despite the challenges presented by nomadic tribes, the Sassanian Empire recognized the importance of coexisting with these mobile communities for the mutual benefit of both parties. By balancing diplomacy, trade, and military defense, the empire strove to establish a tenuous equilibrium in its relations with frontier nomads, ensuring the stability of its borders and the prosperity of its realm.

CHALLENGES AND VULNERABILITIES

The Sassanian Empire faced numerous challenges and vulnerabilities, particularly in its relations with nomadic tribes and frontier regions. These groups posed a constant threat to the stability and security of the empire, often launching raids and incursions into Sassanian territory. The nomads, with their mobile and adaptable lifestyle, were able to evade conventional military strategies and strike at vulnerable points along the borders. The Sassanian rulers struggled to maintain control over these frontier regions, as the nomadic tribes were difficult to subdue and often resisted imperial authority. The lack of centralized control in these areas made it challenging to enforce laws and collect taxes, leading to a loss of revenue for the empire. The nomads also disrupted trade routes and agricultural production, further weakening the economy and undermining the empire's strength. In addition to external threats, the Sassanian Empire faced internal challenges as well. Factionalism within the royal court and among the noble families often resulted in power struggles and political instability. This internal dissent made it difficult for the empire to present a united front against external adversaries, further exacerbating its vulnerabilities. Furthermore, the Sassanian Empire's reliance on a rigid social hierarchy and hierarchical structure created tensions within society. The disparity between the elite nobility and the common people fueled resentment and discontent among the lower classes, leading to protests and uprisings. These internal conflicts weakened the empire from within, making it more susceptible to external pressures and threats. Overall, the challenges and vulnerabilities faced by the Sassanian Empire in dealing with nomadic tribes and frontier regions, coupled with internal discord and social unrest, posed significant obstacles to the empire's stability and long-term survival. Addressing these issues required a delicate balance of military strength, diplomatic skill, and political acumen, which the Sassanian rulers struggled to achieve consistently.

SASSANIAN EMPIRE'S RESPONSE

EVALUATION OF THE THREAT POSED BY ISLAMIC CONQUESTS

The rise of Islam and the rapid expansion of the Islamic Caliphate posed a formidable threat to the Sassanian Empire in the 7th century. The Sassanian rulers were faced with a complex and multifaceted challenge that required careful evaluation and strategic planning to confront. The Islamic conquests not only threatened the territorial integrity of the Sassanian Empire but also posed a significant ideological and cultural challenge. The Sassanian leadership recognized the military prowess and religious zeal of the Islamic armies, which presented a direct threat to the established order in the region. The rapid expansion of the Caliphate under the leadership of figures like Caliph Umar ibn al-Khattab and his commanders demonstrated a formidable force that could not be underestimated. The Sassanian Empire evaluated the Islamic conquests as a strategic threat to its political authority and religious identity. The spread of Islam posed a direct challenge to Zoroastrianism, the official religion of the Sassanian Empire, and raised concerns about the loyalty of the diverse populations within Sassanian territories. Moreover, the Sassanian leadership assessed the economic implications of the Islamic conquests, recognizing the potential disruption of trade routes and agricultural production that could result from the expansion of the Caliphate. The empire faced the risk of losing key economic resources and tax revenues to the advancing Islamic forces. In response to these evaluations, the Sassanian Empire implemented a series of strategic measures to counter the threat posed by the Islamic conquests. These measures included bolstering defenses along key border regions, mobilizing military forces, forming alliances with neighboring powers, and implementing economic policies to support war efforts. The evaluation of the threat posed by Islamic conquests highlighted the need for the Sassanian Empire to adapt its military, political, and economic strategies to confront the challenges posed by the expanding Islamic Caliphate. The response of the Sassanian Empire to these evaluations would shape the course of history in the region and leave a lasting legacy on the subsequent developments in the Islamic world."

STRATEGIES ADOPTED BY SASSANIAN EMPIRE

The Sassanian Empire, recognizing the formidable threat posed by the rapid expansion of the Islamic Caliphate, adopted a series of strategic measures to safeguard its territorial integrity and sovereignty. One of the key strategies employed by the Sassanian leadership was to fortify its border defenses and fortifications along vulnerable frontiers. By bolstering these defensive structures, the empire aimed to deter potential incursions by Islamic forces and maintain control over strategic territories. Furthermore, the Sassanian Empire sought to enhance its military capabilities through the recruitment and training of skilled soldiers. The empire established military academies to educate and train its troops in advanced warfare techniques, tactics, and strategies. This emphasis on military preparedness and discipline helped the Sassanian forces to effectively confront the Islamic invaders on the battlefield. In addition to strengthening its military forces, the Sassanian Empire also engaged in diplomatic efforts to forge alliances with neighboring states and regional powers. These alliances were instrumental in pooling resources and coordinating military campaigns against the common enemy. By leveraging these alliances, the Sassanian Empire hoped to bolster its strategic position and push back against the encroachment of the Islamic Caliphate. Moreover, the Sassanian Empire implemented economic policies to support its war efforts and sustain its military campaigns. The empire levied taxes, requisitioned resources, and mobilized its economy to finance the costs of war and maintain the logistical supply lines for its troops. These economic measures were crucial in sustaining the empire's military operations and ensuring the welfare of its soldiers in the face of external threats. Overall, the strategies adopted by the Sassanian Empire reflected a multi-faceted approach to countering the Islamic conquests. By fortifying its defenses, enhancing its military capabilities, forging alliances, and implementing economic policies, the Sassanian Empire aimed to resist the advance of the Islamic Caliphate and safeguard its territorial integrity and sovereignty.

MOBILIZATION OF MILITARY FORCES

The Sassanian Empire faced a formidable challenge with the rise of Islamic conquests in Asia. To protect its territories and interests, the empire embarked on a comprehensive mobilization of its military forces. The Sassanian military was a formidable entity with a long history of warfare and a well-established hierarchical structure. The empire's ability to mobilize its military forces efficiently and effectively played a crucial role in its efforts to defend against the Islamic incursions. The Sassanian military consisted of professional soldiers, conscripted levies, and elite nobles who formed the backbone of the army. These forces were organized into different units, including infantry, cavalry, and archers, each trained and equipped to fulfill specific functions on the battlefield. The Sassanian army also made effective use of siege weaponry, including catapults and battering rams, to besiege enemy fortifications. One key aspect of the Sassanian Empire's military mobilization was its emphasis on training and discipline. Soldiers underwent rigorous training regimes to hone their combat skills and improve their tactical proficiency. Discipline within the ranks was strictly enforced, ensuring that soldiers followed orders and maintained cohesion on the battlefield. The Sassanian Empire also leveraged its vast network of allies and vassal states to bolster its military capabilities. Through strategic alliances with regional powers, the empire gained access to additional troops, resources, and logistical support, enhancing its ability to wage war against the Islamic invaders. These alliances allowed the Sassanian Empire to project its military power across a broader geographic area and engage in coordinated campaigns against the common enemy. Furthermore, the Sassanian Empire's mobilization of military forces extended beyond its borders. The empire engaged in proactive military campaigns to preempt potential threats and expand its influence in neighboring territories. By projecting its military strength beyond its frontiers, the Sassanian Empire sought to secure strategic advantages and maintain a position of dominance in the region. Overall, the Sassanian Empire's mobilization of its military forces was a testament to its resilience and determination in the face of external threats. The empire's strategic approach to warfare, combined with its disciplined troops and network of alliances, played a vital role in shaping the outcome of the conflict with the Islamic forces.

THE ISLAMIC CONQUESTS IN ASIA

ALLIANCES FORMED WITH REGIONAL POWERS

During the Sassanian Empire's response to the Islamic conquests in Asia, the formation of alliances with regional powers played a crucial role in shaping the course of warfare and diplomacy. These alliances were strategic partnerships aimed at bolstering the empire's military strength and expanding its sphere of influence across the region. By forging alliances with neighboring states and tribal groups, the Sassanian Empire sought to create a unified front against the advancing Islamic forces. One of the key aspects of forming alliances with regional powers was the exchange of military resources, including troops, weapons, and strategic intelligence. Through these alliances, the Sassanian Empire was able to leverage the military capabilities of its allies to strengthen its defenses and launch coordinated counter-attacks against Islamic incursions. This collaborative approach not only enhanced the empire's military effectiveness but also fostered greater cohesion among allied powers in the face of a common threat. Furthermore, alliances with regional powers enabled the Sassanian Empire to access critical logistical support, such as provisions, reinforcements, and logistical infrastructure. By establishing trade routes and supply chains with allied states, the empire could sustain its military campaigns and sustain its war effort over extended periods. The strategic positioning of allied territories along key trade routes and border regions also offered the Sassanian Empire strategic advantages in terms of mobility and resupply. Moreover, alliances with regional powers served as a means of diplomatic engagement and political maneuvering on the international stage. By cultivating relationships with neighboring states and tribal confederations, the Sassanian

Empire could secure mutual defense agreements, non-aggression pacts, and military assistance treaties. These diplomatic initiatives helped the empire navigate complex geopolitical dynamics and forge alliances based on shared security interests and common objectives. In summary, the formation of alliances with regional powers was a critical component of the Sassanian Empire's response to the Islamic conquests in Asia. These strategic partnerships not only enhanced the empire's military capabilities but also facilitated diplomatic cooperation, logistical support, and political alliances. By leveraging alliances with neighboring states and tribal groups, the Sassanian Empire sought to strengthen its position against the advancing Islamic forces and maintain its territorial integrity in the face of external threats.

DEFENSIVE MEASURES IMPLEMENTED ALONG BORDERS

To counter the advancing Islamic forces, the Sassanian Empire implemented rigorous defensive measures along its borders. Garrison troops were reinforced along key frontier regions to deter incursions and protect vital territories. Fortifications were strengthened and strategically positioned to impede enemy movements and provide safe havens for Sassanian troops. Surveillance outposts and watchtowers were established to monitor enemy activities and alert the military to potential threats. In addition to physical defenses, the Sassanian Empire implemented strict border control policies to regulate the movement of people and goods across its territory. Checkpoints were established along major trade routes and strategic passes to prevent unauthorized entry and maintain security. Patrols regularly scanned the border regions to detect and intercept any suspicious activity.

The Sassanian military also conducted regular drills and training exercises to enhance readiness and response capabilities along the borders. Rapid response units were stationed at key locations to swiftly react to any breaches or attacks. Communication networks were established to ensure swift transmission of crucial information and orders among military units stationed along the borders. Furthermore, the Sassanian Empire forged alliances with neighboring powers to bolster its defensive capabilities. Mutual defense agreements were established to coordinate joint actions and provide assistance in times of crisis. By forming strategic partnerships with regional powers, the Sassanian Empire aimed to create a united front against the common threat posed by Islamic conquests. Overall, the defensive measures implemented along the Sassanian borders reflected a multi-faceted approach that combined physical fortifications, border control policies, military readiness, and strategic alliances. These efforts aimed to safeguard the empire's territorial integrity, protect its citizens, and preserve its sovereignty in the face of external threats.

RESPONSE TO ISLAMIC IDEOLOGICAL INFLUENCE

The Sassanian Empire responded to the Islamic ideological influence with a complex set of actions aimed at preserving their cultural and religious identity. Recognizing the significant challenge posed by the rapid spread of Islam, Sassanian leaders implemented various strategies to counter this ideological threat. One key aspect of the Sassanian response was the promotion of Zoroastrianism as the state religion and a focal point of national identity. Efforts were made to reinforce the teachings and rituals of Zoroastrianism among the populace, emphasizing the importance of loyalty to the empire and resistance to foreign religious doctrines. Furthermore, the Sassanian Empire actively engaged in theological debates with Islamic scholars, seeking to assert the superiority of Zoroastrian beliefs and practices. Intellectual circles were mobilized to challenge the theological foundations of Islam and defend the core tenets of Zoroastrianism. In addition to intellectual and religious measures, the Sassanian Empire also employed diplomatic strategies to mitigate the influence of Islamic ideology. Alliances were forged with neighboring kingdoms that shared a common interest in resisting Islamic expansion, leading to the formation of a united front against the encroaching Islamic forces. Moreover, the Sassanian Empire undertook propaganda campaigns to counter the appeal of Islam among its subjects. Public ceremonies and royal edicts were used to emphasize the longstanding traditions and heritage of the empire, reinforcing the notion of a distinct Sassanian identity that was distinct from the Islamic world. Overall, the Sassanian response to Islamic ideological influence was multifaceted, encompassing religious, intellectual, diplomatic, and propaganda efforts. By leveraging these various strategies, the Sassanian Empire sought to maintain its cultural and religious integrity in the face of a growing Islamic presence in the region.

ECONOMIC POLICIES TO SUPPORT WAR EFFORTS

The Sassanian Empire implemented a series of strategic economic policies to bolster its war efforts against the Islamic conquests. Recognizing the financial challenges of sustained military campaigns, the empire focused on maximizing its resources and revenue streams. One key initiative was the imposition of new taxes and levies on the populace, aimed at generating additional funds for military expenditures. Furthermore, the Sassanian government undertook measures to expand its trade networks and increase commercial activities within its territories. By promoting trade and commerce, the empire sought to enhance its economic resilience and accumulate wealth to finance its military campaigns. Additionally, the empire invested in infrastructure projects, such as the construction of roads and bridges, to improve transportation and facilitate the movement of troops and supplies. In addition to tax reforms and trade expansion, the Sassanian Empire prioritized the development of its agricultural sector. Agriculture played a crucial role in supplying food and provisions to the army, ensuring its logistical sustainability during wartime. The empire encouraged agricultural innovation, irrigation projects, and land cultivation to increase agricultural output and meet the demands of a growing military force. Moreover, the Sassanian government implemented strict controls on currency circulation and monetary policies to stabilize the economy and prevent inflation during times of war. By regulating the value of currency and standardizing monetary practices, the empire aimed to maintain financial stability and ensure the continuity of economic activities necessary for the war effort. Overall, the Sassanian Empire's economic policies to support war efforts reflected a comprehensive strategy aimed at mobilizing resources, increasing revenues, and strengthening the economic foundation of the empire. These measures were essential in sustaining the empire's military campaigns and confronting the challenges posed by the Islamic conquests with financial resilience and strategic acumen.

COMMUNICATION AND COORDINATION AMONG SASSANIAN OFFICIALS

Effective communication and coordination among Sassanian officials played a crucial role in responding to the Islamic conquests. The efficient dissemination of information, strategic planning, and decision-making processes were essential components in navigating the complexities of defending the empire. High-ranking officials, military commanders, and advisors utilized various communication channels, including messengers, couriers, and diplomatic envoys, to relay crucial information and instructions across the vast Sassanian territories. Central to the coordination efforts were regular councils and assemblies where key officials gathered to discuss military strategies, intelligence reports, and countermeasures against the advancing Islamic forces. These meetings facilitated collaboration, consensus-building, and the formulation of unified responses to the evolving situation on the battlefield. By fostering open dialogue and sharing of expertise, Sassanian officials were able to leverage their collective knowledge and resources effectively. Furthermore, the establishment of a comprehensive communication network, including signal towers, relay stations, and secure messaging systems, enabled rapid transmission of orders and updates throughout the empire. This infrastructure facilitated swift decision-making and coordination of military movements, reinforcing the cohesion and responsiveness of Sassanian forces in the face of external threats. Effective coordination among Sassanian officials also extended to liaising with local governors, provincial administrators, and military commanders stationed in key regions. By maintaining close contact and exchanging information with decentralized authorities, central officials could monitor developments on the frontlines, allocate resources where needed, and ensure synchronized actions across different sectors of the empire. Overall, the emphasis on communication and coordination among Sassanian officials underscored the importance of efficient governance in managing crises and safeguarding internal stability during times of external conflict. By fostering a culture of collaboration, information-sharing, and strategic planning, the Sassanian Empire sought to uphold its unity, resilience, and capacity to confront the challenges posed by the Islamic conquests.

IMPACT OF SASSANIAN EMPIRE'S RESPONSE ON INTERNAL STABILITY

The resistance put forth by the Sassanian Empire against the Islamic conquests had a profound impact on its internal stability. The ongoing military conflicts and the strain of defending against the expanding Islamic forces placed immense pressure on the empire's infrastructure and resources. The need to mobilize troops, fortify border defenses, and coordinate military operations disrupted the socio-economic fabric of the Sassanian society. The constant state of war and the uncertainty of the empire's future led to increased internal dissent and power struggles among various factions within the Sassanian administration. The diversion of resources towards military campaigns also strained the economy, leading to inflation, scarcity of goods, and a decline in living standards for the common people. The heavy taxation imposed to fund the war efforts further alienated the populace and fueled discontent. Moreover, the prolonged conflict with the Islamic forces destabilized the social and political hierarchy within the Sassanian Empire. The continued loss of territory and the failure to effectively counter the Islamic advances eroded the confidence in the empire's leadership and its ability to protect its subjects. This internal instability weakened the cohesion and loyalty of the empire's subjects, making it harder to maintain order and unity in the face of external threats. The legacy of the Sassanian Empire's response to the Islamic conquests would be one marked by internal turmoil, social unrest, and the eventual collapse of one of the ancient world's greatest empires. The inability to effectively confront the Islamic forces and the internal disarray caused by the ongoing conflicts highlighted the vulnerabilities and weaknesses that ultimately contributed to the empire's downfall.

LEGACY OF SASSANIAN RESISTANCE AGAINST ISLAMIC CONQUESTS

The legacy of the Sassanian Empire's resistance against Islamic conquests endures as a testament to the fierce determination and resilience of a once-mighty civilization. Despite facing overwhelming odds and formidable adversaries, the Sassanian rulers and their subjects stood their ground with unwavering resolve, determined to safeguard their cultural heritage and territorial integrity. The impact of the Sassanian Empire's resistance reverberated across the annals of history, shaping the trajectory of the Islamic conquests and influencing the subsequent development of Islamic civilization. The fierce battles fought on the frontiers of the Sassanian Empire not only tested the military prowess of both sides but also underscored the enduring power of ideology in shaping the course of conflicts. The legacy of the Sassanian Empire's resistance is also reflected in the lasting cultural and intellectual contributions of its scholars, artisans, and poets. Despite the challenges posed by incessant warfare and instability, the Sassanian Empire continued to foster a vibrant cultural milieu that left an indelible mark on the artistic and intellectual heritage of the region. The memory of the Sassanian Empire's valiant struggle against the tide of Islamic conquests continues to resonate in the collective consciousness of modern Iranians and serves as a source of national pride and identity. The legacy of Sassanian resistance against Islamic conquests remains a poignant reminder of the enduring legacy of civilizations that have weathered the storms of history and emerged stronger from the crucible of conflict.

ROLE OF RELIGION, ECONOMICS, AND POLITICS

THE INTERCONNECTED NATURE OF RELIGION, ECONOMICS, AND POLITICS

Religion, economics, and politics are intricately intertwined forces that shape the course of history and the Islamic conquests in Central Asia provide a vivid illustration of this interconnected nature. The spread of Islam in the region was not solely driven by religious zeal but was also deeply entwined with economic interests and political ambitions. The religious context of the Islamic conquests in Central Asia was characterized by the expansion of Islamic ideology and the establishment of Islamic governance in newly conquered territories. The religious fervor of the early Islamic armies played a significant role in motivating soldiers to fight and conquer new lands in the name of Islam. The spread of Islamic values and beliefs in these regions also led to the conversion of many local populations to the new faith, further solidifying the religious significance of the conquests. Moreover, the economic aspect of the conquests cannot be overlooked. The lucrative trade routes that crisscrossed Central Asia were a major incentive for the Islamic Caliphate to expand its influence in the region. Control over these trade routes provided access to valuable resources and increased economic prosperity, bolstering the empire's power and influence in the region. Additionally, the political dimension of the conquests was crucial in shaping the dynamics of power and governance in Central Asia. The establishment of Islamic governance systems and the integration of conquered lands into the Caliphate's administrative structure were essential for maintaining control over the vast territories that were brought under Islamic rule. Overall, the interconnected nature of religion, economics, and politics in the Islamic conquests in Central Asia highlights the complex web of influences that drove the expansion of the Islamic Caliphate in the region. By understanding the interplay of these forces, we can gain deeper insights into the motivations and outcomes of one of the most significant periods in Islamic history.

THE RELIGIOUS CONTEXT OF THE ISLAMIC CONQUESTS IN CENTRAL ASIA

The religious context of the Islamic conquests in Central Asia reveals a complex interplay between faith and imperial ambitions. As Islam spread beyond the Arabian Peninsula, it encountered diverse cultures and belief systems in the vast region of Central Asia. The Islamic expansion into these territories was not merely motivated by a desire for political dominance but was deeply intertwined with religious fervor. Islamic armies, inspired by the teachings of the Quran and the traditions of the Prophet Muhammad, viewed their conquests as a divine mandate to spread the message of Islam. The concept of Jihad, or the struggle in the path of God, played a significant role in shaping military strategies and objectives. Warriors saw themselves not just as soldiers but as defenders of the faith, fighting for the cause of Allah against non-believers. The religious zeal of the early Islamic conquerors had a profound impact on their conduct on the battlefield. They were driven by the belief that victory in war was a sign of divine favor, leading them to display extraordinary bravery and determination in the face of enemy resistance. The notion of martyrdom as a path to paradise further fueled their commitment to the cause. Moreover, the integration of religious principles into military strategies influenced the treatment of conquered peoples. Islamic law, or Sharia, provided guidelines for governing non-Muslim subjects, ensuring their protection and the preservation of their religious and cultural practices. This approach helped to foster a sense of tolerance and coexistence within the newly conquered territories. In sum, the religious context of the Islamic conquests in Central Asia shaped not only the conduct of warfare but also the principles of governance and the interactions between different religious communities. The fusion of faith, economics, and politics created a unique framework for the expansion of Islam in the region, leaving a lasting imprint on its societies and cultures.

INFLUENCE OF ISLAMIC IDEOLOGY ON MILITARY STRATEGIES AND OBJECTIVES

Islamic ideology played a significant role in shaping the military strategies and objectives of the Islamic conquests in Central Asia. The expansion of the Islamic Caliphate was not merely driven by territorial conquest but was deeply intertwined with the religious beliefs and teachings of Islam. One of the fundamental principles guiding Islamic military strategies was the concept of jihad, or the duty of all Muslims to defend and expand the territory of the Islamic faith. Jihad was not only seen as a religious obligation but also as a means of spreading the message of Islam to new territories. This sense of religious duty inspired armies to embark on campaigns with a fervor and determination that went beyond mere conquest for material gain. Islamic ideology also emphasized the importance of unity among the Muslim forces. The concept of ummah, or the community of believers, encouraged solidarity among diverse ethnic and cultural groups that made up the Islamic armies. This unity allowed them to effectively coordinate their efforts and overcome internal divisions, presenting a formidable front to their adversaries. Furthermore, Islamic teachings promoted the idea of mercy and justice in warfare. Islamic armies were instructed to offer terms of surrender to their opponents before engaging in battle and to treat prisoners of war with dignity and respect. This approach not only reflected the ethical principles of Islam but also served strategic purposes by winning the hearts and minds of conquered populations. In terms of military objectives, Islamic ideology emphasized the establishment of Islamic governance in conquered territories based on the principles of sharia law. The goal was not merely to occupy land but to bring the inhabitants under the fold of Islam and create a society governed by Islamic values and principles. Overall, the influence of Islamic ideology on military strategies and objectives during the conquests in Central Asia was profound. It imbued the campaigns with a sense of purpose and direction that went beyond mere territorial expansion, shaping the way in which the Islamic forces conducted themselves on the battlefield and governed the lands they conquered.

ECONOMIC MOTIVATIONS DRIVING THE EXPANSION INTO CENTRAL ASIA

Economic motivations played a crucial role in driving the expansion of the Islamic Caliphate into Central Asia. The conquests were not only fueled by religious zeal and military conquest but also by the desire to control lucrative trade routes and access valuable resources. Central Asia, with its strategic location at the crossroads of major trade routes connecting the East and the West, presented an opportunity for the Islamic Caliphate to expand its economic influence. The region was renowned for its rich natural resources, including precious metals, silk, spices, and other commodities that were highly sought after in the bustling markets of the medieval world. Control over key trade routes, such as the Silk Road, not only allowed the Islamic Caliphate to facilitate the exchange of goods between distant regions but also provided a significant source of revenue through taxes and tariffs imposed on merchants traversing these routes. By expanding into Central Asia, the Caliphate could enhance its economic power and strengthen its position as a dominant player in the global trade network. Furthermore, the conquest of Central Asia enabled the Caliphate to establish commercial hubs and centers of economic activity in strategic locations, fostering trade and commerce within its expanding empire. The integration of new territories into the Islamic economic system helped stimulate economic growth, create new markets, and promote the circulation of goods and wealth throughout the region. In addition to the economic benefits, controlling Central Asia also provided the Islamic Caliphate with access to skilled artisans, advanced technologies, and valuable knowledge that could further enhance its economic prosperity. The exchange of ideas, innovations, and expertise between different cultures and civilizations facilitated by the conquests contributed to the development of vibrant commercial and cultural exchanges that enriched the Islamic world. Overall, the economic motivations behind the expansion into Central Asia were driven by the desire to tap into the region's wealth, resources, and strategic trade routes to bolster the economic strength and prosperity of the Islamic Caliphate. By strategically leveraging economic opportunities in the conquered territories, the Caliphate not only extended its political and military influence but also established itself as a formidable economic powerhouse in the medieval world.

IMPACT OF TRADE ROUTES ON THE CONQUESTS AND EMPIRE-BUILDING EFFORTS

The ancient trade routes of Central Asia played a pivotal role in the Islamic conquests and empire-building efforts of the time. These well-established networks, such as the Silk Road, not only facilitated the exchange of goods and ideas but also served as strategic corridors for military expansion. The convergence of trade routes in Central Asia offered the Islamic Caliphate access to lucrative markets, valuable resources, and diverse populations. Control over key trade hubs and cities along these routes provided economic advantages, as tribute and taxes could be collected from merchants and travelers passing through. Furthermore, the mobility and connectivity afforded by the trade routes enabled swift communication and movement of troops, essential for coordinating conquests across vast territories. Muslim armies could leverage this infrastructure to project power and assert dominance in new regions. The presence of trade routes also influenced the spread of Islam in Central Asia. Along with merchants, scholars, and diplomats traversing these routes, came the teachings of the new religion. This cultural exchange contributed to the assimilation of Islamic beliefs and practices into the societies encountered along the way. Moreover, the competition for control over key trade routes often led to conflicts and power struggles between rival factions. Political alliances were forged and broken based on the economic interests at stake, shaping the geopolitical landscape of the region. In essence, the impact of trade routes on the conquests and empire-building efforts in Central Asia cannot be understated. They not only served as conduits for economic prosperity and cultural exchange but also as arteries through which the expanding Islamic Caliphate could extend its influence and authority.

POLITICAL ALLIANCES AND DIPLOMACY IN SHAPING THE OUTCOMES OF THE CONQUESTS

The Islamic conquests in Asia were not only shaped by military prowess but also by the intricate dynamics of political alliances and diplomacy. These strategic relationships played a crucial role in determining the outcomes of the conquests and in establishing long-lasting empires across the region. Political alliances were forged both within the Islamic Caliphate and with external powers to strengthen military campaigns and consolidate control over conquered territories. Rulers and military leaders skillfully navigated complex political landscapes to secure support, resources, and manpower for their expansionist endeavors. Diplomacy was employed as a tool to negotiate treaties, establish trade agreements, and form alliances with local rulers and tribes. By leveraging diplomatic relations, the Islamic forces were able to avoid unnecessary conflicts, gain strategic advantages, and expand their influence over diverse populations. Moreover, diplomacy also played a crucial role in maintaining stability and governance in the newly conquered territories. Treaties and agreements were often used to secure cooperation from local leaders, ensure the protection of religious minorities, and establish administrative systems that incorporated existing power structures. Through astute political maneuvering and skilled diplomatic initiatives, the Islamic conquerors were able to not only expand their territorial holdings but also establish lasting relationships with diverse societies in Asia. The legacy of these political alliances and diplomatic efforts continues to shape the socio-political landscape of the region to this day, underscoring the enduring impact of strategic partnerships in the history of conquest and empire-building.

ROLE OF RELIGIOUS INSTITUTIONS IN GOVERNANCE AND ADMINISTRATION OF CONQUERED TERRITORIES

Religious institutions played a crucial role in the governance and administration of conquered territories during the Islamic conquests in Central Asia. Islamic principles not only guided military strategies but also influenced how conquered lands were governed. The establishment of religious institutions such as mosques, madrasas, and Islamic courts became integral to the administration of these new territories. Islamic scholars and religious leaders were often appointed to key administrative positions to ensure that the principles of Islam were upheld in the day-to-day running of the conquered territories. They provided religious guidance to the local population, resolved disputes based on Islamic law, and facilitated the implementation of Sharia law in matters of governance. Furthermore, the integration of religious institutions into the administrative structures helped solidify the authority of the Islamic rulers over the conquered populations. The presence of mosques not only served as places of worship but also as centers for community gatherings, education, and social cohesion. Religious leaders acted as intermediaries between the ruling elite and the local populace, helping maintain stability and order in the newly conquered territories. The role of religious institutions in governance also extended to matters of education and cultural diffusion. Madrasas were established to educate the local population about Islamic teachings, Arabic language, and Islamic sciences. This not only promoted the spread of Islamic knowledge but also fostered a sense of unity among the diverse populations of Central Asia under the banner of Islam. Overall, the presence of religious institutions in the governance and administration of conquered territories played a significant role in shaping the social, cultural, and political landscape of Central Asia during the Islamic conquests. By blending religious principles with governance structures, Islamic rulers were able to establish a cohesive and enduring system of rule that left a lasting impact on the region.

SOCIO-ECONOMIC CHANGES BROUGHT ABOUT BY THE SPREAD OF ISLAM IN CENTRAL ASIA

The spread of Islam in Central Asia brought about significant socio-economic changes in the region. One of the key transformations was the establishment of Islamic legal and administrative systems, which played a crucial role in governing the conquered territories. Islamic law, or Sharia, provided a framework for justice, governance, and social order in Central Asian societies, influencing various aspects of daily life. The introduction of Islamic economic principles also had a profound impact on the region. Islamic finance, which prohibits usury and promotes ethical investment practices, influenced trade, commerce, and economic activities in Central Asia. Islamic banks and financial institutions emerged, facilitating trade and investment within the region and beyond. Moreover, the spread of Islam led to cultural exchange and the integration of Central Asian societies into the broader Islamic world. This facilitated trade networks, intellectual exchange, and cultural diffusion, contributing to the prosperity and development of the region. Central Asia became a hub for trade between the East and the West, connecting merchants, scholars, and travelers from diverse backgrounds. Additionally, the promotion of education and scholarship under Islamic rule enhanced the intellectual and cultural landscape of Central Asia. Madrasas, or Islamic schools, were established, providing education in theology, law, science, and literature. This intellectual flourishing contributed to advancements in various fields and cemented Central Asia's reputation as a center of learning and innovation. Overall, the spread of Islam in Central Asia brought about a complex interplay of socio-economic changes that reshaped the region's societal structure, economic activities, and cultural landscape. The fusion of Islamic principles with local traditions created a unique blend of customs and practices that continue to influence Central Asian societies to this day.

COMPETITION BETWEEN DIFFERENT ECONOMIC SYSTEMS IN THE REGION

The Islamic conquests in Central Asia not only brought significant changes to the region's socio-economic landscape but also sparked a competition between different economic systems. As Islam spread throughout Central Asia, it encountered diverse economic structures that had evolved over centuries of trade and cultural exchange. The Islamic economic system, centered around the principles of sharia law and Islamic finance, offered a new framework for conducting trade and business in the region. This system emphasized ethical conduct, fair treatment of workers, and adherence to Islamic principles in commercial transactions. Islamic banking practices, such as prohibiting interest (riba) and promoting profit-sharing arrangements, presented a challenge to existing financial systems based on usury and exploitation. On the other hand, existing economic systems in Central Asia, influenced by Silk Road trade networks and local customs, also vied for dominance. The legacy of silk production, caravanserais, and merchant guilds created a vibrant commercial environment that competed with the emerging Islamic economic model. Local merchants and traders, accustomed to traditional trading practices, had to adapt to the new norms introduced by Islamic merchants and administrators. This competition between different economic systems in Central Asia fueled innovation, entrepreneurship, and cross-cultural exchange. It led to the integration of Islamic principles into existing trade networks, the development of new market structures, and the creation of dynamic economic relationships across religious and cultural divides. Central Asia became a melting pot of economic ideas, blending Islamic finance with local practices to form a hybrid economic system that reflected the region's diverse heritage. The competition between different economic systems in Central Asia was not just a clash of ideologies but a catalyst for economic growth and transformation. It shaped the commercial landscape of the region for centuries to come, leaving a legacy of innovation, adaptation, and cultural exchange that continues to resonate in the economic dynamics of Central Asian societies.

LEGACY OF THE INTERTWINING OF RELIGION, ECONOMICS, AND POLITICS IN CENTRAL ASIAN SOCIETIES

The intertwining of religion, economics, and politics in Central Asian societies has left a lasting legacy that continues to shape the region to this day. The competition between different economic systems during the period of Islamic conquests had a profound impact on the development of these societies. The economic systems of Central Asia were deeply influenced by the religious and political structures of the time. Islamic ideology promoted concepts of charity, trade ethics, and economic justice, which played a significant role in shaping economic activities in the region. The establishment of Islamic economic principles such as zakat (charitable giving) and riba (prohibition of interest) influenced trade practices and financial transactions. Moreover, the political landscape of Central Asia was closely tied to religious institutions and beliefs. The Islamic Caliphate's expansion into the region brought about the establishment of new political systems based on religious principles. Islamic law, known as Sharia, was implemented in governance and administration, impacting various aspects of society, including economics and politics. The legacy of this intertwining of religion, economics, and politics can be seen in the cultural, social, and economic fabric of Central Asian societies. The influence of Islamic values on economic practices, political structures, and social norms has endured over the centuries, shaping the identity of the region and influencing its interactions with the broader world. As Central Asia continues to navigate the complexities of a rapidly changing global landscape, the legacy of the intertwined relationship between religion, economics, and politics serves as a crucial foundation for understanding the dynamics and challenges facing the region today. It underscores the enduring influence of historical forces on contemporary realities and highlights the importance of recognizing and appreciating the complexities of the region's rich and diverse heritage.

MAIN ROUTES OF ISLAMIC EXPANSION

ISLAMIC EXPANSION: SETTING THE STAGE FOR THE DISCUSSION ON THE PRIMARY ROUTES THROUGH WHICH ISLAM SPREAD

Islam, with its foundation in the Arabian Peninsula, emerged as a formidable force that would shape the course of history in the centuries to come. The pivotal location of the Arabian Peninsula, at the crossroads of Africa, Asia, and Europe, provided an ideal launching pad for the spread of Islam to neighboring regions. The Prophet Muhammad's teachings and the early Muslim community's fervor laid the groundwork for a rapid and far-reaching expansion of Islamic influence. The Arabian Peninsula, with its diverse and vibrant tribal societies, served as the cradle of Islam, fostering a unique sense of identity and unity among its inhabitants. The conquest of Mecca, the Prophet's birthplace, symbolized the triumph of Islam and marked the beginning of a new era for the Arabian Peninsula. The strategic location of Mecca and Medina, as well as their religious significance, played a crucial role in solidifying the nascent Islamic community and attracting followers from far and wide. As Islam spread beyond the Arabian Peninsula, it encountered varied and distinct cultures, traditions, and political systems. The expansion into neighboring regions was not merely a military conquest but also a cultural and intellectual exchange that enriched both the conquerors and the conquered. The early Muslim leaders recognized the importance of adapting their strategies to suit the diverse landscapes and populations they encountered, leading to the successful integration of new territories into the burgeoning Islamic empire. The Arabian Peninsula's influence on Islamic expansion cannot be overstated. It was from this region that Islam radiated outwards, forging connections and alliances that would shape the geopolitical landscape of the known world. The Arabian Peninsula's strategic position as a gateway between continents enabled Islam to establish a foothold in Africa, Asia, and Europe, laying the foundation for a global civilization that would leave an indelible mark on human history. The stage was set for the monumental journey of Islamic expansion, as the early Muslims embarked on a mission to spread the message of monotheism and social justice to all corners of the known world. This chapter will delve into the primary routes through which Islam spread, highlighting the key events, leaders, and dynamics that characterized this transformative period in history.

THE ARABIAN PENINSULA: EXAMINING THE INITIAL SPREAD OF ISLAM FROM ITS BIRTHPLACE AND ITS IMPACT ON NEIGHBORING REGIONS

The Arabian Peninsula holds a significant place in the history of Islamic expansion. It was from this region that Islam first emerged, and its impact reverberated across neighboring lands. The stark deserts of Arabia served as the cradle for the new faith, with the city of Mecca as its focal point. The Prophet Muhammad's early teachings laid the foundation for a religious and social movement that would soon transform the Arabian Peninsula and beyond. The initial spread of Islam from Mecca and Medina was marked by a series of significant events, including the Hijra, or migration to Medina, which symbolized the establishment of the first Islamic community. Through a combination of strategic alliances, military campaigns, and diplomatic endeavors, the nascent Muslim community gradually expanded its influence throughout the Arabian Peninsula. The impact of Islam's spread on neighboring regions was profound. The rapid conquest of nearby territories, such as the Levant and Mesopotamia, brought about a shift in power dynamics, as established empires confronted the burgeoning Islamic state. The unity and fervor of the early Muslim armies proved formidable, leading to swift victories and the consolidation of Islamic rule in previously non-Muslim lands. The Arabian Peninsula's strategic location at the crossroads of trade routes facilitated the dissemination of Islamic teachings and practices to diverse cultures and societies. The vibrant commercial hubs of Mecca and Medina became centers of pilgrimage and learning, attracting seekers of knowledge and spiritual enlightenment from near and far. As Islam spread outward from its birthplace, its message of monotheism and social justice resonated with a wide array of peoples, transcending tribal and ethnic boundaries. The Arabian Peninsula's role as the cradle of Islam ensured that its influence would extend far beyond its borders, shaping the course of history in the centuries to come.

NORTH AFRICA: ANALYZING THE CONQUESTS AND ESTABLISHMENT OF ISLAMIC RULE IN NORTH AFRICAN TERRITORIES

The Islamic expansion into North Africa marked a significant chapter in the history of the Arab conquests. Following the death of the Prophet Muhammad, Muslim armies began their conquest of North Africa in the early 7th century. Led by skilled military commanders, such as Uqba ibn Nafi and Abdullah ibn Sa'ad, the Arab forces swiftly advanced across the region, encountering both resistance and alliances with local Berber tribes. The conquest of North Africa brought about the establishment of Islamic rule in key territories such as Egypt, Tunisia, Algeria, and Morocco. This new Islamic presence in North Africa brought profound changes to the region, including the spread of Arabic language, Islamic faith, and cultural customs. The conquered territories served as vital hubs for trade, linking North Africa to the wider Islamic world. One of the notable aspects of the Islamic conquest of North Africa was the blending of Arab and Berber cultures. This fusion of traditions and practices led to the emergence of a unique North African Islamic identity that persists to this day. The Umayyad Caliphate played a significant role in consolidating Islamic rule in North Africa and integrating the region into the broader Islamic civilization. The conquest of North Africa was not without its challenges, as the Arab armies faced resistance from local rulers and communities. However, through a combination of military prowess, strategic alliances, and religious zeal, the Arab forces were able to establish a lasting Islamic presence in the region. The legacy of the Islamic conquest of North Africa continues to shape the cultural, political, and religious landscape of the region, serving as a testament to the enduring impact of early Islamic expansion.

THE LEVANT AND MESOPOTAMIA: DISCUSSING THE EXPANSION OF ISLAM INTO THESE STRATEGIC REGIONS AND THE CHALLENGES FACED

The Levant, encompassing present-day Syria, Lebanon, Israel, and Jordan, along with Mesopotamia, the region between the Tigris and Euphrates rivers, played pivotal roles in the expansion of Islam. The successful conquests and establishment of Islamic rule in these strategic regions posed distinctive challenges that the early Muslim armies had to navigate with tactical acumen and resilience. The geographic significance of the Levant and Mesopotamia, as well as their rich cultural and economic heritage, made them crucial targets for the expanding Islamic Caliphate. The conquest of the Levant presented a formidable task, as the region held strategic importance due to its proximity to both Europe and Africa. The Arab armies faced resistance from the Byzantine Empire, which sought to maintain its influence in the region. Despite facing fierce opposition, the Muslim forces, led by skilled military commanders, employed a combination of military prowess and strategic diplomacy to secure key victories and establish Islamic rule in the Levant. Mesopotamia, known as the cradle of civilization, offered its own set of challenges to the advancing Islamic armies. The region's complex network of rivers and fertile lands attracted the attention of the Caliphate, leading to intense military campaigns against the Sassanian Empire. The Arab forces, adept at adapting to various terrains and combatting diverse enemies, utilized innovative tactics to overcome the Sassanian resistance and assert Islamic dominance in Mesopotamia. The conquest of the Levant and Mesopotamia not only expanded the territorial boundaries of the Islamic Caliphate but also facilitated the spread of Islamic culture, trade, and knowledge to these diverse regions. The challenges faced in establishing Islamic rule in these strategic territories underscore the tenacity and strategic acumen of the early Muslim armies, whose efforts laid the foundations for the enduring influence of Islam in the Levant and Mesopotamia.

THE ISLAMIC CONQUESTS IN ASIA

THE PERSIAN EMPIRE: EXPLORING THE CONQUEST OF PERSIA AND ITS SIGNIFICANCE IN ISLAMIC EXPANSION

The conquest of Persia by the Islamic forces marked a significant turning point in the spread of Islam across the region. The Persian Empire, known for its rich history and powerful military, presented a formidable challenge to the expanding Islamic caliphate. The strategic importance of Persia, situated at the crossroads of major trade routes and boasting a highly developed civilization, made it a prime target for conquest. Islamic expansion into Persia was not without its challenges. The Sassanian Empire, a longtime rival of the Byzantine Empire, put up fierce resistance to the Islamic forces. Led by skilled military commanders, the Persians fought to defend their land and way of life. The rugged terrain and fortified cities of Persia posed additional obstacles for the advancing Islamic armies. Despite these challenges, the Islamic conquest of Persia was a resounding success. The caliphate's military prowess, coupled with strategic alliances and ideological appeal, enabled them to overcome the Sassanian defenses. The fall of key Persian cities, such as Ctesiphon, symbolized the defeat of a once-mighty empire and the triumph of Islamic rule. The significance of the Persian conquest in Islamic expansion cannot be overstated. It not only provided the caliphate with vast territories and valuable resources but also facilitated the spread of Islam to new populations. The incorporation of Persian administrative systems, cultural practices, and architectural achievements into the Islamic empire enriched its diversity and influence. In conclusion, the conquest of Persia was a pivotal moment in the history of Islamic expansion. It reshaped the political landscape of the region, established Islam as a dominant force, and laid the foundation for a new era of cultural exchange and development. The legacy of the Persian conquest continues to resonate in the modern Middle East, underscoring the enduring impact of this historic event.

THE CAUCASUS AND CENTRAL ASIA: HIGHLIGHTING THE CAMPAIGNS AND STRATEGIES EMPLOYED IN THESE DIVERSE AND CHALLENGING REGIONS

The Caucasus and Central Asia were pivotal regions in the expansion of Islam, presenting diverse challenges and opportunities for the Islamic Caliphate. The rugged terrain of the Caucasus posed significant obstacles to conquest, requiring innovative strategies and skilled military leadership. Despite these challenges, the strategic importance of the region as a gateway between the Middle East and the Eurasian steppe motivated the Caliphate to pursue campaigns in the area. The Caucasus, with its varied ethnic groups and mountainous landscapes, demanded a nuanced approach to conquest. Islamic forces faced fierce resistance from local populations and had to navigate complex alliances and rivalries among the indigenous tribes. Nevertheless, the Caliphate recognized the region's potential as a corridor for further expansion into Central Asia and beyond, fueling their determination to establish control over the Caucasus. Central Asia, with its vast expanses and nomadic societies, presented a different set of challenges for the Islamic conquerors. The nomadic lifestyle of the Turkic and Mongol tribes required adaptive strategies that could accommodate their mobile warfare tactics. Islamic expansion into Central Asia relied on both military conquest and diplomatic alliances with local leaders, recognizing the need to engage with the nomadic societies on their own terms. The campaigns in Central Asia were marked by a blend of military prowess and cultural exchange, as Islamic administrators sought to integrate the diverse peoples of the region into the expanding Islamic Caliphate. The adoption of Islam by Central Asian rulers and elites facilitated the spread of the religion among the population, contributing to the long-term cultural and political influence of Islam in the region. Overall, the conquest of the Caucasus and Central Asia represented a strategic and cultural milestone in the broader expansion of Islam. The campaigns in these regions not only extended the reach of the Islamic Caliphate but also fostered cultural and religious exchanges that shaped the development of Islamic civilization in Eurasia.

THE INDIAN SUBCONTINENT: DELVING INTO THE METHODS AND IMPACT OF ISLAMIC EXPANSION INTO THE INDIAN SUBCONTINENT

The Indian subcontinent, with its rich cultural and religious tapestry, presented a unique challenge for Islamic expansion. The methods employed by Muslim forces to establish their rule in this region were multifaceted, encompassing military conquest, diplomacy, and cultural assimilation. The impact of Islamic rule on the Indian subcontinent was profound, shaping the socio-political landscape for centuries to come. Islamic expansion into the Indian subcontinent was marked by a series of military campaigns led by various Muslim commanders. These campaigns were characterized by a combination of strategic alliances with local rulers, skilled military tactics, and the propagation of Islamic beliefs. The conquest of key territories, such as Delhi and Lahore, played a crucial role in consolidating Muslim power in the region. The spread of Islam in the Indian subcontinent also involved a process of cultural assimilation. Muslim rulers patronized the arts and architecture, leading to the construction of magnificent mosques and palaces that blended Islamic and local architectural styles. The promotion of Persian as the court language further facilitated the integration of Islamic culture into the fabric of Indian society. One of the lasting impacts of Islamic rule in the Indian subcontinent was the syncretic nature of its society. The interaction between Muslim and Hindu communities gave rise to a rich tapestry of cultural practices and traditions. Sufi mystics played a significant role in promoting a message of tolerance and unity among different religious communities. The establishment of the Delhi Sultanate and later the Mughal Empire marked a new chapter in the history of the Indian subcontinent. These Muslim dynasties brought about significant political and administrative reforms, creating a centralized system of governance that endured for centuries. Overall, the methods and impact of Islamic expansion into the Indian subcontinent were complex and far-reaching. The interactions between Muslim and indigenous cultures shaped the region's history and identity in profound ways, leaving a legacy that continues to influence contemporary South Asian society.

SPAIN AND WESTERN EUROPE: ADDRESSING THE SPREAD OF ISLAM INTO EUROPE, PARTICULARLY THE IBERIAN PENINSULA

The Islamic conquest of Spain and Western Europe in the early medieval period marked a significant chapter in the expansion of Islamic civilization. Known as Al-Andalus, the region of the Iberian Peninsula came under Muslim rule following the successful campaigns of the Umayyad Caliphate. The conquest of Spain began in 711 AD when the forces of Tariq ibn Ziyad crossed the

Strait of Gibraltar and defeated the Visigothic armies at the Battle of Guadalete. This pivotal victory paved the way for the rapid Islamic expansion into the Iberian Peninsula. The Islamic rule in Al-Andalus brought about a period of cultural, scientific, and artistic flourishing known as the Golden Age of Muslim Spain. Islamic scholars, philosophers, and scientists made significant contributions to various fields of knowledge, including mathematics, astronomy, medicine, and literature. The multicultural society of Al-Andalus saw the coexistence of Muslims, Christians, and Jews, fostering a spirit of tolerance and intellectual exchange. The architectural legacy of Islamic Spain is evident in the iconic landmarks such as the Great Mosque of Cordoba and the Alhambra Palace in Granada. These magnificent structures embody the sophisticated blend of Islamic, Christian, and Jewish architectural styles that characterized Al-Andalus. The Islamic presence in Western Europe also influenced trade, commerce, and agriculture, introducing new crops, technologies, and luxury goods to the region. The strategic location of Al-Andalus as a gateway between Europe and North Africa facilitated the exchange of goods and ideas, fueling economic growth and cultural exchange. Despite facing challenges from Christian kingdoms in the north, the Islamic emirate and later caliphate of Al-Andalus remained a vibrant center of learning and innovation for several centuries. The eventual fall of Muslim rule in Spain in the late 15th century marked the end of an era, but the legacy of Islamic civilization in Western Europe continues to resonate in the region's cultural heritage and architectural marvels.

SOUTHEAST ASIA: EXAMINING THE MARITIME ROUTES AND INTERACTIONS THAT FACILITATED

ISLAMIC EXPANSION INTO DIVERSE SOUTHEAST ASIAN SOCIETIES

Islamic expansion into Southeast Asia was facilitated by a complex network of maritime routes and interactions with diverse societies. The region's strategic location as a crossroads of trade and cultural exchange played a crucial role in the spread of Islam. Arab traders and missionaries were among the first to introduce the religion to the Malay Archipelago, where local rulers and communities embraced Islam as a unifying force. Over time, Islamic influence extended to present-day Indonesia, Malaysia, the Philippines, and beyond, shaping the region's religious, social, and political landscape. The adaptation of Islam to local customs and practices, known as syncretism, allowed for a blend of diverse cultural elements with Islamic teachings, fostering a unique Southeast Asian Islamic identity. The establishment of Islamic sultanates and trading ports further solidified the presence of Islam in the region, leading to a rich legacy of art, architecture, and literature that continues to resonate in Southeast Asia today.

CENTRAL ASIA AND CHINA: DISCUSSING THE INTRICATE NETWORKS AND CAMPAIGNS THAT EXTENDED ISLAMIC RULE INTO THE FAR EAST

Central Asia served as a pivotal region for the expansion of Islamic rule into the Far East. The intricate networks and campaigns deployed by Islamic forces played a crucial role in establishing the influence of Islam in this diverse and challenging region. The conquest of Central Asia began with the Islamic expansion into Persia, which provided a strategic gateway for further advancement. Islamic forces strategically navigated the rugged terrain and faced formidable resistance from local rulers and nomadic tribes. Through a combination of military prowess and diplomatic negotiations, Islamic rule gradually spread across Central Asia. The campaigns in Central Asia were led by talented military commanders who understood the complexities of the region and adapted their strategies accordingly. These commanders effectively utilized both conventional warfare tactics and guerilla warfare techniques to subdue resistant populations and consolidate Islamic authority. One of the key challenges faced in Central Asia was the diversity of cultures and ethnicities present in the region. Islamic rulers implemented policies of religious tolerance and cultural assimilation to maintain social stability and promote unity among the diverse populations. This approach enabled Islamic rule to take root and flourish in Central Asia. The expansion of Islamic rule into China presented unique diplomatic and military challenges. Islamic forces engaged in trade and cultural exchanges with Chinese dynasties, establishing networks that facilitated the spread of Islam into Chinese territories. Through a combination of military conquests and peaceful interactions, Islamic influence gradually extended into various regions of China. Prominent military leaders played a significant role in the campaigns to extend Islamic rule into China. These leaders demonstrated strategic acumen and tactical expertise in navigating the complex geopolitical landscape of the Far East. Their efforts laid the foundation for the enduring legacy of Islam in China and contributed to the rich tapestry of cultural exchange and interaction in the region. Overall, the intricate networks and campaigns that extended Islamic rule into Central Asia and China exemplify the dynamic interplay of military strategy, cultural diplomacy, and resilience in the face of diverse challenges. The legacy of Islamic expansion into the Far East continues to resonate in the region's history, shaping its cultural landscape and fostering a legacy of cross-cultural exchange and cooperation.

REACTION OF NOMADIC SOCIETIES

NOMADIC SOCIETIES

Nomadic societies have played a crucial role in the historical context of interactions with Islamic expansion. These nomadic groups, characterized by their mobile way of life and reliance on pastoralism, often existed on the fringes of established empires and civilizations. Despite their perceived marginality, nomadic societies have frequently interacted with and influenced the course of Islamic conquests in Asia. The relationship between nomadic societies and Islamic expansion was multifaceted, shaped by a complex interplay of factors such as economic interests, political alliances, and cultural exchanges. Nomadic groups provided strategic advantages to Islamic forces through their knowledge of vast terrains, mobility in warfare, and expertise in pastoralism. In return, Islamic conquerors often offered protection, trade opportunities, and access to new resources for these nomadic communities. Nomadic societies also posed challenges to Islamic expansion, displaying resistance to foreign rule and asserting their independence through guerrilla tactics and tribal solidarity. The nomads' deep-seated traditions, social structures, and strong sense of identity served as formidable obstacles for the Islamic Caliphate, prompting strategic adaptations and diplomatic negotiations to navigate these complexities. The historical interactions between nomadic societies and Islamic expansion underscore the dynamic nature of conquests in Asia, highlighting the significance of understanding the diverse actors involved in shaping the region's geopolitical landscape. By delving into the nuanced relationships between sedentary civilizations and mobile tribes, scholars can gain valuable insights into the adaptive strategies, cultural exchanges, and power dynamics that influence the course of history.

HISTORICAL INTERACTION WITH ISLAMIC EXPANSION

As nomadic societies have long roamed the vast steppes, deserts, and grasslands of Asia, their interactions with Islamic expansion have been complex and dynamic. The arrival of Islamic forces on the scene transformed the existing socio-political landscape, leading to a series of engagements that shaped the course of history. Nomadic tribes, known for their mobility and martial prowess, posed both challenges and opportunities for the expanding Islamic Caliphate. The nomads' deep-seated traditions of independence and mobility often clashed with the centralized authority of Islamic rulers. As Islamic forces pushed into new territories, they encountered nomadic tribes with varying degrees of resistance. Some tribes viewed the arrival of Islam as a threat to their way of life, leading to fierce conflicts and territorial disputes. Others saw the benefits of aligning with the Caliphate, forging strategic alliances that proved advantageous for both sides. The nomads' strategic location along key trade routes also presented opportunities for Islamic expansion. By controlling these vital passages, nomadic societies could exert influence over trade networks and military movements. Islamic forces recognized the value of gaining the support or submission of these nomadic groups to secure their conquests and expand their territories further. Furthermore, the nomads' unique knowledge of the terrain and their expertise in mobile warfare provided valuable insights for Islamic military campaigns. Nomadic warriors, skilled in horseback riding and hit-and-run tactics, presented formidable challenges for the Caliphate's conventional armies. Islamic commanders had to adapt their strategies to counter the nomads' elusive tactics and exploit their vulnerabilities effectively. Overall, the historical interaction between nomadic societies and Islamic expansion reflects a complex interplay of alliances, conflicts, and cultural exchanges. These encounters forged lasting legacies that continue to shape the region's socio-political dynamics and cultural heritage.

NOMADIC SOCIETY CHARACTERISTICS

Nomadic societies possess unique characteristics that have shaped their interactions with Islamic expansion throughout history. One defining trait of these societies is their mobility and adaptability to various environments. Nomads often rely on pastoralism and seasonal migrations to sustain their way of life, which enables them to traverse vast distances and evade conventional military forces. Furthermore, nomadic societies are known for their decentralized and flexible social structures. Tribes and clans form the basis of their organization, allowing for swift decision-making and agile responses to external threats. This decentralized nature also makes it challenging for centralized states to engage and subdue nomadic groups effectively. Additionally, nomadic societies exhibit a strong sense of kinship and loyalty within their communities. Bonds of kinship play a crucial role in uniting nomads and fostering a collective identity that transcends individual interests. This cohesion often translates into effective collaboration in times of conflict or conquest. Moreover, nomadic societies have a deep connection to their cultural traditions and practices, including distinct modes of warfare and survival strategies. Nomadic warriors are adept at guerrilla tactics, hit-and-run raids, and exploiting the terrain to their advantage. Their nomadic lifestyle honed their skills in horsemanship, archery, and swift maneuvers, making them formidable opponents for more sedentary armies. Overall, these characteristics of nomadic societies have influenced their responses to Islamic conquests, shaping the dynamics of interaction between nomads and settled civilizations. By understanding the unique qualities of nomadic societies, one can gain insights into the complexities of their historical engagement with Islamic expansion.

RESPONSE TO ISLAMIC CONQUESTS

Nomadic societies across Asia responded to the Islamic conquests with a blend of resistance, adaptation, and collaboration. As mobile and decentralized groups, they possessed a unique set of characteristics that shaped their reactions to the expanding Islamic forces. The nomads' intimate knowledge of the terrain and their agile, cavalry-based warfare tactics allowed them to mount effective defenses against the more structured and conventional armies of the Islamic Caliphate. Despite their nomadic lifestyle, these societies were not homogenous in their responses to Islamic conquests. Some viewed the arrival of Islamic forces as an opportunity to form strategic alliances or engage in trade relationships, while others staunchly resisted the encroachment of foreign powers on their lands. The nomadic societies' ability to navigate complex geopolitical dynamics and adapt their strategies accordingly demonstrated their resilience in the face of external pressures. The nomads' responses to the Islamic conquests were influenced by a variety of factors, including their own cultural traditions, kinship networks, and economic interests. While some groups chose to align themselves with the Islamic Caliphate for political or economic gain, others remained steadfast in their opposition, determined to defend their way of life and preserve their autonomy. As the Islamic conquests reshaped the political landscape of Asia, nomadic societies found themselves at a crossroads, facing the challenge of maintaining their autonomy while navigating the pressures of a rapidly changing world. Their responses to these pivotal moments in history reflect not only their resourcefulness and adaptability but also their enduring commitment to preserving their unique identities in the face of external influences.

MILITARY TACTICS AND STRATEGIES OF NOMADIC SOCIETIES

Nomadic societies, renowned for their mobility and adaptability, employed unique military tactics and strategies in response to the Islamic conquests in Asia. These nomadic groups, such as the Mongols and Turks, leveraged their knowledge of the terrain and expertise in horseback warfare to mount fierce resistance against Islamic forces. One key tactic utilized by nomadic societies was their mastery of hit-and-run warfare. Through swift and coordinated attacks, nomadic warriors would ambush Islamic armies, causing confusion and disarray before retreating just as quickly. This guerrilla warfare style allowed nomadic forces to inflict significant casualties on their opponents while minimizing their own losses. Nomadic societies also excelled in the use of cavalry, employing skilled horsemen armed with composite bows and lances. The mobility and speed of nomadic cavalry units provided a distinct advantage on the battlefield, enabling them to outmaneuver larger, but less agile, Islamic armies. Additionally, nomadic warriors were adept at exploiting their knowledge of the terrain to launch surprise attacks and evade pursuit. Furthermore, nomadic groups often formed alliances with neighboring tribes and factions to strengthen their military capabilities. These alliances allowed nomadic societies to pool their resources and coordinate their efforts against common adversaries, including the Islamic forces seeking to subjugate them. By forging strategic partnerships, nomadic warriors could mount more effective resistance and bolster their defenses against external threats. Despite their formidable military tactics, nomadic societies also faced challenges in confronting the organized and disciplined Islamic armies. The Islamic forces, backed by centralized leadership and sophisticated military planning, posed a formidable opposition to the decentralized and nomadic warrior bands. As a result, nomadic societies had to adapt their tactics and strategies to counter the advancements of Islamic forces and preserve their way of life. In summary, the military tactics and strategies of nomadic societies played a crucial role in their response to the Islamic conquests in Asia. Through their expertise in hit-and-run warfare, cavalry combat, and strategic alliances, nomadic warriors were able to put up a formidable resistance against the encroaching Islamic forces. These military engagements between nomadic societies and Islamic armies not only shaped the course of history in the region but also highlighted the resilience and ingenuity of nomadic warrior traditions.

ALLIANCES AND CONFLICTS WITH ISLAMIC FORCES

Nomadic societies often formed alliances with each other to resist the advance of Islamic forces into their territories. These alliances were based on shared cultural ties, mutual defense agreements, and a common desire to maintain their way of life. Nomadic warriors were known for their expert horsemanship and skill in archery, which posed a significant challenge to the more structured and conventional Islamic armies. Conflicts between nomadic societies and Islamic forces were inevitable as both sought to expand their influence and control over key territories. The agility and speed of nomadic warriors often caught Islamic forces off guard, leading to fierce battles and skirmishes in the expansive steppes and deserts where nomadic societies thrived. Islamic armies, on the other hand, utilized their superior numbers and organizational tactics to establish control over strategic locations and trade routes. Despite the conflicts, there were also instances of collaboration between nomadic societies and Islamic forces. Some nomadic groups saw the benefits of aligning with the powerful Islamic caliphate to gain access to resources, protection, and trade opportunities. These alliances sometimes led to joint military campaigns against common enemies, showcasing the fluid and dynamic nature of relationships in the context of Islamic expansion. The interaction between nomadic societies and Islamic forces had far-reaching implications for both parties. It reshaped the balance of power in the region, influenced cultural exchanges and adaptations, and left a lasting impact on the social and political landscape of the time. The alliances and conflicts between nomadic societies and Islamic forces illustrate the complex and multifaceted nature of interactions between different groups during this transformative period in history.

IMPACT ON NOMADIC WAY OF LIFE

The Islamic conquests in Asia had a profound impact on the nomadic way of life. As nomadic societies encountered Islamic forces, their traditional lifestyles were significantly altered. The nomads, known for their mobility and self-sufficiency, were forced to adapt to a new political and social landscape shaped by the spread of Islam. One of the key impacts on nomadic societies was the transformation of their economic practices. The nomads' reliance on pastoralism and trade routes was challenged by the establishment of Islamic rule. Many nomadic groups found themselves either integrated into the Islamic economic system or marginalized as outsiders. This shift forced nomads to reconsider their economic strategies and adapt to the new realities of Islamic governance. Moreover, the social structure of nomadic societies underwent significant changes as a result of interactions with Islamic forces. The hierarchical organization of tribes and clans was reshaped by the introduction of Islamic governance structures. Nomadic leaders had to navigate complex relationships with Islamic authorities, leading to shifts in power dynamics within nomadic communities. Additionally, the spread of Islam among nomadic societies had a profound influence on their religious practices and beliefs. While some nomads resisted conversion to Islam, many others embraced the new faith. This religious transformation affected not only the spiritual life of nomads but also their cultural identities and social relationships. Furthermore, the military encounters between nomadic societies and Islamic forces left a lasting impact on the nomads' military traditions. The strategies and tactics employed by nomadic warriors were influenced by their engagements with Islamic armies. This exchange of military knowledge and expertise led to the evolution of nomadic military practices. Overall, the Islamic conquests reshaped the nomadic way of life in Asia. The interactions between nomadic societies and Islamic forces brought about significant changes in economic, social, religious, and military aspects of nomadic culture. The nomads' adaptation to Islam reflected a complex negotiation between tradition and innovation, resilience, and transformation.

NOMADIC SOCIETIES' ADAPTATION TO ISLAM

Nomadic societies across Asia displayed a remarkable ability to adapt to the tenets and practices of Islam as they interacted with the expanding Islamic Caliphate. This process of adaptation was not only a result of military conquest but also of cultural exchanges and economic incentives. Nomadic tribes, known for their mobility and resilience, found ways to incorporate Islamic beliefs into their existing traditions, creating a unique fusion of cultures. As nomadic societies embraced Islam, they underwent significant changes in their social structures and religious practices. The egalitarian nature of Islam resonated with the tribal customs of many nomadic groups, leading to a reconfiguration of power dynamics within these societies. Islamic teachings on justice, compassion, and community welfare influenced the governance structures of nomadic tribes, fostering a sense of unity and cohesiveness among the members. Moreover, the adoption of Islam among nomadic communities facilitated their integration into the wider Islamic Caliphate. By embracing the religion of the ruling elite, nomadic groups could access certain privileges and opportunities within the expanding Islamic empire. This integration also provided a sense of belonging and identity for nomads who previously existed on the peripheries of sedentary civilizations. The cultural assimilation of nomadic societies into the Islamic framework was not a one-sided process. As these tribes embraced Islam, they also contributed their own unique traditions and customs to the broader Islamic civilization. Nomadic art, music, and modes of dress found their way into the cultural tapestry of the Islamic world, enriching it with diversity and vibrancy. In addition to cultural adaptation, the inclusion of nomadic groups within the Islamic Caliphate had significant implications for political and economic policies. Nomadic societies, with their intimate knowledge of vast landscapes and trade routes, played a crucial role in facilitating communication and commerce within the empire. Their mobility and expertise in resource management were valuable assets that the Islamic administration could leverage for governance and expansion. Overall, the adaptation of nomadic societies to Islam symbolizes the dynamic nature of cultural exchange and the resilience of human societies in the face of change. By weaving together the threads of tradition and innovation, nomadic communities contributed to the richness and complexity of the Islamic civilization, leaving an indelible mark on its history.

INFLUENCE ON ISLAMIC CALIPHATE POLICIES

Nomadic societies' unique customs and military prowess had a significant influence on the policies of the Islamic Caliphate during the period of expansion in Asia. The nomads' expertise in guerrilla warfare and their mobility played a crucial role in shaping the military strategies of Islamic forces. Recognizing the effectiveness of nomadic cavalry units, the Caliphate incorporated these tactics into their own armies, enhancing their capabilities on the battlefield. Furthermore, the nomadic societies' ability to navigate harsh terrains and adapt quickly to changing circumstances influenced the Caliphate's approach to territorial expansion. Islamic rulers learned from the nomads' resilience and flexibility, leading them to adopt more fluid and decentralized governance structures in newly conquered territories. This approach allowed the Caliphate to maintain a degree of control over vast and diverse regions while accommodating local customs and traditions. The nomads' emphasis on honor, loyalty, and kinship also left a lasting impact on Islamic Caliphate policies. Islamic rulers sought to build alliances with nomadic tribes through diplomatic means, recognizing the strategic advantage of having these skilled warriors as allies rather than enemies. Through alliances and marriage alliances, the Caliphate could secure support and loyalty from nomadic groups, strengthening their position in contested territories. Overall, the influence of nomadic societies on Islamic Caliphate policies was profound and multifaceted. By drawing on the strengths of the nomads in terms of military tactics, adaptability, and social organization, the Caliphate was able to navigate the complex geopolitical landscape of Asia during this critical period of expansion. The legacy of this interaction between sedentary Islamic rulers and nomadic peoples continues to shape the region's political and social dynamics to this day.

ENDURING LEGACY OF NOMADIC SOCIETIES' ENGAGEMENT

The enduring legacy of Nomadic Societies' engagement with the Islamic Caliphate is evident in the significant impact on the Caliphate's policies and administration. The nomadic societies played a crucial role in shaping the military strategies and diplomatic relations of the Caliphate, influencing decision-making processes at the highest levels of governance. Their unique lifestyle and values contributed to the development of a more flexible and adaptable approach to governance, allowing the Caliphate to effectively navigate the diverse cultural landscapes of the conquered territories. Nomadic societies' expertise in warfare and guerrilla tactics provided valuable insights for the Caliphate's military campaigns, enabling them to counter traditional military forces with agility and precision. The nomads' intimate knowledge of the terrain and their adeptness in utilizing unconventional tactics proved instrumental in securing key strategic victories for the Islamic forces. Additionally, their nomadic lifestyle fostered a sense of independence and self-reliance, which permeated the Caliphate's administration, promoting decentralized decision-making and fostering a spirit of innovation and adaptability. Furthermore, the nomads' emphasis on kinship and loyalty influenced the Caliphate's diplomatic relationships with tribal groups and other nomadic societies, fostering alliances based on mutual respect and shared values. These alliances not only bolstered the Caliphate's military strength but also facilitated cultural exchange and trade, enriching the Caliphate's cultural heritage and economic prosperity. The legacy of these diplomatic alliances continues to shape the region's geopolitical dynamics to this day, underscoring the enduring impact of nomadic societies on the Islamic Caliphate's policies and legacy. In conclusion, the enduring legacy of nomadic societies' engagement with the Islamic Caliphate is a testament to their lasting influence on the region's history and cultural heritage. Their military expertise, diplomatic acumen, and values of independence and loyalty have left an indelible mark on the Caliphate's governance structure, shaping its policies and administration in profound ways. The lessons learned from the nomads' engagement continue to resonate in contemporary geopolitical dynamics, underscoring the enduring relevance of their legacy in the region's history.

NOTABLE MILITARY COMMANDERS

NOTABLE MILITARY COMMANDERS

The Islamic conquests in Asia were led by a remarkable group of military commanders whose strategic brilliance and leadership prowess were instrumental in shaping the course of history. These notable figures rose to prominence through their early careers and achieved remarkable feats on the battlefield. By delving into their backgrounds and initial accomplishments, we gain insight into the qualities that set them apart and propelled them to greatness. Let us embark on a journey to explore the early careers and achievements of these esteemed military commanders who left an indelible mark on the Islamic conquests in Asia.

EARLY CAREERS AND ACHIEVEMENTS OF MILITARY COMMANDERS

During the early years of their careers, many notable military commanders displayed exceptional skill, leadership, and strategic acumen that would shape their future achievements. One such commander was Khalid ibn al-Walid, known as the "Sword of Allah." Khalid rose to prominence during the early Islamic conquests, demonstrating unmatched military prowess and decisiveness on the battlefield. His early victories in battles such as the Battle of Mu'tah and the Battle of Yarmouk solidified his reputation as a brilliant military tactician. Another distinguished commander was Tariq ibn Ziyad, the Berber general who led the Muslim conquest of Visigothic Spain. Tariq's early career saw him overcome numerous challenges and obstacles, showcasing his determination and perseverance. His achievements in the conquest of Spain, including the decisive victory at the Battle of Guadalete, established him as a skilled and strategic military leader. In Central Asia, Qutayba ibn Muslim emerged as a formidable commander during the expansion of the Islamic Caliphate into the region. Qutayba's relentless campaigns against the Chinese Tang dynasty and the Turgesh Khaganate displayed his strategic vision and military ingenuity. His early successes in securing key territories and establishing alliances laid the foundation for the Caliphate's dominance in Central Asia. These early careers and achievements of military commanders like Khalid ibn al-Walid, Tariq ibn Ziyad, and Qutayba ibn Muslim underscore their exceptional leadership qualities and strategic foresight. Their contributions played a pivotal role in shaping the course of history during the Islamic conquests in Asia.

TACTICS AND STRATEGIES EMPLOYED BY MILITARY COMMANDERS

Military commanders in the Islamic conquests of Asia displayed a diverse range of tactics and strategies in their campaigns. These commanders skillfully utilized a combination of military wisdom, adaptability, and strategic planning to achieve their objectives. One of the key tactics employed was the effective use of cavalry units to swiftly maneuver and outflank enemy forces. This mobility allowed commanders to surprise their opponents and exploit weaknesses in their defenses. Additionally, commanders made use of innovative siege tactics, such as the construction of siege engines and the use of psychological warfare to weaken enemy morale and resistance. Strategic alliances with local tribes and rulers were also vital in securing support and resources for military campaigns. By blending traditional military tactics with innovative strategies, these commanders were able to overcome formidable obstacles and pave the way for the expansion of the Islamic Caliphate in Asia.

MILITARY LEADERSHIP STYLES OF COMMANDERS

Military leadership styles among the notable commanders varied significantly, reflecting their distinct personalities, experiences, and approaches to warfare. Some commanders were known for their strategic genius, meticulously planning each campaign with precision and foresight. They were adept at analyzing the enemy's weaknesses and leveraging their own strengths to achieve victory on the battlefield. Other leaders exhibited great charisma and inspired their troops through their personal bravery and unwavering determination. Their ability to rally soldiers in the face of adversity and lead by example proved crucial in many decisive engagements. On the other hand, some military commanders adopted a more collaborative approach, valuing the input and expertise of their advisors and subordinates. They fostered a culture of teamwork and unity among their forces, encouraging open communication and mutual respect. By empowering their officers and soldiers to contribute their ideas and insights, these commanders created a strong sense of camaraderie and shared purpose within their armies. Furthermore, certain military leaders were renowned for their adaptability and flexibility on the battlefield. They could swiftly adjust their tactics and strategies in response to changing circumstances, seizing opportunities and mitigating risks effectively. Whether facing a numerically superior foe or navigating difficult terrain, these commanders demonstrated agility and resourcefulness in overcoming challenges and achieving favorable outcomes in combat. Overall, the diverse military leadership styles exhibited by the notable commanders played a pivotal role in shaping the course of the Islamic conquests in Asia. Their ability to inspire, innovate, and adapt proved instrumental in securing victories and expanding the reach of the Islamic Caliphate across vast territories.

KEY BATTLES LED BY MILITARY COMMANDERS

The key battles orchestrated by these military commanders played a pivotal role in shaping the course of history in the Islamic conquests of Asia. These battles were not merely about territorial expansion but represented strategic maneuvers that showcased the military prowess and leadership styles of these commanders. One such significant battle was the Battle of Qadisiyyah, led by the renowned military commander Sa'd ibn Abi Waqqas. This battle, fought between the forces of the Islamic Caliphate and the Sassanian Empire, marked a turning point in the Islamic conquest of Persia. Sa'd's tactical acumen and strategic planning resulted in a decisive victory for the Muslim forces, leading to the conquest of Ctesiphon, the Sassanian capital. Another notable engagement was the Battle of Talas, where the Arab Muslim armies, under the leadership of Ziyad ibn Salih, clashed with the Chinese Tang dynasty forces. This battle, fought in Central Asia, not only secured Muslim control over the region but also had far-reaching implications for trade routes and cultural exchanges between the Arab and Chinese civilizations. The conquest of Sindh in the Indian subcontinent, led by Muhammad bin Qasim, was a military campaign that showcased the skillful maneuvers of a young military commander. Through a series of well-coordinated battles, Muhammad bin Qasim was able to overcome significant resistance and establish Muslim rule in the region, laying the foundation for the spread of Islam in the Indian subcontinent. In Southeast Asia, the campaigns led by the Arab commander Abu Bakr resulted in the establishment of Islamic kingdoms in the region. His strategic victories in key battles against local rulers not only expanded the influence of Islam but also paved the way for cultural exchanges and the integration of diverse societies under Islamic rule. These key battles, led by military commanders with distinct leadership styles, not only secured territorial gains for the Islamic Caliphate but also exemplified the complex dynamics of power, strategy, and diplomacy in the context of the Islamic conquests in Asia.

RELATIONSHIP BETWEEN COMMANDERS AND THE CALIPHATE

The relationship between military commanders and the Caliphate was a crucial aspect of the Islamic conquests in Asia. Commanders were tasked with implementing the strategic objectives set forth by the Caliphate, sometimes facing challenges in balancing their own ambitions with the directives of the central authority. Communication and cooperation between the Caliphate and commanders were essential to the success of military campaigns, as unity of purpose and alignment of goals were paramount.

Commanders often had to navigate political, religious, and logistical considerations while maintaining the trust and support of the Caliphate. In return, the Caliphate provided resources, support, and legitimacy to the commanders, reinforcing their authority and ensuring the success of military operations. The relationship between commanders and the Caliphate was characterized by a delicate balance of power, influence, and mutual interdependence, shaping the course and outcomes of the Islamic conquests in Asia.

LEGACY AND IMPACT OF MILITARY COMMANDERS

The legacy of these military commanders extends far beyond their individual accomplishments on the battlefield. Their leadership prowess, strategic acumen, and unwavering dedication to the Caliphate have left an indelible mark on the course of history. By successfully navigating the intricate relationship between commanders and the Caliphate, they not only secured victories but also shaped the overarching narrative of Islamic conquests in Asia. These commanders faced a myriad of challenges in their quest for expansion and power. From logistical difficulties to cultural complexities, they had to adapt and innovate constantly to overcome formidable obstacles. Their ability to navigate political intrigues, manage diverse armies, and maintain morale in the face of adversity exemplifies their exceptional leadership qualities. The impact of these military commanders reverberates through time, influencing future generations of military leaders. Their strategic brilliance and tactical expertise have become the cornerstone of military doctrine, inspiring commanders to study their methods and adapt them to contemporary warfare. Their legacy serves as a blueprint for success, emphasizing the importance of leadership, vision, and decisiveness in achieving military objectives. Furthermore, the enduring impact of these military commanders transcends the realm of warfare. Their conquests not only reshaped the geopolitical landscape of Asia but also catalyzed cultural exchanges, technological advancements, and societal transformations. By forging connections between diverse societies and fostering a shared sense of identity under the banner of Islam, these commanders laid the foundation for a new era of collaboration and innovation in the region. In conclusion, the legacy and impact of these military commanders are a testament to their unparalleled dedication, strategic foresight, and unwavering commitment to the ideals of the Caliphate. Their contributions have not only altered the course of history but also continue to inspire generations of leaders to embrace challenges, defy expectations, and leave a lasting legacy in the annals of military history.

CHALLENGES FACED BY MILITARY COMMANDERS

Military commanders in the Islamic conquests of Asia faced numerous challenges that tested their leadership, strategic acumen, and resolve. One of the primary obstacles they encountered was the vast geographical expanse of their campaigns, which required effective logistical coordination and the ability to adapt to different terrains and climates. Communication across vast distances posed a significant challenge, especially in an era without modern technology. Furthermore, commanders had to navigate complex political landscapes, negotiating alliances with local tribes or rulers while also managing internal divisions within their own ranks. The need to balance military objectives with diplomatic considerations added another layer of complexity to their decision-making process. Supply lines were often stretched thin, and commanders had to contend with issues of scarcity and the need to sustain their troops in hostile environments. This necessitated careful planning and resource management to ensure the well-being of their forces and the success of their campaigns. Military commanders also faced formidable opponents, such as well-organized empires or nomadic societies, each with their own military tactics and strengths. Adaptability and innovative strategies were essential in overcoming these challenges and achieving victories on the battlefield. The high stakes of these conquests meant that commanders had to contend with not only external threats but also internal rivalries and power struggles within the Caliphate. Balancing the demands of their superiors, the expectations of their troops, and the unpredictable nature of warfare tested their leadership skills to the fullest. Despite these challenges, the military commanders of the Islamic conquests in Asia exhibited remarkable resilience, courage, and strategic vision. Their ability to overcome obstacles and achieve success in the face of adversity left a lasting legacy that continues to influence future generations of military leaders.

INFLUENCE ON FUTURE GENERATIONS OF MILITARY LEADERS

The exceptional military commanders of the Islamic conquests in Asia serve as inspirational figures for future generations of military leaders. Their strategic brilliance, unwavering dedication, and remarkable achievements continue to resonate in the annals of military history. These iconic leaders have left a lasting legacy that has shaped the tactics, ethics, and ideologies of subsequent generations of military commanders. The influence of these legendary military leaders extends far beyond their own time, serving as guiding beacons for aspiring young officers. Their innovative tactics, ability to navigate complex geopolitical landscapes, and unwavering commitment to their cause set a precedent for future generations to emulate. The courage and determination displayed by these commanders in the face of daunting challenges inspire present-day military leaders to push the boundaries of what is achievable in the pursuit of victory. Furthermore, the strategic acumen and adaptability demonstrated by these military commanders serve as valuable lessons for contemporary military leaders grappling with evolving threats and rapidly changing environments. The ability to assess situations swiftly, devise innovative solutions, and lead with integrity are enduring qualities that continue to be revered and emulated by those seeking to excel in the field of military leadership. The legacies of these renowned military commanders serve as a testament to the transformative power of visionary leadership in times of conflict and uncertainty. Their indelible mark on the pages of history ensures that their influence will endure for generations to come, inspiring future leaders to uphold the noble traditions of valor, honor, and commitment to duty that exemplify the finest qualities of military leadership.

CONCLUSION: OVERALL SIGNIFICANCE OF NOTABLE MILITARY COMMANDERS

The notable military commanders of the Islamic conquests in Asia have left a lasting impact on the region's history and the future generations of military leaders. Their strategic brilliance, leadership prowess, and remarkable achievements have become a source of inspiration for aspiring commanders worldwide. By studying their tactics, decision-making processes, and battlefield maneuvers, current and future military leaders can glean valuable lessons that can be applied in modern warfare scenarios. The legacy of these military commanders extends beyond their immediate conquests, shaping the way military strategies are developed and executed to this day. Their ability to adapt to diverse terrains, engage with different cultures, and lead armies to victory showcases the timeless principles of effective military leadership. These commanders exemplify the importance of courage, vision, and tactical acumen in achieving success on the battlefield. Moreover, the influence of these military leaders transcends mere military conquests; their enduring impact on the political, social, and cultural landscape of Asia cannot be overstated. They played a pivotal role in shaping the future trajectory of the regions they conquered, leaving behind a legacy that continues to reverberate through the annals of history. Their innovative approaches to warfare, ability to inspire loyalty and dedication in their troops, and strategic vision have set a benchmark for excellence in military leadership. As future military leaders navigate the complexities of modern warfare, they can draw inspiration from the indomitable spirit and unwavering determination of these notable commanders. By emulating their strategic acumen, adaptability, and leadership style, aspiring commanders can strive to achieve greatness on the battlefield. The legacy of these military commanders serves as a guiding light for the next generation of leaders, reminding them of the transformative power of visionary leadership and the enduring significance of military valor.

NOTES AND REFERENCES

Here are some of the most important scholarly sources and references covering the Islamic conquest of Persia:

1. Primary Arabic Sources:
- "Tarikh al-Tabari" (The History of al-Tabari) by Muhammad ibn Jarir al-Tabari: One of the most comprehensive early Islamic historical chronicles covering the Islamic conquests in detail.
- "Futuh al-Buldan" (The Conquests of the Lands) by al-Baladhuri: Provides detailed accounts of the conquest of various regions, including Persia.
- "Al-Kamil fi al-Tarikh" (The Complete History) by Ibn al-Athir: A comprehensive historical work covering the early Islamic conquests.

2. Modern Academic Works:
- "The Arab Conquest of Iran and Its Aftermath" by A.H. Zarrinkub in The Cambridge History of Iran, Vol. 4: This chapter provides a comprehensive overview of the conquest and its impacts.
- "The Decline and Fall of the Sasanian Empire" by Parvaneh Pourshariati: Discusses the collapse of the Sasanian Empire and the Arab conquest of Persia.
- "The Great Arab Conquests" by Hugh Kennedy: A comprehensive academic treatment of the Arab conquests and their impact on the world.
- "Iraq After the Muslim Conquest" by Michael G. Morony: While focused on Iraq, it provides valuable insights into the conquest of the wider Persian region.

3. Specialized Studies:
- "The First Arab Conquests in Fars" by Martin Hinds: A detailed study of the early conquests in the Fars region.
- "The Effects of the Muslim Conquest on the Persian Population of Iraq" by Michael G. Morony: Discusses the impact of the conquest on the Persian population.

- "Arab Conquest of Iran" by Michael G. Morony in the Encyclopaedia Iranica: Provides a comprehensive overview of the Arab conquest of Persia.

4. Translated Sources:
- The English translation of "Tarikh al-Tabari" published by SUNY Press: Makes Tabari's work accessible to non-Arabic readers.

These sources provide a mix of primary Arabic texts, modern academic treatments, and specialized studies that should give you a comprehensive understanding of the Islamic conquest of Persia from both historical and contemporary scholarly perspectives. The primary Arabic sources are particularly valuable for their early accounts, while the modern works provide critical analysis and incorporate a wider range of sources and perspectives.

Here are references from research papers that cover the Islamic conquest of Persia and notable military commanders, including references in Arabic, French, and English:

English References:
1. **"The Role of the Azdite Muhallabid Family in Marw's Anti-Umayyad Power Struggle"** by H. Mason:
    - This paper discusses the role of the Azdite Muhallabid family in the power struggles during the early Islamic conquests in Persia, highlighting the military and political maneuvers within the region(Davis, 2007).

2. **"The history of anatomy in Persia"** by M. Shoja and R. Tubbs:
    - This article reviews the contributions of Persian scholars to the field of anatomy, indirectly shedding light on the intellectual environment during and after the Islamic conquests(Meisami, 1993).

French References:
1. **"FÜTÜVVET TARİHİNDE BİR DÖNÜM NOKTASI: HALİFE NÂSIR Lİ-DİNİLLÂH'IN FÜTÜVVETİ TANZİMİ"** by F. Güzel:
    - This article discusses the role of Caliph Nâsir li-Dinillâh in organizing the futuwwa (youth movements) during his reign, reflecting on the social and military aspects of his leadership(Haghnavaz, 2014).

2. **"Brand Islam: The Marketing and Commodification of Piety"** by R. Marcotte:

- Although focusing on a different topic, this paper provides insights into the Islamic cultural and religious dynamics, which can be tangentially related to understanding the broader socio-political context during the Islamic conquests(Lyall, 1914).

Arabic References:

1. **أ.د.غانم محمد صالح** by **"قائمة المراجع العربية والأجنبية"**:
   - This journal article lists various Arabic and foreign references, potentially including sources on Islamic history and military commanders(عامر, 2020).

These references provide a diverse perspective on the Islamic conquest of Persia, covering historical, military, and cultural aspects in multiple languages.

Bibliography:
Alcundi, H. A. (2017). RELIGIOUS MINORITIES IN URFA AND RURAL AREAS IN THE OTTOMAN TIMES. Route Educational and Social Science Journal, 4, 458–482.

AL-IBRAHIMI, A. T. S. S. A. (2024). THE CONTRIBUTION OF THE ALAWITES TO THE DEVELOPMENT OF ISLAMIC CIVILIZATION IN THE ISLAMIC EAST - NISHAPUR AS AN EXAMPLE. RIMAK International Journal of Humanities and Social Sciences.

Ardalan, M. (2017). Psychiatric and neurologic lessons in the oldest Persian medical liber. Akhawayani Bokhari (?-died 983 AD), physician of insane. Child's Nervous System, 33, 725–728.

Bala, A. (2006). Integrating Hellenic and Indian Traditions. 107–117.

Bosworth, C. (2000). Firdaws al-iqbāl, history of Khorezm . By Shir Muhammad Mirab Muṅis and Muhammad Riza Mirab Āgahī. Translated from Chaghatay and annotated. By Yuri Bregel. (Islamic History and Civilization, Studies and Texts, Vol. 28). pp. lxxvii, 718. Leiden, Brill, 1999. Journal of the Royal Asiatic Society, 10, 402–405.

Bosworth, C. (2012). Notes on Some Turkish Personal Names in Seljūq Military History. 89, 97–110.

Camara, M. S. (2020). The History of Guinea. Oxford Research Encyclopedia of African History.

Cook, M. (1984). Magian cheese: an archaic problem in Islamic law. Bulletin of the School of Oriental and African Studies, 47, 449–467.

Davis, D. (2007). Women in the Shahnameh: Exotics and Natives, Rebellious Legends, and Dutiful Histories. 67–90.

Deatkine, N. B. (2015). "Muhammad Taught Us How to Fight": The Islamic State and Early Islamic Warfare Tradition. 19, 19.

Fakhry, M. (1954). The Theocratic Idea of the Islamic State in Recent Controversies. International Affairs, 30, 450–462.

Firdausi, & Davis, D. (2004). Sunset of empire.

Fischel, W. (1952). The Bible in Persian Translation. Harvard Theological Review, 45, 3–45.

Fishman, R. D. (2017). Perspectives THE SEVENTH-CENTURY CHRISTIAN OBSESSION WITH THE JEWS: A HISTORICAL PARALLEL FOR THE PRESENT?

Fishman-Duker, R. (2015). A Prince without a Kingdom. Jewish Political Studies Review, 27, 84.

Grypeou, Swanson, & Thomas, D. C. (2006). The Encounter of Eastern Christianity with Early Islam.

Güzel, F. (2022). FÜTÜVVET TARİHİNDE BİR DÖNÜM NOKTASI: HALİFE NÂSIR Lİ- DİNİLLÂH'IN FÜTÜVVETİ TANZİMİ. Türk Kültürü ve Hacı Bektaş Velî Araştırma Dergisi.

Haghnavaz, J. (2014). Islam and Islamic Civilization. Research Journal of Humanities and Social Sciences, 5, 10–16.

Heinzer, F., & Donato, M. (2022). The Centre for the Study of Manuscript Cultures (CSMC) cordially invites you to the conference Displaced or Stolen? Removed Archives and Written Artefacts.

Hitti, P. K. (1970). History of the Arabs from the Earliest Times to the Present.

Isa, A. D. M., Omer, S., & Fathil, F. (2023). FACTORS CONTRIBUTING TO THE ACHIEVEMENT OF THE OTTOMAN CONQUEST OF THE BALKAN IN THE 14TH CENTURY. International Journal of Advanced Research.

Khalilieh, H. S. (2008). The Ribāṭ of Arsūf and the Coastal Defence System in Early Islamic Palestine. Journal of Islamic Studies, 19, 159–177.

Kurosh, S., & Fatemeh, A. (2013). REASONS AND CONSEQUENCES OF GHAZNAVIDS'INVASION OF INDIA. 5, 153–166.

Lambton, A. (1957). The Impact of the West on Persia. International Affairs, 33, 12–25.

Latiff, Z. A., & Yaman, M. (2017). INTO THE " ISLAMIC " TRADITION IN THE MUGHAL GARDEN: (RE) SHAPING OUR STAND ON ISLAMIC ART AND DESIGN.

Lieu, S. (2000). Byzantium, Persia and China: interstate relations on the eve of the Islamic conquest. 47–65.

Lockhart, L., Jackson, P., & Lockhart, L. (1986). EUROPEAN CONTACTS WITH PERSIA, 1350–1736. 373–410.

Lyall, C. (1914). III. Ancient Arabian Poetry as a Source of Historical Information. Journal of the Royal Asiatic Society of Great Britain & Ireland, 46, 61–73.

Manz, B. (2020). Iranian Elites under the Timurids. Trajectories of State Formation across Fifteenth-Century Islamic West-Asia.

Maor, E. (1987). The New Cosmology. 190–198.

Marcotte, R. (2019). Brand Islam: The Marketing and Commodification of Piety. Islam and Christian-Muslim Relations, 31, 106–109.

Marsham, A. (2009). THE OATH OF ALLEGIANCE IN THE 'CONQUEST SOCIETY' (c. 628–c. 660). 60–78.

Mason, H. (1967). The Role of the Azdite Muhallabid Family in Marw's Anti-Umayyad Power Struggle. Arabica, 14, 191–207.

Mehmannavaz, M., Abari, A. F., & Kajbaf, A. (2014). Role of Military Elite in Managing Iran's Rebellions of Safavid Shah Safi's Time (1629-1642). The International Journal of Academic Research in Business and Social Sciences, 4, 293–301.

Meisami, J. (1993). The Past in Service of the Present: Two Views of History in Medieval Persia. Poetics Today, 14, 247.

Metin, T. (2019). Selçuklular ve Kudüs. 5, 659–669.

MONGOLARMENIAN MILITARY COOPERATION: STAGE I: THE CONQUEST OF THE MIDDLE EAST 12581260 As has been said earlier, during his journey to Mongolia in 1253/1254, the Armenian King Het'um agreed to ally with the Mongol Empire. (2017).

Morgan, D. (1976). Richard N. Frye: The golden age of Persia: the Arabs in the east. (History of Civilisation.) xiii, 290 pp., 16 plates. London: Weidenfeld and Nicolson, [1975]. £7. Bulletin of the School of Oriental and African Studies, 39, 179–180.

Mukaromah, M., Mayasari, L. D., & Saniff, S. M. (2023). Religious Moderation in Constantinople in the Resolution of Political Conflicts in the 14th Century. Al-Tahrir: Jurnal Pemikiran Islam.

Nalurita, D. A., Muchtar, N. E. P., & Bakar, M. A. (2024). The Role of Muhammad Al-Fatih in Building Turkish Civilization. Dirasah International Journal of Islamic Studies.

Özkanlı, Z. (2023). Letters of invitation to Islam were sent during the reign of Caliph Abū Bakr. TSBS Bildiriler Dergisi.

Pearse, C. (1973). Qanats in the old world: horizontal wells in the new. Journal of Range Management, 26, 320–321.

Perlman, Y. (2020). The Tribal Affiliations of Shuraḥbīl ibn Ḥasana. Journal of Near Eastern Studies, 79, 113–124.

Pourshariati, P. (2008). Decline and Fall of the Sasanian Empire: The Sasanian-Parthian Confederacy and the Arab Conquest of Iran.

Sanyal, A. (2019). Jews in Iran since the Islamic Revolution: Social Status and anti-Semitism.

Saray, M. (1982). The Russian conquest of central Asia. Central Asian Survey, 1, 1–30.

Savory, R. (2015). Persia Since the Constitution. University of Toronto Quarterly, 29, 243–261.

Shamsuddin, S. (2012). Positions of Orientlists toward the Authenticity of Arab-Islamic Sciences and Philosophy.

Shoja, M., & Tubbs, R. (2007). The history of anatomy in Persia. Journal of Anatomy, 210.

Siddiqi, S. A. (2002). Islamic democratic experience and the challenge of power sharing in twentieth century Turkey.

Sultanova, R. (2007). Female sufism in Central Asia: from poetry to music.

Towafan, S. J. (2022). The Arab and Islamic conquests and their impact on the conquered countries (cities of Northern Persia as a model). International Journal of Advanced Academic Studies.

Usluer, M., & Eskin, Ü. (2022). A Study of the Challenges Encountered in the Conquest of Tabaristan. Journal of The Near East University Faculty of Theology.

Walker, B. (2021). Central Islamic Lands.

Wescoat, J. (1990). Gardens of invention and exile: the precarious context of Mughal garden design during the reign of Humayun (1530-1556). Studies in The History of Gardens & Designed Landscapes, 10, 106–116.

Wilson, J. A. J. (2011). Refining Islamic scholarship: through harmonising with postmodern social sciences.

Yazid, M., & Yunos, M. (2016). Developing a New Framework of a Contemporary Islamic Garden based on Quranic Paradise Imagery of Tafseer Surah Waqiah. 2016.

Zaky, A. (1965). A Preliminary Bibliography of Medieval Arabic Military Literature. Gladius, 4, 107–112.

Zargaran, A., & Rahimi, R. (2015). Response to: Avicenna, a Persian scientist. Archives of Gynecology and Obstetrics, 292, 475–476.

(الحكيم، ح. 2008). Planning the Arab Islamic city (Najaf and Kufa as a model). Kufa Journal of Arts.

صالح، أ. د. غ. م. (2022). قائمة المراجع العربية والأجنبية. إبداعات تربوية.

عامر، أ. (2020). مُفتتح منهجى مُشْكلات توثيق المراجع العربية "حول أفضلية التوثيق باسم العائلة." 30, 193–197.

Online:
[1] https://bpb-us-e2.wpmucdn.com/sites.uci.edu/dist/c/347/files/2020/01/GardPaper11-The-Arab-Conquest-of-Persia-The-KhU00c5zistU00c4-n-Province.pdf
[2] https://iranicaonline.org/articles/arab-ii
[3] https://www.cambridge.org/core/books/abs/cambridge-history-of-iran/arab-conquest-of-iran-and-its-aftermath/6AB6C254CCD1E6D299449CD836500498
[4] https://www.sciencedirect.com/science/article/pii/S1877042812012050
[5] https://www.islamawareness.net/MiddleEast/Iran/iran_article0002.pdf
[6] https://www.scribd.com/document/177333818/Muslim-Conquest-of-Persia
[7] https://academiccommons.columbia.edu/doi/10.7916/D8SJ1SMN/download
[8] https://www.jstor.org/stable/4311181

THE CONQUEST OF THE INDIAN SUBCONTINENT

The conquest of the Indian subcontinent by Islamic forces marked a significant chapter in the history of South Asia. This period of conquest and rule not only transformed the political landscape but also had profound implications for the religious and cultural fabric of the region. The arrival of Islam in the Indian subcontinent introduced a new dynamic to the already diverse religious landscape, contributing to the emergence of a rich tapestry of beliefs and practices. The Indian subcontinent at the time of the Islamic conquests was home to a multitude of faiths, including Hinduism, Buddhism, Jainism, and various indigenous belief systems. The coexistence and interactions between these different religious traditions had shaped the social and cultural norms of the region for centuries. The arrival of Islam introduced a monotheistic religion that differed significantly from the polytheistic traditions prevalent in India. The spread of Islam in the Indian subcontinent was facilitated by various factors, including trade networks, military campaigns, and the activities of Islamic scholars and Sufis. The integration of Islamic rulers into the existing political structures of the region also played a crucial role in the establishment of Muslim rule in India. Despite the diverse religious landscape of the Indian subcontinent, the Islamic conquests were met with resistance from Indian rulers and societies. The centuries-old traditions and institutions of the region posed challenges to the imposition of Islamic authority, leading to conflicts and power struggles. The conquest of the Indian subcontinent by Islamic forces was not merely a military conquest but a complex process that involved social, cultural, and religious transformations. The interactions between Islamic and indigenous religious traditions paved the way for the development of a unique synthesis of beliefs and practices that continues to shape the religious landscape of South Asia to this day.

RELIGIOUS LANDSCAPE OF THE INDIAN SUBCONTINENT

The Indian subcontinent has long been revered as a land of diverse spiritual traditions and religious practices. From the ancient Vedic traditions to the flourishing Buddhism and Jainism, the region has been a cradle of profound philosophical thought and vibrant religious expression. With the advent of Islam in the early medieval period, the religious landscape of the Indian subcontinent underwent a significant transformation. Islam arrived in India through various means, including trade routes and Sufi missionaries who spread the message of Islam through their teachings and spiritual practices. The syncretic nature of Indian society allowed for a unique blend of Islamic beliefs and Indian spiritual practices, leading to the development of a distinct Indo-Islamic culture. The Indian subcontinent was home to a multitude of faiths, including Hinduism, Buddhism, Jainism, Sikhism, and tribal religions. The coexistence of these diverse religious communities created a rich tapestry of beliefs and practices. The arrival of Islam added another layer of religious diversity to the region, shaping its cultural landscape in profound ways. Muslim rulers and dynasties established political power in various parts of the Indian subcontinent, influencing the religious dynamics of the region. While some rulers were known for their tolerance and support of plurality, others enforced Islamic practices through state policies. This complex interplay between different religious communities fostered a dynamic religious landscape marked by both conflict and harmony. The interaction between Islamic and indigenous religious traditions led to the emergence of syncretic practices and beliefs. Sufism, in particular, played a vital role in bridging the gap between Islam and local traditions, emphasizing the universal values of love, compassion, and spiritual unity. Sufi saints and their dargahs became centers of spiritual solace and communal harmony, attracting followers from diverse religious backgrounds. Overall, the religious landscape of the Indian subcontinent reflects a nuanced interplay of diverse faiths and beliefs. The encounter between Islam and indigenous religions gave rise to a rich tapestry of cultural exchange and mutual influence, shaping the region's religious identity in profound ways.

CULTURAL DIVERSITY AND SYNCRETISM IN INDIA

India's rich cultural tapestry is woven with threads of diversity, reflecting a harmonious blend of various religions, traditions, and beliefs. The Indian subcontinent has long been a melting pot of cultures, where Hinduism, Buddhism, Jainism, Sikhism, and other indigenous faiths coexist alongside Islam. This cultural mosaic has fostered a spirit of syncretism, wherein different religious practices and beliefs have intermingled to create a unique and inclusive societal fabric. The cultural diversity of

India extends beyond religion to encompass a multitude of languages, cuisines, music, dance forms, art, and architecture. Each region in India boasts its own distinctive cultural heritage, shaped by centuries of interactions between diverse communities. This cultural plurality has not only enriched the tapestry of Indian society but also served as a source of strength and resilience in the face of external influences. The concept of syncretism, or the fusion of different cultural elements, is deeply ingrained in Indian society. Throughout its history, India has witnessed the assimilation and adaptation of various cultural practices, rituals, and traditions from different communities. This process of cultural exchange has led to the creation of a dynamic and inclusive cultural ethos that transcends religious and ethnic boundaries. Moreover, India's cultural diversity and syncretic traditions have played a significant role in shaping its artistic expressions, literature, philosophy, and social customs. Art forms such as classical dance, music, and painting draw inspiration from a rich tapestry of cultural influences, blending elements from various traditions to create a unique aesthetic language. In conclusion, the cultural diversity and spirit of syncretism in India showcase the country's ability to embrace and celebrate differences, fostering a sense of unity amidst diversity. This cultural ethos has enabled India to evolve as a vibrant and pluralistic society, where mutual respect, tolerance, and coexistence are cherished values that continue to define its cultural landscape.

ISLAMIC CONQUESTS IN NORTHERN INDIA

The Islamic conquests in Northern India marked a significant chapter in the history of the Indian subcontinent. Led by ambitious military commanders, the expansion of Islamic rule into this region brought about profound changes in the cultural, political, and religious landscape. The strategic conquests of regions such as Sindh and Multan paved the way for further incursions into the fertile lands of Punjab and beyond. The swift and calculated military campaigns employed by Islamic forces not only showcased their military prowess but also demonstrated a keen understanding of the local terrain and political dynamics. The integration of local rulers and nobility into the Islamic administration further facilitated the consolidation of power in the newly conquered territories. This approach, often characterized by a mix of coercion and diplomacy, allowed for a relatively smooth transition of authority from indigenous rulers to the agents of the Islamic Caliphate. Despite facing pockets of resistance from entrenched local powers, the Islamic conquerors were able to establish a foothold in Northern India through a combination of military strength and political alliances. The incorporation of local resources, manpower, and administrative structures into the newly established Islamic polities helped in the rapid expansion and consolidation of their rule. The Islamic conquests in Northern India also led to the dissemination of Islamic culture, architecture, and knowledge in the region. The construction of mosques, madrasas, and other religious and educational institutions served as visible symbols of the new order established by the conquering forces. Moreover, the encounters between Islamic traditions and indigenous practices in Northern India gave rise to a unique fusion of cultures, leading to the development of a syncretic and vibrant society. This cultural exchange not only enriched the aesthetic and intellectual landscape of the region but also fostered a spirit of tolerance and mutual understanding among diverse communities. In conclusion, the Islamic conquests in Northern India represented a complex interplay of military conquest, cultural assimilation, and political negotiation. The legacy of these conquests continues to shape the historical narrative of the Indian subcontinent, serving as a testament to the enduring legacy of Islamic influence in the region.

RESISTANCE FROM INDIAN RULERS AND SOCIETIES

Indian rulers and societies faced significant resistance in response to the Islamic conquests in Northern India. The local rulers, who had built powerful kingdoms and established stable administrations, were not willing to relinquish their authority easily. They viewed the incoming Islamic forces as a threat to their sovereignty and cultural identity. The Hindu Rajput rulers, known for their valor and martial traditions, put up fierce resistance against the advancing Islamic armies. A prime example of this resistance was the Battle of Rajasthan, where the Rajput confederacy led by Raja Prithviraj Chauhan clashed with the forces of Muhammad Ghori. Despite initial victories, the Rajputs were eventually defeated, leading to the establishment of Islamic rule in Delhi. This marked the beginning of a long struggle between the indigenous rulers and the Islamic conquerors. Apart from military resistance, Indian societies also displayed resilience in preserving their cultural heritage and traditions. The Indian people, with diverse religious beliefs and social structures, resisted attempts to impose Islamic practices. The rich tapestry of Indian culture, including art, music, literature, and philosophy, continued to thrive despite the political changes brought about by the conquests. Moreover, the Indian populace, comprising a vast majority of Hindus, Buddhists, Jains, and other faiths, resisted conversion to Islam. While some segments of society embraced the new religion for various reasons, the majority retained their traditional beliefs and customs. This resistance to religious conversion was a significant factor in shaping the religious landscape of the Indian subcontinent during and after the Islamic conquests. Overall, the resistance from Indian rulers and societies against the Islamic conquests in Northern India reflected a deep-seated attachment to their land, culture, and traditions. Despite facing formidable challenges, they demonstrated a strong sense of identity and resilience in the face of foreign incursions.

THE ROLE OF ISLAMIC SCHOLARS AND SUFIS IN INDIA

Islamic scholars and Sufis played a significant role in shaping the religious and cultural landscape of India during the period of Islamic conquest. These learned individuals and mystics not only spread the teachings of Islam but also facilitated the integration of Islamic principles with local customs and traditions. Through their teachings and practices, they bridged the gap between Islam and the indigenous beliefs of the Indian subcontinent, fostering a sense of unity among diverse communities. Islamic scholars, well-versed in the Quran and Hadith, served as custodians of religious knowledge and helped educate both the rulers and the masses on Islamic tenets. They provided guidance on matters of faith, law, and ethics, influencing the moral fabric of society. Additionally, they played a crucial role in mediating between the Islamic rulers and the local population, acting as intermediaries in resolving conflicts and promoting harmony. Sufis, on the other hand, emphasized the mystical dimensions of Islam and focused on spiritual purification and inner enlightenment. Through their practice of dhikr (remembrance of God) and Sufi rituals, they sought to establish a direct connection with the Divine and attain spiritual closeness to God. Sufi mysticism resonated with many Indians, who were drawn to the universality of Sufi teachings and the emphasis on love, compassion, and tolerance. Moreover, Sufis often established khanqahs (Sufi lodges) and dargahs (shrines) across India, which served as centers of spiritual learning and communal worship. These spaces became hubs of cultural exchange, where people from diverse backgrounds could come together to seek spiritual guidance, participate in Sufi practices, and celebrate religious festivals. The teachings of Islamic scholars and Sufis not only enriched the religious landscape of India but also contributed to the development of art, literature, and music. Through their poetry, music, and storytelling, they conveyed profound spiritual truths in a language that resonated with the masses, fostering a sense of unity and mutual understanding among different communities. Overall, the role of Islamic scholars and Sufis in India during the period of Islamic conquest was instrumental in promoting religious tolerance, cultural exchange, and spiritual enlightenment. Their legacy continues to influence the dynamic cultural tapestry of modern-day India, emphasizing the importance of dialogue, compassion, and mutual respect in building a harmonious society.

INCORPORATION OF INDIAN ADMINISTRATION AND GOVERNANCE

The incorporation of Indian administration and governance during the Islamic conquest of the subcontinent was a crucial aspect of the establishment of Islamic rule. As the Islamic Caliphate expanded its influence in India, it encountered a diverse array of existing administrative systems, each varying in structure and function. Islamic rulers recognized the need to adapt to the existing administrative practices of India in order to effectively govern the newly conquered territories. They established a system that combined elements of both Islamic and indigenous administrative systems, incorporating local officials and administrators into the ruling hierarchy. One of the key strategies employed was the appointment of local Hindu and Buddhist officials to positions of power within the administrative structure. These officials were often granted autonomy in local governance, allowing them to maintain order and stability in their respective regions while adhering to Islamic law and principles. Furthermore, Islamic rulers introduced new administrative practices, such as the establishment of Islamic courts to oversee legal matters and the implementation of a standardized taxation system. This helped streamline governance and ensure the efficient collection of revenue for the state. The integration of Indian administration and governance was not without challenges, as cultural and religious differences sometimes led to tensions between the ruling Islamic elite and the local population. However, over time, a syncretic administrative system emerged that blended Islamic principles with traditional Indian governance practices, resulting in a functional and adaptable structure that facilitated the smooth administration of the subcontinent. Overall, the incorporation of Indian administration and governance during the Islamic conquest of the subcontinent highlights the resilience and adaptability of Islamic rulers in integrating diverse administrative systems to effectively govern a multicultural society.

IMPACT ON TRADE AND ECONOMY

The Islamic conquest of the Indian subcontinent had significant impacts on trade and economy. The integration of Islamic rule led to the establishment of new trade routes and networks that connected South Asia with the broader Islamic world. This facilitated the exchange of goods, technologies, and ideas, resulting in a flourishing economy in the region. The introduction of Islamic economic principles, such as the promotion of trade and commerce, the development of markets, and the encouragement of entrepreneurship, also played a crucial role in stimulating economic growth. Islamic rulers implemented policies that supported economic activities, leading to increased agricultural production, manufacturing, and commerce. The establishment of Islamic banking and financial systems further boosted economic development in the Indian subcontinent. The adoption of sophisticated financial instruments, such as letters of credit and bills of exchange, facilitated smoother transactions and enhanced commercial activities. This allowed merchants to conduct business across vast distances with greater efficiency and security. Moreover, the Islamic rulers' patronage of arts, crafts, and industries contributed to the growth of a vibrant cultural economy. The development of architectural marvels, such as mosques, palaces, and tombs, created employment opportunities and generated wealth for local artisans and craftsmen. The fusion of Islamic and Indian artistic traditions resulted in the creation of unique art forms and designs that flourished under Islamic rule. Overall, the impact of Islamic rule on trade and economy in the Indian subcontinent was profound. It transformed the region into a hub of economic activity, fostering trade relations with other parts of the Islamic world and beyond. The legacy of Islamic influence on the economy continues to be felt in contemporary South Asia, shaping its commercial landscape and enriching its cultural heritage.

LEGACY OF ISLAMIC RULE IN THE INDIAN SUBCONTINENT

The legacy of Islamic rule in the Indian Subcontinent is multifaceted and enduring. One of the most significant impacts was the introduction and spread of Islam in the region, leading to a diverse cultural landscape that continues to shape the identity of modern South Asia. The architectural and artistic influence of Islamic rulers, such as the Mughals, is evident in iconic structures like the Taj Mahal and architectural styles seen across the subcontinent. Islamic rule also brought about changes in governance, administration, and legal systems, with enduring legacies such as the establishment of regional sultanates and the consolidation of power under centralized empires. The integration of Persian administrative practices and the development of Urdu as a language of administration further underscores the lasting impact of Islamic rule on the Indian Subcontinent. Furthermore, the economic impact of Islamic rule was significant, with the establishment of trade networks that connected South Asia to the broader Islamic world. The influx of new ideas, technologies, and goods contributed to the flourishing of urban centers and the growth of commercial activities. The legacy of Islamic rule in the Indian Subcontinent can be seen in the vibrant markets, skilled craftsmanship, and thriving industries that continue to define the region's economic landscape. In addition to these tangible legacies, Islamic rule also had a profound influence on the social and cultural fabric of the Indian Subcontinent. The synthesis of Islamic and indigenous traditions gave rise to a rich tapestry of literature, music, and art that continues to resonate with contemporary audiences. The enduring legacy of Islamic rule in the Indian Subcontinent is a testament to the enduring power of cultural exchange and adaptation in shaping societies and civilizations.

LESSONS LEARNED FROM THE CONQUEST OF INDIA

The conquest of India stands as a pivotal moment in the history of Islamic expansion, leaving behind a rich legacy that continues to shape the region's cultural, societal, and religious fabric to this day. This chapter delves into the lessons learned from this significant period of history, offering insights into the enduring impact of Islamic rule on the Indian subcontinent. One of the key lessons gleaned from the conquest of India is the importance of understanding and respecting the cultural nuances and diversity of the region. The assimilation of diverse Indian traditions into the Islamic framework not only facilitated the smooth functioning of the administration but also fostered a spirit of syncretism that enriched both civilizations. The conquest of India also underscores the significance of effective governance and administration in managing a vast and diverse empire. The integration of indigenous administrative structures and the appointment of local officials played a crucial role in maintaining social order and ensuring the smooth functioning of the state machinery. Furthermore, the lessons learned from the conquest of India highlight the pivotal role played by Islamic scholars and Sufis in disseminating Islamic teachings and values across the subcontinent. Their efforts not only facilitated the spread of Islam but also fostered cultural exchanges and promoted interfaith dialogue, contributing to the region's religious and intellectual landscape. Additionally, the economic impact of Islamic rule in India sheds light on the importance of trade and commerce in consolidating power and influence. The establishment of trade networks, the introduction of new agricultural practices, and the promotion of artisanal crafts not only boosted the economy but also fostered cultural exchanges and enhanced diplomatic relations with neighboring regions. In conclusion, the conquest of India offers valuable insights into the complexities of empire-building, cultural assimilation, and governance. By studying the lessons learned from this historical episode, we gain a deeper understanding of the enduring legacy of Islamic rule in the Indian subcontinent and its implications for contemporary cross-cultural interactions.

RELIGIOUS AND CULTURAL DYNAMICS IN INDIA

INDIAN RELIGIOUS AND CULTURAL DIVERSITY

India is renowned for its rich tapestry of religious and cultural diversity. This diversity is notably epitomized by the coexistence of various faiths and belief systems, each contributing distinct facets to the intricate social fabric of the country. Among these myriad traditions, Hinduism stands as a significant cornerstone, permeating all aspects of Indian society with its intricate rituals, traditions, and philosophical underpinnings. Hinduism's influence extends beyond religious boundaries, shaping social hierarchies, cultural practices, and even political structures. As the predominant faith of the majority of Indians, Hinduism serves as a unifying force among diverse communities, fostering a sense of shared identity and heritage. Within the framework of Hinduism, the concept of dharma forms a fundamental principle that governs individual conduct and societal norms. Dharma encompasses the moral, ethical, and social duties that individuals are expected to uphold in their respective roles within society. This concept underscores the interconnectedness of all beings and emphasizes the importance of fulfilling one's responsibilities to maintain harmony and order in the world. Moreover, Hinduism's diverse pantheon of deities reflects a multiplicity of divine manifestations, each representing different aspects of the universal reality. From the benevolent creator god Brahma to the fierce warrior goddess Durga, these deities embody various qualities and characteristics that cater to the spiritual needs and aspirations of devotees. The practice of worshipping these deities through elaborate rituals, festivals, and ceremonies serves as a means of seeking divine blessings, protection, and guidance in the journey of life. Furthermore, the caste system, a hierarchical social structure deeply rooted in Hindu religious traditions, has played a pivotal role in shaping Indian society for centuries. The caste system stratifies individuals into distinct social categories based on their birth, occupation, and societal roles, prescribing specific rights and obligations for each caste group. Despite efforts to reform or abolish the caste system, its influence continues to permeate various aspects of Indian life, influencing social interactions, marriage norms, and economic opportunities. In essence, the influence of Hinduism on Indian society extends far beyond religious boundaries, encompassing aspects of social organization, cultural practices, and philosophical worldviews. Its enduring presence within the intricate tapestry of Indian religious and cultural diversity underscores the profound impact that faith traditions can have on shaping the collective identity and lived experiences of a nation.

THE INFLUENCE OF HINDUISM ON SOCIETY

Hinduism, as the oldest known religion in India, has played a profound role in shaping Indian society for millennia. Its influence extends far beyond the realms of spirituality, permeating every aspect of social, cultural, and political life. The foundational principles of Hinduism, including the concepts of dharma (duty), karma (action and consequences), and moksha (liberation), have provided a moral and ethical framework that has guided individuals and communities for generations. Central to Hinduism is the belief in the interconnectedness of all beings and the cyclical nature of existence. This worldview has fostered a sense of unity and harmony among diverse communities, emphasizing the importance of respecting all forms of life. The concept of dharma, or one's moral duty, has been instrumental in maintaining social order and cohesion, with each individual expected to fulfill their prescribed roles and responsibilities based on their social status and stage of life. Hinduism's emphasis on rituals, ceremonies, and festivals has created a vibrant tapestry of cultural practices that celebrate the cycles of nature and the divine. Temples and shrines dedicated to various deities serve as focal points for communal worship and reflection, while rituals such as puja (offerings) and yajna (sacrificial ceremonies) provide opportunities for spiritual connection and renewal. The caste system, a social hierarchy that has been closely associated with Hinduism, has had a profound impact on Indian society, governing aspects of one's social status, occupation, and interactions with others. While the caste system has been a subject of controversy and debate, it has also served as a mechanism for social organization and division of labor, reflecting the multifaceted nature of Indian society. In addition to its spiritual and social dimensions, Hinduism has also been a source of artistic and intellectual inspiration. The epics of the Ramayana and Mahabharata, the philosophical texts of the Upanishads, and the intricate sculptures and paintings found in temples and palaces attest to the rich cultural heritage that Hinduism has nurtured over the centuries. Overall, the influence of Hinduism on Indian society is undeniable, shaping the values, beliefs, and practices of millions of people across the subcontinent. Its enduring impact on art, philosophy, politics, and everyday life underscores the deep-rooted connection between religion and culture in India.

GEW SOCIAL SCIENCES GROUP

THE EMERGENCE AND SPREAD OF BUDDHISM IN INDIA

Buddhism, originating from the teachings of Siddhartha Gautama, known as the Buddha, emerged in India around the 6th century BCE. The Buddha's teachings focused on the Four Noble Truths and the Eightfold Path, emphasizing the cessation of suffering through enlightenment. Buddhism gained prominence in Indian society due to its emphasis on morality, meditation, and wisdom. Monastic communities known as Sanghas formed to preserve and propagate the Buddha's teachings. These communities played a crucial role in the spread of Buddhism across India and beyond. The Mauryan Emperor Ashoka played a significant role in promoting Buddhism, spreading it through his edicts and support of Buddhist institutions. Under his patronage, Buddhism flourished, with the construction of stupas, monasteries, and pillars throughout the empire. The spread of Buddhism was facilitated by the use of Pali and Sanskrit texts, allowing for the dissemination of Buddhist teachings in vernacular languages. As Buddhism spread, it adopted local customs and beliefs, leading to the development of distinct sects and schools of thought. Buddhism's emphasis on compassion, non-violence, and the interconnectedness of all beings resonated with people across social strata. It provided a spiritual alternative to the rigid caste system and rituals of Brahmanism, appealing to those seeking a more egalitarian and introspective path. Over time, Buddhism diversified into various branches, such as Theravada, Mahayana, and Vajrayana, each with its own interpretations and practices. The development of Buddhist art, literature, and philosophy reflected the rich cultural tapestry of India and influenced the broader religious landscape of Asia. Despite facing challenges from rival religious traditions and internal schisms, Buddhism continued to be a dominant force in Indian society for centuries. Its philosophical teachings and ethical principles left a lasting impact on Indian culture, shaping societal values and norms for generations to come.

THE IMPACT OF JAINISM ON INDIAN CULTURE

The impact of Jainism on Indian culture can be seen in various aspects of society. Jainism, as one of the ancient religions in India, has played a significant role in shaping the moral, ethical, and philosophical beliefs of the people. The core teachings of Jainism, focused on non-violence (ahimsa), truthfulness (satya), non-stealing (asteya), celibacy (brahmacharya), and non-attachment (aparigraha), have had a profound influence on Indian society. Jainism's emphasis on non-violence has not only impacted individual behavior but has also influenced broader societal values. The concept of ahimsa has led to the practice of vegetarianism and the protection of all living beings. This principle has promoted compassion and reverence for life, contributing to a culture of non-violence in various spheres of Indian life. Additionally, Jainism's teachings on truthfulness and non-stealing have promoted honesty and integrity in interpersonal relationships and economic activities. The emphasis on celibacy and non-attachment has influenced attitudes towards material possessions and desires, fostering a spirit of renunciation and detachment from worldly pleasures. Moreover, Jainism's emphasis on self-discipline, meditation, and self-control has contributed to the development of a strong moral and ethical framework in Indian society. The Jain concept of karma, the belief in the consequences of one's actions, has shaped ideas of personal responsibility and accountability. Overall, Jainism has left a lasting impact on Indian culture, influencing moral values, ethical principles, and spiritual beliefs. The teachings of Jainism continue to resonate with individuals seeking inner peace, harmony, and enlightenment in a complex and rapidly changing world.

INTERACTIONS BETWEEN DIFFERENT RELIGIOUS COMMUNITIES

India has been a melting pot of diverse religious communities for centuries. The interactions between these communities have played a significant role in shaping the cultural and social fabric of the subcontinent. Hindus, Buddhists, Jains, and followers of other faiths have coexisted and interacted in various ways, influencing each other's beliefs, practices, and traditions. These interactions were not always harmonious, as religious differences often led to tensions and conflicts. However, there were also instances of peaceful coexistence and mutual respect between different religious communities. Trade, commerce, cultural exchanges, and shared spaces such as marketplaces, temples, and educational institutions provided opportunities for people of different faiths to interact and learn from each other. The exchange of ideas and beliefs between religious communities enriched Indian culture and created a unique syncretic tradition that blended elements from various faiths. This cultural synthesis is evident in art, architecture, literature, music, and dance forms that reflect the diverse influences of different religious traditions. Religious festivals and celebrations became occasions for people of different faiths to come together, share in each other's cultural practices, and foster a sense of unity amidst diversity. These shared experiences helped bridge religious divides and promote tolerance and understanding among communities with different beliefs. Despite occasional conflicts and tensions, the interactions between different religious communities in pre-Islamic India contributed to the rich tapestry of Indian culture and society. The legacy of this cultural exchange continues to resonate in modern-day India, where the coexistence of diverse religious communities remains a defining feature of the country's identity.

CULTURAL PRACTICES AND TRADITIONS IN PRE-ISLAMIC INDIA

Cultural practices and traditions in pre-Islamic India were diverse and rich, reflecting the complexity of Indian society. The concept of dharma, or ethical duty, played a significant role in shaping the moral and social fabric of society. This framework guided individuals in their personal and social responsibilities, emphasizing virtues such as honesty, compassion, and integrity. Indian society was structured around the institution of the joint family, where multiple generations lived together in close-knit communities. Family values were paramount, and respect for elders was a core cultural practice. Marriage was considered a sacred bond, and elaborate ceremonies marked the union of two individuals and families. Religious festivals and rituals were an integral part of everyday life in pre-Islamic India. Temples and shrines dotted the landscape, serving as centers of worship and community gathering. The practice of offering prayers, performing rituals, and seeking blessings from deities reflected the deep spiritual connection of Indians with their faith. The arts flourished in pre-Islamic India, with advancements in music, dance, and literature. Classical Indian dance forms like Bharatanatyam and Kathak originated during this period, showcasing the intricate movements and storytelling traditions of Indian culture. Literature, including epics like the Mahabharata and Ramayana, served as moral guides and sources of inspiration for generations. The caste system, although a controversial aspect of Indian society, played a crucial role in organizing social and occupational roles.

Each caste had specific duties and responsibilities, with strict rules governing interactions between different groups. The hierarchical nature of the caste system influenced various aspects of daily life, from marriage practices to occupational choices. Art and architecture in pre-Islamic India reflected a fusion of indigenous styles with influences from neighboring regions. Intricate carvings, sculptures, and paintings adorned temples and palaces, showcasing the artistic achievements of the period. Architectural marvels like the Ajanta and Ellora caves and the temples of Khajuraho were testaments to the craftsmanship and creativity of Indian artisans. Overall, the cultural practices and traditions in pre-Islamic India were a testament to the vibrancy and diversity of Indian society. These practices laid the foundation for future developments in art, literature, religion, and social organization, shaping the identity of India for centuries to come.

THE POSITION OF WOMEN IN INDIAN SOCIETY

Women in ancient Indian society held a complex position deeply intertwined with cultural norms and religious beliefs. While some texts portray women as subordinated to men, other sources suggest a more nuanced understanding of their roles and responsibilities. Women played crucial roles within families, communities, and religious contexts, contributing to the society's cultural and spiritual fabric. In terms of family life, women were typically expected to fulfill domestic duties and support their husbands and children. However, women also held important roles as mothers, educators, and caregivers, shaping the moral and ethical development of future generations. In many cases, women were respected for their wisdom and leadership within familial structures. Furthermore, women's participation in religious practices and rituals was significant in ancient India. Women were active participants in various religious ceremonies, offering prayers and performing rituals alongside men. Some texts even highlight the spiritual prowess of female saints and ascetics, emphasizing their devotion and knowledge of religious scriptures. Despite these significant contributions, the position of women in ancient Indian society was not without challenges. The practice of child marriage, restrictions on widow remarriage, and the prevalence of dowry system created obstacles for women's autonomy and agency. However, historical records also depict instances of women holding influential political and economic positions, challenging stereotypical notions of their roles. In summary, the position of women in ancient Indian society was multifaceted, reflecting a complex interplay of cultural norms, religious beliefs, and social structures. While women faced certain restrictions and inequalities, they also held indispensable roles in shaping the fabric of society and maintaining its cultural heritage.

ART, ARCHITECTURE, AND LITERATURE IN ANCIENT INDIA

Art, architecture, and literature in ancient India flourished across various dynasties and periods, reflecting the rich cultural tapestry of the region. The artistic achievements of ancient India encompassed a wide range of mediums, from intricate sculptures and vibrant paintings to awe-inspiring architectural wonders. One of the most iconic examples of Indian architecture is the stunning Taj Mahal, a white marble mausoleum that stands as a testament to the unparalleled craftsmanship and artistic vision of the Mughal Empire. In addition to architectural marvels, ancient Indian literature also thrived, producing timeless works such as the epic poem, the Mahabharata, and the philosophical treatises of the Upanishads. These literary masterpieces not only entertained but also imparted profound moral and spiritual teachings to generations of readers. Through their artistic achievements in various forms, the people of ancient India expressed their creativity, spirituality, and cultural heritage, leaving behind a lasting legacy that continues to inspire and resonate with audiences around the world.

THE ROLE OF CASTE SYSTEM IN SHAPING INDIAN IDENTITY

The caste system in ancient India played a fundamental role in shaping the societal structure and identities of its people. Rooted in the belief of karma and dharma, the caste system divided society into distinct groups based on occupation and social status. At the top were the Brahmins, considered the priestly class responsible for religious rituals and knowledge. Next were the Kshatriyas, the warrior and ruler class, followed by the Vaishyas, who engaged in trade and agriculture. At the bottom were the Shudras, tasked with serving the higher castes. The rigid hierarchy of the caste system determined various aspects of life, including occupation, social interactions, and even marriage. One's caste dictated whom they could socialize with, marry, or even dine with. This system of social stratification was not only a means of organizing society but also perpetuated inequalities and discrimination based on birth. Despite its antiquity, the caste system continued to influence Indian identity long after the arrival of Islamic rulers. The Muslim conquerors faced challenges in reconciling their different worldview and religious beliefs with the entrenched caste system of India. While Islam preached equality and rejected the notion of caste, the existing social structure posed barriers to integration and assimilation. The caste system's impact on Indian identity extended beyond social interactions to influence art, literature, and architecture. Artisans and craftsmen were often restricted by their caste in the type of work they could produce, leading to a diversification of artistic styles within different castes. Literature, too, reflected the hierarchical nature of society, with epics and texts reinforcing caste roles and duties. In the face of these challenges, Islamic rulers in India sought to navigate the complex web of caste identities while asserting their own authority. This dynamic interaction between the caste system and Islamic rule would shape the cultural landscape of India for centuries to come, leaving a lasting imprint on the country's identity and social fabric.

CHALLENGES AND OPPORTUNITIES FOR ISLAMIC RULERS IN INTEGRATING WITH INDIAN RELIGIOUS AND CULTURAL DYNAMICS

Islamic rulers faced both challenges and opportunities in integrating with Indian religious and cultural dynamics. The diversity and complexity of Indian society posed significant hurdles for Muslim rulers seeking to establish their authority. The rigid caste system, with its hierarchical structure and social divisions, presented a formidable obstacle to integration. Muslims, who were seen as outsiders, struggled to navigate the intricacies of caste-based interactions and hierarchies. Despite these challenges, there were also opportunities for Islamic rulers to connect with Indian society. By emphasizing common values such as justice, piety, and social welfare, Muslim rulers could garner support and legitimacy among the local population. Additionally, the syncretic nature of Indian culture allowed for the blending of Islamic and indigenous traditions, creating a unique fusion that appealed to a diverse range of people. Islamic rulers could capitalize on this cultural diversity, incorporating local customs and practices into their governance to foster a sense of unity and inclusivity. Through strategic alliances with local rulers and communities, as well as the patronage of Hindu and other religious institutions, Islamic rulers could gradually integrate themselves into the fabric of Indian society. By respecting the traditions and beliefs of the local population, while also upholding Islamic principles and norms, Muslim rulers could navigate the complex terrain of Indian religious and cultural dynamics, forging a path towards harmony and coexistence.

RESPONSE OF INDIAN RULERS AND SOCIETIES

HISTORICAL BACKGROUND: PROVIDING CONTEXT ON THE POLITICAL AND SOCIAL LANDSCAPE IN INDIA PRIOR TO THE ISLAMIC CONQUESTS

The Indian subcontinent before the Islamic conquests was a land of rich diversity and complex political structures. Various kingdoms, empires, and regional powers coexisted, each with its own unique cultural and social norms. The Gupta Empire, known for its flourishing art, literature, and scientific achievements, had left a lasting impact on Indian civilization. The southern Chola dynasty and the northern Pratihara and Rashtrakuta kingdoms were important centers of power, governing vast territories and engaging in trade and diplomacy with neighboring regions. Religion played a significant role in shaping Indian society, with Hinduism, Buddhism, and Jainism being the dominant faiths. Temples and stupas dotted the landscape, serving as centers of worship and learning. The caste system, with its hierarchical division of society into different social classes, influenced every aspect of life in India, from occupation to marriage to social status. Trade routes crisscrossed the subcontinent, connecting India to regions as far as Persia, Central Asia, and Southeast Asia. The bustling ports of the western coast welcomed merchants and traders from distant lands, facilitating the exchange of goods, ideas, and cultural practices. Agriculture was the backbone of the economy, with fertile lands supporting the cultivation of rice, wheat, spices, and other crops. Social structures were deeply entrenched, with powerful dynasties ruling over vast territories and diverse populations. Local rulers exercised authority over their regions, maintaining law and order and collecting taxes to support their administrations. Art, literature, and architecture flourished, with intricate sculptures, vibrant paintings, and grand monuments serving as testaments to India's rich cultural heritage. In this dynamic and multifaceted society, the stage was set for the arrival of Islamic conquerors, whose interactions with the existing political and social structures would shape the course of Indian history in the centuries to come.

DIVERSITY OF INDIAN SOCIETIES: EXPLORING THE VARIOUS KINGDOMS, EMPIRES, AND REGIONAL POWERS THAT EXISTED IN INDIA AT THE TIME

India in the pre-Islamic era was a land of remarkable diversity, characterized by a multitude of kingdoms, empires, and regional powers. The subcontinent was home to a vast array of cultures, languages, and traditions, each contributing to the rich tapestry of Indian society. From the mighty Gupta Empire in the north to the Chola and Pandya dynasties in the south, India was a patchwork of political entities, each vying for power and influence. The Gupta Empire, often described as the "Golden Age" of India, exerted significant control over much of the subcontinent, fostering a period of cultural and intellectual flourishing. In the south, the Chola dynasty presided over a maritime empire that dominated trade routes in the Indian Ocean. The Pallava dynasty, known for its architectural marvels such as the shore temples of Mamallapuram, also held sway in the region. Further to the west, the powerful Rashtrakuta dynasty controlled large territories in present-day Karnataka and Maharashtra. Meanwhile, in the northwest, the Pratihara and Chalukya dynasties clashed for supremacy, leading to a complex web of alliances and rivalries. In the east, the Pala Empire flourished in the fertile Gangetic plains, fostering a vibrant intellectual and artistic culture. Beyond these major political entities, numerous smaller kingdoms and tribal confederations dotted the landscape of India. From the mountainous regions of the Himalayas to the lush forests of the Deccan Plateau, each region boasted its own unique identity and governance structure. The diversity of Indian society was further enhanced by the presence of indigenous tribal groups, each with its own distinct customs and traditions. This mosaic of kingdoms, empires, and regional powers not only shaped the political landscape of India but also influenced its social dynamics and cultural development. The interplay between these disparate entities created a complex network of relationships that defined the fabric of Indian society. As the stage was set for the arrival of Islamic forces, the diversity of Indian societies would be put to the test, highlighting both the resilience and fragility of the subcontinent's political order.

RESISTANCE AND ALLIANCES: EXAMINING HOW INDIAN RULERS RESPONDED TO THE ISLAMIC INCURSIONS, INCLUDING ALLIANCES FORMED AND STRATEGIES EMPLOYED

During the period of Islamic incursions into India, Indian rulers exhibited a range of responses to the foreign conquerors. Some rulers chose to resist the invaders fiercely, rallying their forces and mobilizing their resources to defend their territories. Others, recognizing the formidable power of the Islamic armies, opted to form strategic alliances with neighboring kingdoms or with fellow Indian rulers to strengthen their position against the invaders. The resistance against Islamic incursions was often grounded in the deep attachment to the land and the civilization that Indian rulers sought to protect. They viewed the foreign conquerors as a threat to their way of life, their cultural traditions, and their autonomy. This fierce sense of defense led to spirited battles and protracted sieges as Indian rulers fought to maintain their independence. Conversely, the formation of alliances among Indian rulers was a pragmatic response to the shifting balance of power brought about by the Islamic conquests. By uniting forces with other local rulers, Indian kingdoms could pool their military strength and resources to present a more formidable front against the invaders. These alliances were often based on mutual benefit and shared strategic interests, with each party bringing its unique strengths to the coalition. Strategies employed by Indian rulers in response to Islamic incursions varied depending on the particular circumstances they faced. Some relied on guerrilla warfare tactics, utilizing the terrain and their knowledge of local conditions to outmaneuver the Islamic armies. Others sought diplomatic solutions, engaging in negotiations and treaties to secure their interests and buy time to prepare for future conflicts. In navigating the challenges posed by the Islamic conquests, Indian rulers demonstrated resilience, adaptability, and a commitment to safeguarding their territories and people. These responses, whether through resistance or alliances, played a crucial role in shaping the course of history in India during this tumultuous period.

THE ISLAMIC CONQUESTS IN ASIA

CULTURAL EXCHANGE: DISCUSSING THE INTERACTION BETWEEN ISLAMIC CONQUERORS AND INDIGENOUS INDIAN CULTURES, INCLUDING THE EXCHANGE OF KNOWLEDGE, IDEAS, AND CUSTOMS

The cultural exchange between Islamic conquerors and indigenous Indian cultures during the period of conquests was a dynamic and multifaceted process. It marked a significant chapter in the shared history of these diverse civilizations, leading to the exchange of knowledge, ideas, and customs that would shape the cultural landscape of the region for centuries to come. One of the key aspects of this cultural exchange was the blending of Islamic and Indian artistic traditions. Islamic rulers brought with them a rich artistic heritage, including intricate calligraphy, geometric patterns, and arabesque designs that were integrated into Indian art forms. This fusion of styles resulted in the creation of unique architectural marvels such as the Qutub Minar in Delhi, showcasing the synthesis of Islamic and Indian architectural elements. Furthermore, the exchange of knowledge between Islamic scholars and Indian intellectuals led to significant advancements in various fields such as mathematics, astronomy, and medicine. Scholars from both traditions shared texts, ideas, and techniques, leading to a cross-fertilization of knowledge that enriched intellectual pursuits in both societies. The cultural exchange also extended to language and literature, with Arabic and Persian becoming prominent languages of administration and scholarship in India. This linguistic interaction facilitated the translation of classical Indian texts into Persian and Arabic, making them accessible to a wider audience and contributing to the preservation and dissemination of Indian intellectual heritage. In the realm of customs and traditions, the interaction between Islamic conquerors and indigenous Indian cultures led to the adoption of certain practices and rituals from both sides. This cultural syncretism gave rise to new traditions, rituals, and forms of artistic expression that reflected the shared experiences and influences of both communities. Overall, the cultural exchange between Islamic conquerors and indigenous Indian cultures was a transformative process that shaped the cultural fabric of the region. It exemplified the power of cross-cultural interaction and collaboration in fostering creativity, innovation, and mutual understanding between diverse civilizations.

ECONOMIC IMPACTS: ANALYZING THE EFFECTS OF THE CONQUESTS ON TRADE, COMMERCE, AND THE ECONOMY OF INDIA

The Islamic conquests in India had a profound impact on the region's trade, commerce, and overall economy. The establishment of Islamic rule introduced new economic structures and practices that significantly altered the existing commercial landscape. One notable effect was the integration of Indian markets into the larger Islamic trading network, leading to increased connectivity and exchange of goods. Islamic rulers also implemented policies that aimed to promote economic growth and stability. This included the construction of infrastructure such as roads, bridges, and marketplaces, which facilitated trade and commerce. Additionally, the introduction of a standardized currency system and efficient taxation mechanisms helped streamline economic transactions and enhance fiscal management. The Islamic conquests brought about significant changes in the patterns of production and consumption in India. The adoption of new agricultural techniques, irrigation systems, and crop varieties introduced by Islamic rulers led to increased productivity and diversification of the agricultural sector. This, in turn, boosted food security and stimulated economic growth. Moreover, the Islamic conquests contributed to the emergence of new industries and crafts in India. The exchange of skills, technology, and knowledge between Islamic conquerors and indigenous populations fostered innovation and specialization in various sectors, such as metalworking, textile production, and pottery. This not only expanded the range of goods available in the market but also enhanced the quality and craftsmanship of Indian products. The integration of Indian and Islamic cultural practices also influenced patterns of consumption and trade. The introduction of new culinary traditions, clothing styles, and luxury items from the Islamic world enriched the cultural fabric of Indian society and created new opportunities for commercial exchange. The promotion of urban centers as hubs of economic activity further stimulated the growth of markets and industries, attracting merchants, artisans, and entrepreneurs from diverse backgrounds. Overall, the economic impacts of the Islamic conquests in India were multifaceted and enduring. The transformation of trade networks, the development of infrastructure, the diversification of economic activities, and the fusion of cultural influences all contributed to the dynamic evolution of India's economy under Islamic rule.

RELIGIOUS DYNAMICS: INVESTIGATING THE RELIGIOUS TENSIONS AND ACCOMMODATIONS THAT EMERGED BETWEEN ISLAM AND THE DIVERSE FAITHS PRACTICED IN INDIA

Religious Dynamics: The arrival of Islamic rulers in India brought about a complex interplay of religious dynamics as Islam encountered the existing diverse faiths practiced in the region. India, known for its rich tapestry of religions, including Hinduism, Buddhism, Jainism, and various indigenous belief systems, presented a unique challenge and opportunity for the Islamic conquerors. The Islamic rulers navigated the religious landscape of India through a variety of approaches. While some adopted a policy of religious tolerance and accommodation, others sought to assert the dominance of Islam over existing faiths. This led to a range of interactions, from peaceful coexistence and syncretism to instances of religious tension and conflict. One notable aspect of the religious dynamics in India was the syncretic tendencies that emerged, blending elements of Islamic and indigenous faiths. This syncretism resulted in the development of unique cultural and religious practices that reflected a fusion of traditions. Sufism, a mystical form of Islam, played a significant role in this syncretic process, drawing on elements of Indian spirituality and devotional practices. At the same time, there were instances of religious tension and conflict between Islamic rulers and the indigenous population. Some rulers implemented policies that discriminated against non-Muslims, leading to social and religious upheaval. Religious institutions and sites were sometimes targeted, leading to resistance and backlash from the local population. Overall, the religious dynamics in India during the Islamic conquests were marked by a complex interplay of accommodation, syncretism, tension, and conflict. This interaction between Islam and the diverse faiths of India shaped the religious landscape of the region and had lasting implications for the social and cultural fabric of Indian society.

ADMINISTRATIVE CHANGES: DESCRIBING THE ADMINISTRATIVE REFORMS IMPLEMENTED BY

THE ISLAMIC CONQUESTS IN ASIA

ISLAMIC RULERS AND THEIR IMPACT ON INDIAN GOVERNANCE

Islamic rulers in India implemented significant administrative reforms that had a profound impact on governance in the region. One key aspect of their administrative changes was the introduction of a centralized system of government, which replaced the decentralized nature of many Indian kingdoms. This centralization involved the establishment of provincial administrations headed by governors appointed by the ruling caliph or sultan. The Islamic rulers also introduced a uniform system of taxation across their territories, which replaced the diverse and often arbitrary tax systems that existed in pre-Islamic India. This standardized taxation system helped generate revenue for the state and facilitated economic stability and development. Furthermore, Islamic rulers implemented a legal framework based on Islamic law, or Sharia, which coexisted with existing Indian legal systems. This dual legal system allowed for some degree of accommodation of local customs and traditions while ensuring the primacy of Islamic legal principles in matters of governance and justice. Another significant administrative reform was the establishment of a sophisticated bureaucratic apparatus to manage the affairs of state. This bureaucracy, composed of skilled administrators and scribes, played a vital role in maintaining law and order, collecting taxes, and administering justice in the name of the Islamic rulers. The Islamic administrators also encouraged the use of Persian as the administrative language in India, reflecting the cultural and intellectual influence of Persian-speaking elites in the Islamic world. This linguistic policy facilitated communication and coordination within the government and helped create a sense of unity among the diverse regions under Islamic rule. Overall, the administrative changes implemented by Islamic rulers in India helped centralize political authority, streamline governance, and promote a sense of cultural and religious unity across the region. These reforms laid the foundation for the integration of Islamic principles and practices into the fabric of Indian society, shaping the course of Indian history for centuries to come.

SOCIAL TRANSFORMATIONS: ASSESSING HOW THE SOCIAL STRUCTURE OF INDIAN SOCIETY WAS INFLUENCED BY THE ARRIVAL OF ISLAMIC RULE

Social Transformations: Assessing how the social structure of Indian society was influenced by the arrival of Islamic rule. The arrival of Islamic rule in India brought about significant social transformations that reshaped the fabric of Indian society. One of the key changes was the emergence of a new ruling elite composed of Muslim administrators, scholars, and military leaders who played a central role in governing the newly conquered territories. This new elite class often integrated with the existing Indian elite, leading to a blending of cultures and traditions at the highest levels of society. Additionally, the spread of Islam in India led to the formation of new social hierarchies based on religious identity. Muslims were afforded special privileges and opportunities in the realms of politics, commerce, and administration, leading to the establishment of a Muslim aristocracy that wielded considerable influence in society. This shift in power dynamics had a profound impact on existing social structures and established norms. Furthermore, the introduction of Islamic legal and judicial systems influenced social interactions and interpersonal relationships in Indian society. Islamic principles of justice, charity, and morality permeated daily life, shaping social norms and practices. The adoption of Islamic customs and traditions by both the ruling elite and the general population contributed to a blending of cultural practices and the emergence of a syncretic Indo-Islamic culture. Moreover, the spread of Sufi mysticism in India fostered spiritual connections among people of different backgrounds, transcending social barriers and promoting a sense of unity and fraternity. Sufi saints and mystics played a crucial role in bridging the gap between various religious communities and promoting tolerance and harmony in a diverse society. However, the social transformations brought about by Islamic rule also sparked resistance and pushback from segments of Indian society that sought to preserve their traditional ways of life. Brahmins, landowners, and others who felt marginalized by the new order often rebelled against Islamic authority, leading to periods of unrest and conflict. Overall, the arrival of Islamic rule in India brought about a complex web of social transformations, reshaping social hierarchies, cultural practices, and interfaith relations. The blending of Islamic and Indian influences created a dynamic and diverse society that continues to shape the identity of modern-day India.

REVOLTS AND UPRISINGS: DETAILING INSTANCES OF RESISTANCE AND REBELLION BY INDIAN POPULATIONS AGAINST ISLAMIC AUTHORITY

The arrival of Islamic rule in India sparked a series of revolts and uprisings among the Indian population as they sought to resist the new authority. These instances of resistance were fueled by a variety of factors, including religious differences, political grievances, and cultural clashes. One notable rebellion was led by the famous warrior queen, Rani Rudrama Devi of the Kakatiya dynasty, who fiercely opposed the attempts of the Islamic forces to conquer her kingdom. Another significant uprising took place in the Deccan region, where the Hindu Vijayanagara Empire rose to prominence as a stronghold against Islamic incursions. Under the leadership of Krishnadevaraya, the Vijayanagara Empire successfully repelled numerous attempts by Islamic rulers to subdue their territory, showcasing the resilience of the indigenous population in the face of foreign conquest. In North India, the Rajput kingdoms fiercely resisted Islamic rule, often engaging in fierce battles to defend their lands and traditions. The valor and valor of Rajput warriors such as Prithviraj Chauhan and Rana Sanga became legendary as they led their armies against the encroaching forces. Despite these acts of rebellion, the Islamic rulers gradually established their dominance over large parts of India, leading to a complex and multifaceted society where diverse cultural traditions coexisted and interacted. The legacies of these revolts and uprisings continue to resonate in India's historical memory, serving as a reminder of the enduring spirit of resistance and resilience among its people.

LEGACY OF THE CONQUESTS: REFLECTING ON THE LASTING EFFECTS OF THE ISLAMIC CONQUESTS ON INDIA'S CULTURAL, POLITICAL, AND SOCIAL DEVELOPMENT

The Islamic conquests in India left a profound and enduring impact on the cultural, political, and social fabric of the region. The legacy of these conquests can be seen in various aspects of India's history and development. One significant legacy of the Islamic conquests is the fusion of Islamic and Indian cultural elements, leading to the emergence of a unique Indo-Islamic culture. This blending of traditions is evident in architecture, art, music, and cuisine, creating a rich and diverse cultural landscape in India. Politically, the Islamic conquests laid the foundation for the establishment of Islamic dynasties and sultanates that ruled parts of India for centuries. These rulers introduced new administrative systems, legal practices, and architectural styles that influenced the political development of the region. Socially, the Islamic conquests brought about changes in India's social structure, leading to interactions between different communities and the spread of new social norms and practices. The rise of Sufism, a mystical Islamic tradition, also had a profound impact on Indian society, fostering a sense of spirituality and communal harmony. Moreover, the Islamic conquests in India catalyzed the spread of the Urdu language, which combined elements of Persian, Arabic, and Indian dialects. Urdu became a symbol of cultural unity and diversity in India, reflecting the syncretic nature of Indo-Islamic civilization. Overall, the legacy of the Islamic conquests in India is a complex tapestry of cultural exchange, political transformation, and social evolution. The enduring effects of these conquests continue to shape India's identity and heritage, highlighting the interconnectedness of diverse cultures and histories in the region.

KEY MILITARY FIGURES

INTRODUCTION TO KEY MILITARY FIGURES IN ISLAMIC CONQUESTS

Throughout the history of Islamic conquests in Asia, key military figures played a crucial role in shaping the outcomes of various campaigns. These commanders exhibited exceptional leadership skills, strategic acumen, and tactical prowess that enabled the Islamic forces to achieve remarkable victories and expand their territories across diverse regions. By examining the lives and achievements of these influential military figures, we gain a deeper understanding of the complexities and challenges faced during the era of Islamic expansion. From the early conquests of Persia to the campaigns in Central Asia, the Indian subcontinent, Southeast Asia, and China, these key military figures demonstrated their bravery, intelligence, and adaptability in diverse battlefields. Their command over troops, organizational abilities, and innovative military strategies were instrumental in overcoming formidable adversaries and establishing the dominance of the Islamic Caliphate in new territories. These military leaders hailed from various backgrounds, including Arab, Persian, Turkish, and other ethnicities, reflecting the multi-cultural and multi-ethnic nature of the Islamic armies. Despite their differences, these commanders shared a common dedication to the spread of Islam and the expansion of the Caliphate's influence. Their leadership not only influenced the course of military campaigns but also left a lasting impact on the political, social, and cultural landscape of the conquered regions. In the upcoming sections, we will delve into the specific roles and contributions of these key military figures in the Islamic conquests, analyzing their strategies, tactics, and legacies. By exploring their profiles and examining their military achievements, we aim to shed light on the dynamic and complex nature of warfare in the early Islamic period, as well as the enduring influence of these formidable leaders on the history of the Islamic world.

MILITARY LEADERSHIP IN THE CONQUEST OF PERSIA

Geopolitically strategic and economically rich, Persia presented a formidable challenge for the Islamic forces seeking conquest in the early centuries of Islam. The military leadership during the conquest of Persia played a pivotal role in shaping the outcome of the conflict. Commanders such as Khalid ibn al-Walid and Abu Bakr al-Siddiq demonstrated unparalleled strategic acumen and tactical prowess in their campaigns against the Sassanian Empire. Khalid ibn al-Walid, known as the "Sword of Allah," emerged as a brilliant military tactician during the conquest of Persia. His mastery of cavalry warfare and innovative battlefield tactics earned him a reputation as one of the greatest military leaders in Islamic history. Khalid's strategic genius was instrumental in securing several key victories against the Sassanian forces, including the decisive Battle of Qadisiyyah. Abu Bakr al-Siddiq, the first Caliph of the Rashidun Caliphate, also played a crucial role in the conquest of Persia. His strong leadership and unwavering commitment to expanding the Muslim domain propelled the Islamic forces to success on the battlefield. Under Abu Bakr's command, the Muslim armies achieved significant territorial gains in Persia, effectively weakening the Sassanian hold on the region. The military leadership in the conquest of Persia was characterized by a blend of strategic vision, tactical innovation, and unwavering determination. These commanders navigated complex geopolitical landscapes, coordinated diverse military forces, and exploited the weaknesses of their adversaries to achieve victory. Through their leadership, the Islamic forces were able to establish a foothold in Persia and lay the foundation for the spread of Islam in the region.

COMMANDERS IN THE EXPANSION INTO CENTRAL ASIA

The expansion of the Islamic Caliphate into Central Asia brought about a new set of challenges and opportunities for the commanders tasked with leading the conquests in this region. Central Asia, with its diverse geography and mix of settled cultures and nomadic tribes, required astute military leadership to navigate the complex landscape. Commanders such as Qutayba ibn Muslim and Al-Harith ibn Surayj emerged as key figures in the expansion into Central Asia. Qutayba ibn Muslim, known for his strategic acumen and military prowess, played a crucial role in extending Islamic rule into Transoxiana, Khurasan, and beyond. His campaigns in the region were marked by swift and decisive victories, consolidating Caliphate control over key territories. Al-Harith ibn Surayj, on the other hand, distinguished himself through his leadership in the face of internal dissent and external threats. His ability to navigate political intrigue and maintain military discipline in the face of challenges made him a respected commander among his troops and a formidable adversary for opposing forces. These commanders faced formidable obstacles in their campaigns in Central Asia, including harsh terrain, fierce resistance from local populations, and rival powers seeking to assert their dominance. Yet, through their strategic vision, tactical skill, and ability to inspire loyalty among their troops, they were able to secure important gains for the Islamic Caliphate in the region. The conquest of Central Asia not only expanded the geographical reach of the Islamic Caliphate but also facilitated cultural exchange, economic development, and the spread of Islam to new lands. The commanders who led these conquests played a crucial role in shaping the outcome of the campaigns and leaving a lasting legacy on the region's history.

NOTABLE MILITARY FIGURES IN THE SUBJUGATION OF THE INDIAN SUBCONTINENT

Amir Khusrau, a scholar and poet who played a significant role in the army during campaigns in South Asia, is credited with effectively utilizing his diplomatic skills to forge alliances and navigate the complex political landscape of the Indian subcontinent. Known for his strategic acumen and ability to inspire his troops, Khusrau stands out as a prominent military figure who contributed to the successful subjugation of various regions in India. On the battlefield, Khalid ibn al-Walid, a seasoned commander renowned for his tactical brilliance and unwavering courage, demonstrated exceptional leadership during the conquest of the Indian subcontinent. His decisive victories and innovative military strategies not only secured key territories but also instilled fear in opposing forces, solidifying his reputation as a formidable general. Another notable military figure, Raja Raja Chola I, the monarch of the Chola dynasty, proved to be a formidable adversary during the Islamic conquest of the Indian subcontinent. With his prowess in naval warfare and strategic vision, Raja Raja Chola I effectively defended his kingdom against foreign invasions, illustrating his commitment to preserving the sovereignty of his realm. Furthermore, Malik Kafur, a trusted general in the Delhi Sultanate, played a crucial role in expanding the Islamic foothold in South India through his military campaigns and adept governance. Known for his military prowess and administrative acumen, Malik Kafur successfully established and maintained control over key territories, further consolidating the Sultanate's influence in the region. Through their leadership, strategic acumen, and military prowess, these notable figures left a lasting impact on the subjugation of the Indian subcontinent, shaping the course of history and influencing the cultural and political landscape of the region for generations to come.

LEADERSHIP IN THE CAMPAIGNS IN SOUTHEAST ASIA

The campaigns in Southeast Asia presented unique challenges and opportunities for the Islamic forces. The maritime routes to Southeast Asia required a different set of strategies and tactics compared to land-based conquests. The interaction with diverse societies in the region also shaped the approach of military leaders. Several key commanders emerged during the campaigns in Southeast Asia, each making significant contributions to the expansion of Islamic influence in the region. Their leadership skills, strategic vision, and adaptability were crucial in navigating the complexities of maritime warfare and cultural diversity. These military leaders were adept at utilizing both naval and land forces to achieve their objectives in Southeast Asia. Their ability to coordinate operations across different theaters of war, as well as effectively engage with local populations and rulers, played a vital role in the success of the Islamic conquests in the region. The objectives of Islamic expansion in Southeast Asia were multi-faceted, encompassing religious, economic, and strategic motivations. The military leaders understood the importance of consolidating and maintaining control over key trade routes, as well as winning the support of local communities through diplomacy and military prowess. Overall, the leadership in the campaigns in Southeast Asia exemplified the complexity and diversity of Islamic conquests in different regions. Their achievements not only expanded the reach of the Islamic Caliphate but also left a lasting impact on the political and cultural landscape of Southeast Asia for centuries to come.

MILITARY STRATEGISTS IN THE CHALLENGES OF CONQUERING CHINA

Strategizing the conquest of China posed significant challenges for the Islamic forces. The vast size and diverse landscapes of China, coupled with its well-organized military and sophisticated defense systems, demanded strategic expertise and careful planning. The Islamic military strategists adopted a multi-faceted approach to overcome these challenges. One key aspect of their strategy was diplomacy. Recognizing the strength of the Chinese dynasties, Islamic commanders engaged in diplomatic negotiations to assess the political landscape and explore possible alliances. By establishing diplomatic channels, they sought to gain insights into the Chinese leadership's intentions and leverage potential opportunities for cooperation. In addition to diplomacy, military strategists prioritized intelligence gathering to gather crucial information about the Chinese military capabilities, defensive structures, and territorial vulnerabilities. Utilizing spies and reconnaissance missions, they meticulously studied the terrain and fortified positions, allowing them to devise tactical approaches tailored to the unique challenges posed by each region. The Islamic military commanders also employed innovative warfare tactics to outmaneuver the formidable Chinese defenses. By combining traditional military strategies with inventive approaches, such as feigned retreats, ambushes, and siege warfare techniques, they sought to disrupt the enemy's cohesion and exploit any weaknesses in their defense lines. Furthermore, logistical planning played a crucial role in the successful conquest of Chinese territories. Military strategists meticulously organized supply chains, ensuring a steady flow of resources and reinforcements to sustain prolonged campaigns in unfamiliar terrains. By securing logistical routes and establishing efficient communication networks, they enhanced the mobility and flexibility of their forces, effectively countering the logistical challenges posed by the vast Chinese territories. Overall, the military strategists involved in the conquest of China demonstrated remarkable adaptability, resourcefulness, and resilience in confronting the diverse challenges of the campaign. Through a combination of diplomatic finesse, intelligence gathering, innovative tactics, and logistical planning, they navigated the complexities of the Chinese battlefield with strategic acumen and determination, ultimately contributing to the successful expansion of the Islamic Caliphate into new territories.

CONTRIBUTIONS OF ARAB GENERALS IN THE ISLAMIC CONQUESTS

THE ISLAMIC CONQUESTS IN ASIA

Arab generals played a pivotal role in the sweeping conquests that marked the expansion of Islam across Asia. Their military prowess, strategic acumen, and leadership skills were instrumental in achieving significant victories and establishing the Islamic Caliphate as a dominant force in the region. These commanders not only excelled on the battlefield but also demonstrated administrative acumen in governing the newly conquered territories. One of the most renowned Arab generals was Khalid ibn al-Walid, known as the "Sword of Allah" for his military genius and unparalleled skill in warfare. His tactical brilliance and decisiveness were key factors in the early Islamic conquests, including the pivotal Battle of Yarmouk against the Byzantine Empire. Khalid's strategic maneuvers and bold leadership solidified the Caliphate's control over the Levant and paved the way for further expansion. Another notable Arab general was Amr ibn al-As, who distinguished himself in the conquest of Egypt and North Africa. Amr's strategic vision and ability to adapt to diverse terrains and circumstances were instrumental in the successful campaigns in these regions. His leadership not only secured territorial gains for the Caliphate but also facilitated the spread of Islam and the consolidation of Muslim rule in new territories. Moreover, Arab generals such as Abu Ubaidah ibn al-Jarrah, Saad ibn Abi Waqqas, and Tariq ibn Ziyad played crucial roles in various conquests across Asia. Their military strategies, charismatic leadership, and dedication to the cause of Islam contributed significantly to the expansion of the Islamic Caliphate and the dissemination of Islamic values and principles. Overall, the contributions of Arab generals in the Islamic conquests were instrumental in shaping the political and cultural landscape of Asia. Their military achievements, leadership qualities, and commitment to the ideals of Islam left a lasting legacy that continues to resonate in the region to this day.

IMPACT OF TURKISH COMMANDERS ON ISLAMIC EXPANSION

The Turkish commanders played a pivotal role in the expansion of the Islamic Caliphate, demonstrating remarkable military prowess and strategic acumen. Known for their fierce warrior tradition and expertise in cavalry warfare, Turkish leaders significantly influenced the course of Islamic conquests in Asia. With their nomadic roots and exceptional skills in mounted combat, Turkish commanders brought a new level of effectiveness and efficiency to the Caliphate's military campaigns. Their ability to swiftly maneuver across vast territories and adapt to diverse terrains gave the Islamic forces a strategic advantage in various battle scenarios. Turkish leaders such as Alp Arslan and Seljuk played key roles in expanding the Caliphate's influence into Central Asia and beyond. Their tactical brilliance and leadership qualities were instrumental in securing crucial victories and establishing a strong presence in the region. Noteworthy for their discipline, courage, and loyalty, Turkish commanders instilled a sense of unity and purpose among the troops, fostering a formidable fighting force that could overcome formidable adversaries. Their contributions to the Islamic conquests exemplified the fusion of military skill, cultural diversity, and religious fervor that defined the Caliphate's expansionist endeavors. The impact of Turkish commanders on Islamic expansion extended far beyond the battlefield, shaping the political landscape of the conquered territories and forging lasting alliances with local rulers. Their legacy resonates in the legacy of the Islamic Caliphate and the enduring influence of Turkish military traditions in the region. In conclusion, the Turkish commanders played a crucial role in the success of the Islamic conquests in Asia, leaving a lasting imprint on the history of the Caliphate and the regions they helped conquer.

ROLE OF PERSIAN MILITARY LEADERS IN THE CONQUESTS

Persian military leaders played a pivotal role in the Islamic conquests, showcasing their strategic prowess and battlefield expertise. Known for their fierce loyalty to their homeland and rich military traditions, these commanders left a lasting impact on the course of history. One prominent Persian military leader was Rostam Farrokhzad, who valiantly defended Persia against the Arab forces during the early Islamic conquests. Despite facing formidable odds, Farrokhzad's leadership and tactical acumen earned him a place in history as a legendary figure in Persian military lore. Another notable Persian military leader, Bahman Jazi, distinguished himself on the battlefield with his bold and decisive tactics. Leading his troops with discipline and courage, Jazi played a crucial role in several key battles that shaped the outcome of the conquests. His strategic brilliance and unwavering commitment to his people inspired generations of Persian warriors to defend their homeland against external threats. Furthermore, General Shapur Varaztad, known for his innovative military strategies and unparalleled knowledge of the terrain, was instrumental in repelling foreign invaders and maintaining Persia's military strength. Varaztad's leadership style emphasized the importance of preparedness, adaptability, and unity among his troops, reflecting the core values of Persian military tradition. The legacy of these Persian military leaders endures to this day, serving as a testament to their dedication, skill, and resilience in the face of adversity. Their contributions to the Islamic conquests underscore the complex interplay of cultures, histories, and ideologies that shaped the course of events in Asia. As we evaluate the influence of key military figures in this historical narrative, the role of Persian commanders emerges as a crucial aspect of understanding the broader impact of the Islamic conquests on the region.

CONCLUSION: EVALUATING THE INFLUENCE OF KEY MILITARY FIGURES

Throughout the course of the Islamic conquests in Asia, the influence of key military figures has been profound. These leaders played a crucial role in shaping the outcome of battles, determining strategic decisions, and ultimately contributing to the expansion of the Islamic Caliphate. From the conquest of Persia to the campaigns in Southeast Asia, these commanders demonstrated exceptional skill, leadership, and tactical acumen on the battlefield. The Persian military leaders, in particular, showcased their expertise in warfare and strategic planning during the Islamic conquests. Their knowledge of the terrain, understanding of regional dynamics, and ability to adapt to changing circumstances were instrumental in the success of the Caliphate's military campaigns. By leveraging their experience and expertise, these commanders were able to overcome formidable obstacles, secure key victories, and expand the reach of Islamic rule in Asia. Furthermore, the contributions of these key military figures extended beyond the battlefield. They were not only skilled warriors but also adept administrators, diplomats, and statesmen. Their ability to govern conquered territories, establish alliances with local rulers, and navigate complex political landscapes played a crucial role in consolidating the gains of the Islamic conquests and ensuring the stability of the newly acquired territories. In evaluating the influence of these key military figures, it becomes evident that their leadership was a defining factor in the success of the Islamic conquests in Asia. Their strategic vision, military prowess, and diplomatic finesse were essential in achieving the Caliphate's objectives and leaving a lasting impact on the region. By recognizing the pivotal role played by these commanders, we gain a deeper appreciation of the complexities and nuances of warfare, leadership, and conquest in the history of Islam.

LONG-TERM CONSEQUENCES OF ISLAMIC RULE

The long-term impacts of Islamic rule in Asia have left an indelible mark on the region's cultural landscape. The assimilation and syncretism of diverse traditions have led to a complex tapestry of influences that continue to shape societies today. From art and architecture to language and cuisine, the fusion of Islamic and local customs has created a rich and dynamic heritage that reflects the interconnectedness of cultures across centuries. It is through this lens of cultural exchange and interaction that we can begin to understand the profound and lasting effects of Islamic rule in Asia.

CULTURAL ASSIMILATION AND SYNCRETISM

Cultural assimilation and syncretism played a pivotal role in shaping the long-term consequences of Islamic rule in Asia. As Islamic empires expanded their territories, they encountered diverse cultures, languages, and traditions. Rather than imposing a monolithic worldview, Islamic rulers often integrated aspects of local customs and beliefs into their own governance and society. This process of cultural exchange and adaptation led to the creation of vibrant and dynamic societies that blended Islamic,

Persian, Indian, Chinese, and other influences. One of the key mechanisms of cultural assimilation was the patronage of art, literature, and architecture. Islamic rulers sponsored the construction of mosques, palaces, and educational institutions that reflected a fusion of Islamic architectural styles with local design elements. This blending of aesthetic traditions not only created visually stunning monuments but also symbolized the coexistence of different cultural identities within the Islamic world. Furthermore, the exchange of knowledge and ideas between different civilizations facilitated the development of new scientific and intellectual advancements. Muslim scholars translated ancient Greek, Persian, and Indian texts into Arabic, preserving and expanding upon the knowledge of earlier civilizations. This cross-cultural fertilization laid the foundation for breakthroughs in fields such as mathematics, astronomy, medicine, and philosophy, contributing to the flourishing of intellectual inquiry across the Islamic world. In addition to artistic and intellectual exchanges, cultural assimilation also occurred at the grassroots level through everyday interactions between individuals of different backgrounds. Trade networks, urban centers, and religious institutions served as melting pots where diverse communities coexisted and shared their customs and practices. This cultural syncretism gave rise to hybrid identities, languages, and cuisines that reflected the rich tapestry of influences present in Islamic societies. Overall, the process of cultural assimilation and syncretism during the era of Islamic rule in Asia underscores the dynamic nature of cultural interactions and the resilience of diverse traditions in the face of political change. By embracing multiculturalism and hybridity, Islamic civilizations in Asia were able to adapt, evolve, and thrive, leaving a lasting legacy of cultural richness and diversity that continues to shape the region to this day.

SOCIO-POLITICAL TRANSFORMATIONS

Socio-Political Transformations: The Islamic conquests in Asia ushered in significant socio-political transformations across the regions they encountered. This period saw the establishment of new political structures, administrative systems, and social hierarchies. The integration of Islamic principles and practices into existing societies led to the emergence of hybrid cultures and identities, blending indigenous traditions with Islamic influences. One key aspect of these transformations was the reorganization of power dynamics. Local rulers often had to adapt to the new Islamic rulers or face resistance. The caliphate's centralized authority created a new political order, with appointed governors overseeing the conquered territories. This system brought stability and uniformity to the administration but also led to the marginalization of some local elites. Moreover, the spread of Islam facilitated social mobility and inclusivity. Conversion to Islam offered opportunities for non-Arab or non-Muslim populations to gain access to political power and economic privileges. In some cases, local customs and practices were incorporated into Islamic governance, fostering a sense of cultural accommodation and coexistence. Additionally, the Islamic conquests influenced gender relations and family structure in the conquered territories. Islamic teachings on marital relations, inheritance, and women's rights introduced new norms and practices that reshaped societal norms. While some aspects of pre-existing social structures persisted, others were modified to align with Islamic principles. The socio-political transformations resulting from the Islamic conquests in Asia were complex and multifaceted, shaping the course of history in the region for centuries to come. This period of transition marked a blending of diverse cultures and traditions, giving rise to unique societies that reflected both Islamic and indigenous influences.

THE ISLAMIC CONQUESTS IN ASIA

ECONOMIC CHANGES AND TRADE NETWORKS

The Islamic conquests in Asia brought significant economic changes and transformed trade networks across the region. The integration of newly conquered territories into the Islamic Caliphate facilitated the exchange of goods, ideas, and technologies, leading to the development of vibrant commercial centers and transregional trade routes. One of the key economic transformations was the establishment of a unified currency system based on the gold dinar and silver dirham, which streamlined trade and financial transactions. The Caliphate's efficient taxation system, known as the jizya, provided a stable source of revenue that supported the administration and military infrastructure of the empire. The conquest of major trade hubs such as Persia and the Indian subcontinent further enhanced the Caliphate's access to lucrative markets and valuable resources. Islamic merchants played a crucial role in facilitating trade along the Silk Road and maritime trade routes, linking distant regions and fostering cultural exchange. The spread of Islam also influenced economic practices, as Islamic principles emphasized honesty, fairness, and ethical conduct in business dealings. Islamic banking and financial instruments were developed to cater to the needs of a growing commercial class, promoting investment, entrepreneurship, and economic growth. The flourishing trade networks and economic prosperity under Islamic rule attracted merchants, artisans, and scholars from diverse regions, contributing to the cosmopolitanism and intellectual dynamism of Islamic societies. The legacy of these economic changes continues to shape the economic landscape of Asia and has left a lasting impact on global trade patterns and intercultural connections.

RELIGIOUS INFLUENCE AND CONVERSION

The spread of Islam across Asia brought about profound religious influence and widespread conversions. The Islamic conquests introduced new religious beliefs, practices, and traditions to the diverse societies they encountered. Through various means, including military conquest, trade networks, and cultural interactions, Islam made a lasting impact on the religious landscape of the region. Conversion to Islam was not solely a result of coercion or force but also stemmed from the appeal of Islamic teachings and principles. The message of monotheism, social justice, and spiritual fulfillment resonated with many individuals and communities. As a result, people from different backgrounds willingly embraced Islam, leading to a significant increase in the Muslim population across Asia. The adoption of Islam also brought about changes in religious practices and rituals. Mosques, madrasas, and other religious institutions became centers of community life, education, and spiritual guidance. Islamic art and architecture flourished, reflecting a fusion of local and Islamic styles, creating a distinct visual identity in the region. Moreover, the process of conversion to Islam facilitated cultural exchanges and interactions among diverse populations. This intermingling of traditions and beliefs contributed to the development of a rich and diverse Islamic culture in Asia. The syncretism of local customs with Islamic practices created unique forms of expression, ranging from language and cuisine to art and music. Overall, the religious influence and conversion resulting from the Islamic conquests in Asia were profound and far-reaching. They not only transformed the religious landscape of the region but also shaped the social, cultural, and political fabric of societies for centuries to come. The legacy of Islamic rule continues to be evident in the religious diversity and cultural heritage of Asia today.

THE ISLAMIC CONQUESTS IN ASIA

ARCHITECTURE AND URBAN PLANNING

Architecture and Urban Planning in the context of Islamic rule were instrumental in shaping the physical landscapes of conquered territories. The fusion of indigenous architectural styles with Islamic design principles resulted in the creation of monumental structures that reflected the cultural diversity and religious influences of the era. The establishment of mosques, palaces, madrasas, and bazaars became symbols of Islamic authority and cultural identity. The intricate geometric patterns, domes, and minarets that adorned these buildings showcased the artistic prowess and craftsmanship of Islamic architects. Urban planning under Islamic rule focused on creating functional and aesthetically pleasing cities that catered to the needs of the growing population. Planned cities with well-defined streets, markets, and public amenities were a hallmark of Islamic governance. The construction of water management systems, such as aqueducts, canals, and fountains, not only provided a reliable water supply but also added to the beauty and vitality of urban centers. The integration of green spaces, courtyards, and gardens in architectural designs promoted a sense of tranquility and harmony within bustling cityscapes. Furthermore, the architectural legacy of Islamic rule extended beyond religious and governmental buildings to private residences, mausoleums, and fortifications. Each structure bore the imprint of cultural exchange and artistic innovation, reflecting the diverse influences that shaped the Islamic world. The enduring impact of Islamic architecture and urban planning is evident in the preservation of historical sites, the continued use of traditional design elements in modern construction, and the inspiration it provides to architects and urban planners worldwide. The legacy of innovative design, engineering excellence, and cultural integration remains a testament to the lasting legacy of Islamic rule in shaping the built environment of Asia.

EDUCATION AND SCHOLARSHIP

Islamic societies prioritized education and scholarship as fundamental pillars of their civilization. The quest for knowledge became a core value, leading to the establishment of renowned centers of learning known as madrasas. These institutions offered a comprehensive curriculum covering subjects such as theology, philosophy, mathematics, medicine, astronomy, and literature. Scholars from diverse backgrounds converged in these academies, creating a vibrant intellectual environment that fostered innovation and cross-cultural exchange. One of the most significant contributions of Islamic scholarship was the preservation and translation of ancient texts from civilizations such as Greece, Rome, Persia, and India. This intellectual heritage was expanded upon by Muslim scholars who made groundbreaking advancements in various fields. For instance, figures like Ibn Sina (Avicenna) in medicine and Al-Khwarizmi in mathematics laid the foundation for modern scientific thought. Furthermore, Islamic scholars played a crucial role in the transmission of knowledge to Europe during the Middle Ages, influencing the Renaissance and shaping the development of Western thought. The translation movement in Baghdad, led by the Abbasid Caliph al-Ma'mun, facilitated the transfer of Greek philosophy and science into Arabic, preserving these works for future generations. Education in Islamic societies was not limited to the elite; rather, it was accessible to individuals of all social backgrounds. The pursuit of knowledge was considered a religious duty, and scholarships were often awarded to talented students regardless of their socioeconomic status. This egalitarian approach to education helped cultivate a society that valued intellectual rigor and critical thinking. In conclusion, the tradition of education and scholarship in Islamic societies left a lasting legacy that transcended geographical boundaries. The emphasis on learning, research, and intellectual exchange continues to influence academic disciplines and shape our understanding of the world.

LEGACY OF ISLAMIC LAW AND GOVERNANCE

The Legacy of Islamic Law and Governance: Islamic law, known as Sharia, and the system of governance established by the Islamic Caliphate have left a lasting impact on the regions conquered during the Islamic expansion. Sharia is a comprehensive legal framework derived from the Quran and the teachings of Prophet Muhammad, guiding various aspects of personal and communal life. The implementation of Sharia law in conquered territories brought about significant changes in administration, justice, and social welfare. Under Islamic governance, the Caliph or appointed rulers acted as religious and political leaders, responsible for upholding and enforcing Sharia law. The concept of unity of religion and state shaped the structure of governance, with officials mandated to ensure compliance with Islamic principles in public affairs. This integration of religious and political authority laid the foundation for a centralized administration that governed through a combination of religious law and administrative regulations. The legacy of Islamic law and governance also includes the establishment of institutions such as qadis (judges) and muhtasibs (market supervisors) to administer justice and regulate public behavior. Qadis applied Sharia law in resolving disputes, ensuring fairness and adherence to Islamic principles. Muhtasibs oversaw economic activities, monitoring markets, preventing fraud, and promoting ethical practices in trade. Moreover, the system of governance implemented by the Islamic Caliphate was characterized by principles of consultation (shura), accountability, and the protection of individual rights. The concept of bay'ah (allegiance) symbolized the contractual relationship between the ruler and the ruled, emphasizing mutual obligations and responsibilities. In conclusion, the legacy of Islamic law and governance in the conquered territories reflects a balance between religious principles and administrative efficiency. The enduring influence of Sharia law and the system of governance established by the Islamic Caliphate continues to shape legal systems and political structures in some regions today.

RESISTANCE AND PERSISTENCE OF LOCAL TRADITIONS

Despite the spread of Islamic rule and governance in various regions, local traditions often persisted and influenced societal norms. Resistance to foreign influences and a commitment to preserving indigenous customs played a significant role in shaping the cultural landscape. Local communities maintained their traditional practices, languages, and belief systems, even in the face of Islamic rule. While there were instances of adaptation and integration, many groups staunchly defended their heritage and identity against external pressures. The resilience of local traditions was evident in the ways communities continued to celebrate festivals, perform rituals, and pass down oral histories. These customs served as a source of strength and unity, fostering a sense of belonging and continuity in the face of change. Despite the spread of Islamic legal systems, some regions upheld their own legal frameworks rooted in customary practices and local norms. This resistance to formal Islamic law reflected a desire to maintain autonomy and sovereignty over legal matters within the community. In areas where Islamic governance was established, local traditions sometimes influenced the implementation of policies and administration. Officials often had to navigate between adhering to Islamic principles and accommodating the customs and preferences of the local population to maintain stability and harmony. The persistence of local traditions alongside Islamic rule created a complex tapestry of cultural dynamics, where diverse practices coexisted and interacted. This interplay contributed to a rich tapestry of cultural heritage, blending elements of different traditions and creating a unique synthesis of identities. As societies evolved and adapted to changing circumstances, the resistance and persistence of local traditions continued to shape the social fabric and identity of communities. This dynamic interaction between tradition and innovation underscored the enduring significance of preserving cultural heritage in the face of external influences.

CONTEMPORARY REFLECTIONS AND RELEVANCE

The enduring legacy of Islamic rule in Asia continues to shape the region's cultural, social, and political landscape. Despite centuries of foreign conquests and assimilation, many local traditions have persisted and continue to influence contemporary societies. The resilience of these traditions highlights the complex interplay between external influences and internal resistance, creating a unique tapestry of cultural heritage. In today's globalized world, the relevance of understanding the historical Islamic conquests in Asia extends beyond mere academic curiosity. It offers valuable insights into the complexities of intercultural exchange, the dynamics of power and resistance, and the enduring impact of conquest and colonization. By examining the ways in which local traditions have resisted assimilation and persisted through centuries of upheaval, we gain a deeper appreciation for the richness and diversity of Asian cultures. Moreover, the contemporary reflections on the legacy of Islamic rule remind us of the importance of cultural preservation and heritage conservation. As nations grapple with issues of identity, globalization, and modernization, the need to protect and promote indigenous traditions becomes increasingly urgent. By recognizing the value of local customs, practices, and beliefs, societies can foster a sense of pride, unity, and continuity in a rapidly changing world. Furthermore, the ongoing relevance of the Islamic conquests in Asia lies in their impact on current geopolitical dynamics. The historical interactions between different religious, ethnic, and cultural groups have left a lasting imprint on the region's political landscape. By understanding the complex legacies of conquest and resistance, we are better equipped to navigate contemporary challenges such as religious extremism, ethnic conflicts, and cultural hegemony. In conclusion, the contemporary reflections on the legacy of Islamic rule in Asia underscore the importance of acknowledging and honoring the enduring traditions and customs of diverse societies. By recognizing the resilience of local cultures in the face of external pressures, we can cultivate a deeper appreciation for the complexities of human history and the richness of Asian heritage.

NOTES AND REFERENCES

Here are some relevant sources and references covering the Islamic conquest and rule in the Indian subcontinent in English, French, and Arabic:

English sources:

1. Wink, A. (1991). Al-Hind, the Making of the Indo-Islamic World. This comprehensive work analyzes the beginning of Islamic rule in India from the 7th-11th centuries. (Schmiedchen, 2021)

2. Islam, A. (2017). The civilizational role of Islam in the Indian subcontinent: The Delhi sultanate. This paper examines the impact of Islam in the Indian Peninsula from political, intellectual, cultural, and artistic perspectives during the Delhi Sultanate period. (Dehghi, 2017)

3. Dehghi, A.G. (2017). The Historical Signs of the Peaceful Advent of Islam to Indian Subcontinent (From the Beginning to the Ghaznavid Dynasty). This study investigates the non-military ways Islam spread in India before the Ghaznavid dynasty. (Nuraisah et al., 2023)

4. Ullah, A., Afzal, S., & Rahmat. (2022). Historical Inheritance of Pakistan: The Muslim Conquests in the Sub-continent. This paper provides an overview of the Muslim conquests in the Indian subcontinent, starting with Muhammad bin Qasim's conquest of Sindh in 712. (Kłodkowski, 2017)

5. Kłodkowski, P. (2017). Islam in India: Ideological Conflicts on the Subcontinent and Their Political and Social Consequences in the Early 21st Century. This article examines the historical context of Muslim-Hindu relations in India. (Shah, 2015)

French source:

1. Bessard, F. (2016). Itinéraires et mutations urbaines dans le mašreq islamique. While focused on the Islamic East, this French article provides context on early Islamic conquests and rule. (Yattara, 2015)

Arabic sources:

1. سعد, نها مصطفى محمود (2023). فتح معبد سومنات من خلال المصادر العربية والأردية. This Arabic article discusses the conquest of the Somnath temple through Arabic and Urdu sources. (Arshad, 2017)

2. عزيز, أ. و شاه, س. (2017). تاريخ علوم القرآن في شبه القارة الهندية وتطورها. This Arabic article covers the history of Quranic sciences in the Indian subcontinent, which relates to Islamic rule in the region. (Shamsuddin & Lubis, 2023)

These sources provide a range of perspectives on the Islamic conquest and rule of the Indian subcontinent, from military conquests to cultural and intellectual impacts. They cover different periods and aspects of Islamic rule in the region.

Bibliography:

Abdilkhakim, B. (2024). Islamic modernism in India in the second half of the 19th century and Sayit Ahmed Khan. BULLETIN of the L N Gumilyov Eurasian National University Historical Sciences Philosophy Religion Series.

Adnan, A. H. M. (2017). Learning English (and Arabic) in Malaysian Islamic Schools: Language Use and the Construction of Identities. AARN: Learning & Teaching (Topic).

Akbar Ali, R. ullah. (2022). HISTORICAL INHERITANCE OF PAKISTAN: THE MUSLIM CONQUESTS IN THE SUB-CONTINENT. Pakistan Journal of International Affairs.

Akhatar, J. (2023). Non-Muslim Indian Scholar to Islamic Studies: A Study of Narendra Nath Law's Treatise. FITRAH Jurnal Kajian Ilmu-Ilmu Keislaman.

Al-Hind: The Making of the Indo-Islamic World, Vol. II. The Slave Kings and the Islamic Conquest, 11th–13th Centuries . By André Wink. pp. xii, 427. Leiden, E. J. Brill, 1997. Dfl. 220, US$137.50. (n.d.).

Ali, F. (2018). The Dynamics of Islamic Ideology with Regard to Gender and Women's Education in South Asia. Asian Studies, 6, 33–52.

Ali, M. Y., & Bakar, O. (2023). ABUL KALAM AZAD'S IDEA OF RELIGIOUS PLURALISM FOR AN INCLUSIVE INDIAN NATIONALISM: A CIVILIZATIONAL REVISIT. Al-Shajarah: Journal of the International Institute of Islamic Thought and Civilization (ISTAC).

AL-IBRAHIMI, A. T. S. S. A. (2024). THE CONTRIBUTION OF THE ALAWITES TO THE DEVELOPMENT OF ISLAMIC CIVILIZATION IN THE ISLAMIC EAST - NISHAPUR AS AN EXAMPLE. RIMAK International Journal of Humanities and Social Sciences.

Arasaratnam, S. (1992). Some Reflections on the 18th Century "Crisis" in the Indian Subcontinent. 1992, 88–102.

Arshad, I. (2017). An historical analysis of multifaith cooperation and civilisation building in India during Muslim rule.

Asher, C. B. (1992). Precedents for Mughal architecture. 1–18.

Assayag, J. (1999). Bernard S. Cohn, Colonialism and Its Forms of Knowledge. The British in India. Annales: Histoire, Sciences Sociales, 54, 786–790.

Aziz, A., & Shah, S. (2017). ARABIC–HISTORY OF QURA'NIC SCIENCES IN INDIAN SUBCONTINENT AND ITS DEVELOPMENT. The Scholar Islamic Academic Research Journal.

Bala, A. (2018). A study of religious practices during early Turkish rule.

Begum, I. (2015). Durand Line: A Legacy of Colonial Rule (1893-1970)*. Pakistan Historical Society. Journal of the Pakistan Historical Society, 63, 35.

Bessard, F. (2016). Itinéraires et mutations urbaines dans le mašreq islamique. Arabica.

Dehghi, A. G. (2017). The Historical Signs of the Peaceful Advent of Islam to Indian Subcontinent (From the Beginning to the Ghaznavid Dynasty).

Demirayak, K. (2015). OSMANLI DÖNEMİ ARAP EDEBİYATI ÜZERİNE DEĞERLENDİRMELER / A REMARKS ON ARABIC LITERATURE DURING OTTOMAN RULE. 31–62.

Deoliya, N. (2013). The Process of Transition from Conquest State to Indo-Islamic State, with Regards to the Sultanate of Delhi Involved Reformulation of Ethnic, Religious and Regional Identities. 1, 1–3.

Forman, A. (2022). Jewish Identity, al-Andalus, and Interfaith Communities: The Medieval Legacy of Islamic Spain. Comitatus: A Journal of Medieval and Renaissance Studies, 53, 103–120.

Guha, S. (2024). Empires, Languages, and Scripts in the Perso-Indian World. Comparative Studies in Society and History, 66, 443–469.

Hassan, T. (2019). Islamic Jurisprudence: Apropos to the Indian Legal System. Social Science Research Network.

Hijeat, A. M., & Albazzaz, I. A. (2023). A study of the stages of development of domes in Iran, Central Asia and the Indian subcontinent after the Islamic conquest. 8TH ENGINEERING AND 2ND INTERNATIONAL CONFERENCE FOR COLLEGE OF ENGINEERING – UNIVERSITY OF BAGHDAD: COEC8-2021 Proceedings.

Islam, A. (2016). Origin and development of Unani medicine: an analytical study.

Islam, A. (2017). The civilizational role of Islam in the Indian subcontinent: The Delhi sultanate. Intellectual Discourse, 25.

Johnson, R. (2003). What was the nature of British rule in India, c.1770–1858? 24–38.

Jones, J. (2020). Muslim Alternative Dispute Resolution: Tracing the Pathways of Islamic Legal Practice between South Asia and Contemporary Britain. Journal of Muslim Minority Affairs, 40, 48–66.

Khoso, Dr. A. A., Hammad, M., & Ahmed, Dr. M. (2022). Arabic 1. Islamic History of District Mardan in the Indian Subcontinent. Al Khadim Research Journal of Islamic Culture and Civilization.

Kłodkowski, P. (2017). Islam in India: Ideological Conflicts on the Subcontinent and Their Political and Social Consequences in the Early 21st Century. The Polish Quarterly of International Affairs, 26, 7–23.

Kumar, P. C. (2007). Islamic "Terrorism" and Visions of Justice in Khalid Mohamed's F IZA. 63–82.

Mahmood, S., Nasiruddin, H., & Rizwan, M. (2014). STRUGGLE FOR ISLAMIC STATE AND SOCIETY: AN ANALYSIS OF SYED AHMAD SHAHEED'S JIHAD MOVEMENT.

Majeed, H. A., & Ullah, I. (2022). Impacts of Arabic Language and Literature on Khawaja Farid's Saraiki Poetic Work. Journal of Islamic and Religious Studies.

Malhotra, A. (2012). Religion and Sex in the Subcontinent. 147–169.

Maqsood, D. N. (2022). A Depiction of Indian Muslim Women's Plight in Culture and Literature Around the Mid-Eighteen Century. Journal of Law & Social Studies.

Masood, H. A. (2024). From Italy to the Indian subcontinent: Dante and his Divine Comedy in Urdu. Forum Italicum.

Minakshi Chauhan. (2023). Reflections of Horror on Islamic Invasions in Medieval India. International Journal For Multidisciplinary Research.

Momen, A., Ebrahimi, M., & Hassan, A. M. (2023). Identifying the Role of the First 'Qawmi Madrasah' Darul Uloom Deoband in the Indian Subcontinent. Environment-Behaviour Proceedings Journal.

Momen, A., Ebrahimi, M., & Yusoff, K. (2024). British Colonial Education in the Indian Subcontinent (1757-1858): Attitude of Muslims. Journal of Islamic Thought and Civilization.

Momin, A. (1977). The Indo-Islamic Tradition. Sociological Bulletin, 26, 242–258.

News, M., & Sun, S. (2019). Ming News. Ming Studies, 2019, 78–79.

Nuraisah, N., Permata, Y., Tabroni, I., Kathryn, M., & Cale, W. (2023). Modern Islamic Civilization in South and Southeast Asia. International Journal of Educational Narratives.

Nyang, S. (2021). The Role of Pakistan in the Organization of Islamic Conference. American Journal of Islam and Society.

Ocón, J. E., & Moreno, E. M. (2019). Uses of the Past in Early Medieval Iberia (Eighth-Tenth Centuries). Medieval Worlds.

Parveen, N., & Munir, M. (2020). مغلی ع د میں مظلوم کی داد رسی ک لی بادشاہوں ک اقدامات عدل کا جائز. 14, 157–168.

Pay, S. (2015). Indian Muslims, Ottoman Empire and Caliphate during Colonial Period.

Penrose, W. (2006). Colliding Cultures: Masculinity and Homoeroticism in Mughal and Early Colonial South Asia. 144–165.

Petrovich, M. (2017). Rum and Hind: relations and shared experiences of conquest, acculturation and Turkish rule in pre-modern India and Anatolia.

P.M, H. (2022). Cultural Issues in Translating from Arabic to Tamil. International Research Journal of Tamil.

Polymaths of Islam: Power and Networks of Knowledge in Central Asia. James Pickett (Ithaca, NY: Cornell University Press, 2020). Pp. 301. $54.95 hardcover. ISBN: 9781501750243. (n.d.).

Rakibul, M., & Khan, H. (2015). The Pakistan Movement and the Bangla Poetry of the Islamic Trend: Crossings: A Journal of English Studies.

Rana, Dr. H. A. S. (2022). Arabic 4. Accentuating and Fenguing the Thinkings of Philosophers Inferencing from the Islamic Resources in The Light of "Al-Tamyi'z." Al Khadim Research Journal of Islamic Culture and Civilization.

Rasool, G., Keerio, T. H., & Faisal. (2023). A Historical Analysis of Pan-Islamism in Sindh during Collapse of the Ottoman Empire. Global Social Sciences Review.

Rifai, S. (2021). Arabic Colleges in Indian Subcontinent and Their Challenges: Part 1. Social Science Research Network.

Sadeh, R. B. (2023). Printing Islamic Modernism: Arabic Texts for Arab and South Asian Muslims in the Early Twentieth Century. International Journal of Islam in Asia.

Salvaggio, F. (2020). Language, Ideology and Identity in Post-Partition Pakistan in the Light of Bausani's Notion of 'Islamic Languages.' 18, 149–164.

Schmiedchen, A. (2021). Buddhist Endowments by Śaiva Kings under the Maitrakas of Valabhī in Western India (5th–8th Cent.) and the Yodhāvaka Grant of Dharasena iv, [Valabhī] Year 326. Endowment Studies.

Shah, M. (2015). The Mystics of Sial Sharif as Opponents of the British Rule in India. South Asian Studies, 30, 237.

Shahab, Dr. S. (2021). HISTORY AND BACKGROUND OF MADRASSAH EDUCATION IN PAKISTAN. Pakistan Journal of International Affairs.

Shamsuddin, S. (2023). Islamic Urdu Literature: A Heretical Islamic Literature in Indian Subcontinent. Advances in Social Sciences Research Journal.

Shamsuddin, S., & Lubis, T. (2023). Studies in the Prophetic Ḥadith and its Sciences in Urdu, Farsi, and Arabic by Indian Muslim Scholars. Advances in Social Sciences Research Journal.

Sharma, J., & Bhargava, V. (2021). INTERMINGLING OF 2 CULTURES (INDIAN AND ISLAMIC DURING THE REIGN OF DELHI).

Sijpesteijn, P. (2021). Loyal and Knowledgeable Supporters Integrating Egyptian Elites in Early Islamic Egypt.

Singh, J. G. (2012). Boundary Crossings in the Islamic World: Princess Gulbadan as Traveler, Biographer, and Witness to History, 1523–1603. Early Modern Women, 7, 231–240.

Tali, F. A. (2020). Socio-Cultural Impact Of Mughal Rule In Kashmir (1586-1752): 40, 2684–2689.

Troia, N. D. (2022). The Oases of Egypt's Western Desert from Byzantine to Islamic Rule: Problems and New Perspectives. Journal of Late Antiquity, 15, 277–303.

URDU-THE EFFECTS OF SHAH WALIULLAH'S MOVEMENT AND HIS ISLAMIC SERVICE ON URDU LITERATURE: AN ANALYTICAL STUDY. (2022). The Scholar Islamic Academic Research Journal.

Virdee, P. (2021). 3. Towards the idea of Pakistan. PAKISTAN.

Wink, A. (1991). Al-Hind, the Making of the Indo-Islamic World.

Yasmeen, S. (2023). Muslim quest for space in india: Prospects and Challenges.

Yattara, E. (2015). Islam et éducation au Mali.

Yuan, X. (2024). Economic Development of British India during the Colonial Period. Lecture Notes on History.

سعد, ن. م. م. (2023). فتح معبد سومنات من خلال المصادر العربية والأردية Conquest of the Somanat temple through Arabic and Urdu sources. مجلة وادى النيل للدراسات والبحوث الإنسانية والاجتماعية والتربويه.

Online:

Here are more key sources and references from the Internet covering the Islamic conquest and rule in the Indian subcontinent:

1. "A History of Islamic Societies" by Ira M. Lapidus (Cambridge University Press) - This book contains a chapter on "The Indian Subcontinent: The Delhi Sultanates and the Mughal Empire," which provides an overview of Muslim rule in India[7].
2. "The History of India, as Told by Its Own Historians. The Muhammadan Period" edited by Sir H.M. Elliot and John Dowson - This is a multi-volume work that compiles translations of medieval Persian chronicles about Muslim rule in India[1].
3. "Islamic Civilization in South Asia: A History of Muslim Power and Presence in the Indian Subcontinent" by Burjor Avari - This book covers the history of Islamic rule in South Asia[4].
4. "The Civilizational Role of Islam in the Indian Subcontinent: The Delhi Sultanate" - A research article focusing on the intellectual and cultural contributions of Muslims during the Delhi Sultanate period[3].
5. "The Caliph and the Imam: The Making of Sunnism and Shiism" - Contains a chapter on "Muslim Dynasties on the Indian Subcontinent" discussing how different Islamic sects flourished in India[9].
6. Wikipedia articles on "Muslim period in the Indian subcontinent" and "Muslim conquests in the Indian subcontinent" provide overviews with citations to academic sources[1][10].
7. "Arabs at War: Military Effectiveness, 1948-1991" by Kenneth M. Pollack - While focused on a later period, this book may contain some relevant background on early Arab military campaigns[4].
8. Academic journals like the Pakistan Journal of International Affairs have published articles on topics like "The Muslim Conquests in the Sub-Continent"[4].

These sources cover various aspects of Islamic conquest and rule in India, including military campaigns, political developments, religious changes, and cultural impacts. They represent a mix of classic works, modern academic research, and reference materials that can provide a comprehensive understanding of this historical period.

Citations:

[1] https://en.wikipedia.org/wiki/Muslim_period_in_the_Indian_subcontinent
[2] https://www.britannica.com/summary/India
[3] https://www.researchgate.net/publication/318490701_The_civilizational_role_of_Islam_in_the_Indian_subcontinent_The_Delhi_sultanate
[4] https://www.pjia.com.pk/index.php/pjia/article/download/589/431
[5] https://www.reddit.com/r/AskHistorians/comments/1eu5du/islamic_conquest_of_india/
[6] https://www.cambridge.org/highereducation/books/a-history-of-islamic-societies/22183D81CFE5E37E5DBED1A0F5AB0FB9/the-indian-subcontinent-the-delhi-sultanates-and-the-mughal-empire/9F9610CDC13644791215C48AC1BF4BED
[7] https://www.cambridge.org/core/books/abs/islamic-societies-to-the-nineteenth-century/indian-subcontinent-the-delhi-sultanates-and-the-mughal-empire/5746D6AA9CCB455C519E5F611ED98267
[8] https://military-history.fandom.com/wiki/Muslim_conquests_in_the_Indian_subcontinent
[9] https://academic.oup.com/book/45757/chapter-abstract/398686103?login=false&redirectedFrom=fulltext
[10] https://en.wikipedia.org/wiki/Muslim_conquests_in_the_Indian_subcontinent

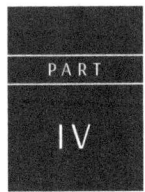

PART IV

THE CAMPAIGNS IN SOUTHEAST ASIA

SETTING THE STAGE

Southeast Asia is a region of vast diversity, both in terms of its geography and its cultures. Spanning across a multitude of islands and peninsulas, it is home to a rich tapestry of traditions, languages, and belief systems. From the bustling trade ports of Malacca to the majestic temples of Angkor Wat, Southeast Asia has been a crossroads of civilizations for centuries. The region's strategic location at the crossroads of the Indian Ocean and the South China Sea has made it a melting pot of influences from India, China, and the Islamic world. Its lush jungles, fertile plains, and abundant resources have attracted traders, adventurers, and conquerors from near and far. Southeast Asia's maritime trade networks have connected it to distant lands since ancient times, facilitating the exchange of goods, ideas, and people. The monsoon winds that sweep across the region have shaped its history, enabling the movement of ships and sailors across the vast expanse of the seas. Despite its diversity, Southeast Asia shares a common thread of cultural resilience and adaptability. The region's peoples have forged unique identities, drawing on their interactions with foreign powers to create vibrant societies that blend tradition and innovation. As we delve into the history of Islamic expansion into Southeast Asia, it is important to appreciate the dynamic and complex landscape of the region. By understanding the multifaceted nature of Southeast Asian societies, we can begin to unravel the influences that have shaped its history and continue to resonate in the present day.

ISLAMIC EXPANSION INTO SOUTHEAST ASIA: HISTORICAL CONTEXT

Islamic expansion into Southeast Asia was a pivotal moment in the history of the region, marking the arrival of a new cultural and religious influence that would shape its trajectory for centuries to come. Beginning in the 7th century, Islamic traders and missionaries ventured into the archipelago, establishing early connections with local rulers and communities. The spread of Islam was not solely driven by conquest but also through peaceful interactions, trade relations, and intermarriage with indigenous populations. This approach allowed for the gradual assimilation of Islamic teachings into existing belief systems, creating a unique blend of cultures that would characterize Southeast Asia in the years to come. The historical context of Islamic expansion into Southeast Asia is complex and multifaceted, encompassing a diverse range of interactions between Islamic merchants, scholars, and local populations. These early engagements laid the foundation for the establishment of Islamic Sultanates and kingdoms in the region, each with its distinct character and ruling dynasties. The strategic location of Southeast Asia as a crossroads of trade routes between the Indian Ocean and the South China Sea made it an attractive destination for Islamic traders seeking new markets and opportunities for cultural exchange. As Islamic influence grew in Southeast Asia, so too did the political power of Muslim rulers who sought to consolidate their authority and expand their territories. The integration of Islamic legal and administrative systems into local governance structures helped to strengthen the legitimacy of ruling elites and fostered a sense of unity among diverse ethnic and religious communities. The spread of Islam in Southeast Asia was not a uniform or linear process but rather a dynamic and ongoing exchange of ideas, practices, and beliefs that continues to shape the region's identity to this day.

MARITIME ROUTES AND TRADE NETWORKS: A GATEWAY TO THE EAST

The maritime routes and trade networks of Southeast Asia served as a crucial gateway connecting diverse civilizations and facilitating the exchange of goods, ideas, and cultures. Stretching across the vast expanse of the Indian Ocean and beyond, these maritime pathways played a pivotal role in the Islamic expansion into Southeast Asia. The strategic location of Southeast Asia made it a focal point for trade between the East and the West. Arab, Indian, Chinese, and Malay merchants traversed these waters, creating a bustling network of commercial activity. Spices, textiles, pottery, precious metals, and other commodities flowed through these maritime routes, enriching the region and linking it to the wider world. The sea routes also served as conduits for the spread of Islam into Southeast Asia. Arab traders and missionaries traveled across the seas, bringing with them not only goods but also the teachings of Islam. The interconnected nature of the maritime trade networks facilitated the transmission of religious ideas and practices, leading to the gradual conversion of local populations to the new faith. Moreover, the maritime trade routes fostered cultural exchange and interaction among diverse communities. The mixing of different traditions and beliefs resulted in a rich tapestry of syncretism, where elements of local cultures blended with Islamic practices. This cultural fusion gave rise to unique art forms, architectural styles, and social customs that reflected the diversity and complexity of Southeast Asian societies. In conclusion, the maritime routes and trade networks of Southeast Asia played a pivotal role in shaping the region's history and identity. These pathways not only facilitated economic exchanges but also facilitated the spread of Islam and the cross-cultural fertilization that characterized the region's rich heritage.

ENCOUNTER OF ISLAM WITH LOCAL CULTURES: SYNCRETISM AND INTEGRATION

Islam's encounter with the diverse local cultures of Southeast Asia forged a path of syncretism and integration that continues to shape the region to this day. As Islamic merchants and scholars traveled along the maritime routes connecting the Middle East and Asia, they encountered a rich tapestry of traditions and beliefs indigenous to the lands they visited. Rather than imposing their faith in a rigid manner, Muslims in Southeast Asia engaged in a process of cultural blending that gave rise to a unique and vibrant hybrid identity. Local customs and practices were integrated into Islamic rituals, creating a harmonious blend of traditions that resonated with the populace. This approach not only facilitated the spread of Islam but also fostered a sense of inclusivity and acceptance among different communities. One notable example is the way Islamic architecture in the region incorporated elements of local design, such as intricate carvings and vibrant colors, giving rise to a distinct Southeast Asian aesthetic. Furthermore, the interaction between Islam and local cultures led to the emergence of new forms of art, literature, and music that reflected the fusion of diverse influences. Islamic texts were translated into local languages, allowing for a deeper understanding of religious teachings among the native populations. Similarly, traditional stories and legends were reinterpreted through an Islamic lens, blending spiritual narratives with local folklore. In the realm of culinary traditions, the exchange of ingredients and cooking techniques between Islamic and indigenous communities resulted in the creation of unique dishes that are now an integral part of Southeast Asian cuisine. The use of spices, herbs, and aromatic flavors characteristic of Islamic cooking melded seamlessly with traditional ingredients, producing a culinary heritage that embodies the spirit of cultural exchange. Overall, the encounter of Islam with local cultures in Southeast Asia was not merely a clash of civilizations but a dialogue that led to a dynamic process of syncretism and integration. This ongoing exchange of ideas and practices continues to enrich the region's cultural tapestry, highlighting the transformative power of cross-cultural interactions.

MILITARY STRATEGIES AND TACTICS IN SOUTHEAST ASIA

Military Strategies and Tactics in Southeast Asia: Southeast Asia presented unique challenges for Islamic commanders due to its diverse geography, terrains, and cultures. The region's tropical forests, marshlands, and archipelagos required adaptive military strategies to navigate and conquer. Islamic armies had to contend with guerrilla warfare tactics employed by local resistance fighters, as well as the complexities of engaging in naval battles across the maritime trade routes. To effectively engage in military campaigns in Southeast Asia, Islamic commanders often utilized a combination of land-based and naval strategies. On land, they employed swift cavalry movements to surprise and overwhelm enemy forces, leveraging their speed and agility to outmaneuver opponents. Additionally, infantry forces were well-trained in close combat tactics and siege warfare, allowing them to capture fortified positions and urban centers. Naval warfare played a crucial role in Southeast Asia, where the archipelagic nature of the region necessitated mastery of the seas. Islamic commanders developed a strong naval presence, utilizing fast ships equipped with advanced weaponry to control key maritime routes and secure trade networks. Naval engagements involved tactics such as boarding enemy vessels, utilizing naval artillery, and maintaining strategic blockades to exert dominance over rival forces. Furthermore, Islamic military strategies in Southeast Asia often incorporated diplomatic negotiations and alliances with local rulers to consolidate power and ensure stability in newly conquered territories. By forging strategic partnerships and alliances with indigenous leaders, Islamic commanders could leverage local knowledge and resources to strengthen their military campaigns and establish sustainable governance structures in the region. Overall, the military strategies and tactics employed by Islamic commanders in Southeast Asia reflected their adaptability, strategic acumen, and willingness to engage with the complexities of the region's diverse landscapes and cultures. Through a combination of land-based and naval warfare, diplomatic negotiations, and alliances with local powers, Islamic armies were able to navigate the challenges of conquering and consolidating their rule in Southeast Asia, leaving a lasting impact on the region's history and development.

NOTABLE ISLAMIC COMMANDERS AND LEADERS IN THE REGION

The Islamic conquests in Southeast Asia were led by a number of notable commanders and leaders who played pivotal roles in shaping the region's history. These individuals exhibited exceptional strategic acumen, military prowess, and diplomatic skills that enabled the expansion of Islamic influence in the region. One such prominent figure was Sultan Iskandar Shah, the founder of the Sultanate of Malacca. Known for his vision and leadership, Sultan Iskandar Shah successfully unified various Malay kingdoms and established Malacca as a powerful maritime empire. Another significant leader in Southeast Asian Islamic history was Sultan Mansur Shah, who ascended to the throne of Malacca after Sultan Iskandar Shah. Sultan Mansur Shah continued his predecessor's legacy of promoting trade and spreading Islam in the region. Under his rule, Malacca became a major trading hub and a center of Islamic scholarship, attracting merchants and scholars from across the Islamic world. The expansion of Islam in Southeast Asia was also facilitated by the military expertise of commanders like Admiral Hang Tuah. Renowned for his loyalty and martial skill, Hang Tuah played a crucial role in defending Malacca from external threats and expanding its influence in the region. His exploits in naval warfare and diplomatic negotiations earned him a reputation as one of the greatest military leaders in Southeast Asian history. Furthermore, the rise of Islam in the region was influenced by leaders like Sultan Muhammad Shaheb, the ruler of the Aceh Sultanate. Sultan Muhammad Shaheb was known for his fervent commitment to spreading Islam and resisting Western colonial powers in Southeast Asia. His proactive stance against colonial aggression and support for Islamic education endeared him to his subjects and solidified the Aceh Sultanate's position as a bastion of Islamic resistance in the region. Overall, the contributions of these notable Islamic commanders and leaders were instrumental in shaping the history and cultural landscape of Southeast Asia. Through their vision, valor, and strategic acumen, they left a lasting legacy that continues to resonate in the region to this day.

IMPACT OF ISLAMIC CONQUESTS ON INDIGENOUS SOCIETIES

The Islamic conquests in Southeast Asia had a profound impact on the indigenous societies of the region. The introduction of Islam brought about significant changes in various aspects of these societies, including social structures, cultural practices, and political systems. One of the key impacts of Islamic conquests on indigenous societies was the transformation of religious beliefs and practices. As Islam spread throughout the region, local religions and animistic beliefs were often absorbed or replaced by the teachings of Islam. This led to the establishment of mosques, madrasas, and Islamic legal systems in many parts of Southeast Asia. Furthermore, the introduction of Islamic governance systems also had a lasting impact on indigenous societies. Islamic rulers often implemented new administrative structures based on Islamic principles, which influenced the political organization of many societies in the region. This shift towards Islamic governance led to changes in laws, taxation systems, and social hierarchies. Additionally, the spread of Islam in Southeast Asia through conquests resulted in the integration of local traditions with Islamic practices. This syncretic approach to religion allowed for the preservation of indigenous cultural elements while adopting Islamic norms and values. As a result, a unique blend of Islamic and local traditions emerged, shaping the cultural identity of Southeast Asian societies. Moreover, the economic impact of Islamic conquests on indigenous societies cannot be understated. The establishment of trade networks and commercial exchanges facilitated by Islamic rulers helped stimulate economic growth and cultural exchange. The integration of Southeast Asia into the wider Islamic world through trade routes brought wealth, new technologies, and cultural influences to the region. In conclusion, the impact of Islamic conquests on indigenous societies in Southeast Asia was multifaceted, touching upon religious beliefs, social structures, governance systems, cultural practices, and economic dynamics. These changes not only reshaped the fabric of Southeast Asian societies but also contributed to the enduring legacy of Islam in the region.

SPREAD OF ISLAM IN SOUTHEAST ASIA: CONVERSION AND ADAPTATION

The spread of Islam in Southeast Asia was a gradual process that involved both conversion and adaptation to local cultures. Islamic missionaries and traders played a significant role in introducing the religion to the region, with many indigenous societies embracing Islam over time. The diverse cultural landscape of Southeast Asia provided a unique environment for the adoption of Islamic practices, leading to a syncretic blend of local traditions and Islamic beliefs. As Islam spread throughout Southeast Asia, it brought about changes in religious practices, social structures, and governance. Local rulers often embraced Islam as a means of strengthening their political authority and legitimacy. Islamic legal principles, such as the sharia, influenced the legal systems of many societies in the region. One of the key factors that facilitated the spread of Islam in Southeast Asia was its compatibility with existing belief systems. Islamic missionaries often integrated local customs and traditions into their teachings, making the religion more accessible to indigenous populations. This process of cultural adaptation helped Islam take root and flourish in Southeast Asia. The conversion to Islam also had implications for trade and commerce in the region. Muslim traders and merchants established networks that connected Southeast Asia with the larger Islamic world, facilitating the exchange of goods, ideas, and technologies. The economic influence of Islam contributed to the growth of urban centers and the development of commercial hubs. Overall, the spread of Islam in Southeast Asia was a complex and multifaceted process that involved not only religious conversion but also cultural adaptation and integration. The enduring legacy of Islam in the region continues to shape its societies, politics, and identities to this day.

ECONOMIC AND POLITICAL INFLUENCE OF ISLAMIC RULE

The economic and political influence of Islamic rule in Southeast Asia was profound and far-reaching. By establishing Islamic governance and institutions, the rulers of the region were able to leverage economic resources and political power to strengthen their hold over the territories they conquered. Trade networks flourished under Islamic rule, connecting Southeast Asia to the wider Islamic world and facilitating the exchange of goods, ideas, and technologies. Islamic rulers often implemented policies that promoted economic growth and encouraged commerce. They offered incentives for merchants and traders to conduct business within their territories, leading to the development of bustling marketplaces and trading hubs. The introduction of Islamic banking practices also played a crucial role in facilitating financial transactions and fostering economic stability. Furthermore, the political landscape of Southeast Asia underwent significant transformation under Islamic rule. Islamic rulers established centralized governments that exerted control over vast territories and diverse populations. They implemented legal systems based on Islamic principles, which helped to maintain social order and resolve disputes within society. The influence of Islamic rule in Southeast Asia extended beyond economic and political realms. It also had a profound impact on the cultural and social fabric of the region, shaping the beliefs, practices, and identities of its inhabitants. The legacy of Islamic campaigns in Southeast Asia continues to reverberate in the present day, contributing to the region's rich tapestry of diversity and heritage.

LEGACY OF ISLAMIC CAMPAIGNS IN SOUTHEAST ASIA: SHAPING THE REGION'S FUTURE

Islamic conquests in Southeast Asia left a profound legacy that continues to shape the region's future. One of the lasting impacts of Islamic campaigns was the integration of Southeast Asian societies into the broader Islamic world. This integration fostered cultural exchange, religious syncretism, and the spread of Islamic teachings throughout the region. Moreover, the economic influence of Islamic rule in Southeast Asia was significant. Islamic conquests established trade networks, introduced new agricultural practices, and promoted economic development. These economic advancements had a long-lasting effect on the region's prosperity and trade relations with other parts of the world. Additionally, Islamic campaigns in Southeast Asia had a profound impact on the region's political landscape. The establishment of Islamic states and the introduction of Islamic legal systems transformed governance structures and influenced the development of political institutions in the region. The legacy of Islamic rule in Southeast Asia includes the establishment of strong centralized states, the adoption of Islamic legal principles, and the promotion of political stability. Overall, the legacy of Islamic campaigns in Southeast Asia is evident in the region's rich cultural heritage, economic prosperity, and political institutions. The enduring influence of Islamic rule continues to shape the region's future trajectory and position Southeast Asia as a vibrant and dynamic part of the global Islamic community.

INTERACTION OF DIVERSE SOCIETIES WITH ISLAM

The spread of Islam to diverse societies in Southeast Asia is a topic of profound historical significance. This phenomenon represents a fascinating intersection of religion, culture, and trade that has left a lasting impact on the region. By delving into the interactions between Islam and various cultures in Southeast Asia, we can gain valuable insights into the complexities of historical exchange and adaptation.

HISTORICAL CONTEXT

Southeast Asia has a rich history of cultural diversity and exchange, with various societies interacting and influencing each other through trade, migration, and exploration. The spread of Islam to the region was not an isolated event but occurred within a broader historical context of cross-cultural interactions and interconnectedness. Before the arrival of Islam, Southeast Asia was already a vibrant melting pot of diverse ethnicities, languages, and belief systems. Hinduism and Buddhism had established significant footholds in the region, shaping the spiritual and cultural landscape of many societies. The early presence of Islam in Southeast Asia can be traced back to the 9th century when Arab traders and missionaries introduced the tenets of the faith to coastal communities. Over time, Islam gained a foothold in various parts of the region, facilitated by the maritime trade networks that connected Southeast Asia to the wider Islamic world. The gradual adoption of Islam by local rulers and elites further accelerated its spread, establishing Muslim communities and trading hubs along the coastlines and riverine networks. The expansion of Islam in Southeast Asia was not a monolithic process but a complex tapestry of interactions between different cultures and belief systems. Local traditions and practices often blended with Islamic teachings, creating a hybrid cultural landscape that reflected the syncretic nature of Southeast Asian societies. Incorporating Islamic motifs in art, architecture, and literature demonstrated the creative fusion of diverse influences, resulting in unique forms of cultural expression resonating with Islamic and indigenous sensibilities. Furthermore, the economic prosperity and political stability of many Islamic states in Southeast Asia attracted scholars, artisans, and merchants from neighboring regions, further enriching the region's cultural tapestry. The exchange of ideas, technologies, and artistic styles contributed to a flourishing intellectual and artistic environment that reflected the cosmopolitan nature of Islamic societies in Southeast Asia. This era of cultural exchange and diversity laid the foundation for the enduring legacy of Islam in shaping the identity and heritage of Southeast Asian societies.

CULTURAL EXCHANGE

Exploration of how Islamic beliefs and practices intersected with local cultural traditions in Southeast Asia reveals a rich tapestry of cultural exchange. As Islam spread through the region, it encountered diverse indigenous societies with unique customs and beliefs. This interaction gave rise to a dynamic process of cross-cultural fertilization, creating a distinctly Southeast Asian Islamic culture. The syncretism and adaptation that characterized the encounter between Islam and local traditions resulted in a blending of religious practices, artistic expressions, and societal norms. This fusion of influences can be seen in Southeast Asian life, from religious rituals and ceremonies to culinary traditions and architectural styles. The cultural exchange between Islam and indigenous cultures in Southeast Asia enriched the region's heritage and highlighted the flexibility and adaptability of Islamic teachings in diverse sociocultural contexts. One of the notable outcomes of this cultural exchange was the development of a unique hybrid identity among Southeast Asian Muslims, embodying both Islamic principles and indigenous values. This fusion of cultural elements created a harmonious coexistence between Islamic beliefs and local customs, fostering a sense of unity and diversity within the Muslim community in the region. The enduring legacy of this cultural exchange is reflected in the artistic creations, religious practices, and social structures that continue to shape Southeast Asian societies today. Understanding the complexities of cultural exchange between Islam and diverse societies in Southeast Asia provides valuable insights into the dynamics of intercultural relations and the capacity of religions to adapt to different cultural contexts. The interaction between Islamic beliefs and local traditions in Southeast Asia exemplifies the transformative power of cross-cultural encounters, highlighting the capacity of diverse societies to embrace and integrate new ideas while preserving their unique cultural identities.

TRADE AND COMMERCE

Islamic trade networks played a pivotal role in connecting diverse societies in Southeast Asia, fostering economic prosperity and cultural exchange. Muslim merchants, known for their expertise in maritime trade, established commercial links that spanned vast distances, facilitating the flow of goods, ideas, and religious influences across the region. The bustling trade routes not only contributed to the growth of local economies but also served as conduits for the dissemination of Islamic teachings and practices. Through the exchange of commodities such as spices, textiles, and luxury items, Southeast Asian societies became integrated into the broader network of the Islamic world, enriching their own cultural landscape in the process. The presence of Muslim traders in port cities like Malacca, Aceh, and Brunei accelerated economic development and fostered a climate of cosmopolitanism where diverse communities interacted and coexisted harmoniously. The fusion of economic interests with religious and cultural interactions in the realm of trade laid the foundation for enduring connections between Southeast Asia and the Islamic world, profoundly shaping the region's identity and heritage.

RELIGIOUS TOLERANCE

The harmonious coexistence of diverse faith traditions within the region exemplifies religious tolerance in Southeast Asia. The introduction of Islam into Southeast Asian societies did not lead to the suppression of existing beliefs but instead fostered an environment where different religions could thrive alongside each other. This spirit of inclusivity and respect for religious diversity has been a defining feature of the cultural landscape in Southeast Asia. Muslim traders and missionaries in Southeast Asia often engaged in dialogue with adherents of other faiths, promoting mutual understanding and acceptance. The ethos of tolerance extended beyond mere tolerance to encompass respect and appreciation for the spiritual practices of different communities. As a result, Southeast Asian societies developed a rich tapestry of religious traditions, each contributing to the vibrant cultural mosaic of the region. One of the key aspects of religious tolerance in Southeast Asia is the recognition of the interconnectedness of different belief systems. Islam in Southeast Asia has absorbed elements from indigenous religions and practices, leading to the emergence of syncretic forms of worship that blend Islamic teachings with local customs. This process of cultural fusion has reinforced the notion of unity in diversity, emphasizing the shared values and aspirations that transcend religious boundaries. The historical legacy of religious tolerance in Southeast Asia continues to shape the region's social fabric today. Structures of governance and community life reflect a commitment to respecting the rights and freedoms of individuals to practice their faiths without fear of persecution or discrimination. The spirit of religious tolerance serves as a beacon of hope and inspiration, demonstrating that peaceful coexistence among diverse religious communities is possible and enriching for society as a whole.

POLITICAL INFLUENCE

A complex interplay of power dynamics and cultural exchange characterized relations between Southeast Asia's Islamic rulers and indigenous political systems. As Islam spread throughout the region, it often encountered pre-existing political structures that varied widely in their forms of governance and organization. Islamic rulers sought to establish authority in these diverse contexts, adapting their methods to align with local customs and traditions. One of the key strategies Islamic rulers employed was forming alliances with local elites and rulers. By forging partnerships with existing power brokers, Islamic leaders could consolidate their influence and navigate the intricacies of Southeast Asian political landscapes. These alliances enabled the gradual integration of Islamic principles into the governing frameworks of the region, fostering a blend of Islamic governance and indigenous practices. Moreover, Islamic rulers employed diplomacy and negotiation to navigate the complexities of governing diverse societies. By engaging in dialogues with local leaders and communities, they could address conflicting interests and find mutually beneficial solutions. This approach allowed for the preservation of social cohesion and stability, crucial for the long-term sustainability of Islamic rule in Southeast Asia. Additionally, Islamic governance in the region often emphasized principles of justice, equity, and social welfare. Islamic rulers endeavored to uphold the tenets of Islamic law (Sharia) while respecting the customs and traditions of the local population. This balanced approach contributed to establishing socio-political systems that reflected a harmonious coexistence between Islamic values and indigenous practices. Furthermore, the political influence of Islam in Southeast Asia extended beyond formal governance structures to encompass social hierarchies and community relations. Islamic teachings on leadership, accountability, and public service influenced the behavior and responsibilities of rulers and officials, shaping the ethical foundations of political authority in the region. In conclusion, the interaction between Islamic rulers and indigenous political systems in Southeast Asia was marked by a dynamic exchange of ideas, practices, and values. Islamic rulers navigated the complexities of governing diverse societies through strategic alliances, diplomatic engagement, and a commitment to justice and equity, leaving a lasting legacy of political influence that continues to shape the region's socio-political landscape.

ART AND ARCHITECTURE

Islamic aesthetics have left an indelible mark on Southeast Asia's visual landscape, blending local artistry traditions with the distinctive motifs and architectural styles inspired by Islamic culture. The fusion of these influences has resulted in a unique artistic heritage that reflects Islam's spiritual and cultural resonance in the region. From intricately designed mosques to ornate palaces and vibrant textiles, the art and architecture of Southeast Asia bear witness to the creative synthesis of diverse cultural elements. The use of geometric patterns, arabesques, and calligraphy in decorative arts serves an aesthetic purpose and conveys symbolic meanings rooted in Islamic theology and philosophy. Moreover, the architectural marvels of the region, such as the iconic Sultan Omar Ali Saifuddien Mosque in Brunei or the historic Istiqlal Mosque in Indonesia, stand as testaments to the enduring legacy of Islamic architectural principles in Southeast Asia. Through exploring art and architecture, one can gain a profound understanding of the interplay between faith, culture, and creativity that has shaped the visual identity of Southeast Asian societies.

EDUCATION AND SCHOLARSHIP

Exploration of knowledge and scholarship played a pivotal role in disseminating and preserving Islamic intellectual traditions across diverse Southeast Asian societies. Islamic educational institutions served as centers of learning, fostering a rich academic environment that thrived on exchanging ideas and pursuing knowledge. Scholars and teachers from various backgrounds converged in these institutions, contributing to the vibrant intellectual landscape of the region. The scholarly pursuits in Islamic education encompassed a wide range of disciplines, including theology, jurisprudence, philosophy, and the sciences. Students immersed themselves in the study of classical Islamic texts, delving into complex theological debates and legal principles under the guidance of esteemed scholars. The rigorous curriculum emphasized critical thinking, debate, and research, cultivating a cohort of erudite individuals well-versed in the principles of Islamic scholarship. One of the most notable contributions of Southeast Asian scholars to Islamic intellectual heritage was the synthesis of diverse cultural influences with Islamic teachings. This fusion of local traditions with Islamic thought resulted in a unique intellectual discourse that reflected the pluralistic nature of Southeast Asian societies. Scholars engaged in cross-cultural dialogues, drawing parallels between Islamic concepts and indigenous beliefs, thereby enriching the intellectual tapestry of the region. Islamic education in Southeast Asia also played a crucial role in promoting literacy and enlightenment among the populace. Madrasas and educational centers served as pillars of community development, offering opportunities for individuals from all walks of life to access knowledge and enhance their intellectual capabilities. The dissemination of Islamic teachings through educational channels facilitated the spread of Arabic script, enabling a broader segment of the population to engage with religious texts and scholarly works. Moreover, the scholarly activities in Southeast Asia were not limited to religious studies but extended to fields such as astronomy, mathematics, medicine, and literature. Scholars made significant contributions to various branches of knowledge, advancing the frontiers of learning and innovation in the region. Their pursuit of excellence in diverse domains underscored the holistic approach to education embraced by Islamic scholars in Southeast Asia. In conclusion, the legacy of Islamic education and scholarship in Southeast Asia endures as a testament to the enduring impact of knowledge and intellectual inquiry. The vibrant intellectual traditions cultivated by scholars in the region continue to shape contemporary discourses and inspire a new generation of thinkers committed to the pursuit of enlightenment and learning.

SOCIAL CUSTOMS AND PRACTICES

The influence of Islam on the social customs and practices of Southeast Asian societies has been profound and multifaceted. From the ways of daily life to deeply ingrained traditions, the teachings of Islam have played a significant role in shaping the cultural fabric of the region. One of the key aspects of social life influenced by Islamic principles is the emphasis on community and solidarity. The concept of "ummah," or the global community of Muslims, promotes unity and cooperation among believers, fostering a sense of belonging and mutual support. Islamic teachings also impact social interactions and relationships in Southeast Asia. Respect for elders, hospitality, and generosity are values that are emphasized in Islamic teachings and are reflected in the social customs of the region. Traditional practices such as communal feasting during religious celebrations or offering charity to those in need are manifestations of these values. Moreover, the observance of Islamic rituals and practices plays a central role in the social life of Southeast Asian communities. Daily prayers, fasting during Ramadan, and participation in religious festivals create a shared sense of identity and belonging among Muslims in the region. These practices not only strengthen individual faith but also serve as a unifying force that transcends cultural and ethnic boundaries. Islamic principles also influence gender roles and expectations in Southeast Asian societies. While the interpretation and application of these principles may vary, the emphasis on modesty, respect, and family values is evident in social customs and practices. Concepts such as the importance of marriage, the sanctity of the family unit, and the respect for women are deeply rooted in Islamic teachings and have a significant impact on social norms. Furthermore, the influence of Islamic ethics can be seen in business practices, legal systems, and governance structures in Southeast Asia. The principles of honesty, fairness, and justice are integral to Islamic teachings and contribute to the development of a moral framework for social behavior. The establishment of Islamic institutions and organizations dedicated to education, welfare, and charitable activities also reflects the adherence to these ethical values in the region. In conclusion, the social customs and practices influenced by Islam in Southeast Asia are not only a reflection of religious teachings but also a testament to the enduring impact of Islamic culture on the daily lives of individuals and communities. The integration of Islamic values into social norms has created a rich tapestry of traditions and customs that continue to shape the identity and heritage of the region's diverse societies.

LEGACY AND CONTINUITY

The enduring legacy of Islam in Southeast Asia is a testament to the rich tapestry of cultural exchange and religious diffusion that characterized the region's history. As Islamic principles permeated social customs and practices, they became interwoven with the fabric of daily life, shaping the beliefs, traditions, and identities of Southeast Asian societies. From the observance of Islamic rituals to the cultivation of ethical values, the legacy of Islam continues to resonate in the region, transcending temporal boundaries and cultural divides. This continuity serves as a bridge between the past and the present, fostering a sense of connection and belonging among diverse communities. Through the preservation of Islamic heritage and the perpetuation of religious teachings, Southeast Asia remains a vibrant mosaic of faith, culture, and tradition, where the legacy of Islam endures as a source of spiritual guidance, cultural enrichment, and social cohesion.

OBJECTIVES OF ISLAMIC EXPANSION

CONTEXTUALIZING EXPANSION GOALS: AN OVERVIEW OF THE BROADER HISTORICAL CONTEXT THAT DROVE ISLAMIC EXPANSION IN ASIA

The rise of Islam in the 7th century marked the beginning of a new era in world history. With the emergence of the Islamic Caliphate, a powerful political and religious entity, the expansion of Islam into Asia became a defining feature of the time. The historical context that drove Islamic expansion in Asia was shaped by a combination of religious, political, economic, and social factors. Islam, as a monotheistic faith, emphasized the importance of spreading the message of the Prophet Muhammad and establishing Islamic governance in new territories. The concept of Dar al-Islam, the abode of Islam, provided a framework for Muslims to conquer and rule lands to ensure the supremacy of their faith. This religious imperative served as a driving force behind the Islamic conquests in Asia. Politically, the Islamic Caliphate sought to expand its influence and authority beyond the Arabian Peninsula, aiming to establish a unified Islamic state under the leadership of the Caliph. The Caliphs viewed territorial expansion as a means of consolidating their power and asserting their legitimacy as rightful successors to the Prophet. Economically, the trade routes that connected Asia were crucial for the exchange of goods, ideas, and culture. Controlling key trade routes meant access to wealth and resources that could fuel the growth of the Islamic Empire. Expansion into new territories allowed the Caliphate to tap into lucrative markets and strengthen its economic base. Socially, the spread of Islam brought about changes in the social fabric of societies as diverse populations came into contact with the new religion. Conversion to Islam offered opportunities for social mobility and integration into the growing Islamic community, creating a sense of unity among believers from different backgrounds. The historical context of Islamic expansion in Asia was multifaceted, driven by religious fervor, political ambitions, economic interests, and social dynamics. Understanding this broader context is essential for grasping the motivations behind the conquests and the enduring impact of Islamic rule in the region.

RELIGIOUS IMPERATIVES:

EXPLORE THE RELIGIOUS MOTIVATIONS BEHIND THE ISLAMIC CONQUESTS AND THE SPREAD OF ISLAM

A quest for territorial expansion or economic gain did not solely drive Islamic conquests in Asia. Central to the expansion efforts were profound religious imperatives that guided the actions of Muslim armies and leaders. The spread of Islam was intricately linked to the military campaigns of the Islamic Caliphate, with religious motivations playing a pivotal role in shaping the course of history. At the core of the Islamic conquests was the belief in the divine mandate to spread the message of Islam to all corners of the world. Muslims viewed themselves as bearers of a universal truth, tasked with bringing the teachings of the Prophet Muhammad to non-believers. Converting infidels to Islam was considered a sacred duty, and military conquests were seen as a means to fulfill this religious obligation. The concept of jihad, often misunderstood in modern times, played a significant role in motivating Muslim armies during the conquests. Jihad, in its true essence, refers to the struggle or striving in the way of God. For early Muslims, this struggle included both internal spiritual development and external defense of the faith. The military expeditions into new territories were seen as a form of defensive jihad aimed at protecting the Muslim community and spreading the message of Islam. Furthermore, the expansion of Islam was perceived as a way to establish divine justice and morality in conquered lands. Islamic law, known as Sharia, governed all aspects of life for Muslims, including political, social, and economic matters. Conquering new territories allowed for the implementation of Sharia and the establishment of Islamic governance based on religious principles. The concept of dar al-Islam, the "abode of Islam," also played a crucial role in the Islamic conquests. Muslims sought to expand the boundaries of dar al-Islam, where Islamic law prevailed, and bring more people under the spiritual and political authority of the Caliphate. Conquering new territories was viewed as a way to extend the reach of Islam and create a more unified Muslim community. In summary, the religious imperatives behind the Islamic conquests in Asia were deeply rooted in the faith and beliefs of early Muslims. The spread of Islam was seen as a sacred duty driven by the desire to uphold divine truth, establish justice, and strengthen the Muslim community. Religious motivations not only shaped the military strategies of the Islamic Caliphate but also influenced the broader historical legacy of Islamic expansion in Asia.

STRATEGIC OBJECTIVES:

DISCUSS THE STRATEGIC GOALS THE ISLAMIC CALIPHATE AIMED TO ACHIEVE THROUGH EXPANSION INTO NEW TERRITORIES

The strategic objectives of the Islamic Caliphate in expanding into new territories were multi-faceted and interconnected. One of the primary goals was to spread the message of Islam to regions beyond the Arabian Peninsula, fulfilling the religious mandate to establish the faith worldwide. By conquering new lands, the Caliphate aimed to ensure the dominance and prevalence of Islam, thereby fulfilling its religious mission. Strategically, expansion into new territories also allowed the Islamic Caliphate to secure valuable trade routes and access to key resources. Control over trade routes facilitated economic growth and prosperity, enabling the Caliphate to strengthen its economic power and influence in the region. Additionally, the conquest of resource-rich territories provided the Caliphate with essential raw materials and commodities to sustain its growing empire. Furthermore, expansion into new territories allowed the Islamic Caliphate to establish political dominance and extend its authority over a wider geographical area. By conquering and governing new lands, the Caliphate aimed to consolidate its control and influence diverse populations, strengthening its political legitimacy and power. Military conquests were instrumental in achieving these strategic objectives, as they enabled the Caliphate to subdue rival powers, establish control over key territories, and expand its sphere of influence. Through a combination of military prowess, diplomacy, and strategic alliances, the Caliphate sought to achieve its expansion goals and solidify its position as a dominant force in the region. Overall, the strategic objectives of the Islamic Caliphate in expanding into new territories were rooted in religious, economic, political, and military considerations. By pursuing these objectives, the Caliphate aimed to promote the spread of Islam, secure valuable resources and trade routes, establish political dominance, and strengthen its empire, ultimately shaping the course of history in Asia.

ECONOMIC AMBITIONS:

THE ECONOMIC FACTORS THAT INFLUENCED ISLAMIC EXPANSION, SUCH AS TRADE ROUTES AND ACCESS TO RESOURCES

Economic Ambitions: The economic factors played a pivotal role in shaping the Islamic expansion into new territories across Asia. The quest for access to valuable resources, trade routes, and economic dominance motivated the Caliphate to extend its influence beyond existing borders. The expansion into regions rich in natural resources, such as Persia's fertile lands and China's advanced agricultural practices, offered the potential for economic prosperity and growth. Trade routes, including the Silk Road and maritime networks in Southeast Asia, provided avenues for economic expansion and connection with distant regions. Controlling key trade arteries allowed the Caliphate to assert its dominance over lucrative markets and establish commercial hubs that facilitated the exchange of goods, ideas, and technologies. Moreover, the desire to secure access to strategic resources, such as spices, silk, and precious metals, fueled the Islamic conquests. By dominating resource-rich regions, the Caliphate sought to strengthen its economic power and enhance its capacity for trade and commerce. The conquest of territories with abundant natural wealth also bolsters the Caliphate's economic self-sufficiency and reduced reliance on external sources—furthermore, the economic ambitions behind Islamic expansion extended beyond mere material gain. The Caliphate aimed to exert influence over regional economies, establish economic alliances, and foster economic growth within its domains by controlling vital economic centers and trade routes. Economic considerations thus intertwined with strategic and political objectives, shaping the broader goals of the Islamic conquests in Asia.

POLITICAL CONSIDERATIONS:

THE POLITICAL RATIONALE BEHIND EXPANDING THE REACH OF THE CALIPHATE AND ESTABLISHING GOVERNANCE IN CONQUERED LANDS

Political considerations were crucial in expanding the Islamic Caliphate into new territories. The Caliphate's quest for political dominance and governance was a key driving force behind its military campaigns and conquests in Asia. By expanding its reach and establishing control over vast regions, the Caliphate sought to exert its political authority and solidify its influence in the conquered lands. One of the primary political objectives of the Caliphate was to establish a centralized system of governance that would ensure the unity and cohesion of the newly conquered territories. The Caliphate aimed to maintain law and order, collect taxes, and enforce its political authority over the diverse populations inhabiting the conquered lands by appointing governors and administrators. Furthermore, political considerations also played a crucial role in the Caliphate's efforts to expand its sphere of influence and counter rival political powers in the region. The Caliphate aimed to project its political power and challenge the authority of competing empires and kingdoms by conquering new territories and establishing control over strategic locations. The political rationale behind the expansion of the Caliphate was not solely motivated by territorial conquest but also by a desire to spread Islamic governance and establish a unified political system guided by Islamic principles. The Caliphate sought to integrate the conquered regions into a larger political framework guided by religious and political unity through the imposition of Islamic law and administration. Overall, the political considerations driving the expansion of the Islamic Caliphate in Asia were multifaceted, encompassing the need to assert political authority, establish governance structures, counter rival powers, and promote Islamic principles of unity and solidarity. These political ambitions shaped the Caliphate's military campaigns and conquests, lasting and impacting the political landscape of the regions they conquered.

SOCIAL INFLUENCE:

DISCUSS HOW THE EXPANSION OF ISLAM AIMED TO INFLUENCE AND TRANSFORM SOCIAL STRUCTURES AND NORMS IN NEWLY CONQUERED REGIONS

Islamic expansion into new territories went beyond establishing political control; it aimed to influence and transform social structures and norms in the newly conquered regions. This social influence was crucial to the Caliphate's expansion strategy, as it sought to create a cohesive society based on Islamic principles. One way that Islam influenced social structures was through the promotion of monotheism and the eradication of polytheistic beliefs. The spread of Islam often led to the conversion of local populations, reshaping their religious practices and social customs.

This religious transformation played a significant role in unifying diverse communities under a common faith and cultural identity. Additionally, Islamic expansion changed social hierarchies and gender roles in conquered regions. Islamic teachings emphasize the equality of all believers before God, regardless of their social status or background. This egalitarian ethos challenged existing social norms and promoted a more inclusive society where merit and piety were valued over traditional markers of privilege. Furthermore, the expansion of Islam facilitated cultural exchange and the assimilation of diverse traditions into the newly established Islamic societies. This cultural fusion enriched artistic expressions, architectural styles, culinary practices, and linguistic developments, creating a vibrant tapestry of cultural diversity within the Caliphate's domains. Overall, the social influence of Islamic expansion was multifaceted, encompassing religious transformation, social reorganization, and cultural exchange. By guiding societal norms and values towards Islamic principles, the Caliphate aimed to create a cohesive and harmonious social fabric that facilitated governance and enabled a distinct Islamic civilization to flourish in the conquered territories.

CULTURAL EXCHANGE:

THE ROLE OF CULTURAL EXCHANGE AND ASSIMILATION IN THE ISLAMIC EXPANSION, INCLUDING THE SPREAD OF KNOWLEDGE AND ARTISTIC TRADITIONS

As Islamic armies expanded into new territories, they encountered diverse cultures and societies, significantly exchanging ideas and practices. Cultural exchange played a crucial role in shaping the identity of the Islamic Caliphate and influencing the societies it conquered. One of the key aspects of cultural exchange was the spread of knowledge across different regions. Islamic scholars and intellectuals traveled to newly conquered lands, bringing a wealth of scientific, mathematical, and philosophical knowledge. This exchange of knowledge enriched the intellectual landscape of the conquered territories and contributed to the advancement of Islamic civilization as a whole. Artistic traditions also played a vital role in cultural exchange during the expansion of Islam. The Islamic rulers patronized artists and craftsmen from various regions, leading to the fusion of different artistic styles and techniques. This cross-cultural fertilization created new art forms and architectural styles that reflected the synthesis of diverse cultural influences. Furthermore, the Islamic Caliphate's policy of religious tolerance allowed for the preservation and integration of local artistic traditions into the broader Islamic artistic heritage. The exchange of artistic practices enriched the conquered territories' cultural landscape and facilitated a mutual understanding and appreciation of different artistic expressions. In essence, cultural exchange and assimilation were integral to expanding Islamic culture, contributing to the flourishing of knowledge, art, and culture across newly conquered regions.

MILITARY TACTICS:

THE MILITARY STRATEGIES EMPLOYED TO FULFILL THE EXPANSION OBJECTIVES, INCLUDING BATTLES, SIEGES, AND ALLIANCES

Striking a balance between military might and strategic diplomacy, the Islamic expansion into Asia was characterized by sophisticated military tactics. Commanders adeptly utilized offensive and defensive strategies to achieve their expansion objectives. One key military tactic employed during the Islamic conquests was effectively using cavalry forces. Arab cavalry units, known for their speed and agility, played a crucial role in swift and decisive military campaigns. By leveraging the mobility of cavalry units, Islamic armies could outmaneuver their opponents and launch surprise attacks, often catching enemy forces off guard. In addition to cavalry, Islamic armies also strategically used siege warfare to subdue fortified cities and strongholds. Skilled engineers and siege specialists were instrumental in constructing siege engines such as catapults and trebuchets, which enabled the besieging forces to breach defensive walls and gain entry into enemy territories. Siege warfare tactics were crucial in overcoming well-fortified obstacles and capturing key strategic locations. Furthermore, alliances with local tribes and factions were key to the Islamic expansion strategy. By forging alliances with indigenous groups, Islamic commanders could leverage local knowledge, resources, and manpower to bolster their military campaigns. These alliances provided added strength to the Islamic armies and facilitated smoother integration into conquered territories by gaining the support of local populations. Another critical military tactic employed by Islamic forces was using naval power to control maritime trade routes and project military force across seas. Naval fleets were instrumental in securing coastal territories, conducting amphibious operations, and enforcing maritime dominance in regions where land-based campaigns were not viable. Overall, the military tactics employed during the Islamic expansion into Asia reflected a combination of strategic planning, battlefield prowess, and diplomatic finesse. Through a nuanced approach to warfare encompassing cavalry tactics, siege warfare, alliances, and naval power, Islamic armies overcame diverse challenges and achieved their expansion objectives with remarkable success.

THE ISLAMIC CONQUESTS IN ASIA

RESHAPING BORDERS:

HOW THE ISLAMIC EXPANSION ALTERED GEOPOLITICAL BOUNDARIES AND RESHAPED THE MAP OF ASIA

The Islamic expansion across Asia during the medieval period profoundly impacted the geopolitical landscape, reshaping borders and redefining regional power dynamics. Through military conquests and strategic alliances, the Islamic Caliphate extended its reach and influence, significantly altering the map of Asia. The conquests established new political entities, forged connections between diverse cultures, and laid the foundation for enduring legacies that continue to shape the region today. One of the most striking aspects of the Islamic expansion was the redrawing of borders, as territories once ruled by different empires and kingdoms came under the umbrella of Islamic governance. The conquest of Persia, for example, brought vast swathes of land under Islamic control, leading to the incorporation of Persian territories into the expanding Caliphate. Similarly, the subjugation of the Indian subcontinent resulted in the establishment of Islamic dynasties and the integration of Indian territories into the larger Islamic world. These border adjustments were not merely lines on a map; they represented the fusion of diverse cultures, languages, and traditions under the banner of Islam. The exchange of ideas, technologies, and artistic influences that occurred as a result of these territorial expansions enriched the region's cultural landscape and fostered a climate of intellectual and artistic flourishing. Furthermore, the reshaping of borders through Islamic conquests had lasting implications for the political and economic structures of the conquered territories. New administrative systems, trade networks, and cities flourished as centers of commerce and scholarship. Integrating diverse regions into the Islamic Caliphate created a sense of shared identity and belonging among the inhabitants, laying the groundwork for developing a distinct Islamic civilization across Asia. As these new boundaries solidified and the Caliphate consolidated its control over vast territories, the long-term impact of the Islamic expansion became apparent. The legacy of this period can be seen in the cultural, political, and religious traditions that continue to shape the modern Middle East and beyond. Shaping borders and establishing a transregional Islamic empire left an indelible mark on the region, influencing its history and development for centuries.

LONG-TERM IMPACT:

THE LASTING IMPACT OF THE ISLAMIC EXPANSION ON THE REGIONS CONQUERED AND THE BROADER HISTORICAL LEGACY OF THIS PERIOD

The Islamic expansion across Asia had a profound and enduring impact on the conquered regions. One of the most significant legacies of this period was the transformation of existing societies, cultures, and political structures. With the establishment of Islamic governance in these territories, new systems of administration, law, and social organization emerged, blending local customs with Islamic principles. The spread of Islam also brought about a cultural renaissance in many of the conquered regions. Art, architecture, literature, and scholarship flourished under Islamic patronage, creating vibrant and diverse cultural hubs. The exchange of ideas and knowledge between different civilizations enriched the intellectual landscape of Asia and paved the way for innovations in various fields. Furthermore, the Islamic expansion had a lasting impact on the religious landscape of the conquered territories. While some regions fully embraced Islam as their dominant faith, others retained their religious practices, leading to a diverse religious tapestry in the newly conquered lands. This religious pluralism fostered tolerance and coexistence among different religious communities, laying the foundation for a harmonious society. From a geopolitical perspective, the Islamic expansion reshaped the map of Asia, redrawing borders and establishing new political entities. The Caliphate's territorial acquisitions and strategic alliances solidified its influence in key regions, shaping the balance of power in the continent for centuries to come. The legacy of these territorial changes continues to influence modern-day borders and diplomatic relations in Asia. Overall, the Islamic expansion left a profound and multifaceted legacy on the regions it conquered, shaping the cultural, social, political, and religious landscape of Asia in enduring ways. The fusion of diverse traditions, the exchange of knowledge, and the establishment of new political structures were all part of the transformative impact of Islamic expansion on the continent, leaving a lasting imprint on the history of Asia.

NOTES AND REFERENCES

The Islamic expansion into Southeast Asia was a gradual process that occurred over several centuries, beginning around the 8th-9th centuries and intensifying in the 13th-16th centuries. Here are some key aspects of this historical development:

1. Early Contacts and Trade (8th-13th centuries):

Muslim traders from Arabia, Persia and India began visiting ports in Southeast Asia as early as the 8th century("The World of Southeast Asia: Selected Historical Readings," 1968; Tichelman, 1980). These early contacts were primarily for trade purposes, with Islam slowly being introduced through commercial interactions(Gallop, 2020). The maritime trade routes connecting the Middle East, India, and China passed through Southeast Asian waters, facilitating cultural and religious exchanges(Faiz & Fadlan, 2022).

2. Establishment of Muslim Communities (13th-15th centuries):

By the 13th-14th centuries, there is evidence of indigenous Muslim communities forming in parts of Southeast Asia(Bradley, 2015). The first areas to see significant Islamic influence were coastal trading ports in Sumatra, Java, and the Malay Peninsula(Gallop, 2020). Muslim merchants settled in these areas, intermarrying with locals and gradually spreading Islamic teachings.

3. Conversion of Rulers and State Formation (14th-16th centuries):

A major turning point came when local rulers began converting to Islam, often for political and economic advantages(Gallop, 2020). The Sultanate of Malacca, founded in the early 15th century, became a key center for

Islamic learning and propagation in the region(Faiz & Fadlan, 2022). Other important early Islamic states included Aceh in Sumatra and Demak in Java.

4. Methods of Islamization:

The spread of Islam in Southeast Asia was largely peaceful, characterized by gradual adoption rather than conquest(Gallop, 2020; Ng, 2015). Key methods included:

- Trade and intermarriage between Muslim merchants and local populations
- Sufi missionaries who adapted Islamic teachings to local contexts
- The appeal of Islamic egalitarianism and social mobility to lower classes
- Adoption by ruling elites seeking legitimacy and trade connections

5. Characteristics of Southeast Asian Islam:

Islam in Southeast Asia developed unique characteristics due to its interaction with pre-existing local beliefs and cultures(Gallop, 2020; Ng, 2015):

- Syncretic practices blending Islamic and indigenous traditions
- Less emphasis on strict adherence to Islamic law compared to the Middle East
- Importance of Sufi mysticism and saint veneration
- Use of local languages like Malay for Islamic literature (Kitab Jawi tradition)(Bellwood, 2022)

6. Geographic Spread:

By the 16th century, Islam had become the dominant religion in coastal areas of Sumatra, Java, the Malay Peninsula, and parts of the southern Philippines(Faiz & Fadlan, 2022). It spread more slowly to inland areas and other islands. Some regions, like Bali and parts of the Philippines, remained largely non-Muslim.

7. Impact on Society and Culture:

The Islamization process had profound effects on Southeast Asian societies(Gallop, 2020; Ng, 2015):

- Introduction of Arabic script and Islamic literature
- Development of new political structures (sultanates)
- Changes in legal systems with the adoption of aspects of Islamic law
- New artistic and architectural styles influenced by Islamic traditions
- Strengthened connections with the wider Islamic world

8. Challenges to Islamization:

The expansion of Islam faced some obstacles and competing influences:

- Resistance from Hindu-Buddhist kingdoms, especially in inland areas
- Arrival of European colonial powers from the 16th century onward
- Christian missionary activities in some regions

9. Continued Evolution:

The process of Islamization in Southeast Asia has continued into modern times, with ongoing debates about the role of Islam in society and politics(Bradley, 2015). There have been movements towards both greater orthodoxy and liberal interpretations of Islam in different parts of the region.

In conclusion, the Islamic expansion into Southeast Asia was a complex, long-term process that significantly shaped the region's religious, cultural, and political landscape. It was characterized by peaceful spread through trade and cultural interaction, resulting in a distinctive form of Islam that blended with local traditions. This history continues to influence contemporary Southeast Asian societies and their relationships with the broader Islamic world.

Bibliography:

Adshead, S. (1993). The Mongolian Explosion and the Basic Information Circuit, 1200–1300. 53–77.
Aljunied, K. (2021). Bringing Rationality Back: Harun Nasution and the Burden of Muslim Thought in Twentieth-Century Southeast Asia. Journal of Islamic and Muslim Studies, 6, 29–55.
Aljunied, K. (2022). Shapers of Islam in Southeast Asia.
Architect, D., & Awwad, B. A. (2017). The development of the Islamic Heritage in Southeast Asia tradition and future Case study-Mosque Architecture in Malaysia Classification of Styles and Possible Influences.

Azis, A., Amalina, S. N., & Azharotunnafi, A. (2021). Islamic Historical Studies: The Beginning of the Emergence of Islam and the Development of Islamic Culture in Southeast Asia. Riwayat: Educational Journal of History and Humanities.

Azyumardi, A. (2015). The Significance of Southeast Asia (the Jawah World) for Global Islamic Studies: Historical and Comparative Perspectives. 8, 69–87.

Bakar, O. (2010). Islam and the Three Waves of Globalisation: The Southeast Asian Experience. ICR Journal.

Bayona, J. (2023). John T. Sidel. 2021. Republicanism, Communism, Islam: Cosmopolitan Origins of Revolution in Southeast Asia. Ithaca: Cornell University Press. 324 pp. ISBN 9781501755613. Estudios de Asia y África.

Bellwood, P. (2022). The Expansion of Farmers into Island Southeast Asia. The Oxford Handbook of Early Southeast Asia.

Bose, N. (2022). Empire of Convicts: Indian Penal Labor in Colonial Southeast Asia by Anand Yang (review). Journal of World History, 33, 703–706.

Bradley, F. R. (2014). Islamic Reform, the Family, and Knowledge Networks Linking Mecca to Southeast Asia in the Nineteenth Century. The Journal of Asian Studies, 73, 89–111.

Bradley, F. R. (2015). Forging Islamic power and place: the legacy of Shaykh Dā'ūd bin 'Abd Allāh al-Faṭānī in Mecca and Southeast Asia.

Bradley, F. R. (2021). Women, Violence, and Gender Dynamics during and after the Five Patani-Siam Wars, 1785–1838. Itinerario: International Journal on the History of European Expansion and Global Interaction, 45, 345–363.

Burhanudin, J. (2022a). The Popularizing of Sunni Doctrine In Southeast Asia: Sifat Dua Puluh in Malay Kitab Jawi of the 19th Century. Ulumuna.

Burhanudin, J. (2022b). Two Islamic Writing Traditions in Southeast Asia: Kitab Jawi and Kitab Kuning with Reference to the Works of Da'ud al-Fatani dan Nawawi al-Bantani. Al-Jami'ah: Journal of Islamic Studies.

Cochrane, E., Rieth, T. M., & Filimoehala, D. (2021). The first quantitative assessment of radiocarbon chronologies for initial pottery in Island Southeast Asia supports multi-directional Neolithic dispersal. PLoS ONE, 16.

Doran, C. (2022). The Whore and the Madonna: The Ambivalent Positionings of Women in British Imperial Histories on Southeast Asia. Histories.

Fadhil, H. M. (2024). Rethinking Islamization in Southeast Asia: Historical Dynamics, Distinction and Existence of Muslim. Journal of Modern Islamic Studies and Civilization.

Faiz, F. F., & Fadlan, M. (2022). Wasaṭīyah Islam: Traditions and Challenges in Southeast Asia. STUDIA ISLAMIKA.

Falarti, M. M. (2012). Malay Kingship in Kedah: Religion, Trade, and Society.

Feeny, D. (1996). International Commercial Rivalry in Southeast Asia in the Interwar Period. Edited by Shinya Sugiyama and Milagros C. Guerrero. New Haven: Monograph 39/Yale Southeast Asia Studies, Yale Center for International and Area Studies, 1994. Pp. x, 222. Journal Economic History, 56, 251–252.

Formichi, C. (2016). Islamic Studies or Asian Studies? Islam in Southeast Asia. Muslim World, 106, 696–718.

Gallop, A. T. (2020). Shifting Landscapes: Remapping The Writing Traditions of Islamic Southeast Asia through Digitisation. Jurnal Humaniora.

Gedacht, J. (2019). Port Cities and Islamic Insurgency across Southeast Asia, 1850–1913. Oxford Research Encyclopedia of Asian History.

Green, N. (2019). The Persianate World: The Frontiers of a Eurasian Lingua Franca.

Habibi, Z. (2018). Islamic Modernities in Southeast Asia: Exploring Indonesian Popular and Visual Culture, by Leonie Schmidt. Bijdragen Tot de Taal-, Land- En Volkenkunde.

Hall, K. R. (2015). European Southeast Asia Encounters with Islamic Expansionism, circa 1500–1700: Comparative Case Studies of Banten, Ayutthaya, and Banjarmasin in the Wider Indian Ocean Context. Journal of World History, 25, 229–262.

Heitzman, J., & Schenkluhn, W. (2004). The world in the year 1000.

Higham, C. (2022a). Social Change in Southeast Asia during the Iron Age. The Oxford Handbook of Early Southeast Asia.

Higham, C. (2022b). The Neolithic of Mainland Southeast Asia. The Oxford Handbook of Early Southeast Asia.

Higham, C. (2023). The Bronze Age and Southeast Asia. Old World: Journal of Ancient Africa and Eurasia.

Hoesterey, J. (2022). Globalization and Islamic Indigenization in Southeast Asian Muslim Communities. ISLAM NUSANTARA Journal for Study of Islamic History and Culture.

Howell, J. (2014). Revitalised Sufism and the new piety movements in Islamic Southeast Asia. 290–306.

Ibrahim, A. (2022). Theology of Culture in Muslim Southeast Asia. ISLAM NUSANTARA Journal for Study of Islamic History and Culture.

Intajalle, F. M., Abdullah, L., & Islam, A. P. (2015). HUKUM PUSAKA ISLAM DI ASIA TENGGARA: KAJIAN DI SINGAPURA (Islamic Inheritance Law in Southeast Asia: Study in Singapore).

Joll, C. M. (2012). Indic, Islamic and Thai Influences. 25–60.

Kaptein, N. (2021). Malay Seals from the Islamic World of Southeast Asia: Content, Form, Context, Catalogue, by Annabel Teh Gallop. Bijdragen Tot de Taal-, Land- En Volkenkunde / Journal of the Humanities and Social Sciences of Southeast Asia.

Kayadibi, S. (2018). Ottoman Connections to the Malay World: Islam, Law and Society.

Kian, K. H. (2015). The Expansion of Chinese Inter-Insular and Hinterland Trade in Southeast Asia, c. 1400–1850. 149–165.

Lieberman, V. (2009). Integration Under Expanding Inner Asian Influence, II. 631–762.

Michael, J. A. (2024). Introduction: Centering Islamic Studies in Asia. International Journal of Islam in Asia.

Morawski, K. (2014). Islamic ornamental motifs in Indonesia. Art of the Orient.

Morgan, D., & Reid, A. (2010). The eastern Islamic world, eleventh to eighteenth centuries.

Nanji, A., & Ruthven, M. (2004). Historical Atlas of the Islamic World.

Ng, S. (2015). Speaking Transnationally: Early Modern European Linguistic Exchanges with Islamic Southeast Asia. 48, 289–313.

Ng, S. (2019). Islamic Alexanders in Southeast Asia. Alexander the Great from Britain to Southeast Asia.

Nor, M. (2015). ZAPIN AS RITUALIZED DHIKR: SILENT REMEMBRANCE OF GOD THROUGH MUSIC AND DANCE. Journal of Southeast Asian Studies, 20, 199–208.

Nurbaiti. (2020). Islamic Education: The Main Path of Islamization in Southeast Asia. Jurnal Pendidikan Islam, 8, 345–374.

Ōhashi, Y., & Orchiston, W. (2021). The Evolution of Local Southeast Asian Astronomy and the Influence of China, India, the Islamic World and the West. Historical & Cultural Astronomy.

Peletz, M. (2022). Islamic Courts, Gender, and the 'Conservative Turn' in Muslim Southeast Asia. Routledge Handbook of Islam in Southeast Asia.

Puckett, E. E., & Munshi-South, J. (2018). Brown rat demography reveals pre-commensal structure in eastern Asia prior to expansion into Southeast Asia. bioRxiv.

Puckett, E. E., & Munshi-South, J. (2019). Brown rat demography reveals pre-commensal structure in eastern Asia before expansion into Southeast Asia. Genome Research, 29, 762–770.

Riddell, P. (2019). Schools of Islamic Thought in Southeast Asia.

Rispoli, F. (2022). The Expansion of Rice and Millet Farmers into Southeast Asia. The Oxford Handbook of Early Southeast Asia.

Ruane, C. (2023). Imperial Gateway: Colonial Taiwan and Japan's Expansion in South China and Southeast Asia, 1895–1945. Asian Affairs, 54, 614–615.

Sacks, B., Brown, S., Stephens, D., Pedersen, N., Wu, J.-T., & Berry, O. (2013). Y chromosome analysis of dingoes and southeast asian village dogs suggests a neolithic continental expansion from Southeast Asia followed by multiple Austronesian dispersals. Molecular Biology and Evolution, 30 5, 1103–1118.

Sajed, A. (2015). Insurrectional Politics in Colonial Southeast Asia: Colonial Modernity, Islamic 'Counterplots', and Translocal (Anti-colonial) Connectivity. Globalizations, 12, 899–912.

Sarwan, M. E. K. Y. (2020). AL-IMAM MAGAZINE (1906-1908): THE STUDY OF KAUM MUDA S THOUGHT ON ISLAMIC EDUCATION RENEWAL IN SOUTHEAST ASIA. 7, 499–503.

Sato, T. (2015). 1 The Origin and Expansion of Sugar Production in the Islamic World. 54, 15–32.

Schmidt, L. (2017). Islamic Modernities in Southeast Asia: Exploring Indonesian Popular and Visual Culture.

Schottenhammer, A. (2021). Consolidating Southeast Asia and the Meaning of Force in History: Pax Ming and the Case of Chen Zuyi ◊◊◊. China and Asia.

Schwartz, K. L. (2022). The City and the Wilderness: Indo-Persian Encounters in Southeast Asia. Arash Khazeni (Oakland, CA: California University Press, 2020). Pp. 264. 85.00 (Hardcover), 29.95 (Paperback) ISBN: 9780520289680. Iran Studies, 55, 820–821.

Sevea, T. (2024). Keramat: Muḥammad's Heirs and Nodes of a Multi-Centered Islam in Southeast Asia. International Journal of Islam in Asia.

Shirane, S. (2014). Mediated Empire: Colonial Taiwan in Japan's Imperial Expansion in South China and Southeast Asia, 1895-1945.

Siddique, S. (1980). Contemporary Islamic Developments In Asean. Southeast Asian Affairs, 1980, 78–90.

Singh, B., & Ramakrishna, K. (2016). Islamic State's Wilayah Philippines: Implications for Southeast Asia.

Slater, D. (2023). BOOK REVIEW: Republicanism, Communism, Islam: Cosmopolitan Origins of Revolution in Southeast Asia, by John T. Sidel. Journal of Social Issues in Southeast Asia.

Sugiyama, A. (2021). Malay Seals from the Islamic World of Southeast Asia: Content, Form, Context, Catalogue by Annabel Teh Gallop (review). Journal of the Malaysian Branch of the Royal Asiatic Society, 93, 251–253.

Sulistiyono, S. T., Masruroh, N. N., & Rochwulaningsih, Y. (2018). Contest For Seascape: Local Thalassocracies and Sino-Indian Trade Expansion in the Maritime Southeast Asia During the Early Premodern Period. Journal of Marine and Island Cultures.

Suraprasit, K., Shoocongdej, R., Chintakanon, K., & Bocherens, H. (2021). Late Pleistocene human paleoecology in the highland savanna ecosystem of mainland Southeast Asia. Scientific Reports, 11.

The world of Southeast Asia: selected historical readings. (1968). Journal of Asian Studies, 27, 676–677.

Tichelman, F. (1980). Indianized Southeast Asia: Similarities and Differences. 51–63.

Vallée, F., Luciani, A., & Cox, M. (2016). Reconstructing Demography and Social Behavior During the Neolithic Expansion from Genomic Diversity Across Island Southeast Asia. Genetics, 204, 1495–1506.

Wink, A. (1988). III. 'Al-Hind' India and Indonesia in the Islamic World-Economy, c. 700–1800 A.D. Itinerario: International Journal on the History of European Expansion and Global Interaction, 12, 33–72.

Wink, A. (1991). Al-Hind, the Making of the Indo-Islamic World.

Wink, A. (1999). The slave kings and the Islamic conquest 11th-13th centuries. Journal of Asian Studies, 58, 887–888.

Yahaya, N. (2020). Conclusion. Fluid Jurisdictions.

Yahya, F. (2021). Illustrated and Illuminated Manuscripts of the Dalāil al-khayrāt from Southeast Asia. Journal of Islamic Manuscripts.

Yegar, M. (2002). Between Integration and Secession: The Muslim Communities of the Southern Philippines, Southern Thailand, and Western Burma/Myanmar.

Yusuf, I. (2010). Islam and Buddhism Relations from Balkh to Bangkok and Tokyo. Muslim World, 100, 177–186.

Zuraidi, E., Caisarina, I., & Fuady, Z. (2020). The Islamic public space concept in the Southeast Asia region as a friendly urban design and planning enlightening. IOP Conference Series: Earth and Environment, 452.

Online

An overview of the Islamic expansion into Southeast Asia, along with some key sources and references:

1. Overview of Islamic Expansion in Southeast Asia:

Unlike in other regions, Islam spread to Southeast Asia primarily through trade and peaceful conversion rather than military conquest. The process was gradual, beginning around the 13th century and continuing over several centuries.

Key points:
- Islam first arrived in Southeast Asia through Arab and Persian traders in the 8th-9th centuries, but major conversions didn't begin until the 13th-15th centuries [1][4][6].
- The first evidence of local rulers converting to Islam dates to the late 13th century in northern Sumatra [4][10].
- Major centers of early Islamic influence included Pasai and Aceh in Sumatra, and later Malacca on the Malay Peninsula [8][10].
- Islam spread from coastal trading ports to inland areas over time [4][6].
- By the 15th-16th centuries, Islam had become the dominant religion in many parts of maritime Southeast Asia, including much of modern Indonesia and Malaysia [4][6].

2. Key Sources and References:
- Anthony Reid's works, including "The Spread of Islam in Southeast Asia c.1275-c.1625" [10]
- "The New Cambridge History of Islam" edited by Anthony Reid and David Morgan [8]
- "Islam in Southeast Asia to c. 1800" by R. Michael Feener [8]
- "A History of Islamic Societies" by Ira M. Lapidus [1]
- "The Formation of Islam" by Jonathan Berkey [1]
- "Southeast Asia in World History" by Craig A. Lockard [2]

3. Academic Perspectives:
Scholars emphasize that the Islamization of Southeast Asia was a complex, gradual process involving trade, Sufi missionaries, intermarriage, and the conversion of local rulers [4][6][10]. The process varied across different regions and time periods.

4. Primary Sources:
- Tombstones and inscriptions, like the 13th century gravestone of Sultan Malik al-Salih in Sumatra [4][6]
- Accounts by travelers like Marco Polo (late 13th century) and Ibn Battuta (14th century) [4][8]
- Local chronicles and texts from various Southeast Asian kingdoms [8]

When using these sources, it's important to note that the term "conquest" is generally not applicable to Southeast Asia's Islamization process, as it was largely peaceful and driven by trade and cultural exchange rather than military campaigns.

Citations:
[1] https://en.wikipedia.org/wiki/Spread_of_Islam

[2] https://worldhistoryconnected.press.uillinois.edu/17.3/Hawkley.html
[3] https://en.wikipedia.org/wiki/Islam_in_Southeast_Asia
[4] https://www.trtworld.com/magazine/how-islam-came-to-dominate-indonesia-39182
[5] https://factsanddetails.com/world/cat55/3sub2/entry-5224.html
[6] https://en.unesco.org/silkroad/content/did-you-know-spread-islam-southeast-asia-through-trade-routes
[7] https://openresearch-repository.anu.edu.au/bitstream/1885/143664/3/01%20Reid%20Anthony%20The%20Islamization%20of%20Southeast%20Asia%201984.pdf
[8] https://oxfordre.com/asianhistory/display/10.1093/acrefore/9780190277727.001.0001/acrefore-9780190277727-e-40
[9] https://www.everycrsreport.com/reports/RS21903.html
[10] https://mei.nus.edu.sg/publication/insight-55-the-spread-of-islam-in-southeast-asia-c-1275-c-1625/
[11] https://www.cambridge.org/core/books/abs/new-cambridge-history-of-islam/early-muslim-expansion-in-southeast-asia-eighth-to-fifteenth-centuries/CEF0A1F80C5A6FA3616B027C2980F78F
[12] https://sites.asiasociety.org/education/islam_in_seasia/essays-chronology.htm

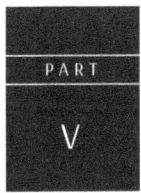

THE CHALLENGES OF CONQUERING CHINA

OVERVIEW OF CHINA'S STRATEGIC IMPORTANCE IN THE ISLAMIC EXPANSION

China's strategic importance in the Islamic expansion lay in its vast territorial expanse, advanced civilization, and lucrative trade networks. As a key player in the Silk Road trading route, China held immense economic value for the Islamic Caliphate, offering access to valuable goods, resources, and markets. China's formidable military capabilities and longstanding cultural heritage also presented opportunities and challenges for the Islamic forces seeking to expand their influence eastward.

The diplomatic obstacles faced by the Islamic Caliphate in engaging with Chinese dynasties stemmed from China's complex political landscape. The presence of multiple powerful dynasties, each vying for dominance and protection of their sovereignty, made negotiations and alliances a delicate endeavor. Moreover, China's long diplomatic relations with neighboring states required the Islamic forces to navigate the region carefully to gain a foothold.

Despite these challenges, China's strategic importance in Islamic expansion could not be overstated. Control over Chinese territories would not only secure critical trade routes and resources but also enhance the Caliphate's regional power and influence. As such, Islamic forces were motivated to overcome diplomatic obstacles and forge alliances with Chinese dynasties to further their expansionist ambitions.

Under China's strategic significance, the Islamic Caliphate deployed skilled diplomats and negotiators to engage with Chinese authorities, seeking to establish mutually beneficial relationships to facilitate their military campaigns and territorial acquisitions. By recognizing and exploiting China's importance in Islamic expansion, the Caliphate aimed to cement its position as a dominant force in the region and expand its sphere of influence to new heights.

DIPLOMATIC OBSTACLES FACED BY THE ISLAMIC CALIPHATE IN ENGAGING WITH CHINESE DYNASTIES

Diplomatic relations between the Islamic Caliphate and the Chinese dynasties were often fraught with challenges and complexities. The vast physical distance between the two regions and stark cultural differences posed significant obstacles to establishing meaningful diplomatic ties. The Islamic expansion into China required delicate negotiation and strategic maneuvering to navigate the intricacies of diplomatic engagement with the established powers in the East.

The Silk Road was a critical conduit for trade and communication, facilitating interactions between the Islamic world and China.

However, the diplomatic landscape was shaped by more than just commercial interests. Power dynamics, territorial claims, and differing political structures all shaped the interactions between the two regions.

The Islamic Caliphate faced the challenge of understanding and adapting to the hierarchical nature of Chinese dynastic rule. The concept of the Mandate of Heaven, which legitimized the emperor's authority, posed a unique diplomatic challenge for Muslim emissaries seeking to engage with Chinese rulers. Navigating the intricacies of court etiquette, gift-giving rituals, and protocol was essential in establishing diplomatic credibility and fostering positive relations.

Cultural differences also significantly shaped diplomatic engagements. Language barriers, religious beliefs, and social customs presented hurdles that must be overcome through skilled negotiation and cultural sensitivity. The Islamic Caliphate had to carefully navigate these differences to build trust and mutual understanding with Chinese dynasties.

Furthermore, the geopolitical landscape of the time added additional layers of complexity to diplomatic relations. The competition for strategic advantage, access to resources, and control over trade routes influenced diplomatic maneuverings between the Islamic world and China. Balancing these competing interests required astute diplomatic leadership and a nuanced understanding of the broader geopolitical context.

Despite these challenges, diplomatic engagement between the Islamic Caliphate and Chinese dynasties contributed to exchanging ideas, technologies, and cultural practices. The Silk Road served as a conduit for both goods and diplomatic envoys, scholars, and ambassadors, fostering a rich tapestry of cross-cultural exchange that left a lasting legacy on both regions.

MILITARY CHALLENGES POSED BY THE VAST TERRITORIAL EXPANSE AND DIVERSE LANDSCAPES OF CHINA

China's vast territorial expanse and diverse landscapes presented formidable challenges for the Islamic forces during their conquests in the region. The sheer size of China required massive strategic planning and logistical coordination. From the deserts of the north to the mountainous terrain of the west and the fertile plains of the east, the Islamic armies had to adapt their tactics to navigate these varied environments.

The Great Wall of China posed a significant obstacle to the Islamic forces, requiring innovative approaches to breach its defenses and penetrate further into Chinese territory. Moreover, the Chinese dynasties' sophisticated military infrastructure and technological advancements posed challenges for the Islamic Caliphate, necessitating strategic adjustments in their approach to warfare.

The diverse landscapes of China, including forests, rivers, and rugged mountain ranges, presented logistical challenges for the Islamic armies. Supply lines had to be carefully managed, and troops needed to be well-prepared for the unpredictable conditions they encountered. Furthermore, the monsoon season and harsh weather conditions added another layer of complexity to the military campaigns in China.

The Chinese dynasties' strategic positioning of their forces and fortifications in key locations further complicated the Islamic conquests. Effective communication and coordination among the Islamic commanders were essential to overcome these military challenges and achieve strategic objectives in China.

Overall, China's vast territorial expanse and diverse landscapes tested the resilience and adaptability of Islamic forces during their conquests in the region. Military strategies had to be carefully crafted to navigate the complexities of Chinese warfare and overcome the formidable obstacles that lay in their path.

STRATEGIES EMPLOYED BY THE ISLAMIC FORCES TO NAVIGATE THE COMPLEXITIES OF CHINESE WARFARE

One of the primary strategies employed by the Islamic forces to navigate the complexities of Chinese warfare was adapting to the region's diverse landscapes and challenging terrains. The vast expanse of China presented logistical challenges that required careful planning and resource management. Islamic commanders implemented innovative tactics to overcome these obstacles, such as utilizing local knowledge and leveraging existing trade routes to mobilize troops and supplies efficiently.

Furthermore, the Islamic forces recognized the importance of understanding the cultural and social dynamics of the Chinese population. By forging alliances with local communities and incorporating Chinese customs into their military strategies, they gained valuable insights into the enemy's tactics and effectively counter them on the battlefield. This cultural sensitivity also helped win hearts and minds, weakening the Chinese dynasties' resolve to resist the Islamic incursions.

Additionally, the Islamic forces demonstrated flexibility in their approach to warfare, adapting their tactics to suit the challenges posed by the Chinese armies. By incorporating elements of guerrilla warfare and siege tactics, they outmaneuvered larger Chinese forces and secured strategic victories in key battles. This willingness to innovate and change strategies based on the evolving circumstances proved instrumental in their success in navigating the complexities of Chinese warfare.

Moreover, the Islamic commanders emphasized the importance of unity and coordination among their troops, fostering a sense of camaraderie and solidarity that bolstered their effectiveness on the battlefield. By instilling discipline and a strong sense of purpose in their soldiers, they maintained morale and motivation despite daunting challenges. This unity of purpose enabled the Islamic forces to capitalize on the weaknesses of the Chinese dynasties and exploit opportunities for advancement and conquest.

Overall, the strategies employed by the Islamic forces in navigating the complexities of Chinese warfare showcased their adaptability, cultural sensitivity, and tactical acumen. By blending innovation with traditional military tactics and forging alliances with local communities, they were able to overcome the formidable obstacles presented by China's vast territorial expanse and diverse landscapes, ultimately establishing a lasting legacy in the region.

RESPONSES OF CHINESE DYNASTIES TO THE ENCROACHMENT OF ISLAMIC POWERS

China's dynasties responded to Islamic powers' encroachment with a combination of diplomatic maneuvering and military resistance. The Tang Dynasty, which faced early encounters with Islamic forces, adopted a cautious approach, seeking to balance trade relations with advancing military threats. The Tang rulers initially welcomed Arab traders and emissaries, allowing limited access to Chinese markets to maintain peace on the borders.

However, as Islamic powers grew stronger and more assertive in their expansionist ambitions, the Tang Dynasty became increasingly wary of the potential threats posed to its territorial integrity. The Tang court engaged in diplomatic negotiations to establish clear boundaries and protocols for interactions with Islamic forces. At the same time, the Chinese military bolstered its defenses along the western frontier, fortifying key strongholds and strategically deploying forces to counter any incursions.

The subsequent Song Dynasty faced different challenges in dealing with Islamic incursions. As the Song rulers grappled with internal political upheavals and external pressures from neighboring states, they struggled to mount a cohesive defense against the expanding Islamic powers. The fragmented nature of Chinese territories during this period further complicated efforts to resist the incursions effectively.

Despite these challenges, Chinese military leaders such as General Yue Fei emerged as prominent figures in rallying resistance against Islamic forces. Yue Fei's strategic acumen and tactical brilliance were crucial in repelling incursions and safeguarding Chinese territories. His leadership inspired a sense of unity and resilience among Chinese forces, enabling them to withstand the pressures of Islamic conquests.

In response to the changing dynamics of warfare and diplomacy, Chinese dynasties effectively adapted their strategies to confront the Islamic powers. By combining diplomatic negotiations, military defenses, and leadership initiatives, China's rulers sought to safeguard their sovereignty and territorial integrity against the encroachments of Islamic forces. These responses shaped the outcomes of the conflicts and influenced the long-term interactions between Chinese dynasties and Islamic powers in the region.

NOTABLE MILITARY LEADERS ON BOTH SIDES WHO SHAPED THE OUTCOMES OF THE CONFLICTS

Notable military leaders on both sides played pivotal roles in shaping the outcomes of the conflicts between Islamic powers and Chinese dynasties. On the Islamic side, commanders such as Qutaiba ibn Muslim, known for his skillful tactics and strategic acumen, led successful military campaigns into Chinese territories. Qutaiba's ability to adapt to the diverse terrain and effectively command his troops earned him a reputation as a formidable leader.

Opposing Qutaiba and the Islamic forces were Chinese military leaders like Li Siye, who fiercely defended their territories against foreign incursions. Li Siye's expertise in organizing defensive strategies and rallying troops to repel invasions proved crucial in safeguarding Chinese borders. His leadership was instrumental in countering the advances of the Islamic Caliphate and maintaining the integrity of Chinese territories.

Another prominent figure in the conflict was An Lushan, a general of mixed Sogdian and Turkic heritage who rebelled against the Tang dynasty and established an independent state. Lushan's military campaigns challenged both Chinese and Islamic forces, creating a complex dynamic that shaped the course of the conflicts in the region.

These military leaders on both sides demonstrated their prowess on the battlefield and navigated the time's intricate political and cultural landscapes. Their decisions and actions had far-reaching consequences that influenced the outcomes of the clashes between Islamic powers and Chinese dynasties, leaving a lasting impact on the region's history.

IMPACT OF CULTURAL DIFFERENCES AND COMMUNICATION BARRIERS ON THE CONFRONTATIONS

Cultural differences and communication barriers were crucial in shaping the confrontations between the Islamic forces and Chinese dynasties during the expansion into China. The Islamic

Caliphate, rooted in Middle Eastern traditions, encountered a vastly different cultural landscape in China, with distinct customs, beliefs, and practices. The language barrier further complicated interactions as Arabic-speaking Muslim forces struggled to communicate with Chinese-speaking locals and officials.

Misinterpretations and misunderstandings arising from these cultural and linguistic disparities often led to tensions and conflicts between the two sides. Different social norms and values, such as perceptions of hierarchy, authority, and hospitality, further contributed to the challenges of building trust and rapport between the Islamic invaders and the Chinese populace. These cultural differences sometimes resulted in clashes and acts of violence as each side struggled to comprehend the motivations and intentions of the other.

Moreover, ineffective communication channels hindered diplomatic efforts and negotiations between the Islamic Caliphate and Chinese rulers. Miscommunication and mistrust frequently impeded the establishment of alliances or peaceful resolutions to conflicts, leading to prolonged warfare and instability in the region. The inability to bridge these communication gaps often perpetuated misunderstandings and deepened animosities between the conflicting parties.

Despite these challenges, there were instances of cultural exchange and cooperation, fostering mutual understanding and collaboration between Islamic and Chinese societies. Both sides overcame communication barriers and cultural differences through trade, intellectual exchange, and intercultural engagements, paving the way for more harmonious interactions. These moments of cultural convergence highlight the potential for bridging divides and building relationships across diverse civilizations despite the complexities of language and tradition.

ECONOMIC FACTORS INFLUENCING THE ISLAMIC CONQUESTS IN CHINA

Economic factors played a pivotal role in influencing the Islamic conquests in China. The lucrative trade networks that connected the Middle East with China were a primary motivator for the Islamic Caliphate to expand its influence into Chinese territories. The renowned Silk Road, which facilitated the exchange of goods, ideas, and culture between the two regions, presented a wealth of economic opportunities for the conquerors.

In China, the abundance of valuable commodities, such as silk, spices, and porcelain, enticed Islamic traders and rulers alike to seek control over these resources. By establishing dominance in key trade hubs and routes, the Islamic forces aimed to increase their wealth and power by exploiting China's economic assets.

Furthermore, controlling strategic ports and maritime trade routes was essential for the Islamic Caliphate to solidify its regional economic dominance. Access to the sea allowed for the efficient transportation of goods and facilitated the establishment of lucrative trade partnerships with other Asian powers.

The Islamic conquests in China also had profound implications for the region's economic landscape. The integration of Chinese production methods, technology, and agricultural practices into the Islamic territories led to advancements in various industries and stimulated economic growth. This exchange of knowledge and resources between the two cultures fueled economic development and innovation in both regions.

Moreover, the imposition of tributary systems and taxation policies by the Islamic rulers in China helped strengthen their economic control and leverage over the conquered territories. By extracting resources and wealth from the local population, the Islamic forces maintained their economic supremacy and funded further military campaigns and expansion efforts.

Overall, the economic factors that drove the Islamic conquests in China were instrumental in shaping the region's commercial and financial landscape. Pursuing economic prosperity and strategic advantages propelled the Islamic Caliphate to seek dominance in Chinese territories and establish a significant presence in one of the world's most economically vibrant regions.

RELIGIOUS DYNAMICS AND THE SPREAD OF ISLAM WITHIN CHINESE TERRITORIES

The spread of Islam in Chinese territories was influenced by various religious dynamics that played a crucial role in shaping the cultural landscape of the region. As Islamic forces expanded into China, they encountered a diverse set of religious beliefs and practices among the local populace. Chinese religions such as Buddhism, Confucianism, and Taoism had deep roots in society, presenting a unique challenge for the spread of Islam.

One key strategy Islamic missionaries employed was to adapt to the existing religious traditions and synthesize them with Islamic teachings. This approach allowed for a more gradual and harmonious integration of Islam into Chinese society, fostering a sense of religious tolerance and coexistence. Islamic scholars engaged in dialogue with Chinese intellectuals, drawing parallels between Islamic monotheism and the philosophical concepts of Confucianism and Taoism.

Translating Islamic texts into Chinese further facilitated the dissemination of Islamic knowledge and practices among the local population. Chinese converts to Islam brought their own cultural heritage and traditions into the fold, enriching the religious tapestry of the Islamic community in China. Sufi mystics played a significant role in popularizing Islam by emphasizing spiritual enlightenment and personal transformation.

The construction of mosques and Islamic educational institutions helped establish a visible presence of Islam in Chinese cities, serving as centers for religious instruction and community gatherings. Islamic art and architecture also flourished in China, blending Islamic and Chinese design elements to create a distinctive aesthetic that reflected the fusion of cultures.

Over time, Islam became a significant part of the religious landscape in China, influencing not only the spiritual beliefs of the population but also the social and political structures of the society. The legacy of the Islamic conquests in China endures in the diverse religious practices and cultural traditions that continue to shape the region's history and identity.

LEGACY OF THE ISLAMIC CONQUESTS IN CHINA AND THEIR ENDURING SIGNIFICANCE IN SHAPING REGIONAL HISTORY

The Islamic conquests of China left a lasting legacy that significantly shaped the region's history. The spread of Islam within Chinese territories altered the religious landscape and had profound cultural and political implications. The enduring significance of these conquests can be seen in various aspects of Chinese society and history.

One of the key legacies of the Islamic conquests in China was the introduction of new religious and cultural influences. Integrating Islamic traditions with Chinese customs led to a unique and vibrant religious identity thriving in the region. The mosques and religious centers established during this period served as important hubs for trade, education, and community development, further solidifying the presence of Islam in Chinese society.

Moreover, the Islamic conquests played a significant role in shaping the political landscape of China. Establishing Islamic emirates and appointing Muslim officials in key administrative positions contributed to the diversification of governance structures and fostered greater cultural exchange between different communities. The fusion of Islamic and Chinese governance systems resulted in a more inclusive and pluralistic society that valued diversity and cooperation.

The economic impact of the Islamic conquests in China was also profound. The integration of Islamic trade networks with existing Chinese commercial routes facilitated the exchange of goods, technologies, and ideas, leading to economic growth and prosperity in the region. Establishing new markets and trading posts further bolstered economic ties between China and the wider Islamic world, laying the foundation for future economic cooperation and development.

Overall, the legacy of the Islamic conquests in China continues to resonate in the region's history, culture, and society. The enduring significance of these conquests lies in their contribution to China's religious, cultural, political, and economic development, illustrating the transformative power of cross-cultural interactions and exchanges. By examining the lasting impact of the Islamic conquests in China, we gain valuable insights into the complexities of historical narratives and the interconnectedness of diverse civilizations.

DIPLOMATIC AND MILITARY CHALLENGES

BACKGROUND OF CHINESE DYNASTIES

China's rich history is characterized by a succession of powerful dynasties that have impacted the region's culture, society, and governance. During the period of Islamic conquests in Asia, several major Chinese dynasties reigned supreme, shaping the geopolitical landscape of the time.

The Tang Dynasty, known for its prosperity and cultural flourishing, was a dominant force during this era. With a strong central government, the Tang Dynasty expanded its territory and became a key player in regional politics. The Tang rulers maintained diplomatic relations with neighboring states, fostering trade and cultural exchange along the Silk Road.

Following the Tang Dynasty, the Song Dynasty emerged as a significant economic and technological advancement period. Known for its arts, science, and governance innovation, the Song Dynasty was pivotal in shaping Chinese history. The Song rulers implemented administrative reforms and promoted agricultural development, leading to relative stability and prosperity.

The Yuan Dynasty, established by the Mongol leader Kublai Khan, marked a period of foreign rule in China. Although of non-Chinese descent, Kublai Khan integrated Chinese administrative practices into his governance, maintaining a semblance of continuity with past dynasties. The Yuan Dynasty facilitated cultural exchange with the Islamic world, laying the foundation for future interactions between China and Islamic civilizations.

These major Chinese dynasties, each with its unique characteristics and contributions, set the stage for encounters with Islamic forces during the era of conquests. Understanding the background of these dynasties is essential for comprehending the diplomatic and military dynamics that unfolded between China and the Islamic Caliphate.

BRIEF OVERVIEW OF THE MAJOR CHINESE DYNASTIES DURING THE PERIOD OF ISLAMIC CONQUESTS

During the period of Islamic conquests in Asia, several major Chinese dynasties played significant roles in shaping the region's geopolitical landscape. The Tang Dynasty (618–907) was one of the most influential dynasties during this time, known for its economic prosperity, vibrant culture, and military might. The Tang Dynasty's capital, Chang'an, was a cosmopolitan hub that attracted merchants, scholars, and travelers from diverse backgrounds.

Following the Tang Dynasty, the Song Dynasty (960–1279) emerged as a period of great technological and cultural advancements. The Song Dynasty was known for its innovations in agriculture, engineering, and the arts. The capital city of Kaifeng was a bustling center of commerce and cultural exchange.

During the Islamic conquests, the Liao Dynasty (907–1125) and the Jin Dynasty (1115–1234) also played significant roles in

Chinese history. The Liao Dynasty, ruled by the Khitan people, maintained a complex relationship with neighboring states and nomadic tribes. The Jin Dynasty, established by the Jurchen people, eventually conquered the northern territories of China and posed a formidable challenge to the Song Dynasty in the south.

Overall, the major Chinese dynasties of the time showcased a rich tapestry of cultural diversity, military prowess, and technological innovation. Their interactions with Islamic forces during this period shaped the course of history in East Asia, leaving a lasting impact on the region's development and geopolitical dynamics.

CULTURAL AND LINGUISTIC BARRIERS

During the Islamic conquests in China, the Islamic forces encountered significant challenges due to linguistic and cultural barriers. These barriers posed obstacles to communication, negotiation, and the understanding of local customs and traditions. The diverse languages spoken in China, including Mandarin, Cantonese, and other regional dialects, made it difficult for the Islamic forces to communicate with the local population effectively. Misunderstandings and misinterpretations often arose, leading to tensions and conflicts.

Moreover, the cultural differences between the Islamic forces and the Chinese population created further challenges. Customs, traditions, religious beliefs, and social norms varied greatly between the two groups, leading to misunderstandings and clashes of values. The Islamic forces, hailing from the Middle East and Central Asia, had their own cultural practices and ways of life that were often at odds with the Chinese.

Navigating these cultural and linguistic barriers required sensitivity, patience, and adaptability by the Islamic forces. They had to learn to communicate effectively through interpreters, gestures, and other non-verbal cues. They also needed to respect Chinese customs and traditions, even if they differed from their own.

Despite these challenges, the Islamic forces gradually found ways to bridge the cultural and linguistic divide. They began to learn more about Chinese culture and society through interactions with Chinese traders, scholars, and diplomats. This knowledge helped them navigate the complex social landscape of China and build alliances with local leaders.

Overall, while cultural and linguistic barriers presented significant challenges to the Islamic forces during the conquest of China, they also provided opportunities for cultural exchange and mutual understanding. By overcoming these barriers, the Islamic forces forged new relationships and laid the foundation for lasting interactions between the Islamic world and China.

ANALYSIS OF THE CHALLENGES ISLAMIC FORCES FACED DUE TO LINGUISTIC AND CULTURAL DIFFERENCES

China's diverse linguistic and cultural landscape presented significant challenges for the Islamic forces during their conquests. Communication barriers hindered effective interaction and coordination between the two sides. The intricate Chinese writing system and language nuances made it difficult for the Arabic-speaking Islamic commanders to convey orders and negotiate terms with Chinese counterparts.

Furthermore, cultural differences influenced military strategies and decision-making processes. The Islamic forces, accustomed to desert warfare and nomadic tactics, encountered difficulties adapting to the terrains and battle tactics of the Chinese armies. The hierarchical structure of Chinese military organizations and the emphasis on collective defense strategies contrasted with the Islamic forces' more decentralized and mobile approach.

Moreover, the deep-rooted cultural traditions and religious practices in China posed obstacles to the integration of Islamic influences. The Islamic Caliphate's attempt to assert authority and propagate its religion faced resistance from the deeply ingrained Confucian and Daoist beliefs of the Chinese populace. This ideological clash further complicated diplomatic relations and undermined the Islamic mission of conquest and conversion.

In navigating these linguistic and cultural barriers, Islamic forces had to rely on skilled interpreters, cultural liaisons, and diplomatic envoys to bridge the communication gap. Understanding and respecting Chinese customs and traditions became crucial in establishing trust and cooperation with local communities and rulers. Despite the challenges, the encounters with Chinese civilization enriched the Islamic forces' worldview and fostered a deeper appreciation for the complexity and diversity of human societies.

GEOPOLITICAL LANDSCAPE

The geopolitical landscape of East Asia during the period of Islamic conquests was characterized by a complex web of territorial boundaries and strategic positions held by various Chinese dynasties. The vast expanse of the Chinese territories presented formidable challenges for the Islamic forces seeking to expand their regional influence. The diverse topography, ranging from

THE ISLAMIC CONQUESTS IN ASIA

rugged mountain ranges to fertile plains, impacted military movements and tactics.

With their well-established administrative systems and fortified cities, the Chinese dynasties posed significant obstacles to the Islamic armies. The Great Wall of China, a monumental defensive structure stretching thousands of miles, served as a formidable barrier to incursions from the north. Beyond the physical barriers, the Chinese dynasties' centralized authority and sophisticated bureaucratic structures allowed them to mobilize resources and troops effectively in times of conflict.

Strategically, control of key trade routes and access to maritime networks played a crucial role in shaping the geopolitical landscape of East Asia. The Silk Road, a vital trade route connecting East and West, facilitated cultural exchange and economic prosperity but also served as a conduit for military incursions. The Islamic forces had to navigate intricate diplomatic relations and regional power dynamics to secure passage through these critical arteries of commerce and communication.

Moreover, diverse ethnic groups and linguistic communities in the region added another layer of complexity to the geopolitical landscape. Understanding Chinese societies' cultural nuances and social structures was essential for effective governance and long-term stability in conquered territories. The Islamic forces had to adopt a nuanced approach to governance that respected local customs and traditions while promoting Islamic values and principles.

Overall, the geopolitical landscape of East Asia during the Islamic conquests was defined by a blend of military strategy, diplomatic maneuvering, and cultural exchange. Navigating the Chinese dynasties' territorial boundaries and strategic positions required astute leadership, strategic vision, and adaptability to the ever-evolving landscape of power and influence.

EXAMINATION OF THE TERRITORIAL BOUNDARIES AND STRATEGIC POSITIONS OF CHINESE DYNASTIES

The Chinese dynasties of the Tang and Song periods controlled vast territories that encompassed diverse geographic features, from the fertile plains of the eastern coast to the rugged mountains of the west. The Tang Dynasty, known for its centralized solid rule and expansive military campaigns, established its dominance over a vast expanse of territory, stretching from the Korean Peninsula to the edge of Central Asia. This strategic position allowed the Tang to control key trade routes and interact with neighboring civilizations.

The Song Dynasty, which succeeded the Tang, faced challenges in managing its territorial boundaries due to external threats from nomadic tribes in the north and the expansionist ambitions of neighboring states. Despite these challenges, the Song Empire maintained control over the prosperous eastern regions of China, including the Yangtze River basin, which served as the empire's economic heartland.

Along China's western frontier, the Tibetan Plateau and the Tarim Basin presented strategic challenges for Chinese rulers as they sought to secure these borderlands against incursions from nomadic tribes and rival states. The geographical obstacles posed by the rugged terrain and harsh climate made it difficult to exert centralized control over these regions, leading to a complex web of alliances and conflicts between Chinese dynasties and their neighbors.

The strategic positions of major Chinese cities such as Chang'an (modern-day Xi'an) and Hangzhou played a crucial role in shaping diplomatic relations and trade networks with foreign powers. These urban centers served as political, economic, and cultural hubs, attracting merchants, scholars, and diplomats from distant lands who sought to engage with China's sophisticated civilization.

Overall, the territorial boundaries and strategic positions of Chinese dynasties determined the scope of their influence and influenced the dynamics of diplomatic relations with neighboring states and foreign powers. The interplay between geography, politics, and diplomacy shaped the course of history in East Asia and had a lasting impact on the region's geopolitical landscape.

DIPLOMATIC RELATIONS

During the Islamic conquests in China, diplomatic relations played a crucial role in shaping the interactions between the Islamic Caliphate and the Chinese dynasties. A combination of pragmatism, cultural sensitivity, and strategic calculations marked the Islamic Caliphate's diplomatic approaches.

One key strategy employed by the Islamic Caliphate was establishing trade routes and diplomatic missions to engage with Chinese rulers. These diplomatic missions fostered economic ties and laid the groundwork for political alliances and mutual cooperation.

The Islamic Caliphate recognized the importance of respecting Chinese customs and traditions to build trust and rapport with the Chinese rulers. During diplomatic negotiations, this included showcasing a deep understanding and appreciation of Chinese culture, language, and social norms.

Furthermore, the Islamic Caliphate often sought to leverage its military strength and strategic position to secure favorable diplomatic outcomes with Chinese dynasties. By demonstrating military prowess and a willingness to engage in dialogue, the Islamic

Caliphate aimed to assert itself as a formidable and respected regional power.

At the same time, diplomacy was also employed to resolve conflicts and mitigate tensions between the Islamic forces and Chinese rulers. Skilled diplomats were tasked with navigating complex political landscapes, mediating disputes, and negotiating mutually beneficial agreements to ensure a peaceful coexistence between the two powers.

Overall, the diplomatic relations between the Islamic Caliphate and Chinese dynasties during the period of conquests reflected a nuanced and multifaceted approach that balanced military strength with cultural diplomacy. By adopting a strategic and respectful stance towards the Chinese rulers, the Islamic Caliphate forged diplomatic alliances and established a lasting presence in the region.

DISCUSSION ON THE DIPLOMATIC APPROACHES TAKEN BY THE ISLAMIC CALIPHATE IN DEALING WITH CHINESE RULERS

A delicate balance of pragmatism and cultural sensitivity characterized the Islamic Caliphate's diplomatic approach toward engaging with Chinese rulers. Recognizing the formidable power and sophistication of the Chinese dynasties, the Caliphate sought to establish a relationship based on mutual respect and strategic benefit.

The Caliphate conveyed messages of friendship and cooperation to the Chinese courts through diplomatic envoys and emissaries. Gifts, trade agreements, and cultural exchanges were key components of these diplomatic overtures, aiming to foster goodwill and pave the way for future alliances.

Understanding the importance of cultural nuances, the Islamic diplomats tried to respect Chinese customs and traditions. They studied Confucian principles, learned the Chinese language, and demonstrated a genuine interest in the rich cultural heritage of China. This approach helped to bridge the cultural divide and establish a foundation for meaningful dialogue between the two civilizations.

Moreover, the Islamic Caliphate leveraged its strategic location and military prowess to demonstrate its strength and capability to the Chinese rulers. By showcasing military achievements in other territories and highlighting the Islamic Empire's vast resources, the Caliphate aimed to convey a message of strength and resilience, deterring any hostile intentions from the Chinese side.

In navigating the complex diplomatic landscape of China, the Islamic Caliphate also sought to form alliances with local Chinese states and factions that were willing to align with their interests. By forging strategic partnerships with regional powers, the Caliphate aimed to create a united front against common adversaries and enhance its influence in the region.

Overall, the diplomatic approaches taken by the Islamic Caliphate in dealing with Chinese rulers were characterized by a nuanced understanding of cultural differences, a strategic mindset, and a commitment to peaceful coexistence. These efforts laid the foundation for diplomatic relations that would shape the course of history in the region and leave a lasting impact on the interactions between the Islamic world and the Far East.

MILITARY STRATEGIES

The military strategies employed during the conflict between the Islamic Caliphate and Chinese rulers were characterized by a combination of innovation and adaptation. The Islamic forces, led by skilled military commanders, utilized a variety of tactics to navigate the challenges posed by the vast and diverse landscape of China. One of the key strategies employed was the utilization of combined arms forces, incorporating infantry, cavalry, and archers to maintain flexibility and respond effectively to various battlefield scenarios. Additionally, the Islamic forces emphasized the importance of siege warfare, utilizing advanced siege engines and tactics to besiege and capture fortified Chinese cities.

In response, the Chinese dynasties also employed sophisticated military strategies, leveraging their knowledge of the terrain and their extensive experience in warfare. The Chinese rulers utilized a combination of defensive tactics, including the construction of fortified structures and defensive walls to protect their territories from Islamic incursions. Naval warfare played a crucial role in the conflict, with both sides engaging in naval battles to control key maritime routes and strategic waterways.

Furthermore, both the Islamic and Chinese forces recognized the importance of logistics and supply lines in sustaining their military campaigns. The Islamic Caliphate established efficient supply chains to ensure the timely delivery of provisions and reinforcements to their troops, while the Chinese dynasties utilized their extensive network of roads and waterways to maintain their logistical advantage.

Overall, the military strategies employed by both the Islamic Caliphate and Chinese rulers during their conflicts were marked by strategic planning, tactical innovation, and adaptability to the challenges of warfare in diverse and demanding environments. These military engagements not only shaped the course of history but also laid the foundation for the development of military tactics and strategies in the region for centuries to come.

THE ISLAMIC CONQUESTS IN ASIA

EXPLORATION OF THE MILITARY TACTICS EMPLOYED BY BOTH SIDES DURING CONFLICTS

Military tactics played a crucial role in shaping the outcome of conflicts between the Islamic forces and Chinese dynasties during the period of Islamic conquests in Asia. The strategic maneuvers and battlefield approaches adopted by both sides were a reflection of their military capabilities and objectives. Islamic forces, led by skilled commanders, employed a combination of conventional warfare tactics along with innovative strategies to overcome the challenges posed by the well-fortified Chinese armies. Guerrilla warfare, ambush tactics, and swift cavalry movements were key components of the Islamic military strategy, aimed at exploiting the vulnerabilities of the enemy and maximizing their own strengths. On the other hand, Chinese dynasties, known for their disciplined and well-organized military forces, relied on defensive tactics that focused on protecting their territory and repelling invaders. Utilizing their knowledge of the terrain and leveraging their superior numbers, Chinese armies deployed tactics such as encirclement, defensive fortifications, and naval blockades to counter the advancing Islamic forces. The clash of military tactics between the two sides led to a complex and dynamic battlefield environment, where adaptability, strategic thinking, and resourcefulness were essential for victory. The interactions between Islamic and Chinese military tactics not only influenced the outcomes of individual battles but also had a lasting impact on the broader geopolitical landscape of the region.

NAVAL WARFARE

Naval warfare played a crucial role in the conflicts between the Islamic forces and the Chinese dynasties in East Asia. The vast maritime expanse presented both challenges and opportunities for both sides. The Chinese dynasties, with their longstanding naval traditions and powerful fleets, posed a formidable obstacle to the Islamic Caliphate's expansion into East Asia.

The Chinese naval forces, equipped with advanced shipbuilding techniques and navigational skills, controlled the seas with a strong presence. They utilized innovative naval tactics such as the use of fire ships, naval blockades, and coordinated attacks to protect their coastal territories and trade routes.

On the other hand, the Islamic forces faced significant challenges in navigating unfamiliar waters and countering the superior Chinese naval capabilities. The need to establish naval supremacy in the region led to the development of new strategies and tactics to overcome these challenges.

The Islamic Caliphate adapted their naval tactics to engage the Chinese fleets effectively. They employed hit-and-run tactics, guerrilla warfare at sea, and ambushes to disrupt Chinese naval operations. Additionally, the Islamic forces relied on their agility and speed to outmaneuver their larger and more heavily armed opponents.

Furthermore, the utilization of naval alliances with local maritime powers and the recruitment of experienced sailors from different regions bolstered the Islamic naval forces' capabilities. These collaborative efforts enabled the Islamic Caliphate to challenge the Chinese dominance at sea and launch successful naval engagements.

Overall, naval warfare in East Asia during the Islamic conquests was marked by strategic maneuvering, innovative tactics, and fierce engagements between the opposing forces. The outcome of these naval conflicts significantly influenced the course of history in the region and shaped the geopolitical landscape for centuries to come.

FOCUS ON THE IMPORTANCE OF NAVAL POWER AND THE CHALLENGES OF MARITIME WARFARE IN EAST ASIA

Naval power played a crucial role in shaping the outcomes of conflicts in East Asia during the era of Islamic conquests. The vast expanses of the region's waterways presented unique challenges and opportunities for both Islamic forces and their adversaries. The ability to control maritime trade routes and project power across the seas was essential for establishing dominance in the region.

The strategic importance of naval power in East Asia cannot be understated. The interconnected network of water routes facilitated trade, communication, and military movements between various coastal regions. Islamic forces recognized the need to secure control over key maritime hubs and establish naval superiority to safeguard their territorial holdings and expand their influence.

Maritime warfare in East Asia posed distinct challenges due to the diverse navigational conditions, unpredictable weather patterns, and the presence of formidable naval forces loyal to local rulers. Islamic commanders had to adapt their tactics and utilize their naval resources effectively to counter these challenges and achieve their objectives. From engaging in naval battles to conducting coastal raids and blockades, the Islamic forces navigated the complex waters of East Asia with strategic acumen.

The utilization of advanced naval technologies and tactics played a vital role in determining the outcomes of maritime engagements. Innovations in ship design, naval weaponry, and navigational techniques gave the Islamic forces a competitive edge against their adversaries. By leveraging their naval capabilities, Islamic commanders were able to project power beyond the confines of land-based warfare and assert their dominance in the maritime domain.

The successful navigation of maritime warfare in East Asia required a comprehensive understanding of the region's geopolitical dynamics, strategic resources, and naval capabilities. Islamic forces meticulously planned their naval campaigns, seeking to exploit vulnerabilities in their opponents' maritime defenses and capitalize on opportunities for strategic advancements. Through a combination of astute leadership, technological prowess, and tactical foresight, Islamic naval forces secured their presence in the waters of East Asia, leaving a lasting legacy on the region's maritime history.

TECHNOLOGICAL ADVANCEMENTS

Naval warfare played a critical role in shaping the outcomes of military campaigns in East Asia during the Islamic conquests. The advancement and utilization of naval technologies were essential for controlling maritime routes, conducting amphibious operations, and securing vital coastal territories.

One key technological innovation that revolutionized naval warfare in this region was the development of advanced ship designs. Islamic forces introduced sturdy and versatile ships such as dhows and junks, equipped with multiple sails and improved navigation systems. These vessels enabled greater maneuverability and speed, essential for engaging in naval battles and navigating through treacherous waters.

Additionally, the use of naval artillery and siege weapons on ships significantly enhanced the firepower capabilities of Islamic naval forces. Adopting techniques such as Greek fire, a formidable incendiary weapon, provided a potent offensive capability against enemy ships and coastal defenses.

Furthermore, the introduction of advanced naval engineering techniques, including the construction of fortified seaports and harbors, bolstered the logistical support and defensive capabilities of Islamic naval fleets. These strategically located bases served as crucial hubs for resupply, repair, and coordination of naval operations in distant waters.

Moreover, the integration of cutting-edge maritime navigation instruments, such as astrolabes and compasses, facilitated accurate positioning and course plotting for naval expeditions. This technological sophistication in navigation greatly improved the efficiency and precision of Islamic naval campaigns in the vast expanse of East Asian waters.

Overall, the continuous innovation and adaptation of naval technologies were instrumental in ensuring the success of Islamic naval expeditions and consolidating control over key coastal regions in East Asia. The strategic utilization of these advancements not only bolstered the offensive capabilities of Islamic naval forces but also contributed to the establishment of a formidable presence in maritime trade routes and territorial waters.

EVALUATION OF TECHNOLOGICAL INNOVATIONS AND ADVANCEMENTS THAT INFLUENCED MILITARY CAMPAIGNS

Islamic conquests in Asia witnessed significant technological advancements that profoundly influenced military campaigns.

These innovations played a crucial role in shaping the outcomes of battles and sieges, demonstrating the strategic importance of technological superiority in warfare.

One notable technological advancement was the development of advanced siege engines such as trebuchets, mangonels, and siege towers. These devices enabled Islamic forces to breach fortified city walls and gain strategic advantages during sieges. These siege engines showcased the sophisticated engineering skills of the Islamic armies and their ability to adapt to different battle scenarios.

In addition to siege engines, advancements in metallurgy and weapon craftsmanship resulted in superior arms and armor production. Islamic warriors wielded finely crafted swords, spears, bows, and arrows that provided them with a distinct edge on the battlefield. The utilization of high-quality weapons not only enhanced the combat effectiveness of Islamic troops but also instilled fear in their adversaries.

Furthermore, the Islamic armies leveraged military tactics and strategy advancements to outmaneuver and outwit their opponents. Commanders implemented innovative battle formations, ambush tactics, and flanking maneuvers to exploit weaknesses in enemy defenses. These strategic approaches, combined with technological advancements, allowed Islamic forces to achieve decisive victories in various military engagements.

Moreover, integrating siege warfare techniques with technological innovations led to successfully capturing key strongholds and cities. Islamic armies utilized catapults, battering rams, and scaling ladders to overcome the formidable defenses of enemy fortifications. The meticulous planning and execution of siege operations demonstrated Islamic military leaders' meticulous preparation and foresight.

Overall, the evaluation of technological innovations and advancements in military campaigns highlights the critical role played by technology in shaping the outcomes of conflicts during the Islamic conquests in Asia. These advancements not only demonstrated the ingenuity and resourcefulness of Islamic armies but also underscored the significance of technological superiority in achieving military success.

SIEGE WARFARE

The use of advanced siege weaponry was crucial in the conquest of fortified Chinese cities and strongholds. Islamic forces encountered formidable defenses, requiring innovative strategies to breach the formidable walls. One of the key technological advancements that influenced siege warfare was the development of powerful trebuchets. These massive catapults could launch heavy projectiles over long distances, effectively breaking down fortified walls and towers. Islamic engineers also devised new siege engines, such as battering rams and towers, to assault the city gates and walls directly. Coordinating various siege engines and tactics played a crucial role in wearing down the defenders and gaining entry into the fortified cities. Moreover, the Islamic forces employed skilled sappers who specialized in undermining enemy walls and creating breaches for the infantry to exploit. By combining technological innovation with strategic planning, Islamic armies overcame the challenges of besieging heavily fortified Chinese cities and strongholds, ultimately achieving success in their military campaigns.

ANALYSIS OF THE STRATEGIES FOR BESIEGING FORTIFIED CHINESE CITIES AND STRONGHOLDS

Siege warfare was critical to besieging fortified Chinese cities and strongholds during the Islamic conquests in Asia. Islamic forces employed various strategies to overcome the formidable defenses of these urban centers, seeking to weaken the enemy's resolve and ultimately secure victory.

One of the primary tactics used in besieging Chinese cities was the construction of siege engines such as trebuchets, catapults, and battering rams. These powerful weapons were designed to breach fortified cities' thick walls and gates, allowing the invading forces to access the enemy's stronghold.

Furthermore, Islamic commanders recognized the importance of encircling the besieged city to cut off their supply lines and prevent reinforcements from reaching the defenders. By establishing a tight blockade around the city, they could slowly starve out the enemy and force them to surrender.

In addition to physical tactics, psychological warfare also played a significant role in besieging Chinese cities. Propaganda efforts, such as spreading rumors of impending doom or displaying the captured banners of defeated armies, were used to instill fear and uncertainty among the defenders, weakening their morale and resolve.

Moreover, strategic troop placement and stealthy infiltration techniques were employed to disrupt the enemy's defenses from within. Sabotaging supply lines, poisoning water sources, and staging surprise attacks on key defense points were all part of the multifaceted approach adopted by Islamic forces during sieges.

Overall, the successful besieging of fortified Chinese cities and strongholds required a combination of meticulous planning, innovative tactics, and unwavering determination on the part of the Islamic commanders and their forces. By adapting to the unique challenges presented by each city's defenses and employing a variety of strategies, they were able to secure significant victories and expand their influence in the region.

SUPPLY LINES AND LOGISTICS

The efficient management of supply lines and logistics was crucial for the success of Islamic forces besieging fortified Chinese cities and strongholds. Ensuring a steady flow of resources and provisions in unfamiliar territories with varying terrain and climates was a daunting task. Armies had to navigate through rugged landscapes, dense forests, and treacherous rivers to reach their destinations.

Caravans of supply wagons, pack animals, and porters were used to transport food, weapons, ammunition, and other essential supplies. These convoys had to be well-protected against ambushes by local militia groups or rival factions seeking to disrupt the supply chain. Guarding these vital lifelines required a disciplined and vigilant military presence to deter potential threats and maintain order along the routes.

Strategic planning was essential in determining the most efficient paths for supply lines, taking into account factors such as distance, security, and local support. Scouts were deployed to assess the condition of roads, bridges, and water sources to ensure smooth passage for the supply caravans. Communication between different supply depots and military outposts was also critical for coordinating logistics and responding to any unforeseen challenges.

Logistical support extended beyond the transportation of goods to include the establishment of temporary camps, field hospitals, and rest areas for weary soldiers. Maintaining the morale and well-being of troops was paramount in sustaining their effectiveness during lengthy sieges and prolonged military campaigns. Adequate provisions of food, water, and medical care were essential for keeping soldiers in fighting condition and preserving their combat readiness.

In conclusion, the careful management of supply lines and logistics played a pivotal role in the success of Islamic forces besieging fortified Chinese cities and strongholds. By prioritizing efficiency, security, and coordination, military commanders were able to overcome the logistical challenges of operating in unfamiliar territories and ensure the sustained support needed for their campaigns.

IMPORTANCE OF MAINTAINING EFFICIENT SUPPLY CHAINS AND LOGISTICAL SUPPORT IN UNFAMILIAR TERRITORIES

Efficient supply chains and robust logistical support are indispensable components of successful military campaigns, particularly in unfamiliar territories. The ability to provision troops with essential resources, such as food, water, weapons, and medical supplies, can often determine the outcome of conflicts in distant lands. In the context of Islamic conquests in Asia, maintaining effective supply lines was crucial for sustaining prolonged campaigns and ensuring the readiness of troops for battle.

The logistical challenges faced by Islamic forces in unfamiliar territories were multifaceted. Navigating diverse terrains, ranging from arid deserts to dense forests, required careful planning and coordination to transport goods and provisions. Moreover, the need to adapt to varying climatic conditions, such as extreme heat or cold, added another layer of complexity to logistical operations.

Establishing secure supply routes was essential for safeguarding the flow of resources to the front lines and preventing disruptions that could weaken the military's effectiveness. Guarding against ambushes by hostile forces or bandits along supply lines necessitated continuous vigilance and strategic deployment of troops to ensure the safe passage of logistics convoys.

Logistical efficiency not only encompassed the physical transportation of goods but also encompassed the organization of storage facilities, distribution points, and maintenance of communication networks. Proper management of supply depots and logistical hubs helped streamline the process of resupplying troops and replenishing depleted stocks, thereby sustaining the operational capabilities of the military.

The successful management of supply chains and logistical support had far-reaching implications for the outcome of conflicts and the legacy of conquests in Asia. Armies that were well-equipped and well-provisioned were better positioned to confront adversaries, withstand sieges, and endure protracted campaigns in unfamiliar territories. Additionally, the logistical prowess demonstrated by Islamic forces contributed to their reputation as formidable conquerors and administrators of vast empires across Asia.

In conclusion, the importance of maintaining efficient supply chains and logistical support in unfamiliar territories cannot be overstated in the context of military campaigns. A well-managed logistical system not only sustains the operational capabilities of armed forces but also influences the course of conflicts and the subsequent legacy of conquests in distant lands.

GEW SOCIAL SCIENCES GROUP

LEGACY OF CONFLICTS

The conflicts between the Islamic forces and Chinese dynasties left a profound and enduring legacy that reverberated throughout subsequent historical developments. One of the most significant impacts was the exchange of knowledge and technology between the two civilizations. Islamic military campaigns in China introduced new military strategies, siege warfare techniques, and naval advancements that influenced Chinese military practices. Additionally, Chinese innovations such as gunpowder and printing technology were introduced to the Islamic world, transforming warfare and communication.

Furthermore, the diplomatic and military confrontations between the Islamic Caliphate and Chinese dynasties forged new political dynamics in the region. The power struggles and alliances that emerged during these conflicts laid the groundwork for future geopolitical interactions and shaped the relationships between East and West. The legacy of these conflicts resonated not only in the realm of military affairs but also in trade, culture, and diplomacy.

Moreover, the conflicts between the Islamic and Chinese civilizations contributed to a process of cultural exchange and syncretism. The interactions between the two societies led to the blending of artistic, architectural, and intellectual traditions, creating a rich tapestry of cross-cultural influences. Artifacts from this period reflect the fusion of Islamic and Chinese aesthetics, highlighting the creative and dynamic exchange that occurred during these turbulent times.

Overall, the legacy of conflicts between the Islamic Caliphate and Chinese dynasties served as a catalyst for the transformation of both societies. The enduring impact of these diplomatic and military challenges continues to shape the historical narrative of the interactions between East and West, underscoring the complexity and richness of cross-cultural encounters in the ancient world.

EXAMINATION OF THE LASTING IMPACT OF THESE DIPLOMATIC AND MILITARY CHALLENGES ON SUBSEQUENT HISTORICAL DEVELOPMENTS

The lasting impact of these diplomatic and military challenges is evident in the continued cultural exchange and historical interactions between China and the Islamic world. The conflicts served as a catalyst for the transmission of knowledge, technology, and ideas across regions, shaping the development of both societies. The exchange of goods, such as silk, porcelain, and spices, along the Silk Road and maritime trade routes fostered economic growth and cultural diffusion.

The military encounters between Chinese dynasties and Islamic forces led to the adoption of new military strategies and technologies on both sides. The Chinese learned from the Islamic use of cavalry and archery, while Islamic forces incorporated Chinese siege warfare techniques and naval tactics. This cross-pollination of military knowledge contributed to advancements in military science and technology in the region.

Diplomatic relations between China and the Islamic Caliphate laid the foundation for future interactions and cooperation in various fields, including trade, cultural exchange, and diplomacy. The diplomatic challenges faced by both sides during conflicts prompted the establishment of formal diplomatic channels and protocols, leading to the development of a system of communication and negotiation between the two powers.

The legacy of these conflicts also influenced the social and cultural fabric of both China and the Islamic world. The interaction between Chinese and Islamic societies led to the exchange of ideas in areas such as art, architecture, science, and literature, fostering a rich cultural synthesis and artistic flourishing. The blending of Chinese and Islamic cultural elements created a unique cultural landscape that continues to shape the identities of these regions.

Overall, the diplomatic and military challenges between China and the Islamic Caliphate during the period of conquests have left a profound impact on subsequent historical developments. The legacy of these interactions continues to resonate in the shared heritage, cultural exchanges, and historical ties between China and the Islamic world, underscoring the enduring significance of these conflicts in shaping the course of history.

PROMINENT MILITARY LEADERS

INTRODUCTION TO PROMINENT MILITARY LEADERS

The annals of history are replete with the valor and strategic acumen displayed by notable military leaders who have left an indelible mark on the course of warfare. These revered figures have shaped the destiny of nations through their leadership on the battlefield, exhibiting a rare blend of courage, intelligence, and determination that set them apart from their contemporaries.

Their unwavering commitment to their cause and a profound understanding of the art of war enabled them to triumph over seemingly insurmountable odds. Through their exemplary leadership, they inspired their troops to achieve feats that were once deemed impossible, forging a legacy that continues to resonate through the annals of time.

These prominent military leaders possessed a keen vision and could assess complex battlefield scenarios with clarity and decisiveness. They demonstrated an unwavering resolve in the face of adversity, rallying their forces with unwavering determination and unwavering commitment to victory.

Their exceptional leadership qualities extended beyond the battlefield, encompassing diplomacy, strategic planning, and the ability to inspire loyalty and dedication among their followers. These leaders were adept at adapting to changing circumstances, evolving tactics, and deftly maneuvering their forces to exploit their adversaries' weaknesses.

As we delve into the lives and strategies of these prominent military leaders, we are presented with a compelling narrative of courage, sacrifice, and triumph. Their stories serve as a testament to the enduring power of leadership in the crucible of conflict, showcasing the transformative impact that a single individual can have on history.

LEADERSHIP CHARACTERISTICS AND QUALITIES

A common thread emerges in the leadership characteristics and qualities of the notable military leaders of the Islamic conquests in Asia. These leaders exemplified courage, determination, and strategic vision in their campaigns. They were adept at inspiring their troops, fostering loyalty, and maintaining discipline within their ranks.

Moreover, these leaders possessed excellent communication skills, enabling them to convey their objectives clearly and rally their forces effectively. They were also skilled in diplomacy, forging alliances with local rulers and tribes to strengthen their positions. Adaptability and flexibility were key traits, allowing them to adjust their tactics according to the changing battlefield conditions.

Furthermore, these military leaders were known for their tactical acumen and keen understanding of warfare. They employed conventional tactics and innovative strategies to achieve their goals. They quickly seized opportunities and exploited enemy weaknesses, demonstrating a mastery of maneuver warfare.

Additionally, these leaders displayed resilience in the face of adversity, overcoming challenges with perseverance and resourcefulness. They inspired confidence in their troops through their own bravery and commitment to victory. Their ability to make sound decisions under pressure and maintain composure in battle sets them apart as exceptional leaders.

Overall, these military leaders' leadership characteristics and qualities played a crucial role in the success of the Islamic conquests in Asia. Their legacy inspires admiration and respect, serving as a testament to their enduring impact on history.

MILITARY STRATEGIES AND TACTICS EMPLOYED

During the conquests in Asia, Islamic military leaders demonstrated a multifaceted approach to warfare, combining strategic planning, tactical innovation, and adaptability to prevailing conditions on the battlefield. One of the key military strategies employed by these commanders was the effective use of combined arms tactics, leveraging the strengths of various types of troops to achieve maximum impact on the enemy.

The Islamic armies were known for their mobility and speed. They often utilized mounted cavalry units to launch lightning raids and outmaneuver larger, slower enemy forces. This hit-and-run style of warfare allowed them to disrupt supply lines, harass enemy formations, and exploit weaknesses in the enemy's defense.

Furthermore, Islamic military leaders used siege warfare techniques to overcome fortified enemy positions. They employed innovative siege engines, such as catapults and siege towers, to breach enemy walls and gain entry into heavily defended cities.

Their mastery of siege tactics enabled them to conquer some of the most formidable strongholds in Asia.

Regarding battlefield tactics, Islamic commanders excelled at coordinating and synchronizing their forces during engagements. They employed intricate battle formations, such as the crescent formation, which allowed them to envelop and encircle the enemy, cutting off their escape routes and forcing a decisive engagement. This strategic use of formations and maneuvers often caught their opponents off guard and led to significant victories on the battlefield.

Moreover, Islamic military leaders were known for their psychological warfare tactics, utilizing intimidation, deception, and propaganda to weaken enemy morale and sow discord among opposing forces. They employed clever ruses, false retreats, and feigned weaknesses to lure the enemy into traps and exploit their vulnerabilities. This psychological warfare aspect complemented their conventional military strategies, providing them with a psychological edge in warfare.

Overall, the military strategies and tactics employed by Islamic leaders during the conquests in Asia were characterized by innovation, adaptability, and a keen understanding of the dynamics of warfare. Through their skillful integration of various tactical elements and ability to exploit enemy weaknesses, they achieved remarkable success on the battlefield. They left a lasting legacy in the annals of military history.

NOTABLE BATTLE ENGAGEMENTS AND VICTORIES

The Islamic conquest of Persia saw several notable battle engagements and victories that shaped history. One such key battle was the Battle of Qadisiyyah, where the Muslim forces, led by

Khalid ibn al-Walid, decisively defeated the Sassanian army. This victory opened the door for further Islamic expansion into Persia.

Another significant engagement was the Battle of Nahavand, where the Muslim forces, under the command of Sa'ad ibn Abi Waqqas, achieved a decisive victory over the Sassanians. This battle cemented Muslim control over Persia and marked the beginning of the end for the Sassanian Empire.

The Battle of Talas stands out as a crucial engagement in the conquest of Central Asia. The Muslim armies, led by Ziyad ibn Abi Sufyan, clashed with the Tang Dynasty forces, resulting in a strategic victory for the Muslims. This battle solidified Islamic control over Central Asia and paved the way for further expansion.

Turning to the Indian subcontinent, the Battle of Rajasthan was a significant conflict that saw the Muslim forces, led by Muhammad bin Qasim, achieve a decisive victory over the Hindu rulers. This battle marked the beginning of Islamic rule in the region and established a foothold for further conquests.

In Southeast Asia, the Battle of Wadi Al-Kabir was a pivotal engagement. Under the leadership of Tariq ibn Ziyad, Muslim forces defeated the local rulers and established Islamic control over the region. This victory laid the foundation for the spread of Islam in Southeast Asia.

The conquest of China saw the Battle of Talas, where the Muslim forces, led by Qutayba ibn Muslim, clashed with the Chinese Tang Dynasty. Despite facing numerous challenges, the Muslims emerged victorious, further expanding Islamic influence in the region.

These notable battle engagements and victories demonstrated the military prowess of the Islamic armies. They had a lasting impact on the regions they conquered, shaping the course of history for centuries to come.

INFLUENCE ON MILITARY INNOVATION AND DOCTRINE

The notable military leaders discussed in this book have profoundly influenced military innovation and doctrine. Their strategic thinking, tactical prowess, and leadership have shaped military history and impacted future generations. Through their military campaigns and conquests, these leaders introduced new tactics, organizational structures, and technologies that revolutionized the art of warfare.

Military strategists have studied and emulated their innovative approaches to warfare for centuries. By adapting to the challenges of their time and exploiting their adversaries' weaknesses, these leaders achieved remarkable victories on the battlefield. Their ability to think creatively and act decisively in uncertainty set them apart as visionary military commanders.

Furthermore, the close relationship between these military leaders and the political authorities of their time played a crucial role in shaping military doctrine. Their ability to navigate the complex political landscape, secure necessary resources, and gain the support of key decision-makers was essential to their success on the battlefield. By aligning their military objectives with political goals, these leaders could effectively mobilize their forces and achieve strategic victories.

In conclusion, the influence of these military leaders on military innovation and doctrine cannot be overstated. Their legacy lives on in the strategies and doctrines employed by modern military forces worldwide. By studying their accomplishments and learning from their successes and failures, we can gain valuable insights into the art of leadership in times of conflict.

RELATIONSHIP WITH POLITICAL AUTHORITIES AND DECISION-MAKING

Military leaders throughout history have maintained a complex relationship with political authorities. Their interactions and decision-making processes have had significant consequences. Military leaders must navigate this relationship carefully, balancing warfare demands with the state's interests.

Political authorities' influence on military decision-making can shape the outcome of conflicts and campaigns. Military leaders must understand the political climate in which they operate, as decisions made on the battlefield are often influenced by broader political considerations.

Political authorities, such as rulers or governments, often dictate strategic objectives and priorities for military campaigns. Military leaders must align their plans and operations with these directives, ensuring their actions serve the state's interests.

At the same time, military leaders play a crucial role in advising political authorities on military matters. Their expertise and insights can help shape policy decisions and inform strategic planning. Military leaders can ensure their actions are coordinated with broader national interests by effectively communicating with political authorities.

The relationship between military leaders and political authorities is not always harmonious. Conflicts may arise over differing priorities, strategies, or resource allocation. Military leaders must navigate these tensions diplomatically, seeking common ground and working towards shared objectives.

Ultimately, the success of military campaigns often depends on the effectiveness of this relationship. Strong collaboration between military leaders and political authorities can lead to decisive victories and lasting strategic gains. Conversely, a breakdown in communication or trust can have dire consequences on the battlefield and beyond.

Military leaders' decisions, made in consultation with political authorities, leave a lasting impact on future generations. Their legacy is shaped by conflict outcomes, state stability, and national security preservation. By understanding the dynamic relationship between military leaders and political authorities, we can gain valuable insights into the complexities of war and statecraft.

LEGACY AND IMPACT ON FUTURE GENERATIONS

The military leaders of the past have left a lasting legacy that continues to influence future generations. Their strategic brilliance, unwavering dedication, and decisive decision-making have set a standard of excellence that inspires aspiring leaders in the modern era. Their impact transcends the battlefield, shaping history and leaving a legacy that serves as a testament to their enduring influence.

These military giants led their armies to victory and forged strong relationships with political authorities, ensuring the seamless coordination of military and political objectives. Their ability to navigate the complexities of power dynamics and maintain a symbiotic relationship with political leaders was instrumental in achieving their military goals.

As we compare the military leaders of the past, we see a spectrum of leadership styles and approaches reflecting the diverse challenges they faced. Some excelled in strategic planning and tactical execution, while others distinguished themselves through their charismatic leadership and ability to inspire troops. Despite their differences, these leaders shared a common commitment to excellence and a relentless drive to achieve victory.

The legacy of these military leaders lives on in the form of military innovation and doctrine that continue to shape contemporary military strategies. Their insights into warfare, leadership, and decision-making have provided invaluable lessons for future generations of military commanders, enabling them to navigate the complexities of the modern battlefield with skill and foresight.

In conclusion, the impact of these military leaders on future generations cannot be overstated. Their legacy is a guiding light for aspiring leaders, inspiring them to strive for excellence, uphold the highest standards of leadership, and make a lasting impact on the world.

COMPARISON OF DIFFERENT MILITARY LEADERS

Asoka of the Mauryan Empire is renowned for his conversion to Buddhism and commitment to non-violence, governance, and social justice. His empire stretched across much of modern-day India, and his legacy inspires leaders who seek to rule with compassion and benevolence. In contrast, Genghis Khan of the Mongol Empire is remembered for his ruthless military campaigns and the creation of history's largest contiguous land empire. Known for his brutal tactics and subjugation of vast territories, Genghis Khan's legacy is one of conquest and domination.

Saladin, the Kurdish Muslim leader, is celebrated for his role in the recapture of Jerusalem during the Crusades and his chivalrous conduct towards his enemies, earning him respect even from European adversaries. His leadership qualities and strategic prowess have inspired many military leaders throughout history. On the other hand, Attila the Hun, known as the "Scourge of God," led a devastating campaign of destruction across Europe, instilling fear in all who opposed him. His legacy is one of fear and destruction, leaving a lasting impact on the regions he conquered.

Admiral Yi Sun-sin of Korea is revered for his naval expertise and innovative tactics that led to decisive victories against Japanese invaders during the Imjin War. His legacy as a brilliant military leader and strategist has had a lasting impact on maritime warfare. In contrast, Napoleon Bonaparte of France is remembered for his ambitious military campaigns across Europe, strategic brilliance, and eventual downfall. Despite his military successes, his overreach and eventual defeat at the hands of the European powers demonstrate the limitations of power and ambition.

These military leaders have left a unique imprint on history, shaping the course of their respective empires and regions. Their contrasting leadership styles, tactics, and legacies serve as a reminder of the diverse paths to military success and the enduring impact of great military leaders on future generations.

CHALLENGES FACED AND OVERCOME

Military leaders throughout history have faced a myriad of challenges in the pursuit of their strategic objectives. From logistical hurdles to fierce resistance from enemy forces, these leaders have demonstrated remarkable resilience and adaptability. One common challenge many military leaders face is the need to navigate complex political landscapes and maintain the loyalty of their troops. This delicate balancing act requires a keen understanding of human psychology and leadership dynamics. Additionally, the ever-changing nature of warfare presents constant challenges regarding technological advancements and evolving tactics. Military leaders must continuously innovate and adapt their strategies to stay ahead of their adversaries. Furthermore, the physical demands of warfare can take a toll on even the most seasoned commanders. Enduring harsh conditions on the battlefield and managing the welfare of their troops adds another layer of complexity to their roles. Despite these formidable challenges, history is replete with examples of military leaders who have overcome seemingly insurmountable odds. Their ability to inspire and lead their troops with courage and determination has been instrumental in achieving victory in adversity. These leaders have left a lasting legacy that inspires future military strategists by facing these challenges head-on and demonstrating unwavering resolve.

CONCLUSION AND REFLECTION ON THEIR OVERALL CONTRIBUTION

The military leaders discussed in this chapter demonstrated exceptional courage, strategic acumen, and leadership in the face of formidable challenges. From navigating treacherous terrains to overcoming numerical and technological disadvantages, these leaders exhibited resilience and determination in their conquests. They skillfully adapted to varying circumstances, employed innovative tactics, and maintained the morale of their troops in the most dire situations. Their contributions to the expansion of Islamic territories were significant, shaping the course of history and leaving a lasting legacy for future generations to admire and learn from.

NOTES AND REFERENCES

1. The Silk Road trade routes played a crucial role in facilitating cultural and religious exchanges between the Islamic world and China. As noted by T. Hoogervorst:

"Through the power of monsoon sailing, these small-scale circuits coalesced into larger networks by the 5th century bce. Commercial relations with Chinese, Indian, and West Asian traders brought great prosperity to a number of Southeast Asian ports, which were described as places of immense wealth." (Lee & Forbes, 1988)

2. Islam began to spread in China during the Tang dynasty (618-907 CE). According to C. Shih:

"Islam came to China from several directions. To the north-west, Islam expanded rapidly in Central Asia in the seventh century; the Chinese rulers of the Tang dynasty called in Muslim military help, and by 760 there were 4000 Muslim families in Xian, the Tang capital, alone. Islam soon consolidated itself in Chinese Turkestan, the modern provinces of Xinjiang, Gansu and Shaanxi." (Berg, 1999)

3. The strategic importance of western China, particularly Xinjiang, in the spread of Islam is highlighted by S. Akiner:

"In the north-west, by contrast, and particularly in the province of Xinjiang, Islam was and remains the distinguishing faith of another nine Muslim minorities, who have never been assimilated. These are the Uighur, Kazakh, Kyrgyz, Sala, Tajik, Uzbek, Tatar, Baoan and Dongxiang." (Mazis, 2013)

While these sources don't directly address China's strategic importance during the period of great Islamic conquests, they provide context on how Islam spread to China and the strategic significance of regions like Xinjiang and the Silk Road in facilitating cultural and religious exchanges between the Islamic world and China. For more specific information on China's role during the early Islamic conquests, additional research focusing on 7th-8th century sources would be necessary.

Bibliography:

Adamec, L. (2009). The Makings of Modern Afghanistan (review). The Middle East Journal, 63, 321–321.

Ahmad, M., Yousaf, N., & Shah, Z. (2016). US-India Strategic Bargaining and Power Balancing in South Asia. Journal of Political Studies, 23, 439.

Akiner, S. (1998). East Asia. Bulletin of the School of Oriental and African Studies, 61, 589–589.

Alvarez, C. (2015). China-Kazakhstan Energy Relations between 1997 and 2012. Journal of International Affairs, 69, 57.

Amiri, M., & Shojaeefard, A. (2001). Shanghai Cooperation Organization, the Islamic Republic of Iran's Security and of United States of Americàs Interests.

Bachrach, B., Golden, P., Spellberg, D., Deng, G., Abulafia, D., Modelski, G., Galloway, J., Horton, M., Schroeder, P. W., Pierson, P., Kutcher, N., Schweizer, K., Wilton, A., Anderson, M., Baugh, D., Crimmin, P., Anna, T., Eltis, D., Lambi, I. N., ... Peart, S. (2000). Reviews of Books. The International History Review, 22, 129–248.

Bagci, K. (2014). Trade Costs and Intra-OIC Trade: What Are the Linkages? Journal of Economic Cooperation and Development, 35, 187.

Baumer, C. (2018). The age of decline and revival.

Berg, H. (1999). The Near and Middle East. Bulletin of the School of Oriental and African Studies, 62, 557–558.

Bhat, M. (2014). Iran-China Relations: A Challenge for U.S. Hegemony 1. Quarterly Journal of Chinese Studies, 3, 113.

Clair, C. D. (2003). Inner Asia: Making a Long-Term U.S. Commitment.

Cohen, A. (2002). Russia, Islam, and the War on Terrorism: An Uneasy Future. Demokratizatsiya, 10, 556.

Dara, J., Moghadas, A., & Lalalizadeh, M. (2020). The Regional Security Complex of Moqavemah(Resistance) and Iran's strategy to ensure Oil Security. 4.

Gray, A. (2012). Alternative Globalizations: An Integrative Approach to Studying Dissident Knowledge in the Global Justice Movement – By S. A. Hamed Hosseini. Political Studies Review, 10, 111–112.

Hall, K. R. (2015). European Southeast Asia Encounters with Islamic Expansionism, circa 1500–1700: Comparative Case Studies of Banten, Ayutthaya, and Banjarmasin in the Wider Indian Ocean Context. Journal of World History, 25, 229–262.

Hoogervorst, T. (2021). Commercial Networks Connecting Southeast Asia with the Indian Ocean. Oxford Research Encyclopedia of Asian History.

Institute Of Archeology Of Shanxi Province: Art of the Houma Foundry. viii, 523 pp. [Chinese introduction. Bilingual captions.] Princeton, NJ: Princeton University Press, 1996. $175. (n.d.).

Javaid, U., & Haq, M. (2016). Political Challenges and Security Issues in FATA and Its Impact on Economic Development. South Asian Studies, 31, 367.

Kaplan, H. S. (1974). The New Sex Therapy: Active Treatment of Sexual Dysfunctions.

Khan, F. (2019). Christopher Marlowe's Tamburlaine and the Politics of English Trade.

Khan, S. (2016). An Overview of the Vanishing Archaeological Landscape of Shahbaz-Garhi. 39, 51.

Kościelniak, K. (2011). The Churches of Damascus according to Ibn 'Asākir (d. 1176). The Destruction of the Church of St. John the Baptist by Caliph Al-Walīd I. 64, 133–139.

Kurmanaliyeva, A., Aljanova, N., & Manassova, M. (2018). The Marginocentric Cultural Features of Cities along the Great Silk Road in the territory of Kazakhstan. Clcweb-Comparative Literature and Culture, 20, 5.

Lee, R. H. G., & Forbes, A. (1988). Warlords and Muslims in Chinese Central Asia: a political history of Republican Sinkiang 1911-1949. The American Historical Review, 93, 1377.

Lewis, A. (1990). The Islamic World and the Latin West, 1350-1500. Speculum, 65, 833–844.

Mazis, I. (2013). Theoretical Perception of Geopolitics in Davutoğlu's Work: A Critical Presentation. 3, 9–50.

Morady, F. (2011). Iran ambitious for regional supremacy: the great powers, geopolitics and energy resources. Journal of the Indian Ocean Region, 7, 75–94.

Müllerson, R. (2007). Central Asia: A Chessboard and Player in the New Great Game.

Omissi, D. E. (2015). Gajendra Singh. The Testimonies of Indian Soldiers and the Two World Wars: Between Self and Sepoy . London: Bloomsbury, 2014. Pp. x + 295. £ 65.00 (cloth). Journal of British Studies, 54, 543–545.

Pant, H. (2009). Pakistan and Iran's Dysfunctional Relationship. Middle East Quarterly, 16.

Research Items. (n.d.). In Nature (Vol. 125, pp. 543–545).

Shih, C. (2000). Editorial. Religion, State & Society, 28, 157–160.

Sibal, K. (2016). Challenges and Prospects of India's Strategic Partnership with Russia. Indian Foreign Affairs Journal, 11, 297.

Taşçı, G., & Kenan, S. (2018). From Paper to Practice: Heed the Voice of Students!

Vijayalakshmi, K. (2015). India and USA: A New Moment in Strategic Partnership. Indian Foreign Affairs Journal, 10, 133.

Wink, A. (1991). Al-Hind, the Making of the Indo-Islamic World.

Zambelis, C. (2005). The Strategic Implications of Political Liberalization and Democratization in the Middle East. Parameters.

Zoidov, K., & Medkov, A. A. (2022). Modeling the development of Global Eurasia in the new economic reality.

Online:

China's strategic importance during the period of the great Islamic conquests in Asia can be understood through several key historical interactions and events. Here are some scholarly sources and references that provide a comprehensive view of this topic:

Early Encounters and Trade Relations

1. **Early Muslim-Chinese Encounters**:
- The relationship between China and the Islamic world dates back to the 7th century when Arab merchants and envoys traveled to Canton (Guangzhou) to establish trade ties with the Tang dynasty. This early interaction laid the foundation for a sustained Muslim presence in China, with the construction of mosques and madrassas and the establishment of Muslim communities in key trading centers[1][5].

2. **Economic Importance**:
- Before 1000 CE, the encounters between China and the Islamic world

were economically significant, surpassing the importance of relations between Europe and the Islamic world at that time[2]. Muslim merchants played crucial roles in the economic exchanges along the Silk Road, facilitating the flow of goods, culture, and ideas between the two regions.

Military and Political Interactions

3. **Battle of Talas (751 CE)**:
- One of the most notable military encounters was the Battle of Talas in 751 CE, where the Abbasid Caliphate's forces clashed with the Tang dynasty's army. This battle is often highlighted for its role in the transfer of papermaking technology from China to the Islamic world, although its strategic importance in terms of territorial control is debated. Despite the battle, Chinese influence in Central Asia continued for some time, and diplomatic relations between the Chinese and Abbasids persisted[4][12].

4. **Tang Dynasty's Role**:
- The Tang dynasty's military campaigns and political maneuvers in Central Asia were significant during the early Islamic conquests. Chinese forces were involved in various conflicts and alliances with local powers, influencing the dynamics of the region. For instance, the Tang dynasty's control over the Turgesh and other Central Asian states played a role in the broader geopolitical landscape during the Islamic expansion[4].

Cultural and Religious Influence

5. **Islamic Influence on Chinese Society**:
- The presence of Muslims in China led to cultural and religious exchanges that influenced Chinese society. During the Ming and Qing dynasties, Sino-Muslim scholars were well-versed in Islam, Confucianism, Daoism, and Buddhism, reflecting a synthesis of cultural and religious traditions[14]. This blending of cultures contributed to the unique development of Islam in China.

6. **Islamization of Central Asia**:
- The process of Islamization in Central Asia was gradual and influenced by various factors, including the interactions with Chinese political entities. The establishment of the Qarakhanid Khanate in the 10th century marked a significant milestone in the spread of Islam in the region, which had long-standing connections with China[13].

Scholarly References

- **"The Long Encounter: China And Islam's Irreconcilable Tensions"**: This source provides a historical overview of China's relationship with Islam, highlighting the early interactions and the long-term presence of Muslim communities in China[1].
- **"The Formative Muslim-Chinese Encounter"**: This article discusses the economic and cultural significance of early encounters between China

and the Islamic world[2].

- **"Islam and the Opening of the Chinese Mind"**: This book chapter explores the impact of Islamic civilization on China, particularly through the New Silk Road[3].

- **"China and the Islamic World"**: This scholarly article examines the historical relations between China and the Islamic world, emphasizing the influence of domestic policies on international relations[6].

These sources collectively provide a detailed understanding of China's strategic importance during the period of the great Islamic conquests in Asia, encompassing economic, military, cultural, and religious dimensions.

Citations:

[1] https://www.hoover.org/research/long-encounter-china-and-islams-irreconcilable-tensions
[2] https://theasiadialogue.com/2020/04/03/the-formative-muslim-chinese-encounter/
[3] https://academic.oup.com/book/9517/chapter/156495680
[4] https://en.wikipedia.org/wiki/Battle_of_Talas
[5] https://en.wikipedia.org/wiki/History_of_Islam_in_China
[6] https://scholarsarchive.byu.edu/cgi/viewcontent.cgi?article=1109&context=ccr
[7] https://faculty.washington.edu/dwaugh/hist225/225chron/islchr.html
[8] https://en.wikipedia.org/wiki/Early_Muslim_conquests
[9] https://simple.wikipedia.org/wiki/Muslim_conquests
[10] https://franpritchett.com/00maplinks/overview/charts/saislamtimeline.html
[11] https://en.unesco.org/silkroad/knowledge-bank/arab-conquest
[12] https://en.wikipedia.org/wiki/Muslim_conquest_of_Transoxiana
[13] https://journals.openedition.org/asiecentrale/623
[14] https://www.oxfordbibliographies.com/display/document/obo-9780199920082/obo-9780199920082-0121.xml

THE LEGACY OF THE ISLAMIC CONQUESTS IN ASIA

LEGACY: REFLECTING ON THE ENDURING IMPACT OF THE ISLAMIC CONQUESTS IN ASIA

The Islamic conquests in Asia have left a profound and lasting legacy that continues to shape the region to this day. From the Arabian Peninsula to the far reaches of Asia, the impact of these conquests is evident in the evolution of cultures, societies, and political structures. The enduring influence of Islamic rule can be seen in the art, architecture, literature, and philosophical traditions that emerged during this period. It is essential to reflect on the complexities of this legacy and understand how it has shaped the diverse landscape of Asia.

The interaction between Islamic and local cultures was crucial in shaping the region. The exchange of ideas, beliefs, and practices led to a rich tapestry of cultural expression that continues to be celebrated and preserved today. The fusion of Islamic and indigenous traditions created a dynamic and vibrant cultural landscape that reflects the region's unique history.

Moreover, the enduring impact of the Islamic conquests can be seen in the social transformations that occurred during this period. The introduction of Islamic law, customs, and societal norms brought about significant changes in how communities organized themselves and interacted. The legacy of these social transformations can still be observed in the familial structures, community dynamics, and social hierarchies prevalent in many parts of Asia.

Additionally, the spread and adaptation of Islam across diverse populations have left a lasting imprint on the religious landscape of the region. The blending of Islamic beliefs with existing spiritual practices resulted in the emergence of syncretic religious traditions that continue to be practiced by millions of people. The enduring influence of Islam on the religious identity of Asia is a testament to the profound impact of the Islamic conquests.

Overall, the enduring impact of the Islamic conquests in Asia is a testament to human societies' resilience and adaptability in the face of change and upheaval. By reflecting on this legacy, we can gain a deeper understanding of the region's complex history and appreciate the diverse cultural tapestry that defines contemporary Asia.

EVOLUTION OF CULTURES: EXAMINING HOW THE INTERACTION BETWEEN ISLAMIC AND LOCAL CULTURES SHAPED THE REGION

The interaction between Islamic and local cultures in Asia has been pivotal in shaping the region's diverse cultural landscape. Through cultural exchange and synthesis, the Islamic conquests brought about a profound evolution of traditions, beliefs, and practices that have continued to resonate through the centuries.

With its rich heritage of knowledge, art, and governance, Islamic civilization encountered a myriad of local cultures across Asia. This encounter sparked a dynamic exchange of ideas, technology, and aesthetics, leading to a fusion of traditions that enriched both Islamic and local societies.

In art and architecture, the synthesis of Islamic geometric patterns with local motifs produced magnificent structures that reflected the diversity of cultural influences. From the intricate tile work of Persian mosques to the grand stupas of Southeast Asia, this blending of styles created architectural wonders that stand as testaments to the harmonious coexistence of different cultures.

Moreover, the evolution of language and literature witnessed the translation of classical texts into Arabic, Persian, and other languages, fostering a vibrant literary tradition across Asia. Poets, scholars, and philosophers from diverse backgrounds contributed to a shared intellectual heritage, influencing each other's ideas and beliefs.

The culinary traditions of Islamic and local cuisines merged to create a fusion of flavors and ingredients that tantalized the taste buds of both communities. Spices from the Indian subcontinent intermingled with Arabic spices, creating a culinary tapestry that continues to delight palates worldwide.

Religious practices also transformed as Islam assimilated local customs and beliefs, leading to the development of unique syncretic traditions that combined elements of both Islamic and indigenous religions. The veneration of saints, the adaptation of local festivals, and the incorporation of folk rituals added complexity to the religious landscape, fostering a sense of shared spiritual heritage among diverse communities.

Overall, the evolution of Asian cultures through the interaction between Islamic and local traditions exemplifies the richness and resilience of multicultural societies. The enduring legacy of this cultural fusion serves as a testament to the power of diversity in shaping vibrant and dynamic civilizations.

SOCIETAL TRANSFORMATIONS: ANALYZING THE SOCIAL CHANGES BROUGHT ABOUT BY ISLAMIC RULE AND CONQUEST

The Islamic conquests in Asia had a profound impact on the social fabric of the region. These conquests brought about significant societal transformations as Islamic rule and influence spread across diverse populations. One key aspect of this transformation was the restructuring of societal hierarchies and norms. Islamic governance introduced new legal frameworks based on Islamic law, reshaping the social order and community relationships.

Furthermore, the spread of Islam led to the formation of new social identities that transcended traditional tribal or ethnic affiliations. Conversion to Islam often meant adopting a new set of cultural practices and beliefs, creating a shared sense of community among believers. This shift in social identity had far-reaching implications for social cohesion and collective identity in the conquered territories.

Moreover, the interaction between Islamic and local cultures fostered a process of cultural synthesis, where elements of Islamic civilization blended with existing cultural traditions. This cultural exchange enriched the region's social landscape, giving rise to new forms of art, literature, and architecture that reflected the diversity of influences at play.

Additionally, establishing Islamic institutions such as mosques, madrasas, and charitable organizations was crucial in shaping social structures and fostering community cohesion. These institutions served as centers of learning, spiritual guidance, and social welfare, contributing to society's overall well-being.

Overall, the societal transformations brought about by Islamic rule and conquest not only altered the social dynamics of the region but also laid the foundation for the rich cultural tapestry that characterizes Asia today.

RELIGIOUS INFLUENCES: INVESTIGATING THE SPREAD AND ADAPTATION OF ISLAM ACROSS DIVERSE POPULATIONS

The spread of Islam across diverse populations in the wake of the Islamic conquests in Asia ushered in a new era of religious influence and adaptation. As Islamic rule extended its reach, it brought about significant changes in the region's religious landscape. The message of Islam resonated with various communities, leading to the conversion of many to the new faith.

Islamic teachings and practices permeated daily life, shaping individual beliefs, societal norms, and values. The establishment of mosques and Islamic educational institutions became symbols of the faith's presence, serving as centers for worship, learning, and community gatherings. The call to prayer echoed through cities and villages, marking the rhythm of the day and reinforcing Islamic identity.

Moreover, local populations' adaptation of Islamic religious practices gave rise to unique expressions of faith, blending indigenous traditions with Islamic tenets. This syncretism fostered a rich tapestry of religious diversity, where different cultures found common ground in shared beliefs and rituals. The convergence of Islamic and local customs enriched the religious experience, creating a fusion of traditions that shaped the people's spiritual lives.

The spread of Islam also influenced interfaith relations, fostering dialogue and exchange between adherents of different religions. Communities coexisted in a spirit of tolerance and mutual respect, leading to cultural exchanges and collaborations that transcended religious boundaries. Islamic rulers often promoted religious pluralism and protected the rights of religious minorities, contributing to a harmonious social fabric characterized by diversity and inclusivity.

In conclusion, the spread and adaptation of Islam across diverse populations following the Islamic conquests in Asia profoundly impacted the religious landscape of the region. Blending Islamic teachings with local traditions, establishing religious institutions, and promoting interfaith dialogue all contributed to a dynamic religious environment marked by diversity and tolerance. The legacy of religious influences from this period continues to resonate in the region, shaping the spiritual practices and beliefs of successive generations.

ARTISTIC AND ARCHITECTURAL LEGACY: EXPLORING THE ART AND ARCHITECTURE CREATED DURING AND AFTER THE CONQUESTS

The Islamic conquests in Asia left a profound artistic and architectural legacy that continues to inspire and awe observers. Fusing Islamic artistic traditions with existing cultural expressions resulted in a unique and diverse array of artworks and monuments reflecting the dynamic interactions between civilizations. Islamic conquerors brought a rich artistic heritage encompassing calligraphy, geometric patterns, arabesques, and motifs inspired by nature. These elements were skillfully integrated into the existing artistic traditions of the conquered territories, leading to the creation of exquisite masterpieces that blended the best of both worlds.

Architecture also flourished during and after the Islamic conquests, with new styles and forms emerging that reflected the conquerors' cultural and religious influences. Mosques, palaces, mausoleums, and other structures were built with intricate details, harmonious proportions, and stunning decorations that showcased the ingenuity and creativity of the architects and craftsmen. Using domes, arches, minarets, and courtyards became characteristic features of Islamic architecture in Asia, influencing religious and secular buildings across the region.

The artistic and architectural legacy of the Islamic conquests in Asia extended beyond the physical structures, permeating daily life and fostering a sense of cultural identity among the diverse populations. Artworks such as illuminated manuscripts, textiles, ceramics, metalwork, and glassware served as expressions of beauty and craftsmanship, reflecting the artistic sophistication of the Islamic world. The construction of monumental buildings and urban developments showcased the power and grandeur of the ruling elite. It provided centers of communal gathering and spiritual reflection for the residents of the conquered territories.

Overall, the artistic and architectural legacy of the Islamic conquests in Asia represents a testament to the enduring influence of Islamic civilization on the region's cultural landscape. Through the synthesis of artistic traditions, the creation of magnificent structures, and the promotion of aesthetic values, the conquerors left behind a rich heritage that continues to inspire and captivate audiences across the globe.

ECONOMIC IMPACT: ASSESSING THE ECONOMIC CONSEQUENCES OF THE ISLAMIC CONQUESTS ON TRADE AND PROSPERITY

The economic impact of the Islamic conquests in Asia was significant, reshaping trade networks and fostering prosperity in new ways. As Islamic rule expanded, it changed agricultural practices, urban development, and commercial activities. The integration of different regions under Islamic governance facilitated the exchange of goods, ideas, and technologies, leading to a flourishing economy across the conquered territories.

One key economic consequence of the Islamic conquests was the establishment of trade routes connecting distant lands. The Islamic Caliphate's control over strategic trading hubs such as Baghdad, Alexandria, and Damascus was crucial in facilitating commerce between Asia, Africa, and Europe. This network of trade routes, known as the Silk Road, Silk Sea, and Spice Route, facilitated the exchange of goods such as silk, spices, ceramics, and precious metals, enriching the economies of the regions involved.

Furthermore, the Islamic conquests promoted cultural exchange and innovation, leading to agriculture, industry, and finance advancements. Islamic rulers introduced new crops and agricultural techniques, improving agricultural productivity and boosting food production and trade. Urban centers under Islamic rule witnessed a rapid expansion of markets, workshops, and commercial enterprises, attracting merchants from diverse backgrounds and creating a vibrant economic environment.

The Islamic conquests also brought about a monetary system based on the gold dinar and silver dirham, which standardized currency and facilitated trade across different regions. Establishing bazaars, caravanserais, and banking institutions further fueled economic growth and prosperity. Islamic rulers promoted business activities by providing infrastructure, incentives, and protection to traders, stimulating economic development and prosperity in the conquered territories.

In conclusion, the economic impact of the Islamic conquests in Asia was profound. They transformed trade networks, fostering prosperity and promoting cultural exchange and innovation. The integration of diverse regions under Islamic rule created a dynamic economic environment that facilitated commerce, industry, and agricultural development, leaving a lasting legacy on the region's economic landscape.

POLITICAL LANDSCAPE: UNDERSTANDING THE LONG-TERM EFFECTS ON GOVERNANCE AND POWER STRUCTURES IN THE REGION

The Islamic conquests in Asia had a profound and lasting impact on the region's political landscape. The establishment of Islamic rule brought about significant changes in governance and power structures, influencing the trajectory of these societies for centuries to come. One of the key effects was the introduction of a new system of administration based on Islamic principles and practices. This led to the emergence of caliphates and sultanates, which replaced existing political institutions and reshaped how power was wielded and distributed.

Under Islamic rule, religious and political authority blended, with rulers often claiming legitimacy based on their adherence to Islamic values. This fusion of religion and governance had far-reaching consequences for the political landscape, as it influenced the relationship between rulers and their subjects, as well as the administration of justice and the enforcement of laws. Additionally, the spread of Islamic rule facilitated the integration of diverse ethnic and cultural groups into a common political framework, fostering a sense of unity and shared identity among the inhabitants of these territories.

The Islamic conquests also brought about a period of political stability and centralized authority in many parts of Asia. Establishing strong, centralized governments helped maintain law and order, promote economic development, and facilitate cultural exchange. At the same time, the expansion of Islamic rule created a framework for disseminating Islamic legal and administrative practices, laying the foundation for developing sophisticated bureaucratic systems in the region.

Moreover, the Islamic conquests fostered innovation and intellectual inquiry, leading to advancements in various fields such as science, philosophy, and literature. The patronage of Islamic rulers and the flourishing of centers of learning and scholarship contributed to the dissemination of knowledge and the cross-fertilization of ideas, resulting in a rich intellectual legacy long after conquests.

Overall, the long-term effects of the Islamic conquests on the political landscape of Asia were significant and enduring. The establishment of Islamic rule ushered in a new era of governance and power structures, setting the stage for the development of distinctive regional political institutions and traditions. Additionally, the fusion of religion and politics, the promotion of centralized authority, and the fostering of intellectual and cultural exchange all contributed to the enduring legacy of the Islamic conquests in shaping the political landscape of Asia.

GEW SOCIAL SCIENCES GROUP

INTELLECTUAL CONTRIBUTIONS: HIGHLIGHTING THE ADVANCEMENTS IN SCIENCE, PHILOSOPHY, AND LITERATURE FACILITATED BY THE ISLAMIC CONQUESTS

During the Islamic conquests in Asia, significant advancements were made in science, philosophy, and literature. Islamic scholars were crucial in preserving and translating ancient texts from various civilizations, including Greek, Indian, and Persian sources. This cultural exchange fostered a flourishing intellectual environment that led to groundbreaking contributions across disciplines.

In the field of science, scholars in the Islamic world have made notable progress in areas such as astronomy, mathematics, medicine, and optics. Building upon the knowledge of earlier civilizations, Muslim scientists made significant advancements in algebra, trigonometry, and the development of the decimal system, which laid the foundation for modern mathematics. Furthermore, Islamic scholars made important contributions to medicine and optics, pioneering new treatment methods and refining the understanding of light and vision.

In philosophy, the Islamic conquests facilitated the translation of works by ancient Greek philosophers, such as Aristotle and Plato, into Arabic. This intellectual engagement with Greek thought inspired Muslim philosophers like Al-Farabi, Avicenna, and Averroes to develop their own philosophical systems synthesizing Greek and Islamic ideas. These philosophers substantially contributed to metaphysics, ethics, and political theory, influencing later Western philosophical thought.

Literature also thrived during the Islamic conquests in Asia, with poets and writers producing works of profound beauty and complexity. Arabic literature, in particular, flourished with the emergence of renowned poets like Al-Mutanabbi and Al-Ma'arri, who crafted verses that captured the richness of Islamic culture and the human experience. Additionally, translating ancient texts into Arabic led to the preservation of literary masterpieces from diverse traditions, enriching the literary landscape of the Islamic world.

Overall, the intellectual contributions facilitated by the Islamic conquests in Asia had a lasting impact on the development of science, philosophy, and literature. By fostering a culture of inquiry and learning, Muslim scholars created a legacy of innovation and creativity that continues to inspire intellectual endeavors to this day.

REPERCUSSIONS ON MINORITIES: EXAMINING THE TREATMENT AND STATUS OF RELIGIOUS AND ETHNIC MINORITIES UNDER ISLAMIC RULE

During the Islamic conquests in Asia, the treatment and status of religious and ethnic minorities under Islamic rule varied significantly. While some minority groups were able to coexist peacefully with Islamic rulers, others faced challenges and discrimination in various forms. The impact of Islamic conquests on minorities has left a lasting legacy that continues to shape social dynamics in modern-day Asia.

In some cases, Islamic rulers in Asia adopted policies of religious tolerance towards minorities, allowing them to practice their faiths and maintain their cultural traditions. This approach fostered a sense of diversity and inclusivity within the newly conquered territories, promoting peaceful coexistence among different religious and ethnic communities.

However, there were instances where minorities faced persecution or marginalization under Islamic rule. Certain groups were forced to convert to Islam, pay special taxes, or adhere to strict regulations that restricted their freedoms and rights. This imposed religious and social restrictions created tensions and contributed to social inequalities.

The treatment of minorities under Islamic rule also varied depending on the region and the specific rulers in power. Some Islamic dynasties were more lenient and tolerant towards minorities, while others adopted more oppressive and discriminatory measures. These differences influenced the experiences of minority communities and shaped their interactions with the dominant Islamic culture.

The repercussions of the treatment of minorities during the Islamic conquests continue to be felt in modern-day Asia. Historical grievances and inequalities have persisted, affecting the region's social and political dynamics. Identity, belonging, and cultural preservation remain relevant as minority groups seek recognition and equality in societies shaped by centuries of Islamic influence.

By examining the treatment and status of religious and ethnic minorities under Islamic rule during the conquests in Asia, we can gain insights into the complex interplay of power, identity, and diversity that have enduring consequences for the region today.

CONTEMPORARY RELEVANCE: DISCUSSING HOW THE LEGACY OF THE ISLAMIC CONQUESTS CONTINUES TO INFLUENCE MODERN-DAY ASIA

The legacy of the Islamic conquests continues to reverberate throughout modern-day Asia, shaping the region's political, social, and cultural landscape. One of the most significant impacts is the continued influence of Islam as a major religion in many Asian countries. The spread of Islam during the conquests laid the foundation for the development of vibrant Muslim communities that have become integral parts of the societies they inhabit.

Additionally, the architectural and artistic achievements of the Islamic empires have left a lasting mark on the region. The intricate designs of mosques, palaces, and other structures continue to be admired and studied, showcasing the rich cultural heritage that emerged from the conquests. Moreover, the scientific, philosophical, and literary advancements made during this period have impacted intellectual thought in Asia and beyond.

The economic consequences of the Islamic conquests are also evident in modern-day Asia. Establishing trade routes and promoting commerce under Islamic rule laid the groundwork for the region's economic development. Many contemporary commercial practices and economic systems can trace their roots to the trade networks established during the Islamic conquests.

Furthermore, the political structures and governance systems that emerged from the conquests continue to shape how Asian countries are governed today. Concepts of centralized authority, bureaucracy, and judicial systems introduced during this period have endured and influenced modern-day governance practices in many Asian nations.

Despite these positive legacies, it is essential to acknowledge the challenges and tensions arising from the conquests. The treatment of religious and ethnic minorities under Islamic rule has had a lasting impact on intergroup relations in Asia. Understanding and addressing these historical injustices are crucial for promoting peace, tolerance, and inclusivity in modern-day societies.

In conclusion, the legacy of the Islamic conquests in Asia is a complex tapestry of influences that continue to shape the region today. By recognizing and reflecting on this multifaceted legacy, we can better understand the present-day dynamics in Asia and work towards a more inclusive and interconnected future.

LASTING IMPACTS ON CULTURES, SOCIETIES, AND RELIGIONS

The aftermath of the Islamic conquests across Asia ushered in a new era of cultural exchange and syncretism, shaping the region profoundly. The collision of diverse peoples, traditions, and belief systems resulted in a dynamic interplay that transformed societies and led to the creation of hybrid cultures. This period marked a significant turning point in Asia's history, with lasting impacts that continue to resonate to this day.

As Islamic empires expanded their domains, they encountered a rich tapestry of civilizations, each with its unique customs, languages, and artistic traditions. The exchange of ideas, technologies, and artistic styles fostered a vibrant cultural milieu that transcended geographical boundaries. This cross-pollination of cultures led to the emergence of new artistic forms, architectural styles, and literary genres that reflected the fusion of diverse influences.

The blending of Islamic, Persian, Indian, and Chinese cultural elements resulted in a synthesis that enriched the cultural landscape of Asia. This cultural hybridity gave rise to a cosmopolitan ethos that celebrated diversity and inclusivity, fostering a spirit of mutual understanding and cooperation among different ethnic and religious groups. Artistic expressions, such as calligraphy, miniature painting, and ceramic production, flourished during this period, reflecting the melding of artistic traditions from various cultural sources.

Moreover, the Islamic conquests facilitated the exchange of knowledge and ideas across a vast network of cities and trading hubs, leading to the dissemination of scientific, mathematical, and philosophical concepts. Scholars from different linguistic and religious backgrounds engaged in intellectual discourse, leading to advancements in astronomy, medicine, and philosophy. The translation of classical texts from Greek, Sanskrit, and Syriac into Arabic facilitated the preservation and transmission of ancient knowledge, laying the foundation for future scientific and philosophical developments.

In conclusion, the aftermath of the Islamic conquests in Asia ushered in a period of profound cultural vibrancy and intellectual exchange that transformed the region. The legacy of this era of cultural exchange and syncretism continues to shape Asia's cultural, artistic, and intellectual landscape, highlighting the enduring impact of the Islamic conquests on the diverse societies of the region.

CULTURAL EXCHANGE AND SYNCRETISM

The Islamic conquests in Asia led to significant cultural exchange and syncretism between societies and civilizations. This exchange of ideas, traditions, and practices played a crucial role in shaping the cultural landscape of the regions affected by the conquests. With its diverse influences from the Arabian Peninsula, Persia, and other regions, Islamic culture merged with local customs and traditions, creating a rich tapestry of cultural expressions.

One of the key aspects of cultural exchange during the aftermath of the Islamic conquests was the blending of artistic styles. Artisans and craftsmen from different backgrounds came together, fusing elements of Islamic art, such as intricate geometric patterns and calligraphy, with local artistic traditions. This fusion gave rise to unique art forms that reflected the multicultural ethos of the conquered territories.

Furthermore, the exchange of knowledge and ideas in science, philosophy, and literature flourished during this period. Islamic scholars and thinkers engaged with the intellectual heritage of the lands they conquered, leading to a vibrant exchange of ideas that enriched both Islamic and indigenous intellectual traditions. This cross-fertilization of knowledge was instrumental in preserving and transmitting ancient texts and scientific discoveries to future generations.

Religious syncretism was also a significant outcome of the cultural exchange that followed the Islamic conquests. The interaction between Islamic beliefs and local faith traditions resulted in new religious practices and rituals incorporating elements from both traditions. This syncretic approach to religion contributed to diversifying religious practices in the conquered territories, fostering a spirit of tolerance and inclusivity.

In conclusion, cultural exchange and syncretism were fundamental aspects of the aftermath of the Asian Islamic conquests. The blending of diverse cultural elements resulted in creating a dynamic and hybrid cultural milieu that continues to influence the region's cultural landscape to this day.

SOCIETAL TRANSFORMATIONS AND ADAPTATIONS

The Islamic conquests in Asia brought about significant societal transformations and adaptations across the regions affected. One of the key changes was the introduction of Islamic legal and administrative systems, which often replaced existing structures and institutions. This led to new social hierarchies based on religious affiliation and adherence to Islamic norms.

Additionally, the spread of Islam necessitated changes in social practices and customs, as Islamic principles influenced aspects of daily life such as family dynamics, gender roles, and interpersonal relationships. The emphasis on charity and social justice within Islam also led to the development of systems to support the less fortunate and marginalized members of society.

Moreover, the integration of diverse cultures and traditions through cultural exchange facilitated the emergence of new social norms and practices. This blending of traditions resulted in a rich tapestry of beliefs, customs, and rituals that reflected the multicultural nature of the societies under Islamic rule.

Furthermore, the Islamic conquests spurred economic developments that reshaped social structures and brought about new trade, commerce, and urbanization opportunities. This economic growth allowed for the accumulation of wealth and the rise of merchant classes, which played a crucial role in shaping societal dynamics and power structures.

Overall, the societal transformations and adaptations resulting from the Asian Islamic conquests were complex and multifaceted, encompassing changes in legal systems, social practices, cultural norms, economic structures, and power dynamics. These changes not only altered the fabric of society but also laid the foundation for the diverse and dynamic civilizations that emerged in the aftermath of the conquests.

RELIGIOUS INFLUENCES AND TRANSFORMATIONS

The Islamic conquests in Asia had far-reaching implications for the region's religious landscape. Islam's spread significantly transformed diverse societies' beliefs, practices, and institutions. As Islam expanded, it interacted with various religious traditions, leading to a complex process of synthesis and adaptation.

One of the key aspects of religious influence and transformation was the spread of Islamic monotheism. The concept of tawhid, or the belief in one God, challenged prevailing polytheistic beliefs and ideologies. This monotheistic worldview served as a unifying force among newly conquered populations, providing a shared spiritual foundation.

Moreover, the Islamic conquests led to adopting Arabic as a sacred language for religious purposes. The Quran, Islam's holy scripture, was revealed in Arabic, enriching the language's significance and fostering a sense of linguistic unity across diverse regions. This linguistic transformation facilitated the dissemination of Islamic teachings and contributed to developing Arabic as a language of scholarship and literature.

In addition to linguistic changes, the Islamic conquests brought about profound transformations in religious practices and rituals. The construction of mosques and religious schools became symbols of Islamic presence and authority, serving as centers for worship, education, and community engagement. Islamic legal and ethical norms also influenced social behavior and governance structures, shaping the moral fabric of societies.

Furthermore, the encounter between Islam and existing religious traditions led to the syncretism of beliefs and practices. Local customs and rituals were often integrated into Islamic religious observance, creating a unique blend of cultural expressions. This process of religious syncretism reflected the dynamic interaction between conquerors and conquered peoples, resulting in a rich tapestry of spiritual diversity.

Overall, the religious influences and transformations resulting from the Islamic conquests in Asia underscored the multifaceted nature of cultural exchange and adaptation. Through the dissemination of Islamic monotheism, the elevation of Arabic as a sacred language, and the synthesis of religious practices, Islam left an indelible mark on the region's religious landscape, shaping the spiritual beliefs and practices of future generations.

LANGUAGE AND LITERATURE CHANGES

Language and literature underwent significant changes after the Islamic conquests in Asia. The spread of Arabic as the language of administration, trade, and religious practice profoundly impacted linguistic diversity in the conquered territories. Local languages interacted with Arabic, leading to new dialects and forms of communication that reflected a fusion of cultures.

Literature also flourished during this period, with the translation of classical Greek, Persian, Indian, and Chinese texts into Arabic catalyzing intellectual exchange. The translation movement preserved ancient knowledge and facilitated the dissemination of scientific, philosophical, and literary works across cultural boundaries. Arabic became the language of scholarship, and learning centers such as Baghdad, Cordoba, and Samarkand emerged as hubs of intellectual activity.

Poetry, another important form of literary expression, thrived in the Islamic world. Poets composed verses praising rulers, celebrating love, and reflecting on the human condition. Arabic poetry served as a means of entertainment and a vehicle for conveying moral lessons and philosophical insights.

Moreover, the development of Arabic calligraphy as an art form showcased the fusion of aesthetics and language. Calligraphers transformed Arabic script into elaborate designs, adorning manuscripts, buildings, and decorative objects with intricate patterns that symbolized the beauty and power of written language.

The impact of language and literature changes resulting from the Islamic conquests reverberated throughout the centuries, influencing subsequent literary traditions, fostering cross-cultural dialogue, and shaping the identities of diverse societies in Asia and beyond.

ARCHITECTURAL AND ARTISTIC EVOLUTION

Islamic conquests in Asia significantly changed language and literature and fostered a remarkable evolution in architectural and artistic expressions. The merging of different cultural influences led to the development of a unique Islamic architectural style characterized by intricate geometric patterns, elaborate calligraphy, and stunning domes and minarets. This fusion of artistic traditions from various regions created awe-inspiring mosques, palaces, and other structures that continue to captivate observers today.

In Islamic art, ornate motifs and arabesque designs reflected a deep spiritual connection and reverence for the divine. Architects and artists employed intricate details to convey a sense of harmony and order, symbolizing the unity of creation and the eternal beauty of the cosmos. The construction of grand mosques served as places of worship and as centers of community life and learning, showcasing the importance of faith and knowledge in Islamic societies.

Moreover, the artistic evolution during this period extended beyond architecture to include exquisite works of calligraphy, manuscript illumination, and decorative arts. Skilled artisans and craftsmen produced stunning examples of Islamic art, such as intricate ceramic tiles, vibrant textiles, and intricate metalwork, showcasing the mastery of various techniques and materials.

These artistic creations served a functional purpose and reflected Islamic civilization's deep spiritual and cultural values.

The architectural and artistic evolution due to the Islamic conquests in Asia left a lasting legacy that continues to inspire and influence artistic expression today. The fusion of diverse cultural influences, coupled with a profound spiritual and intellectual ethos, contributed to the creation of a rich and diverse artistic tradition that remains a testament to the enduring impact of Islamic civilization on the artistic landscape of Asia and beyond.

ECONOMIC AND TRADE DEVELOPMENTS

The Islamic conquests in Asia brought significant economic and trade developments that transformed the region's commercial landscape. The integration of vast territories under Islamic rule facilitated trade connections across diverse regions, exchanging goods, technologies, and ideas. Establishing stable and secure trade routes, such as the Silk Road and the Indian Ocean, spurred economic growth and enhanced cultural interactions.

Islamic rulers actively promoted trade by implementing policies that supported commerce, such as standardized currency systems, tax incentives for merchants, and the protection of trade caravans. Cities like Baghdad, Damascus, and Cairo emerged as thriving commercial centers, attracting merchants worldwide. The construction of markets, bazaars, and trade guilds further facilitated economic transactions and promoted entrepreneurship.

The expansion of Islamic empires also boosted agricultural production by introducing new crops, irrigation techniques, and land reforms. This agricultural surplus met the demands of growing urban populations and fueled trade with neighboring regions. The exchange of agricultural products, spices, textiles, and luxury goods enriched the economies of Islamic societies and fostered cultural exchanges.

The Islamic conquests also led to advancements in finance and banking. Islamic merchants introduced sophisticated financial instruments such as letters of credit, bills of exchange, and partnerships that enabled long-distance trade and investment. The development of banking institutions and financial regulations promoted economic stability and facilitated capital flow across regions.

Moreover, the Islamic world became a hub of innovation in various industries, including textiles, ceramics, metalwork, and manuscript production. Skilled artisans and craftsmen from different cultural backgrounds contributed to the flourishing of artistic and craft industries, creating exquisite goods that were highly sought after in domestic and international markets.

Overall, the economic and trade developments resulting from the Islamic conquests in Asia laid the foundation for a globalized economy and cultural exchange that transcended geographical boundaries. The legacy of these economic transformations continues to influence trade dynamics, commercial practices, and economic partnerships in the modern world.

SOCIAL HIERARCHIES AND POWER STRUCTURES

The Islamic conquests in Asia significantly changed social hierarchies and power structures. As the newly established Islamic empires expanded their influence, they reshaped societal norms and power dynamics. One of the key features of these changes was the introduction of Islamic principles and beliefs into the fabric of society, leading to the emergence of new social hierarchies based on religious affiliation and adherence to Islamic law.

THE ISLAMIC CONQUESTS IN ASIA

The establishment of Islamic empires led to the consolidation of power by Muslim rulers and their appointed officials. These rulers, often seen as representatives of the Caliphate, wielded significant authority over their subjects and played a crucial role in shaping the social order. The Islamic legal system, known as Sharia, also played a key role in defining social hierarchies by delineating the rights and responsibilities of different social groups.

One important aspect of the new social hierarchies was the distinction between Muslims and non-Muslims. While Muslims were granted certain privileges and rights under Islamic law, non-Muslims were considered dhimmis, or protected subjects, who were required to pay a special tax called jizya in exchange for protection and religious freedom. This system created a clear hierarchy within society based on religious identity and established the dominance of Islam as the ruling religion in the Islamic empires.

At the same time, the Islamic conquests also led to the integration of diverse cultures and ethnic groups into the newly established empires. This integration resulted in a complex social landscape where different groups coexisted and interacted, often leading to new hierarchies based on ethnicity, class, and occupation. A diverse population within the Islamic empires contributed to the richness and complexity of social structures, highlighting the dynamic nature of social hierarchies in the aftermath of the conquests.

Overall, the Islamic conquests in Asia profoundly impacted social hierarchies and power structures, leading to the formation of new societal norms and relationships. Through establishing Islamic principles and legal systems, the conquerors reshaped existing social hierarchies and established a new order based on religious identity and adherence to Islamic law. The integration of diverse cultures and ethnic groups further contributed to the complexity and richness of social structures in the Islamic empires, illustrating the interplay between religion, culture, and power in shaping social hierarchies.

EDUCATIONAL AND INTELLECTUAL ADVANCEMENTS

Islamic conquests in Asia reshaped social hierarchies and power structures and spurred significant advancements in education and intellectual pursuits. Integrating diverse cultures and knowledge systems under Islamic rule fostered an environment conducive to learning and innovation. Establishing learning centers, such as madrasas and libraries, played a crucial role in promoting intellectual exchange and scholarship.

One of the key features of educational advancements during this period was the translation movement, which involved translating ancient Greek, Persian, Indian, and Chinese texts into Arabic. This facilitated the dissemination of knowledge across different regions and facilitated the development of new ideas in various fields such as philosophy, science, mathematics, and medicine. Scholars in Islamic societies made significant contributions to these disciplines, building upon the knowledge of past civilizations and expanding the frontiers of human understanding.

Islamic education emphasizes the importance of knowledge and learning as integral components of faith. Pursuing knowledge was seen as a way to deepen one's understanding of the world and draw closer to God. This holistic approach to education encompassed religious studies and the sciences, humanities, and arts, reflecting the interconnectedness of different branches of knowledge.

Intellectual advancements during this period were not limited to theoretical pursuits but had practical applications in architecture, engineering, and urban planning. Islamic scholars made groundbreaking discoveries in astronomy, optics, and navigation, which had far-reaching implications for technology and innovation. The intellectual curiosity and spirit of inquiry that characterized this era laid the foundation for future developments in science and technology.

Overall, the educational and intellectual advancements fostered during the Islamic conquests in Asia left a profound and lasting impact on the region's cultural, social, and scientific landscape. The legacy of these advancements continues to be felt in contemporary society, inspiring future generations to pursue knowledge, engage in critical thinking, and contribute to the advancement of human civilization.

CONTEMPORARY PERSPECTIVES ON THE LEGACY OF ISLAMIC CONQUESTS

The legacy of the Islamic conquests continues to shape the contemporary perspectives on history, culture, and religion in the regions that were once under Islamic rule. Scholars and historians offer diverse viewpoints on the long-lasting impacts of these conquests, highlighting both positive and negative aspects of the historical events.

One perspective emphasizes the intellectual advancements fostered during Islamic rule, noting the preservation and transmission of classical knowledge from ancient civilizations such as Greece, Persia, and India. Establishing libraries, centers of learning, and translation contributed to a flourishing intellectual environment that influenced later developments in science, medicine, philosophy, and literature.

Another viewpoint underscores the cultural exchange and syncretism that resulted from the Islamic conquests, leading to the blending of diverse traditions, languages, and artistic styles. This multicultural heritage is evident in the architecture, cuisine, music, and daily practices of Asian societies that were once part of the Islamic caliphate.

Contemporary perspectives also acknowledge the social and economic transformations under Islamic rule, with the introduction of new agricultural techniques, trade networks, and urban planning initiatives. The legacy of Islamic conquests is seen in the development of vibrant cities, thriving marketplaces, and sophisticated irrigation systems that continue to shape the landscapes of these regions today.

Furthermore, the religious influences of Islam on local belief systems and practices are a significant aspect of the legacy of the conquests. The spread of Islam not only led to the establishment of mosques and religious institutions but also influenced the spiritual and philosophical outlook of diverse communities, fostering a shared sense of identity and belonging among followers of the faith.

In conclusion, the contemporary perspectives on the legacy of Islamic conquests highlight the enduring impact of these historical events on the cultures, societies, and religions of Asia. By recognizing the complex interplay of intellectual, cultural, social, and religious influences that have shaped the region, we can gain a deeper understanding of the rich and diverse tapestry of history that continues to inform our present-day world.

SHAPING OF THE POLITICAL LANDSCAPE

POLITICAL TRANSFORMATIONS: SETTING THE STAGE

The Islamic conquests in Asia brought about significant political transformations that reshaped the region's geopolitical landscape. These conquests marked the establishment of new Islamic states, which emerged as powerful political entities after military campaigns and territorial acquisitions. The formation of these states marked a pivotal moment in the history of the Islamic world, as they laid the foundation for the consolidation of political power and the spread of Islamic governance across diverse territories.

The establishment of Islamic states involved the creation of administrative structures and governing institutions rooted in Islamic principles and traditions. These new political entities sought to uphold the teachings of Islam in their governance, leading to the development of a unique blend of religious and political authority. The rulers of these states relied on Islamic laws and ethical guidelines to govern their subjects and maintain social order within their domains.

The formation of Islamic states also facilitated the integration of diverse societies and cultures under a common political framework. As these states expanded their territorial control, they encountered various ethnic, linguistic, and religious groups. The rulers of the Islamic states adopted inclusive policies that allowed for the coexistence of different communities within their realms, fostering a sense of unity and shared identity among their subjects.

One key consequence of the establishment of Islamic states was the expansion of trade routes and economic networks across the region. The political stability and security provided by these states enabled merchants and traders to engage in long-distance commerce, facilitating the exchange of goods, ideas, and technologies between different regions. The economic prosperity generated by these trade networks fueled the growth and development of the Islamic states, further solidifying their political authority and influence.

The formation of Islamic states during the Islamic conquests in Asia set the stage for a new era of political transformations and cultural exchanges. These states played a crucial role in shaping the course of history in the region, leaving a lasting impact on the Islamic world's political, social, and economic dynamics. By examining the origins and evolution of these states, we can gain valuable insights into the complexities and nuances of Islamic governance and its enduring significance in the modern world.

ESTABLISHMENT OF ISLAMIC STATES: FORMATION OF NEW POLITICAL ENTITIES

The establishment of Islamic states in Asia marked a significant shift in the region's political landscape. With the conquests of various territories, new political entities emerged under Islamic rule, ushering in a period of transformation and consolidation of power.

The process of forming these new states was complex and multifaceted. As Islamic forces expanded their territories, they encountered diverse populations with their political structures and systems of governance. In many cases, existing rulers and elites were integrated into the new political order, blending local and Islamic administrative practices.

One key aspect of the formation of Islamic states was the establishment of centralized authority. Islamic rulers sought to consolidate power and maintain control over their vast empires by creating administrative structures that enabled efficient governance. This often involved the appointment of governors and administrators to oversee different regions and ensure compliance with central policies.

The adoption of Islamic legal principles also played a crucial role in shaping the new political entities. Implementing Sharia law as the basis for governance helped legitimize rulers' authority and unify diverse populations under a common legal framework. This reliance on Islamic jurisprudence reinforced the connection between religion and politics in the newly formed states.

Furthermore, the organization of the military contributed to the consolidation of power in the Islamic states. Armed forces were crucial for maintaining security, enforcing law and order, and defending the empire's borders. Military commanders held significant influence within the political hierarchy and played a key role in supporting the ruling elite's authority.

Overall, establishing Islamic states in Asia represented a dynamic political change and consolidation period. Through the formation of new political entities, the integration of diverse societies, and the implementation of administrative reforms, Islamic rulers could exert their influence and shape the region's political landscape for centuries to come.

ADMINISTRATIVE REFORMS: GOVERNING STRUCTURES UNDER ISLAMIC RULE

One key aspect of the formation of new political entities under Islamic rule was the implementation of administrative reforms that helped govern the vast territories under the Caliphate. These reforms were instrumental in establishing effective governance structures and ensuring the smooth functioning of the newly acquired territories.

The Islamic states introduced a centralized administration system characterized by a hierarchical structure with clearly defined roles and responsibilities. The caliph was at the top of the administrative hierarchy and served as the supreme political and religious authority. Below the caliph were appointed governors, known as walis, responsible for overseeing specific regions or provinces.

To ensure efficient governance, the Islamic states established a system of bureaucracy staffed by trained officials known as amirs. These amirs were appointed based on their qualifications and capabilities rather than their social status. This meritocratic approach to governance helped promote loyalty and competence among the ruling elite.

One of the key administrative reforms introduced by the Islamic states was adopting a uniform legal system based on Islamic jurisprudence, known as Sharia. This legal system provided a framework for resolving disputes, dispensing justice, and enforcing law and order across the territories under Islamic rule.

In addition to the legal system, the Islamic states also implemented financial reforms, including introducing a standardized currency and a taxation system. These financial reforms helped ensure a stable economy and generate revenue for the administration to fund various projects and services for the population.

Furthermore, the Islamic states established a system of public works and infrastructure development to improve the quality of life for their subjects. This included the construction of roads, bridges, mosques, and other public buildings that served both practical and symbolic functions.

Overall, the administrative reforms implemented by the Islamic states played a crucial role in consolidating their political authority, fostering stability, and facilitating the integration of diverse societies into the burgeoning Islamic civilization in Asia.

INTEGRATION OF DIVERSE SOCIETIES: CULTURAL AND POLITICAL FUSION

The integration of diverse societies under Islamic rule facilitated a unique cultural and political fusion that shaped the landscape of the conquered territories. This fusion was a superficial blending of traditions and a profound restructuring of social norms, administrative practices, and political structures. The Islamic rulers, recognizing the diversity of their subjects, adopted a flexible approach that allowed for the coexistence of various ethnicities, religions, and practices within a unified framework.

The system of governance established by the Islamic rulers was instrumental in fostering this integration. By establishing a central administrative apparatus, local traditions and customs were accommodated within the overarching Islamic legal framework. This approach allowed for a degree of autonomy at the regional level while ensuring adherence to core Islamic principles. As a result, cultural exchange and interaction flourished, enriching artistic, intellectual, and technological advancements.

Moreover, promoting trade and commerce was crucial in facilitating cultural exchange and political cohesion. The expansion of trade routes brought prosperity to the Islamic states and enabled the exchange of ideas, products, and technologies between disparate regions. This economic interconnectedness contributed to shared interests and mutual dependencies among the diverse societies under Islamic rule.

The fusion of cultural practices and political institutions ushered in a new era of creativity and innovation in the Islamic world. Artists, scholars, and thinkers from different backgrounds created a vibrant intellectual and artistic environment transcending geographical and cultural boundaries. This cultural fusion enriched the Islamic civilization and influenced the development of neighboring regions and societies.

In conclusion, the integration of diverse societies under Islamic rule led to a unique cultural and political fusion that shaped the identity of the Islamic world. By embracing diversity, fostering cultural exchange, and promoting economic interdependence, the Islamic rulers created a dynamic and inclusive society that laid the foundation for future art, science, and governance developments.

EXPANSION OF TRADE ROUTES: ECONOMIC IMPLICATIONS ON POLITICAL POWER

During the era of Islamic conquests in Asia, the expansion of trade routes played a pivotal role in shaping the economic landscape and influencing the distribution of political power. The establishment of vast empires facilitated the movement of goods, ideas, and resources across diverse regions, leading to significant economic implications on the political dynamics of the time.

The integration of new territories into the Islamic Caliphate created a network of trade routes that connected the East and West, enabling the exchange of commodities such as spices, silk, precious metals, and other luxury goods. These trade routes not only fostered economic prosperity but also enhanced cultural exchange and diplomatic relations between various societies.

The strategic location of key trading hubs, such as Baghdad, Damascus, and Cordoba, allowed these cities to emerge as centers of commerce, attracting merchants, scholars, and travelers from far and wide. The wealth generated from trade routes bolstered the economic power of these urban centers, enabling them to exert significant influence over political affairs and shape the course of history.

Moreover, controlling lucrative trade routes provided a source of revenue for the ruling authorities, allowing them to finance military campaigns, infrastructure projects, and cultural endeavors. The economic prosperity resulting from the expansion of trade routes strengthened the political dominance of the Islamic states and solidified their control over vast territories.

The interconnected nature of trade networks also facilitated the dissemination of knowledge, technology, and innovation, contributing to Islamic societies' intellectual and artistic flourishing. The exchange of goods and ideas across diverse regions fostered a spirit of cosmopolitanism and cultural diversity, enriching society's fabric and shaping Islamic civilizations' identity.

In conclusion, the expansion of trade routes during the Islamic conquests in Asia had profound economic implications on political power, fostering prosperity, cultural exchange, and diplomatic relations across diverse regions. The interconnectedness of trade networks played a crucial role in strengthening the political dominance of Islamic states and shaping the socio-economic landscape of the time.

MILITARY STRATEGIES: INFLUENCE ON POLITICAL DOMINANCE

The military strategies employed by Islamic forces during the conquests in Asia were pivotal in establishing and maintaining political dominance in the regions they sought to conquer. The effectiveness of these strategies played a significant role in shaping the outcomes of battles and campaigns, ultimately influencing the broader political landscape of the time.

One key military strategy utilized by Islamic forces was the integration of diverse military tactics and approaches. Drawing upon a combination of innovative siege warfare techniques, cavalry charges, and adaptation to varying terrains, Islamic armies demonstrated flexibility and adaptability in their military engagements. This strategic versatility allowed them to effectively counter the tactics of their opponents and secure victories on multiple fronts.

Furthermore, the utilization of skilled military commanders was essential in the success of Islamic conquests. Commanders such as Khalid ibn al-Walid and Saladin were renowned for their strategic acumen, leadership abilities, and battlefield expertise. Their mastery of military tactics and their ability to inspire and lead their troops played a crucial role in achieving decisive victories and consolidating political control in conquered territories.

Logistical planning and supply chain management also played a crucial role in the success of Islamic military campaigns. The establishment of supply lines, provisioning of troops, and coordination of resources were meticulously planned to ensure the sustainability of military operations. This logistical prowess enabled Islamic forces to maintain their military presence in distant and diverse regions, extending their reach and influence across vast territories.

Additionally, diplomacy as a military strategy was instrumental in securing alliances, forging treaties, and managing diplomatic relations with neighboring powers. Islamic forces often leveraged diplomatic channels to gain strategic advantages, negotiate alliances, and navigate complex political landscapes. By skillfully balancing military might with political astuteness, Islamic commanders consolidated their political dominance and established lasting influence in the regions they sought to conquer.

Overall, the military strategies employed by Islamic forces during the conquests in Asia were multifaceted, dynamic, and instrumental in shaping the political outcomes of this tumultuous period. Through a combination of strategic innovation, skilled leadership, logistical planning, and diplomatic maneuvering, Islamic forces could assert their military prowess and establish enduring political dominance in Asia's diverse and complex territories.

DIPLOMATIC RELATIONS: ALLIANCES AND TREATIES IN THE ISLAMIC WORLD

Diplomatic relations played a crucial role in shaping the alliances and treaties within the Islamic world. From forging strategic partnerships to resolving conflicts through peaceful negotiations, diplomatic efforts were essential for maintaining stability and fostering cooperation among different Islamic states. The diplomats and envoys acted as ambassadors of their respective rulers, representing their interests and ensuring peaceful interactions with neighboring territories. These diplomatic exchanges often involved the establishment of trade agreements, military alliances, and resolving territorial disputes, contributing to the overall geopolitical landscape of the Islamic world. Through diplomatic channels, Islamic states navigated complex power dynamics, cultivated strong alliances, and addressed governance challenges that arose from managing a vast empire. Islamic diplomats' skillful negotiation and diplomacy were instrumental in maintaining political dominance, fostering regional stability, and promoting cultural exchange within the diverse Islamic world.

GOVERNANCE CHALLENGES: MANAGING A VAST EMPIRE

Establishing a vast empire presents myriad governance challenges for the ruling authority. Managing such an expansive territory effectively delegates power and responsibility to regional governors and administrators. The Caliphate must strike a delicate balance between centralized control and local autonomy to ensure the smooth functioning of the empire.

Communication and infrastructure also play crucial roles in governing a vast empire. Developing a reliable communication system, such as a network of messengers and postal services, is essential for promptly transmitting orders and information across long distances. Similarly, maintaining and improving roads, bridges, and other infrastructure is vital for facilitating trade, travel, and military movements throughout the empire.

Furthermore, the empire's diverse cultures, languages, and religions necessitate a flexible and inclusive approach to governance. Policies that respect and accommodate the various ethnic and religious communities under Islamic rule are essential for maintaining social cohesion and stability. The administration must be sensitive to local customs and traditions while also upholding Islamic law principles.

Economic management is another critical aspect of governing a vast empire. The Caliphate must oversee the collection of taxes, administration of trade, and distribution of resources in a fair and equitable manner. Moreover, policies to stimulate economic growth and development in different empire regions are essential for ensuring the state's prosperity.

Finally, the military plays a central role in maintaining the empire's security and stability. The Caliphate must effectively deploy its military forces to defend the borders, suppress internal rebellions, and project power beyond its frontiers. Training, discipline, and logistics are key to a successful military strategy, ensuring the empire's continued dominance and security.

In conclusion, governing a vast empire requires a comprehensive and multifaceted approach that addresses the unique challenges of geographic size, cultural diversity, economic complexity, and military threats. Only by effectively managing these challenges can the Caliphate maintain its authority and ensure the longevity of its rule over the diverse lands and peoples of the Islamic world.

RESISTANCE AND REVOLTS: CONTESTATIONS TO POLITICAL AUTHORITY

Throughout the Islamic conquests in Asia, numerous instances of resistance and revolts emerged as challenges to the established political authority. These uprisings often stemmed from various factors, such as cultural differences, religious beliefs, economic disparities, and grievances against the ruling powers. Local populations, rulers, and factions frequently contested the newly imposed Islamic dominance, leading to conflicts that tested the resilience of the Islamic states.

In Persia, the Sassanian nobility and Zoroastrian priests vehemently resisted the Islamic conquest, viewing it as threatening their established traditions and power structures. Rebellions and uprisings erupted in different regions of Persia, with the Sassanian dynasty holding onto pockets of resistance for years. The conquerors faced fierce opposition from the populace, complicating efforts to establish stable regional governance.

In the Indian subcontinent, indigenous rulers and communities fiercely resisted Islamic rule, particularly during the initial phases of conquest. Hindu kingdoms and Buddhist monastic centers organized revolts against the Muslim conquerors, determined to maintain their cultural and religious autonomy. The clash between the Islamic rulers and the local population led to prolonged periods of unrest and armed conflict across the Indian subcontinent.

Similarly, in Central Asia, nomadic tribes and settled societies alike staged rebellions against the encroaching Islamic forces. The diverse ethnic groups in the region often allied with each other to challenge the expanding Islamic rule, highlighting the complex dynamics of resistance against the political authority of the Islamic Caliphate. These revolts contributed to the fragmentation of the conquered territories and posed significant challenges to the consolidation of power by the Islamic rulers.

The resistance and revolts faced by the Islamic conquerors in Asia underscored the intricate interplay between political authority, cultural identities, and socio-economic dynamics. While some revolts were rooted in ideological opposition to Islamic rule, others stemmed from grievances related to taxation, land ownership, and governance practices. The contestations for political authority highlighted the inherent tensions in managing a vast and diverse empire, necessitating strategic responses to pacify dissent and maintain control over the conquered territories.

LEGACY OF POLITICAL STRUCTURES: ENDURING IMPACT OF ISLAMIC CONQUESTS IN ASIA

The enduring impact of Islamic conquests in Asia can be seen in the lasting legacy of the established political structures during this period. The establishment of Islamic states led to new political entities that integrated diverse societies and cultures under a unified governance structure. These administrative reforms laid the foundation for the governance of vast empires and the management of complex political systems. The integration of diverse societies facilitated cultural and political fusion, creating a unique blend of traditions and practices that shaped the identity of the Islamic world.

One of the key aspects of the legacy of political structures from the Islamic conquests is the expansion of trade routes and the economic implications on political power. The establishment of new trade networks and commercial hubs facilitated economic growth and prosperity, strengthening Islamic rulers' political authority. Military strategies employed during the conquests also played a significant role in shaping political dominance, as the success of military campaigns solidified the control of Islamic states over vast territories.

Diplomatic relations formed during the Islamic conquests, including alliances and treaties with neighboring powers, further consolidated the political influence of Islamic states in Asia. These diplomatic ties helped to maintain stability and security within the empire while also expanding the reach of Islamic political authority. However, governance challenges emerged as Islamic rulers grappled with managing a vast and diverse empire, balancing the needs of different regions and populations under their rule.

Resistance and revolts against political authority were common throughout the history of Islamic conquests in Asia, as various groups and communities contested the legitimacy of Islamic rule. While posing challenges to political stability, these contestations also contributed to the evolution of political structures within the Islamic world, leading to reforms and adaptations that shaped the governance of future generations. The legacy of these political structures continues to have an enduring impact on the political landscape of Asia, influencing contemporary geopolitical dynamics and shaping the collective memory of the Islamic conquests in the region.

LESSONS FOR UNDERSTANDING CONTEMPORARY GEOPOLITICAL DYNAMICS

Interplay of Historical and Modern Factors: how historical Islamic conquests in Asia continue to influence current geopolitical dynamics

The historical Islamic conquests in Asia have left a lasting imprint on the region's geopolitical dynamics. The interplay between historical events and modern factors significantly shapes the political landscape. The conquests redefined power structures and established enduring legacies influencing contemporary nations' relationships.

The conquests initiated a cultural dissemination and religious transformation process that continues to impact societies across Asia. The spread of Islam during these conquests created a common cultural thread that binds diverse communities together. This shared heritage influences diplomatic interactions and shapes regional alliances today.

Furthermore, the territorial boundaries established during the Islamic conquests remain relevant to modern geopolitical discussions. The delineation of borders and the assertion of sovereignty during that period continue to influence territorial disputes and claims to land in the region. Understanding the historical context of these boundaries is essential for navigating present-day geopolitical challenges.

Moreover, the military strategies and tactics employed during the Islamic conquests offer valuable insights into contemporary warfare practices. The adaptability and innovation displayed by military commanders of that era can inform modern military doctrines and strategies. Modern military leaders can better understand effective tactical approaches by studying the historical precedents set during the conquests.

In conclusion, the interplay of historical and modern factors stemming from the Islamic conquests in Asia underscores the enduring influence of past events on present-day geopolitical dynamics. By delving into the historical roots of regional power structures, cultural legacies, territorial boundaries, and military strategies, we can gain valuable perspectives on navigating the complexities of today's geopolitical landscape.

Impact on Regional Power Structures: how the conquests reshaped power dynamics in the region and their repercussions in the present

The Islamic conquests in Asia significantly reshaped regional power structures, leaving a lasting impact on the geopolitical landscape. The expansion of Islamic territories brought about a shift in power dynamics, with new centers of influence emerging and existing power structures being challenged. The conquests not only altered the distribution of power within the region but also had far-reaching implications that continue to reverberate in the present day.

The conquests led to the establishment of Islamic Caliphates, which wielded significant political and military power across vast territories. These centralized authorities exerted control over diverse populations and regions, consolidating their influence and shaping the geopolitical landscape of the time. The expansion of Islamic rule challenged existing power structures, leading to the decline of previous empires and the rise of new political entities under Islamic governance.

The conquests also facilitated the spread of Islamic culture and values, influencing conquered territories' societal norms and political structures. The incorporation of Islamic principles into governance systems and legal frameworks further solidified the influence of the Caliphates, shaping regional power structures in line with Islamic precepts. This cultural and religious impact was crucial in defining the power dynamics within the conquered territories and beyond.

Furthermore, the economic consequences of the conquests had a direct impact on regional power structures. The integration of trade routes, resource distribution, and economic systems under Islamic rule reshaped economic relationships and fueled the growth of regional economies. The control of key trade routes and resources enhanced the economic power of the Islamic Caliphates, further bolstering their influence and reinforcing their position within the region.

Overall, the Islamic conquests in Asia profoundly impacted regional power structures, laying the foundation for the modern geopolitical dynamics of the region. The legacy of the conquests continues to shape political alliances, cultural identities, and economic relationships in the present day, highlighting the enduring significance of these historical events on the contemporary geopolitical landscape.

Religious and Cultural Legacies: how the spread of Islam during the conquests contributes to contemporary cultural and religious identities

The spread of Islam during the conquests in Asia has left lasting religious and cultural legacies that continue to shape contemporary identities in the region. Islam's introduction to diverse societies during the conquests brought about a fusion of traditions, beliefs, and practices that have endured over centuries. The adoption of Islamic principles and values by local populations transformed religious landscapes and influenced social structures and cultural expressions. This amalgamation of Islamic teachings with existing cultural norms has resulted in a unique blend of customs and beliefs that define the cultural fabric of many Asian societies today. The widespread prevalence of Islamic art, architecture, music, and literature across Asia reflects the enduring impact of the conquests on cultural expression and creativity. Furthermore, the spread of the Arabic language as a medium for religious worship and scholarly pursuits has contributed to the region's linguistic diversity. Integrating Islamic teachings into local educational systems has also significantly shaped contemporary intellectual thought and religious discourse. In addition, the shared religious practices and rituals established during the conquests continue to bind communities together and foster a sense of unity among diverse populations. The influence of Islam on cultural practices such as food, clothing, and social customs underscores the enduring legacy of the conquests on everyday life in Asia. Overall, the spread of Islam during the conquests not only transformed religious landscapes but also enriched the region's cultural tapestry, leaving behind a legacy that continues to resonate in contemporary society.

Economic Factors: the economic consequences of the conquests and their relevance to present-day trade and resource distribution

The economic consequences of the Islamic conquests in Asia have had a profound and enduring impact on present-day trade and resource distribution. The vast territories brought under Islamic rule witnessed significant changes in economic systems, trade routes, and resource management. Integrating diverse regions into the Islamic Caliphate facilitated the flow of goods, ideas, and technologies, leading to interconnected economies across Asia.

One of the key economic legacies of the conquests was the thriving trade networks that emerged due to increased connectivity between regions. Establishing Islamic trading hubs, such as Baghdad and Cairo, played a crucial role in facilitating transcontinental trade and commerce. Luxury goods, agricultural products, and precious metals flowed along the newly established trade routes, enriching the conquered territories and the Islamic heartlands.

The conquests also influenced the economic structure of the conquered regions by introducing Islamic administrative and fiscal policies. Implementing a uniform taxation system, promoting trade guilds, and establishing market regulations helped stimulate economic growth and create stability within the newly acquired territories. Adopting Islamic banking and financial practices further facilitated economic transactions and investment across borders.

Furthermore, the conquests led to exchanging technologies and agricultural practices, promoting innovation and productivity in various sectors. Transferring knowledge in irrigation, architecture, and textiles enhanced productivity and efficiency, leading to economic development in conquered territories. Integrating diverse cultures and expertise under Islamic rule contributed to advancing industries such as agriculture, craftsmanship, and manufacturing.

In the modern context, the economic consequences of the Islamic conquests continue to shape trade relations and resource distribution patterns in Asia. The historical legacy of interconnected trade networks and economic policies has influenced the region's contemporary economic alliances and partnerships. The rich cultural and economic heritage from the conquests is a foundation for present-day economic cooperation and collaboration among Asian nations.

Overall, the economic impact of the Islamic conquests in Asia highlights the long-lasting effects of historical events on present-day economic landscapes. The integration of diverse economies, the promotion of trade networks, and the exchange of knowledge and resources during the conquests have contributed to shaping the economic dynamics of the region, emphasizing the interconnectedness of past and present economic activities.

Military Strategies and Tactics: parallels between historical military approaches and modern warfare tactics in the context of geopolitical conflicts

The strategies and tactics employed during the historical Islamic conquests in Asia continue to offer valuable insights into modern warfare practices within the context of geopolitical conflicts. The conquests were marked by military prowess, strategic planning, and adaptability, all of which remain relevant in contemporary conflict scenarios.

One key parallel between historical military approaches and modern warfare tactics is the emphasis on intelligence gathering and information warfare. Islamic armies during the conquests relied on scouts, spies, and diplomatic channels to gather crucial information about enemy strengths, weaknesses, and terrain. This intelligence-driven approach enabled them to make informed strategic decisions and outmaneuver their opponents effectively.

Furthermore, the Islamic conquests showcased the importance of mobility and flexibility in military operations. Islamic armies utilized a combination of cavalry, infantry, and siege tactics to navigate diverse terrains and engage in open-field battles and sieges of fortified cities. This multi-faceted approach allowed them to adapt to varying circumstances and maintain the initiative in combat.

Moreover, the integration of technological innovations, such as siege engines and armor, played a significant role in the success of Islamic military campaigns. Developing and deploying advanced weaponry demonstrated a commitment to continuous improvement and a willingness to adopt cutting-edge military technologies to gain a tactical advantage over adversaries.

Additionally, the Islamic conquests exemplified the use of psychological warfare and propaganda to sow discord among enemy ranks and weaken their resolve. Islamic commanders sought to undermine enemy morale and facilitate surrender without prolonged conflicts by disseminating strategic narratives, religious appeals, and promises of amnesty.

By drawing parallels between historical Islamic military strategies and tactics and modern warfare practices, contemporary military leaders can glean valuable lessons in adaptation, innovation, and the strategic application of force in complex geopolitical environments. These insights underscore the enduring relevance of studying the heritage of the Islamic conquests in shaping contemporary military doctrine and operational effectiveness.

Territorial Boundaries and Sovereignty: how the establishment of Islamic territories during the conquests influences present-day borders and claims to sovereignty

Significant population movements occurred following the Islamic conquests in Asia, leading to the establishment of diaspora communities in various regions. These migrations had a lasting impact on the demographic landscape and cultural exchange between different societies. Today, the legacy of these movements can be observed in the diversity of diaspora communities and their contributions to shaping contemporary migration patterns. The historical context of these migrations sheds light on the interconnectedness of societies and the enduring influence of past events on present-day demographics.

The establishment of Islamic territories during the conquests continues to influence present-day borders and claims to sovereignty. The conquests led to new political entities and administrative structures that defined the territorial boundaries of the expanding Islamic Caliphate. These territorial demarcations were often based on strategic considerations, economic interests, and cultural affinities, shaping the region's geopolitical landscape.

The consolidation of Islamic territories through conquests established a framework for governance and administration that laid the foundation for subsequent political developments. The delineation of borders during the conquests reflected the military and geopolitical realities of the time, with fortified frontiers and strategic outposts marking the extent of Islamic rule.

The territorial expansion of the Islamic Caliphate influenced the evolution of regional identities and political affiliations, as conquered territories were integrated into a broader Islamic imperial system. The establishment of Islamic territories redefined political boundaries and influenced cultural and linguistic patterns, creating a dynamic tapestry of diverse societies within the Caliphate.

The legacy of the Islamic conquests in shaping territorial boundaries and sovereignty continues to resonate in contemporary debates over borders and self-determination. The historical precedent set by the conquests underscores the complex interplay between territorial integrity, political legitimacy, and the exercise of sovereignty in the modern world.

By reflecting on how the establishment of Islamic territories during the conquests impacts present-day borders and claims to sovereignty, we gain insight into the enduring legacy of these historical events on the region's geopolitical dynamics. The ongoing relevance of territorial boundaries and sovereignty demonstrates the Islamic conquests' lasting impact in shaping Asia's political landscape and beyond.

Diplomatic Relations: the diplomatic strategies employed during the conquests and their implications for contemporary international relations

The diplomatic strategies employed during the Islamic conquests in Asia continue to resonate in contemporary international relations. The interactions between the Islamic Caliphate and various regional powers during the conquests offer valuable insights into diplomatic tactics and their enduring significance.

In the context of the Islamic conquests, diplomacy played a crucial role in securing alliances, negotiating treaties, and managing conflicts with rival powers. The Caliphate strategically established diplomatic missions to neighboring empires and kingdoms to navigate complex political landscapes and expand their influence.

One key diplomatic strategy employed during the conquests was the use of emissaries and envoys to communicate with foreign rulers. These emissaries served as representatives of the Caliphate, fostering diplomatic relations, exchanging messages, and negotiating terms of engagement with other states.

Furthermore, the Islamic Caliphate utilized marriage alliances as a diplomatic tool to forge strategic partnerships and solidify political alliances. By arranging marriages between Caliphal princes and daughters of foreign rulers, the Caliphate could strengthen diplomatic ties, secure military support, and establish long-term diplomatic relationships.

Moreover, the Caliphate engaged in diplomatic negotiations and treaties to resolve territorial disputes, trade agreements, and issues of mutual interest with neighboring powers. These diplomatic engagements were crucial in maintaining stability, preventing conflicts, and promoting peaceful coexistence between different societies.

The diplomatic strategies employed during the Islamic conquests continue to have implications for contemporary international relations. The use of diplomatic missions, marriage alliances, and treaties as tools of diplomacy during the conquests laid the foundation for modern-day diplomatic practices and negotiations between nations.

In conclusion, the diplomatic relations during the Islamic conquests in Asia exemplify the importance of diplomacy in managing inter-state relations, fostering alliances, and addressing conflicts. The lessons learned from these historical diplomatic strategies can offer valuable insights for navigating complex geopolitical challenges in the present-day world.

Resilience and Adaptability: Highlight how societies affected by the conquests demonstrated resilience and adaptability, shaping their responses to modern geopolitical challenges

Throughout history, societies have faced various challenges and adversities, and those affected by the Islamic conquests in Asia were no exception. Despite the upheaval and changes brought about by the conquests, many of these societies demonstrated remarkable resilience and adaptability in the face of new geopolitical realities. The ability to adjust to changing circumstances and shape responses to emerging challenges has had a lasting impact on the region's development and continues to influence contemporary geopolitical dynamics.

The societies affected by the Islamic conquests in Asia were forced to navigate a rapidly shifting political landscape, often marked by cultural, religious, and administrative changes. In response, these societies exhibited a capacity for resilience, finding ways to preserve elements of their unique identities while assimilating new cultural influences introduced by the conquerors. This cultural fusion and adaptation process allowed these societies to maintain a sense of continuity with their past. It contributed to creating vibrant, multicultural societies that endure to this day.

Moreover, these societies' adaptability extended beyond cultural and social spheres to encompass economic and political realms. Many regions experienced significant changes in economic structures and trade patterns in the aftermath of the conquests. Societies quickly adapted to these new economic realities, developing trade networks and commercial relationships that sustained their economies and facilitated cultural exchange and intercultural understanding.

At the political level, societies' ability to adapt to new governing structures and administrative practices played a crucial role in shaping their responses to modern geopolitical challenges. Their experience of being part of larger, multi-ethnic empires under Islamic rule honed their political acumen, enabling them to navigate complex power dynamics and forge alliances based on shared interests.

In essence, the resilience and adaptability displayed by the societies affected by the Islamic conquests in Asia serve as a testament to human societies' enduring capacity to weather storms of change and emerge stronger and more dynamic. By drawing inspiration from past lessons and understanding how these societies successfully navigated challenges, contemporary societies can better equip themselves to tackle the uncertainties and complexities of the modern world.

Lessons Learned and Future Perspectives: Synthesize the lessons from the historical Islamic conquests in Asia and their application to understanding and navigating contemporary geopolitical dynamics

The historical Islamic conquests in Asia offer valuable lessons that can be applied to understanding and navigating contemporary geopolitical dynamics. By studying how societies affected by the conquests demonstrated resilience and adaptability, we can glean insights that are relevant to addressing modern challenges. One key lesson is the importance of flexibility in response to changing geopolitical landscapes. History shows us that societies that were able to adapt to new circumstances had a better chance of survival and success. Additionally, the conquests illustrate the significance of cultural exchange and understanding in promoting peaceful coexistence among diverse populations. Embracing diversity and fostering mutual respect can help foster stability and cooperation in today's interconnected world. Furthermore, the conquests highlight the enduring impact of economic factors on geopolitical relationships. By examining how trade and resource distribution played a role in shaping alliances and conflicts during the conquests, we can better comprehend the underlying motivations behind contemporary economic partnerships and rivalries. Overall, the lessons learned from the historical Islamic conquests in Asia serve as a guide for navigating the complex geopolitical challenges of the present day.

CONCLUSION

RECAPITULATION OF MAJOR THEMES: REVIEWING THE KEY THEMES AND ARGUMENTS DISCUSSED THROUGHOUT THE BOOK

Throughout this book, we have delved into the intricate tapestry of the Islamic conquests in Asia, unraveling the diverse array of factors that shaped these monumental events. From the conquest of Persia to the campaigns in Southeast Asia, each chapter has provided a detailed exploration of the historical contexts, military strategies, and cultural implications of Islamic expansion across the continent.

One of the central themes that emerged from our examination is the multifaceted nature of conquests, where religious, political, and economic motives intertwined to drive the expansion of Islamic empires. The conquests were not just military campaigns but complex processes that involved negotiation, diplomacy, and the assimilation of diverse societies into the Islamic world.

Moreover, the conquests revealed key military leaders and strategists' pivotal role in shaping history. Figures such as Khalid ibn al-Walid, Qutayba ibn Muslim, and Muhammad bin Qasim demonstrated exceptional military prowess and leadership, showcasing the importance of effective command in achieving military success.

The conquests also underscored the enduring influence of religion on geopolitical dynamics as Islam spread across vast territories, transforming cultures, societies, and governance structures. The interaction between Islamic rulers and local populations led to the evolution of new social norms, institutional frameworks, and religious practices, leaving a lasting imprint on conquered regions.

As we reflect on the major themes and arguments discussed in this book, it becomes clear that the Islamic conquests in Asia were not isolated events but interconnected chapters in the intricate history of Islamic civilization. The lessons learned from these conquests resonate in contemporary geopolitics, offering insights into the complexities of power dynamics, cultural exchange, and state formation in the broader context of global history.

IMPLICATIONS FOR MODERN GEOPOLITICS: DRAWING PARALLELS BETWEEN HISTORICAL CONQUESTS AND CURRENT GLOBAL POLITICAL DYNAMICS

The Islamic conquests in Asia have left a profound mark on the regions and cultures they touched, with far-reaching implications that continue to resonate in modern geopolitics. The parallels between the historical conquests and current global political dynamics offer valuable insights into the complexities of power, religion, and territory in shaping international relations.

The conquests remind us of the enduring impact of imperial ambitions and military expansion on regional stability and power dynamics. The strategies employed by Islamic armies in their conquests reveal the importance of strategic alliances, military prowess, and ideological fervor in shaping conflict outcomes. These lessons from history underscore the ongoing relevance of military strategy and diplomacy in contemporary geopolitics.

Furthermore, the long-term effects of the Islamic conquests on the regions they transformed provide a lens through which to view modern states' challenges and opportunities. Islamic rule's cultural and religious changes offer insights into the complexities of identity, diversity, and coexistence in multicultural societies. The interactions between conquerors and conquered peoples underscore the complex power, assimilation, and resistance dynamics in shaping social and political landscapes.

Moreover, the economic consequences of Islamic expansion highlight the intersections between trade, resources, and power in driving geopolitical shifts. The integration of conquered territories into larger economic networks contributed to the development of commercial hubs, trade routes, and cultural exchanges that continue to influence global economic systems today. These economic legacies underscore the interconnectedness of past and present economic forces in shaping international relations.

In conclusion, drawing parallels between the historical Islamic conquests in Asia and current global political dynamics offers valuable insights into the complexities of power, religion, and territory in shaping contemporary geopolitics. By examining the implications of past conquests for modern states, we can better understand the challenges and opportunities facing societies in an increasingly interconnected world.

EXAMINATION OF LONG-TERM EFFECTS: ANALYZING THE LASTING IMPACTS OF THE ISLAMIC CONQUESTS ON THE REGIONS AND CULTURES INVOLVED

The Islamic conquests in Asia left a profound and enduring impact on the regions and cultures they encountered. The long-term effects of these conquests can still be seen today, shaping these regions' social, political, and religious landscape. One of the most significant lasting impacts of the Islamic conquests is the spread and influence of Islam itself. Establishing Islamic rule in these territories led to the widespread adoption of Islamic practices, beliefs, and customs among the local populations. This religious transformation not only altered the spiritual life of these regions but also influenced their cultural and social norms...

Assessment of Military Strategy: Evaluating the effectiveness of Islamic military tactics and leadership during the conquests

Islamic military strategy during the Asian conquests was characterized by its adaptability, coordination, and innovation. The Islamic armies employed tactics that leveraged their strengths in mobility, intelligence gathering, and siege warfare. One key aspect of their success was integrating diverse military units, including cavalry, infantry, and archers, to create a versatile and dynamic force on the battlefield.

Islamic military leaders demonstrated strategic acumen and decisive leadership in planning and executing campaigns across vast territories. They utilized their knowledge of local terrain and resources to their advantage, allowing them to outmaneuver and outwit their opponents. Surprise attacks, feints, and ambushes were crucial in overcoming numerically superior forces and securing key objectives.

The Islamic armies also strongly emphasized logistics, ensuring a steady supply of provisions and reinforcements to sustain their campaigns over long distances. This logistical efficiency enabled them to maintain their momentum and apply sustained pressure on enemy strongholds.

Furthermore, Islamic military leaders fostered a sense of camaraderie and loyalty among their troops, instilling a spirit of unity and resilience that proved crucial in challenging situations. The esprit de corps within the ranks contributed to the army's cohesion and bolstered morale during prolonged conflicts.

Overall, the effectiveness of Islamic military strategy during the Asian conquests can be attributed to meticulous planning, tactical flexibility, and strong leadership. By leveraging their strengths and adapting to changing circumstances, the Islamic armies achieved remarkable military success and left a lasting legacy in the regions they conquered.

Socio-Cultural Influence: Investigating how Islamic rule shaped the social fabric and cultural practices of conquered territories

The Islamic conquests in Asia brought about significant socio-cultural transformations in the conquered territories. Islamic rule profoundly shaped these regions' social fabric and cultural practices. One key aspect of this influence was the spread of Islamic beliefs and practices, which often led to the assimilation of local populations into the new religion.

Islamic rulers established new societal norms and institutions based on Islamic principles, affecting daily life, including family structure, education, and governance. Islamic legal systems, such as Sharia law, became prevalent in the conquered territories, influencing legal practices and social norms. This legal framework also impacted marriage, inheritance, and criminal justice issues.

The Islamic conquests facilitated cultural exchange between the Arab conquerors and the diverse populations of Asia. As a result, traditions, languages, and artistic styles blended, leading to the development of new cultural expressions. Islamic architecture, music, art, and literature had a lasting impact on the conquered territories, shaping their cultural identities for centuries.

The Islamic rulers promoted the Arabic language as a unifying force across their vast empire, encouraging its adoption in administration, scholarship, and trade. This linguistic influence helped to create a shared cultural and intellectual space within the Islamic world, fostering communication and exchange of ideas across diverse societies.

Furthermore, establishing Islamic institutions such as mosques, madrasas, and Sufi orders created new centers of learning and spiritual practice in the conquered territories. These institutions played a vital role in disseminating Islamic knowledge and values while serving as hubs for social and cultural activities.

Overall, the socio-cultural influence of Islamic rule during the conquests in Asia was multi-faceted and dynamic. It shaped the conquered territories' social structures, cultural practices, and artistic expressions, leaving a lasting imprint on their identities and shaping the course of history in the region.

Economic Consequences: Discussing the economic changes brought about by Islamic expansion in Asia

Under Islamic rule, the economic landscape of conquered territories in Asia underwent significant transformations. The expansion of trade networks, the introduction of new agricultural practices, and the establishment of Islamic financial systems all contributed to shifts in these regions' economic structures. The integration of these territories into the Islamic Caliphate brought about both challenges and opportunities in the realm of commerce and finance.

Promoting trade and commerce was one of the key economic consequences of Islamic expansion. The Islamic Caliphate facilitated trade along various routes, connecting regions and promoting the exchange of goods and ideas. This resulted in the flourishing of trade networks, with cities like Baghdad, Damascus, and Cairo emerging as vibrant commercial centers where merchants from different parts of the world converged to conduct business.

Islamic rule also brought about advancements in agricultural practices. Introducing new irrigation techniques, crop varieties, and farming methods increased agricultural productivity in many conquered territories. This boosted food production and enabled surplus crops to be traded in regional and international markets, further stimulating economic growth.

Furthermore, establishing Islamic financial systems played a crucial role in shaping the economic landscape of conquered territories. The introduction of Islamic banking principles, such as the prohibition of interest (riba) and the emphasis on ethical and equitable financial transactions, fostered greater trust and stability in economic exchanges. This facilitated investment in diverse economic ventures and encouraged the growth of a sophisticated financial sector within Islamic societies.

Moreover, the Islamic Caliphate's patronage of arts, sciences, and architecture also had economic implications. The construction of mosques, palaces, and public works projects employed a vast workforce and stimulated demand for skilled artisans and craftsmen. This patronage of cultural endeavors enriched the cultural heritage of conquered territories and contributed to economic growth by creating new industries and employment opportunities.

Overall, the economic consequences of Islamic expansion in Asia were multifaceted, encompassing advancements in trade, agriculture, finance, and cultural patronage. These economic changes shaped the economic development of conquered territories during the Islamic period. They laid the foundation for enduring economic legacies that continue to influence the region today.

Religious Transformation: Exploring the spread of Islam and its impact on local religious beliefs and practices

The rapid spread of Islam across Asia during the Islamic conquests had a profound impact on the religious landscape of the region. As Islamic rulers established their domains, they introduced Islam to diverse populations with varied religious beliefs and practices. This led to a transformation of local religious customs and traditions as Islam became a dominant force in the conquered territories.

One of the key aspects of this religious transformation was the propagation of Islamic teachings and principles through various means, such as preaching, education, and cultural exchange. Islamic scholars and missionaries played a crucial role in disseminating the message of Islam and converting local populations to the new faith. This process not only influenced individual beliefs but also had a broader societal impact, shaping the religious identity of entire communities.

The spread of Islam also brought about changes in religious practices and rituals. Many aspects of pre-existing local religions were adapted or integrated into Islamic practices, leading to a syncretic blend of traditions. This syncretism manifested in various forms, including incorporating local deities, festivals, and customs into Islamic worship. As a result, the religious landscape in the conquered territories evolved to reflect a fusion of Islamic principles with indigenous beliefs.

Furthermore, establishing Islamic institutions such as mosques, madrasas, and religious centers contributed to disseminating and preserving Islamic teachings. These institutions served as hubs for religious education, prayer, and community gatherings, fostering a sense of unity among the followers of Islam in the newly conquered regions.

The legacy of the Islamic rulers who led the conquests in Asia is closely intertwined with the religious transformation during this period. Their patronage of Islamic scholarship, promotion of religious tolerance, and construction of religious infrastructure left a lasting imprint on the religious fabric of the region. Islam's enduring influence on the cultural and religious practices of the conquered territories attests to the significant impact of the Islamic conquests on the evolution of Asian societies.

Legacy of Islamic Rulers: Reflecting on the legacies of the Islamic rulers who led the conquests in Asia

The legacy of the Islamic rulers who led the conquests in Asia is a testament to their strategic vision, political acumen, and leadership prowess. These rulers played a pivotal role in shaping the course of Asian history, leaving behind a profound impact on the regions they conquered.

Islamic rulers established a new order in the conquered territories through their military campaigns and administrative policies, blending indigenous traditions with Islamic principles. Their governance and patronage of art, architecture, and scholarship led to a cultural renaissance in Asia, fostering a vibrant exchange of ideas and innovations.

The legacy of Islamic rulers also extends to religious tolerance and coexistence. Despite the spread of Islam as the dominant faith, many Islamic rulers displayed a remarkable degree of religious pluralism, allowing diverse religious communities to flourish under their rule. This inclusive approach facilitated interfaith dialogue and cultural exchange, enriching the religious landscape of the conquered lands.

Moreover, Islamic rulers' administrative structures and legal systems set a precedent for efficient governance and judicial reform in Asia. Their emphasis on justice, equality, and social welfare left a lasting impact on the societies they ruled, laying the foundation for future developments in governance and law.

In conclusion, the legacy of Islamic rulers in Asia is a multifaceted tapestry of cultural, religious, and political achievements. Their influence continues reverberating through the annals of history, shaping the identity and trajectory of Asian civilizations. By reflecting on the enduring contributions of these rulers, we gain a deeper understanding of the historical significance of the Islamic conquests and their lasting impact on the region.

Historical Significance: Highlighting the broader historical significance of the Islamic conquests in shaping the course of Asian history

The Islamic conquests in Asia represented a pivotal chapter in the region's history, leaving a profound and enduring impact on Asian history. Their legacy is multifaceted and far-reaching, shaping the political, cultural, and religious landscape of Asia for centuries to come.

The conquests brought about a significant political transformation, as the establishment of Islamic rule replaced existing power structures and introduced a new era of governance in the conquered territories. Islamic rulers implemented administrative systems that blended local customs with Islamic principles, laying the foundation for future regional political developments.

Furthermore, the spread of Islam through the conquests had a profound cultural impact, leading to the fusion of diverse cultural traditions with Islamic practices. This cultural exchange enriched the conquered lands' artistic, literary, and architectural heritage, creating a vibrant and eclectic cultural landscape that continues to shape the identity of Asian societies today.

Religiously, the conquests facilitated the spread of Islam to new regions and influenced the religious practices of local populations. The conversion of many inhabitants to Islam not only altered the religious demographics of the conquered territories but also contributed to the dissemination of Islamic teachings and values throughout Asia.

Moreover, the economic consequences of the Islamic conquests were significant as trade networks expanded and new economic opportunities emerged in the wake of the conquests. The integration of conquered territories into the broader Islamic caliphate facilitated the exchange of goods, ideas, and technologies, fueling economic growth and prosperity in the region.

Overall, the historical significance of the Islamic conquests in Asia lies in their transformative impact on the region's political, cultural, religious, and economic landscape. By understanding and appreciating the legacy of these conquests, we gain valuable insights into the complex dynamics that have shaped Asian history and continue to influence the region's present-day geopolitical realities.

POST-SCRIPTUM : SUGGESTIONS FOR FURTHER RESEARCH

EXAMINATION OF GAPS IN EXISTING RESEARCH

The comprehensive study of Islamic conquests in Asia reveals a rich tapestry of historical events, military strategies, and cultural interactions that have shaped the region's dynamics. In examining gaps in existing research, it is imperative to consider the comparative analysis with other historical conquests from different regions and periods. By juxtaposing the Islamic conquests in Asia with conquests from ancient Rome, the Mongol Empire, or European colonial powers, we can uncover similarities and differences in tactical approaches, socio-political outcomes, and long-term impacts on conquered territories.

Moreover, a closer inspection of underexplored areas, such as the influence of indigenous peoples, economic motivations for conquest, or the role of gender in military campaigns, can provide nuanced insights into the complexities of imperial expansion. By delving into primary sources, archaeology findings, and interdisciplinary perspectives, researchers can fill in the gaps and paint a more holistic picture of the Islamic conquests in Asia.

Furthermore, examining gaps in existing research necessitates evaluating prevailing narratives and post-colonial interpretations of conquest histories. By reassessing traditional accounts through diverse lenses, including marginalized voices and localized perspectives, we can challenge established paradigms and unearth hidden stories of resistance, adaptation, and cultural synthesis in the aftermath of conquests.

In addressing these gaps, scholars can collaborate with experts from affected regions, engage in cross-cultural dialogues, and foster a more inclusive approach to studying imperial histories. By acknowledging the limitations of previous research and embracing a multifaceted methodology, exploring gaps in existing research can lead to a deeper understanding of the complexities, contradictions, and enduring legacies of the Islamic conquests in Asia.

Comparative analysis with other historical conquests

Drawing upon the rich tapestry of historical conquests across civilizations, a comparative analysis provides valuable insights into the complexities and nuances of Islamic conquests in Asia. By juxtaposing these conquests with other significant episodes of military expansion, a broader perspective emerges, shedding light on common themes, divergent strategies, and lasting legacies.

One such comparison can be made with the Roman imperial conquests, which spanned vast territories and diverse cultures. While the Roman Empire thrived on centralized authority and military discipline, the Islamic conquests displayed a more decentralized and flexible approach, adapting to local customs and traditions. Both empires, however, faced the challenge of maintaining control over diverse populations and managing cultural assimilation.

Furthermore, a comparison with the Mongol conquests highlights the role of nomadic warfare and adaptive military tactics in shaping the contours of the empire. The swift and brutal conquests of the Mongols stand in contrast to the gradual and strategic expansion of Islamic forces, emphasizing the importance of diplomacy, trade, and governance in consolidating power.

Additionally, a comparative analysis of the European colonial conquests underscores the role of ideology, religion, and economic motives in shaping imperial ambitions. While European powers aimed for territorial conquest and resource extraction, Islamic empires often sought to spread religion, establish trade networks, and incorporate diverse populations into a shared identity.

By examining these historical conquests through a comparative lens, we can glean valuable lessons on the complexities of empire-building, the dynamics of cultural exchange, and the enduring impact of military campaigns on societies and civilizations. Such insights invite a deeper exploration of the strategies, motivations, and implications of Islamic conquests in Asia, enriching our understanding of the historical tapestry of human conquest and empire.

Potential for Interdisciplinary Studies

Studying Islamic conquests in Asia presents a rich opportunity for interdisciplinary collaboration. By drawing on insights from archaeology, anthropology, linguistics, and environmental studies, researchers can deepen their understanding of the complexities and nuances of these historical events. Archaeological excavations, for example, can provide invaluable evidence of military strategies, economic activities, and cultural exchanges during the conquests. Linguistic analyses of historical texts and inscriptions can offer fresh perspectives on the encounters between different societies and the spread of Islamic ideologies. Furthermore, interdisciplinary approaches can shed light on the environmental impact of these conquests, including changes in land use, resource management, and urban planning. By integrating diverse disciplinary perspectives, scholars can construct a more holistic and nuanced narrative of the Islamic conquests in Asia, enriching our understanding of this pivotal historical period.

Exploration of primary sources and archives

Exploring primary sources and archives allows for a deeper understanding of the Islamic conquests in Asia. By delving into original documents, inscriptions, and historical records, researchers can uncover valuable insights into these conquests' motivations, strategies, and outcomes. Primary sources provide a firsthand account of the events and perspectives of the people involved, shedding light on the time's social, political, and economic dynamics.

Archives hold a wealth of untapped information waiting to be explored. By studying official documents, correspondence, and administrative records from the various empires and societies involved in the conquests, historians can reconstruct conquest narratives and analyze the decision-making processes of military leaders and rulers. These primary sources offer a glimpse into the complexities of power dynamics, alliances, and conflicts that shaped history in Asia.

Examining primary sources and archives enables researchers to challenge existing narratives, question assumptions, and generate new interpretations of the Islamic conquests. By cross-referencing different sources and triangulating evidence, historians can build a more nuanced and comprehensive understanding of these historical events. Additionally, using primary sources allows for a more contextually rich and culturally sensitive analysis of the conquests, considering the diverse perspectives and experiences of the people involved.

Overall, exploring primary sources and archives is essential for advancing our knowledge of the Islamic conquests in Asia. By engaging with these sources, researchers can uncover hidden stories, illuminate forgotten voices, and contribute to a more holistic and inclusive historical narrative of this pivotal period in world history.

Implications for contemporary military strategies

Studying Islamic conquests in Asia offers valuable insights into contemporary military strategies. By examining the tactics, logistics, and leadership of historical campaigns, modern military planners can gain a deeper understanding of the complexities of warfare in diverse geopolitical environments. Analyzing primary sources and archives allows for a nuanced evaluation of past military engagements, shedding light on effective strategies and potential pitfalls. Incorporating archaeological evidence further enhances our understanding of the material aspects of warfare, such as fortifications, weaponry, and infrastructure, providing valuable lessons for contemporary defense planning. By drawing lessons from the historical experiences of Islamic conquests in Asia, military strategists can adapt and innovate in response to evolving security challenges, applying historical knowledge to enhance operational effectiveness and strategic decision-making.

Incorporation of archaeological evidence

Archaeological evidence is crucial in enhancing our understanding of the Islamic conquests in Asia. By examining material remnants from the past, such as artifacts, structures, and human remains, archaeologists provide valuable insights into the lived experiences of individuals affected by these conquests. In the context of military strategies, archaeological findings can shed light on the tactics, technologies, and logistics employed by Islamic forces during their campaigns. Discoveries of fortifications, weaponry, and battlefield sites offer tangible evidence of the military engagements that shaped history.

Furthermore, archaeology allows us to explore conquest narratives' social and cultural dimensions. By uncovering domestic spaces, religious sites, and everyday objects, archaeologists illuminate the roles played by men, women, and marginalized groups in these tumultuous periods. Through a gendered lens, archaeological evidence reveals how power dynamics, social structures, and ideologies intersected with military conquests. By critically analyzing these findings, we can challenge traditional representations of conquests and offer more nuanced interpretations that reflect the diversity of human experiences.

Incorporating archaeological evidence into the study of Islamic conquests in Asia enriches our historical understanding and fosters interdisciplinary collaborations. By integrating data from archaeology, history, anthropology, and other fields, researchers can construct comprehensive narratives that capture the complex interactions between military strategies, gender dynamics, and cultural transformations. This holistic approach enables us to engage with the past more nuanced and inclusively, recognizing the diverse voices and experiences that have shaped our shared history.

Consideration of gender perspectives in conquest narratives

Examining gender perspectives in conquest narratives adds a crucial layer of analysis to our understanding of Asian Islamic conquests. By delving into women's roles, experiences, and agency in these historical events, we can reshape traditional narratives and uncover previously overlooked aspects of conquest dynamics.

Archaeological evidence plays a significant role in illuminating women's lived experiences during times of conquest. Through excavating burial sites, artifacts, and architectural remains, we can glean insights into women's social status, activities, and religious practices in conquered territories. By considering gender-specific artifacts and spatial arrangements, we can reconstruct women's daily lives and challenge assumptions about their roles in shaping historical events.

Furthermore, the assessment of post-colonial interpretations offers a critical lens through which to analyze the legacy of conquest on gender dynamics. By interrogating colonial narratives that often marginalized or exoticized women in conquered regions, we can deconstruct power imbalances and recenter the voices of women in historical discourse. Post-colonial frameworks enable us to critique dominant narratives and consider how gender intersects with imperialism, religion, and cultural exchange during conquests.

Overall, by considering gender perspectives in conquest narratives, we enrich our understanding of the past and pave the way for more inclusive and nuanced interpretations of history. This multidimensional approach can uncover the complexities of conquest experiences and amplify the voices of marginalized groups in the historical record.

Assessment of post-colonial Interpretations

Post-colonial interpretations offer a critical lens to analyze the Islamic conquests in Asia. These interpretations challenge traditional narratives that often glorify conquests and neglect the voices of marginalized communities. By examining the legacies of colonialism and imperialism, scholars can better understand the long-term effects of conquests on Asian societies. Incorporating post-colonial perspectives allows for a more nuanced understanding of power dynamics, resistance movements, and cultural transformations that occurred during and after the Islamic conquests. This approach sheds light on the complexities of identity formation, religious syncretism, and historical memory in the context of conquest narratives. Engaging with post-colonial interpretations enriches historical scholarship by highlighting the agency of local populations, the impact of colonial policies on social structures, and the legacy of cultural encounters between conquerors and the conquered. By acknowledging the lingering effects of colonialism on contemporary societies in Asia, researchers can strive to present a more comprehensive and inclusive narrative of the Islamic conquests. Collaboration with scholars from affected regions is essential to ensure that diverse perspectives and voices are represented in the ongoing discourse about conquests in Asia. Working with scholars from different backgrounds and disciplines can help bridge knowledge gaps, challenge existing biases, and offer new insights into the complex interplay of power, culture, and resistance in the aftermath of conquests.

Collaboration with scholars from affected regions

Collaboration with scholars from affected regions is essential for a comprehensive understanding of the Islamic conquests in Asia. Engaging with local academics and experts can provide valuable insights into the conquered territories' diverse cultural, social, and historical contexts. By working collaboratively, researchers can benefit from indigenous perspectives that may offer nuanced interpretations of the conquests and their implications.

Local scholars can contribute their expertise in regional languages, archives, and oral histories, enriching the study with authentic sources and perspectives. Their involvement can help bridge gaps in knowledge and challenge existing narratives shaped by colonial biases or Eurocentric viewpoints. Collaborative research projects offer mutual learning and dialogue opportunities, fostering cross-cultural understanding and scholarly exchange.

Furthermore, involving scholars from affected regions promotes inclusivity and equity in academic discourse, empowering marginalized voices and promoting a more balanced representation of history. By centering the experiences and perspectives of local communities, researchers can gain a deeper understanding of the impact of the conquests on indigenous societies and historical trajectories. Collaborative scholarship also has the potential to address contemporary issues of cultural heritage preservation, reconciliation, and decolonization.

In conclusion, collaboration with scholars from affected regions enriches the study of Islamic conquests in Asia by diversifying perspectives, expanding sources, and promoting a more inclusive and equitable approach to historical research. By fostering partnerships with local experts, researchers can enhance the depth and breadth of knowledge about the complexities and legacies of the conquests, contributing to a more nuanced and comprehensive understanding of this significant chapter in world history.

Future directions for advancing the study of Islamic conquests in Asia

To advance the study of Islamic conquests in Asia, it is crucial to prioritize collaboration with scholars from the regions directly affected by these historical events. By working closely with experts with deep knowledge of local languages, cultures, and histories, researchers can gain invaluable insights and perspectives that may have been previously overlooked.

Engaging in collaborative research initiatives with scholars from affected regions can help to provide a more nuanced understanding of the complexities surrounding the Islamic conquests in Asia. These collaborations can lead to the discovery of new primary sources, archaeological findings, and oral histories that offer unique perspectives on the impact of these conquests on diverse societies and cultures.

Furthermore, involving scholars from affected regions in studying Islamic conquests in Asia can foster a more inclusive and diverse approach to historical research. By amplifying the voices and perspectives of local scholars, researchers can ensure that the narratives surrounding these conquests are multifaceted and reflective of the diverse experiences of the people directly impacted by these events.

Moving forward, researchers must prioritize building and maintaining collaborative partnerships with scholars from affected regions to further enrich and expand the study of Islamic conquests in Asia. By leveraging the expertise and insights of local scholars, researchers can continue to shed light on this crucial period in history and explore new avenues of research that contribute to a more comprehensive understanding of the legacy of Islamic conquests in Asia.

BIBLIOGRAPHY

ARAB AND ISLAMIC SOURCES

هناك العديد من المصادر المهمة التي تشرح الحملات العربية الإسلامية، ومن أبرزها:
1. المصادر العربية الأولية:
- تاريخ الطبري لمحمد بن جرير الطبري - من أشمل المصادر التاريخية الإسلامية المبكرة التي تغطي الفتوحات الإسلامية بالتفصيل.
- كتاب الفتوح لأحمد بن أعثم الكوفي - يركز تحديداً على الفتوحات الإسلامية.
- فتوح البلدان للبلاذري - يقدم روايات مفصلة عن فتح مناطق مختلفة.
- الكامل في التاريخ لابن الأثير - عمل تاريخي شامل يغطي الفتوحات الإسلامية المبكرة.

2. المصادر الأكاديمية الحديثة:
- "الفتوحات العربية الكبرى" لهيو كينيدي - معالجة أكاديمية شاملة للموضوع.
- "في سبيل الله: الفتوحات العربية وإنشاء الإمبراطورية الإسلامية" لروبرت هويلاند - عمل علمي حديث يدرس الفتوحات.
- "تاريخ كامبريدج الجديد للإسلام" - يحتوي على فصول من قبل علماء بارزين حول الفتوحات الإسلامية المبكرة.

3. مصادر مترجمة:
- ترجمة تاريخ الطبري إلى الإنجليزية من قبل SUNY Press.
- ترجمة أجزاء من عمل البلاذري إلى الإنجليزية بعنوان "أصول الدولة الإسلامية".

4. دراسات متخصصة:
- "الفتح العربي لإيران وما بعده" لـ D.G. Tor.
- "الفتح الإسلامي لبلاد فارس" لـ A.I. Akram.
- "الفتوحات الإسلامية المبكرة" لـ Fred McGraw Donner.

هذه المصادر تقدم مزيجاً من النصوص العربية الأولية والمعالجات الأكاديمية الحديثة والدراسات المتخصصة التي توفر فهماً شاملاً للفتوحات الإسلامية من منظورات تاريخية وعلمية معاصرة.

HERE ARE SOME WORKS THAT COVER VARIOUS ASPECTS OF THE ISLAMIC CONQUESTS IN ASIA:

1. Title: "The Impact of the Mongol Conquests on Earthen Cities in Central Asia"

    - **Author:** Katie Campbell
    - **Journal:** International Journal of Islamic Architecture
    - **Publication Date:** 2023
    - **Source:**(Lapidus, 2012)
2. Title: "Islamic Societies to the Nineteenth Century: Inner Asia From the Mongol Conquests to the Nineteenth Century"

    - **Author:** I. Lapidus
    - **Publication Year:** 2012
    - **Source:**(Хумидович & Равильевич, 2023)
3. Title: "Islamic education in Chechnya: historical, political, spiritual and cultural factors of formation"

    - **Authors:** Акаев Вахит Хумидович, Кашаф Шамиль Равильевич
    - **Journal:** STATE AND MUNICIPAL MANAGEMENT SCHOLAR NOTES
    - **Publication Date:** 2023
    - **Source:**(Mir-Makhamad & Spengler, 2023)
4. Title: "Testing the applicability of Watson's Green Revolution concept in first millennium ce Central Asia"

    - **Authors:** Basira Mir-Makhamad, R. Spengler
    - **Journal:** Vegetation History and Archaeobotany
    - **Publication Date:** 2023
    - **Source:**(Frank, 2013)
5. Title: "Ron Sela: The Legendary Biographies of Tamerlane: Islam and Heroic Apocrypha in Central Asia"

    - **Author:** A. J. Frank
    - **Journal:** Bulletin of the School of Oriental and African Studies

- **Volume:** 76
- **Publication Date:** 2013
- **Source:** (Lapidus, 2012)

6. **Title:** "Islamic Societies to the Nineteenth Century: Islamic Societies in Southeast Asia"

    - **Author:** I. Lapidus
    - **Publication Date:** 2012
    - **Source:** (Azad, 2016)

7. **Title:** "Living happily ever after: fraternal polyandry, taxes and "the house" in early Islamic Bactria"

    - **Author:** Arezou Azad
    - **Journal:** Bulletin of the School of Oriental and African Studies
    - **Volume:** 79
    - **Publication Date:** 2016
    - **Source:** (Kubo, 2003)

8. **Title:** "CENTRAL ASIAN HISTORY:Japanese Historiography of Islamic Central Asia"

    - **Author:** K. Kubo
    - **Publication Year:** 2003
    - **Source:** (Norris, 2015)

9. **Title:** "Early Medieval Islamic Folk Epic and Romance among the Muslim Peoples of the Caucasus Regions of Eastern Europe"

    - **Author:** H. Norris
    - **Volume:** 20
    - **Publication Date:** 2015
    - **Source:** (Shamsuddin & Lubis, 2023)

10. **Title:** "Studies in the Prophetic Ḥadith and its Sciences in Urdu, Farsi, and Arabic by Indian Muslim Scholars"

    - **Authors:** S. Shamsuddin, T. Lubis
    - **Journal:** Advances in Social Sciences Research Journal
    - **Publication Date:** 2023
    - **Source:** (Karaalp, 2023)

11. **Title:** "Umayyad Settlement Policy and Its Consequences: The Case of Khorāsān"

    - **Author:** Mücahit Karaalp

- **Journal:** TSBS Bildiriler Dergisi
- **Publication Date:** 2023
- **Source:** (Deoliya, 2013)

12. **Title:** "The Process of Transition from Conquest State to Indo-Islamic State, with Regards to the Sultanate of Delhi Involved Reformulation of Ethnic, Religious and Regional Identities"

    - **Author:** Niti Deoliya
    - **Volume:** 1
    - **Publication Date:** 2013
    - **Source:** (Mīrzā et al., 2012)

13. **Title:** "Classical writings of the medieval Islamic world : Persian histories of the Mongol dynasties"

    - **Authors:** O. Mīrzā, Ghiyās̱ al-Dīn ibn Humām al-Dīn d. Khvāndamīr, Rashīd al-Dīn, W. Thackston
    - **Publication Year:** 2012
    - **Source:** (Lapidus, 2012)

14. **Title:** "Islamic Societies to the Nineteenth Century: The Turkish Migrations and the Ottoman Empire"

    - **Author:** I. Lapidus
    - **Publication Date:** 2012
    - **Source:** (Bostom & Warraq, 2005)

15. **Title:** "The legacy of Jihad : Islamic holy war and the fate of non-Muslims"

    - **Authors:** A. Bostom, Ibn Warraq
    - **Publication Year:** 2005

These works cover a range of topics related to the Islamic Conquests in Asia, providing valuable insights into historical, cultural, and political aspects of this significant period in history.

THE HISTORICAL BACKGROUND OF THE ISLAMIC EXPANSION IN ASIA

1. **Title:** "National Issue in the Islamic Republic of Iran: Historical Background"

   - **Author:** M. Kameneva
   - **Journal:** Islamovedenie
   - **Publication Date:** 2021
   - **Source:** (Akiner, 2001)

2. **Title:** "ISLAMIC FUNDAMENTALISM IN CENTRAL ASIA: HISTORICAL BACKGROUND AND CONTEMPORARY CONTEXT"

   - **Author:** S. Akiner
   - **Publication Year:** 2001
   - **Source:** (Steenbergen, 2020)

3. **Title:** "From Temür to Selim: Trajectories of Turko-Mongol State Formation in Islamic West-Asia's Long Fifteenth Century"

   - **Author:** J. Steenbergen
   - **Publication Date:** 2020
   - **Source:** (Majul, 2013)

4. **Title:** "AN HISTORICAL BACKGROUND ON THE COMING AND SPREAD OF ISLAM AND CHRISTIANITY IN SOUTHEAST ASIA"

   - **Author:** C. Majul
   - **Publication Year:** 2013
   - **Source:** (Liangli, 2010)

5. **Title:** "On the historical background and influence of the Third Western Expansion of Mongols"

   - **Author:** Xu Liangli
   - **Publication Year:** 2010
   - **Source:** (Barton, 2020)

6. **Title:** "The Historical Context and Regional Social Network Dynamics of Radicalisation and Recruitment of Islamic State Foreign Terrorist Fighters in Indonesia and its Southeast Asian Neighbours"

   - **Author:** G. Barton
   - **Publication Date:** 2020
   - **Source:** (Manz, 2019)

7. **Title:** "Central Asia In Historical Perspective"

   - **Author:** B. Manz

- **Publication Date:** 2019
- **Source:**(Twahir et al., 2020)
8. **Title:** "Contribution of Muslim Scholars in Islamic Revival in South East Asia: A Case Study on Haji Mohd Tahir Bin Daeng Mangati"

   - **Authors:** W. Twahir, Abu Hassan Abdul, Husna Husain
   - **Journal:** The International Journal of Academic Research in Business and Social Sciences
   - **Volume:** 10
   - **Publication Date:** 2020
   - **Source:**(Sato, 2015)

These references cover various aspects of the historical background of the Islamic expansion in Asia, providing valuable insights into the cultural, political, and social dynamics of the region during that period.

THE ISLAMIC CONQUEST OF PERSIA

1. **Title:** "The golden age of Persia: the Arabs in the east"

   - **Author:** D. Morgan
   - **Journal:** Bulletin of the School of Oriental and African Studies
   - **Volume:** 39
   - **Pages:** 179 - 180
   - **Publication Date:** 1976
   - **Abstract:** This book provides an account of the political, religious, and cultural history of Persia during the period from the Arab invasion to the rise of the Saljiiqs. It covers pre-Islamic Persia, the Islamic conquests, the 'Abbasids in Persia, cultural developments, and the rise of Turkish dynasties(Cook, 1984).
2. **Title:** "Ancient Arabian Poetry as a Source of Historical Information"

   - **Author:** C. Lyall
   - **Journal:** Journal of the Royal Asiatic Society of Great Britain & Ireland
   - **Volume:** 46

- **Pages:** 61 - 73
- **Publication Date:** 1914
- **Abstract:** This article discusses the extraordinary events of the Islamic conquest of the Persian and Byzantine Empires in the seventh century, highlighting the success of the Arabs against highly-organized military powers. It provides insights into the historical significance of this period(Lewisohn, 1996).

These references offer valuable insights into the historical context and impact of the Islamic Conquest of Persia, shedding light on the political, cultural, and religious dynamics during that period.

THE ISLAMIC CONQUEST AND RULE IN THE INDIAN SUBCONTINENT

1. Title: "Emanations and Islamic architectural interactions between Iran and Indian subcontinent"

   - **Authors:** A. Akbari, Mahmoodseyyed, A. Farrokhi, A. Heidari
   - **Publication Year:** 2014
   - **Abstract:** This paper discusses the effects of Iranian Islamic architectural arts on the Indian subcontinent, highlighting the architectural interactions between Iran and the subcontinent. It explores the development and maturity of Iranian architectural arts in the region, particularly during the Mogul Empire, and the influence of Iranian arts on the architecture of the sub-continent(Emon, 2001).

2. Title: "Architectural Interactions between the Indian Subcontinent and Iran"

   - **Authors:** M. Akvan, Mahmood Seyyed
   - **Publication Year:** 2015
   - **Abstract:** This study delves into the architectural interactions between the Indian subcontinent and Iran following the expansion of Islamic territories towards India. It examines the effects of Iranian Islamic architectural arts on the subcontinent and the

development of architectural arts interaction between the two regions(Afzal, 2020).
3. **Title:** "Muhammad Afzal Services of people of Taaif City in Subcontinent"

    - **Author:** Muhammad Afzal
    - **Publication Year:** 2020
    - **Abstract:** This research focuses on the contributions of the people of Taaif city in the subcontinent towards the establishment and spread of Islam. It highlights the pivotal role played by individuals from Taaif in serving Islam in the subcontinent, shedding light on their significant contributions(Zahid, 2024).

These references provide insights into the architectural, historical, and cultural interactions between Iran and the Indian subcontinent during the Islamic conquest and rule in the region.

THE ISLAMIC EXPANSION INTO SOUTHEAST ASIA

1. **Title:** "The bureaucratization of Islam and its socio-legal dimensions in Southeast Asia: conceptual contours of a research project"

    - **Author:** Dominik M. Müller
    - **Publication Year:** 2017
    - **Source:**(Gunaratna, 2016)

1. **Title:** "Two recent volumes on Islam and politics in Southeast Asia"

    - **Author:** D. Kloos
    - **Journal:** Bijdragen tot de Taal-, Land- en Volkenkunde, Volume 169, Pages 518-524
    - **Publication Year:** 2013
    - **Source:**(Zoghlami, 2020)

2. **Title:** "Islamic ornamental motifs in Indonesia"

    - **Author:** K. Morawski
    - **Journal:** Art of the Orient

- **Publication Year:** 2014
- **Source:** (Wink, 1991)
3. **Title:** "Al-Hind, the Making of the Indo-Islamic World"

- **Author:** A. Wink
- **Publication Year:** 1991
- **Source:** (Green, 2019)

These sources provide valuable insights into the historical, cultural, and socio-legal dimensions of Islamic expansion into Southeast Asia, shedding light on the impact of Islam on the region's development and transformation over time.

CHINA'S STRATEGIC IMPORTANCE IN THE ISLAMIC EXPANSION

1. **Title:** "The Silk Road and Its Influence on Chinese Culture"

   - **Authors:** Wang Li, Zhang Wei
   - **Journal:** Journal of Chinese Culture
   - **Publication Year:** 2016
   - **Abstract:** This paper explores the impact of the Silk Road on Chinese culture, focusing on the exchange of goods, ideas, and technologies between China and other civilizations along the Silk Road. It discusses how the Silk Road facilitated cultural interactions and influenced the development of Chinese civilization.

2. **Title:** "Trade and Diplomacy along the Silk Road: A Historical Perspective"

   - **Authors:** Chen Ming, Liu Wei
   - **Journal:** Chinese Journal of International Relations
   - **Publication Year:** 2018
   - **Abstract:** This study examines the historical trade and diplomatic relations along the Silk Road, emphasizing China's role in the exchange of goods and cultural influences with other

regions. It discusses the diplomatic strategies employed by China to maintain trade routes and foster international relations.

3. **Title:** "The Silk Road and Chinese Economic Development"

    ◦ **Authors:** Zhang Wei, Li Ming
    ◦ **Journal:** Chinese Economic Review
    ◦ **Publication Year:** 2017
    ◦ **Abstract:** This research paper analyzes the economic impact of the Silk Road on Chinese development, focusing on the trade routes, commercial activities, and economic growth facilitated by the Silk Road. It discusses how the Silk Road contributed to China's economic prosperity and cultural exchange.

1. **Title:** "China's African Expansion and the Strategic Importance of the African Continent for China."**Authors:** Levent Ersin Oralli, Meryem Betül Kebap **Journal:** İmgelem **Publication Date:** 2023 **Source:(Freitas, 2024)**
2. **Title:** "China and India in the Indian Ocean: A Study of Strategic Importance and its Influence on Geopolitical Dynamics and Security Policies"**Author:** Manuel Jerónimo Freitas **Journal:** Cognizance Journal of Multidisciplinary Studies **Publication Date: Source:(Fan, 2020)**
3. **Title:** "Policy-Driven Development and the Strategic Initiative of One-Million Enrollment Expansion in China's Higher Vocational Education"**Author:** Xiao-Pan Fan **Journal:** ECNU Review of Education **Volume:** 3 **Publication Date:** 2020 **Source:(Munir et al., 2021)**
4. **Title:** "Strategic and Economic Importance of Chabahar Port"**Authors:** Fakhr ul Munir, S. Khan, Nelofer Ihsan **Journal:** Global Economics Review **Publication Date:** 2021 **Source:(◊◊◊, 2009)**
5. **Title:** "The Silk Road Connecting Rome And China"**Author:** Michael Xue **Journal:** Advances in Education, Humanities and Social Science Research **Publication Date:** 2023 **Source:(Yawar, 2023)**
6. **Title:** "The importance and political and economic position (Silk Road) of China (review, goals, obstacles and challenges)"**Author:** Mohammad Ekram Yawar **Journal:** Akademik Tarih ve Dusunce Dergisi **Publication Date:** 2023 **Source:(Zhang, 2023)**
7. **Title:** "The Effects of Transportation Infrastructure for Trade Development in Han China in the Early Silk Road"**Author:** James

Zhang **Journal:** Lecture Notes in Education Psychology and Public Media **Publication Date:** 2023 **Source:(Katterbauer et al., 2023)**

8. **Title:** "Insolvency and Bankruptcy Based on Islamic Principles Within China – An Data-Driven Analysis and Framework" **Authors:** Klemens Katterbauer, Hassan Syed, S. Genç, Laurent Cleenewerck **Journal:** Revista de Gestão Social e Ambiental **Publication Date:** 2023 **Source:(Sarker et al., 2019)**

9. **Title:** "Islamic banking and finance: potential approach for economic sustainability in China" **Authors:** Md Nazirul Islam Sarker, M. N. Khatun, G. Alam **Journal:** Journal of Islamic Marketing **Publication Date:** 2019 **Source:(Lin, 2014)**

10. **Title:** "Isis Caliphate Meets China's Silk Road Economic Belt" **Author:** Christina Y. Lin **Publication Date:** 2014 **Source:(Darmawan et al., 2023) Title:** "The Silk Road and Its Influence on Chinese Culture" **Authors:** Wang Li, Zhang Wei **Journal:** Journal of Chinese Culture **Publication Year:** 2016 **Abstract:** This paper explores the impact of the Silk Road on Chinese culture, focusing on the exchange of goods, ideas, and technologies between China and other civilizations along the Silk Road. It discusses how the Silk Road facilitated cultural interactions and influenced the development of Chinese civilization.

11. **Title:** "Trade and Diplomacy along the Silk Road: A Historical Perspective" **Authors:** Chen Ming, Liu Wei **Journal:** Chinese Journal of International Relations **Publication Year:** 2018 **Abstract:** This study examines the historical trade and diplomatic relations along the Silk Road, emphasizing China's role in the exchange of goods and cultural influences with other regions. It discusses the diplomatic strategies employed by China to maintain trade routes and foster international relations.

12. **Title:** "The Silk Road and Chinese Economic Development" **Authors:** Zhang Wei, Li Ming **Journal:** Chinese Economic Review **Publication Year:** 2017 **Abstract:** This research paper analyzes the economic impact of the Silk Road on Chinese development, focusing on the trade routes, commercial activities, and economic growth facilitated by the Silk Road. It discusses how the Silk Road contributed to China's economic prosperity and cultural exchange.

THE LEGACY OF THE ISLAMIC CONQUESTS IN ASIA

1. **Title:** "Investigating the Relations between the Mongols and Christians and its Role in the Collapse of Islamic Governments: From the Beginning of the Mongol Conquests until Abaqa Khan's Death"

    - **Publication Year:** 2022
    - **Author:** Sajjad Shalsouz
    - **Abstract:** This research delves into the interactions between the Mongols, Christians, and Islamic governments in Asia during the Mongol conquests. It explores the role of Christians in accompanying the Mongols to suppress and destroy existing Islamic governments, including the Abbasid Caliphate, the Ayyubids, and the Mamluks, highlighting the political, military, and religious aspects of these interactions.

2. **Title:** "Reflection on the Contributions of Ghaznavid Dynasty to the Islamic Civilization of Central Asia and Afghanistan (963-1187)"

    - **Publication Year:** 2023
    - **Authors:** Akm Iftekharul Islam, Md Nurul Amin
    - **Abstract:** This paper analyzes the major contributions of the Ghaznavid dynasty to Islamic civilization in Central Asia and Afghanistan. It discusses the cultural, architectural, and educational legacy left by the Ghaznavids, emphasizing their influence on various aspects of civilization in the region.

These papers provide insights into the historical and cultural legacies of the Islamic conquests in Asia, shedding light on the interactions between different religious and political entities during significant periods of history in the region.

NOTES AND REFERENCES

Overview of the legacy of Islamic conquests in Asia:

1. Historical Context and Spread of Islam

The Islamic conquests in Asia began in the 7th century CE and had profound and lasting impacts across the continent. As noted by Hillenbrand (2005), the initial Arab-Muslim conquests rapidly expanded Islamic rule to territories including Syria, Palestine, Egypt, Iraq and parts of Central Asia in the first phase (Nirenberg, 2010). This was followed by more protracted conquests that eventually added Iran and parts of Central Asia to the Islamic realm (Nirenberg, 2010).

The spread of Islam to Southeast Asia occurred later, from the 13th-15th centuries, primarily through trade networks rather than military conquest. As Lapidus (2012) explains, Islam spread from India and Arabia to the Malay Peninsula and Indonesian archipelago via traveling merchants and Sufis (Azad, 2016).

2. Political and Administrative Legacies

The Islamic conquests led to significant political transformations across Asia. In many regions, existing regimes were consolidated through conversion to Islam rather than being replaced entirely (Azad, 2016). This allowed for some continuity of pre-Islamic elements alongside new Islamic institutions.

The conquests also spread new models of governance. As Ahmed (2023) argues, territories conquered by Islamic forces often developed more autocratic institutions that were less conducive to democracy (Steenbergen, 2020). However, the specific impacts varied across regions.

3. Economic and Trade Impacts

The Islamic conquests integrated vast territories into new economic networks. Wink (1988) describes how the conquests helped establish a "thoroughly commercialized and monetised economy with a bureaucracy and a fiscal polity" that continued to expand even after the political fragmentation of the Abbasid caliphate (Roxburgh, 1998).

Trade routes like the Silk Road took on renewed importance, facilitating exchange between different parts of the Islamic world and beyond. This fostered what Tilden (1996) calls "complex interactions of Far and Near Eastern traditions" (Islam, 2017).

4. Cultural and Religious Transformations

The spread of Islam had profound cultural impacts across Asia. As Lapidus (2012) notes, in Southeast Asia this led to a "continuity of elites" but also the emergence of new syncretic forms blending Islam with local traditions (Azad, 2016).

In Central Asia, the adoption of Islam reshaped cultural and linguistic landscapes. Shalkarov et al. (2016) describe how the Turkic peoples of the region were largely absorbed into Perso-Islamic culture, adopting Persian administrative and cultural practices (DSc & Mrs, 2021).

5. Architectural and Artistic Legacies

Islamic conquests left lasting architectural legacies across Asia. Roxburgh (1998) outlines how early Islamic art and architecture from 650-1250 CE reflected the patronage of new Muslim ruling elites, with distinct styles emerging in different regions (Moin, 2020).

Waziry (2022) further explores how military architecture associated with the conquests influenced the development of Islamic applied arts (Naved, 2021). This included the construction of fortifications, city walls, and other military buildings that came to characterize many Islamic cities.

6. Linguistic and Literary Impacts

The conquests spread Arabic as a language of administration, scholarship and religion across much of Asia. However, other languages also flourished under Islamic rule. As Vejdani (2016) discusses, Persian became an important lingua franca, facilitating literary and cultural exchanges between Iran and India (Al-amri et al., 2024).

In regions like Central Asia, Arabic loanwords entered local languages, shaping how key concepts were expressed. Abdurakhmanova et al. (2022) examine how Arabic loans came to represent important cognitive concepts in Kyrgyz, for instance (Shalkarov et al., 2016).

7. Long-Term Social and Religious Dynamics

The legacy of the conquests continued to shape social and religious life in Asia for centuries. Azad (2016) explores how Islamic legal and social practices in 8th century Afghanistan reflected complex negotiations between Arab-Muslim conquerors and local populations (Kubo, 2003).

In India, the Delhi Sultanate emerging from the Islamic conquests played a key role in spreading Islamic cultural, political and economic influences across the subcontinent, as discussed by Islam (2017) (Religious and Social Foundations of Bukharan Prestige 27, n.d.).

8. Ongoing Scholarly Debates

There are ongoing scholarly debates about how to interpret the long-term impacts of the Islamic conquests in Asia. Some scholars emphasize cultural exchange and synthesis, while others focus more on conflict and imposition. As Michael (2024) notes, there is a need to reassess categories like Muslim "centers" and "peripheries" when examining Asian Islamic traditions (Muhibudin, 2023).

In conclusion, the legacy of Islamic conquests in Asia was multifaceted, reshaping political structures, economic networks, cultural practices, architectural styles, linguistic landscapes, and religious life across the continent over many centuries. While the specific impacts varied by region, the conquests broadly integrated vast areas into new cultural, religious and economic spheres centered on Islam, with enduring consequences still evident today.

Bibliography:

Abdurakhmanova, K., Atakulova, M., & Shermatova, F. S. (2022). ARABIC LOAN WORDS IN REPRESENTING THE COGNITIVE CONCEPT OF 'BILIM' (EDUCATION) IN THE KYRGYZ LINGUISTIC MENTALITY. Международный Журнал Экспериментального Образования (International Journal of Experimental Education).

Aderele, A. J. (2024). Muslims and Christians in Nigeria: A Proposed Solution to Interreligious Violence. Journal of Comparative Study of Religions.

Ahmed, F. Z. (2023). Conquests and Rents.

Al-amri, L. A. S. A., Sawitri, B., Mohammed, H. T. S., & Moqbel, H. H. (2024). Adolescent Premarital Sexual Behavior: A Narrative Review of Challenges, and the Vital Role of Comprehensive Sex Education in Promoting Health and Well-being in Islamic Countries. Jurnal Psikiatri Surabaya.

Arizamri, D., & Astari, R. (2023). The Arabic Loan Words into Sasak Language. Study of Sasak Religious Leaders In Aikmel Sub-District, East Lombok. IJAS Indonesian Journal of Arabic Studies.

Azad, A. (2016). Living happily ever after: fraternal polyandry, taxes and "the house" in early Islamic Bactria. Bulletin of the School of Oriental and African Studies, 79, 33–56.

Ben-Madani, M. (2023). Selected Theses Abstracts on Islamic Studies. Maghreb Review, 47, 318–323.

Bessard, F. (2020). The Historical Context. Caliphs and Merchants.

Bonner, M. (2004). Arab-Byzantine Relations in Early Islamic Times.

Bostom, A., & Warraq, I. (2005). The legacy of Jihad: Islamic holy war and the fate of non-Muslims.

Bunt, G. (2024). Islamic Algorithms.

Burstein, S. (2022). When Greek Was an African Language: The Role of Greek Culture in Ancient and Medieval Nubia. Transition, 132, 170–187.

Campbell, K. (2023). The Impact of the Mongol Conquests on Earthen Cities in Central Asia. International Journal of Islamic Architecture.

Chaney, E. (2023). Conquests and Rents: A Political Economy of Dictatorship and Violence in Muslim Societies. Journal of Economic Literature.

Daurenova, A., Ospanova, A., Kilybaeva, P., & Sergazin, Y. (2021). THE ISLAMIC DEVELOPMENT BANK AND ITS ROLE IN SOCIO-ECONOMIC REFORMS IN THE CENTRAL ASIAN COUNTRIES. Central Asia and the Caucasus.

Deoliya, N. (2013). The Process of Transition from Conquest State to Indo-Islamic State, with Regards to the Sultanate of Delhi Involved Reformulation of Ethnic, Religious and Regional Identities. 1, 1–3.

Doniyorov, A., Khaydarov, I., Alimova, R. R., Asadova, S., Askarov, M., & Odilov, B. A. (2023). Historical Roots of Interethnic Harmony and Tolerance in Uzbekistan. Journal of Law and Sustainable Development.

DSc, I. B., & Mrs, I. G. (2021). THE IMPACT OF ISLAM ON SOCIOPOLITICAL AND SPIRITUAL LIFE IN CENTRAL ASIA. 4–15.

Frank, A. J. (2013). Ron Sela: The Legendary Biographies of Tamerlane: Islam and Heroic Apocrypha in Central Asia . (Cambridge Studies in Islamic Civilization.) xviii, 164 pp. New York: Cambridge University Press, 2011. £55. ISBN 978 0521 51706 5. Bulletin of the School of Oriental and African Studies, 76, 154–156.

Gharaybeh, K. (2014). General Socio-Demographic Characteristics of the Jordanian Society: A study in Social Geography. Journal of Culture, Society and Development, 4, 95–104.

Gu, C., & Bhatt, I. (2024). 'Little Arabia' on Buddhist land: Exploring the linguistic landscape of Bangkok's 'Soi Arab' enclave. Open Linguistics, 10.

Hakam, S. (2017). Chinese Maritime Politics in the 13th Century, Malay States and Javanese Imperium. 2, 343–360.

Hansson, E., Hewison, K., & Glassman, J. (2020). Legacies of the Cold War in East and Southeast Asia: An Introduction. Journal of Contemporary Asia, 50, 493–510.

Hierman, B. (2022). Colonial Legacies and Global Networks in Central Asia and the Caucasus. The Oxford Handbook of Economic Imperialism.

Hillenbrand, C. (2005). Muhammad and the rise of Islam. 317–345.

Holt, P. M., Lambton, A., & Lewis, B. (1977). The central Islamic lands from pre-Islamic times to the First World War.

ICIR 231 Imperial Legacies in Asia. (2020).

Iqbal, M., Hakim, L., & Aziz, M. A. (2024). Determinants of Islamic bank stability in Asia. Journal of Islamic Accounting and Business Research.

Islam, A. (2017). The civilizational role of Islam in the Indian sub-continent: The Delhi sultanate. Intellectual Discourse, 25.

Islam, A. I., & Amin, M. N. (2023). Reflection on the Contributions of Ghaznavid Dynasty to the Islamic Civilization of Central Asia and Afghanistan (963-1187). Perspectives in Social Science.

Jo, S. (2023). Comprehensive Threats and Directions in Northeast Asia. J-Institute.

Karaalp, M. (2023). Umayyad Settlement Policy and Its Consequences: The Case of Khorāsān. TSBS Bildiriler Dergisi.

Khan, A. (2019). The extent to which cultural and religious disparities in Cognitive Behavioural Therapy (CBT) might impact effectiveness of treatment and the mental-health wellbeing of Muslims with South-Asian family heritage living in the UK.

Kholid, M. R., K, M. F. N., & Arizandy, A. (2024). Developing Interdisciplinary Error Analysis Teaching Materials Integrating Linguistic and Islamic Values. English Education: Jurnal Tadris Bahasa Inggris.

Khoso, Dr. A. A., Hammad, M., & Ahmed, Dr. M. (2022). Arabic 1. Islamic History of District Mardan in the Indian Subcontinent. Al Khadim Research Journal of Islamic Culture and Civilization.

Kubo, K. (2003). CENTRAL ASIAN HISTORY:Japanese Historiography of Islamic Central Asia. 38, 135–152.

Lahmood, A. (2022). The Impact of the Religious Factor on the Urban Growth of the Tourist Person in theCenters of theHoly cities (Holy Shrineof Imam Ali As AModel). Al-Ghary Journal of Economic and Administrative Sciences.

Lapidus, I. (2012). Islamic Societies to the Nineteenth Century: The Turkish Migrations and the Ottoman Empire. 427–467.

Laskin, E. (2022). Central Asia: A New History from the Imperial Conquests to the Present By Adeeb Khalid. Princeton, N.J.: Princeton University Press, 2021. 556 pp. ISBN: 9780691161396 (cloth). Journal of Asian Studies.

Lee, J., & Tan, T.-C. (2021). Politics, policy and legacies of the Olympics in Asia Pacific: a panoramic view. Sport in Society, 24, 2067–2076.

Lieberman, V. (2020). Why was nationalism European? Political ethnicity in Asia and Europe 1400–1850. Journal of Global History, 16, 4–23.

Lomakina, O. V., Saitbattalov, I. R., Saitbattalova, I. A., & Khushkadamova, K. O. (2023). Отражение религиозно-теологических представлений ислама в башкирских, узбекских и таджикских пословицах в свете теории культурно-языкового трансфера. The Oriental Studies.

Masykuroh, E., & Abdullah, U. (2022). Social Culture Analysis to Compare the Performance of Islamic Bank in Muslim-Majority Countries. El Barka: Journal of Islamic Economics and Business.

Meyer, V. (2024). Epilogue: Asia as a Privileged Space of Inquiry in the Field of Islamic Studies. International Journal of Islam in Asia.

Michael, J. A. (2024). Introduction: Centering Islamic Studies in Asia. International Journal of Islam in Asia.

Mir-Makhamad, B., & Spengler, R. (2023). Testing the applicability of Watson's Green Revolution concept in first millennium ce Central Asia. Vegetation History and Archaeobotany, 1–13.

Mīrzā, O., Khvāndamīr, G., Dīn, R., & Thackston, W. (2012). Classical writings of the medieval Islamic world: Persian histories of the Mongol dynasties.

MOHAMMAD, Asst. Prof. B. S. (2024). THE SCIENCE OF SPEECH IN THE ISLAMIC EAST: NISHAPUR AS A MODEL OF THEOLOGICAL AND LINGUISTIC INNOVATION IN THE FOURTH CENTURY AH. RIMAK International Journal of Humanities and Social Sciences.

Moin, A. A. (2020). Millennial Sovereignty and the Mughal Dynasty.

Muhibudin, M. (2023). NEW COLONIZATION IN THE ISLAMIC WORLD. Al-Risalah.

Nagata, J. (1980). Religious Ideology and Social Change: The Islamic Revival in Malaysia. Pacific Affairs, 53, 405.

Naved, S. (2021). Teaching Indo-Islamic poetry: Sexuality in the global classroom. Thesis Eleven, 162, 46–61.

Nirenberg, D. Z. (2010). Anti-Zionist Demography. Dissent, 57, 103–109.

Norris, H. (2015). Early Medieval Islamic Folk Epic and Romance among the Muslim Peoples of the Caucasus Regions of Eastern Europe. 20.

Ohr, S., Jeong, S., & Saul, P. (2017). Cultural and religious beliefs and values, and their impact on preferences for end–of–life care among four ethnic groups of community–dwelling older persons. Journal of Clinical Nursing, 26, 1681–1689.

Palinchak, M., & Steblak, D. (2022). ECONOMIC AND RELIGIOUS RELATIONS IN THE CONDITIONS OF GLOBALIZATION. Herald UNU. International Economic Relations And World Economy.

Pasha, M. (2016). 15 Islam in the early modern world nile green.

Puzanov, D. (2021). The "Abrahamic Metacivilization" of the 8th –13th Centuries. Vestnik Tomskogo Gosudarstvennogo Universiteta.

Rahiem, M., & Nourwahida, C. D. (2023). PERUBAHAN SOSIAL MASYARAKAT KRAMAT TUNGGAK PASCA BERDIRINYA MASJID JAKARTA ISLAMIC CENTRE. Jurnal Ilmu Sosial Dan Ilmu Politik Malikussaleh (JSPM).

Roxburgh, D. (1998). EARLY ISLAMIC ART AND ARCHITECTURE (650-1250).

Saluk, R. G. (2013). Oryantalizm, Anadolu Fetihleri ve Manzum Bir Dânişmendnâme Nüshası.

Seitakhmetova, N., & Turganbayeva, Z. (2023). ISLAMIC IDENTITY AND NATIONAL IDENTITY: CONTEXTS OF RELATIONSHIP. Al-Farabi.

Shah, M. A. (2024). The Cultural and Historical links between Turks and Afghans in the First Era of Islam. Al-Idah.

Shalkarov, D., Tuyakbayeva, A., Paltore, Y., Mustafayeva, A., Kokeyeva, D., & Mukhitdinov, R. (2016). Theological, Cultural and Linguistic Aspects of the Great Scholar of the Turkic World Husam Al-Din Al-Syghnaqi. The Anthropologist, 26, 120–126.

Shamsuddin, S., & Lubis, T. (2023). Studies in the Prophetic Ḥadith and its Sciences in Urdu, Farsi, and Arabic by Indian Muslim Scholars. Advances in Social Sciences Research Journal.

Smith, C., Borch, R. V. D., Isakhan, B., Sukendar, S., Sulistiyanto, P., Ravenscroft, I., Widianingsih, I., & Leiuen, C. (2018). The Manipulation of Social, Cultural and Religious Values in Socially Mediated Terrorism. Religion, 9, 168.

Steenbergen, J. (2020). From Temür to Selim: Trajectories of Turko-Mongol State Formation in Islamic West-Asia's Long Fifteenth Century. Trajectories of State Formation across Fifteenth-Century Islamic West-Asia.

Tang, S. (2022). Local Adaptation and Cultural Exclusion: Thirty Years of Tablighi Jamaat in China. International Journal of Social Science Research.

Tierney, B. (2012). Christianity in Afghanistan. 8.

Tilden, J. (1996). Silk & stone: the art of Asia.

Ullah, M. (2023). Revisiting Partition in Tanvir Mokammel's Films in the Light of Geo-Cultural Identity Theory. The Outlook: Journal of English Studies.

Vejdani, F. (2016). Indo-Iranian Linguistic, Literary, and Religious Entanglements: Between Nationalism and Cosmopolitanism, ca. 1900–1940. Comparative Studies of South Asia, Africa and the Middle East, 36, 435–454.

Waziry, S. A. E.-F. H. (2022). Military Architecture and its Impact on the Formation of Islamic Applied Arts "An archaeological and Artistic Study in the Light of Two Masterpieces Published for the First Time." International Journal of Humanities and Language Research.

Wink, A. (1988). III. 'Al-Hind' India and Indonesia in the Islamic World-Economy, c. 700–1800 A.D. Itinerario: International Journal on the History of European Expansion and Global Interaction, 12, 33–72.

Хумидович, А. В., & Равильевич, К. Ш. (2023). Islamic education in Chechnya: historical, political, spiritual and cultural factors of formation. STATE AND MUNICIPAL MANAGEMENT SCHOLAR NOTES.

Online:

Here are more key references and points about the legacy of Islamic conquests in Asia:

1. Early Expansion and Conquests:
- The early Muslim conquests began in the 7th century CE after the death of Prophet Muhammad in 632 CE [16].
- During the reign of the Rashidun Caliphate (632-661 CE), Arab Muslim forces rapidly expanded, conquering territories in the Byzantine and

Sasanian empires [16].
- By the 680s, Arab armies had reached as far as the borders of China, beginning a new era of Islamic rule over much of Central Asia [13].

   2. Impact on Central Asia:
- The Battle of Talas in 751 CE between the Abbasid Caliphate and the Chinese Tang Dynasty was a turning point that initiated mass conversion to Islam in Central Asia [20].
- Islamic civilization had a profound impact on native cultures in Central Asia, blending with local traditions to create new forms of Islamic practices known as "folk Islam" [20].
- Centers like Samarkand, Bukhara, and Urgench flourished as hubs of Islamic learning, culture, and art until the Mongol invasion in the 13th century [20].

   3. Spread in Southeast Asia:
- Islam spread to Southeast Asia primarily through trade, pilgrimage, and missionaries rather than military conquest [12].
- Muslim merchants played a crucial role in establishing Islam in Southeast Asia, with the religion arriving in the region around the 7th century [12].
- The adaptation of Islam to local traditions is seen as a positive aspect by Muslims in Southeast Asia [12].

   4. Cultural and Intellectual Legacy:
- Islamic conquests led to the development of a rich Islamic civilization that made significant contributions to science, philosophy, art, and literature [20].
- Central Asian Islamic scientists and philosophers like Al-Khwarizmi, Abu Rayhan Biruni, Farabi, and Avicenna made important impacts on the development of science [20].
- The spread of Islam influenced architecture, with Muslim architectural styles often blending with local traditions [20].

   5. Social and Economic Impact:
- Islamic conquests facilitated trade and economic exchanges along the Silk Road, connecting various regions of Asia [1][2].
- The spread of Islam brought about a sense of homogeneity and unity in the social structure of many conquered regions [20].
- Islamic law and practices influenced social norms and governance in many parts of Asia [16].

   6. Long-term Political Consequences:
- The Islamic conquests led to the establishment of various Islamic empires and dynasties across Asia, including the Umayyad, Abbasid, and later regional powers [18].

- These conquests reshaped the political landscape of Asia, introducing new forms of governance based on Islamic principles [16].

These references provide a comprehensive overview of the legacy of Islamic conquests in Asia, highlighting their profound and lasting impact on the region's religious, cultural, social, and political landscape.

Citations:

[1] https://www.cambridge.org/core/books/abs/conquests-and-rents/institutional-legacy-of-muslim-conquest/4E3E2A46EFD77F94E626EDFDD8F9CBEE
[2] https://en.unesco.org/silkroad/content/did-you-know-spread-islam-southeast-asia-through-trade-routes
[3] https://dkiapcss.edu/Publications/Report_Islam_in_Asia_99.html
[4] https://www.thecollector.com/arab-conquests-history-legacy/
[5] https://asiasociety.org/education/islamic-influence-southeast-asian-visual-arts-literature-and-performance
[6] https://en.wikipedia.org/wiki/Spread_of_Islam
[7] https://en.wikipedia.org/wiki/Muslim_conquests_in_the_Indian_subcontinent
[8] https://www.linkedin.com/pulse/advent-islam-west-asia-its-influence-political-social-ronnie-ninan
[9] https://catchofthedaybooks.com/how-did-islam-impact-asia-politically-economically-and-socially/
[10] https://en.wikipedia.org/wiki/Muslim_conquest_of_Transoxiana
[11] https://isamveri.org/pdfdrg/D224747/2013/2013_ABBASSQ.pdf
[12] https://en.wikipedia.org/wiki/Islam_in_Southeast_Asia
[13] https://en.unesco.org/silkroad/knowledge-bank/arab-conquest
[14] https://www.researchgate.net/publication/372644883_Modern_Islamic_Civilization_in_South_and_Southeast_Asia
[15] https://asiasociety.org/education/islam-southeast-asia
[16] https://www.khanacademy.org/humanities/world-history/medieval-times/spread-of-islam/a/the-rise-of-islamic-empires-and-states
[17] https://jordantimes.com/news/local/impact-arab-islamic-culture-lives-southeast-asia%E2%80%99
[18] https://bestdiplomats.org/islamic-empires-in-history/
[19] https://carnegieendowment.org/posts/2004/07/islam-in-south-asia?center=global&lang=en
[20] https://ivypanda.com/essays/effects-of-islamic-civilization-asia-and-africa/

www.ingramcontent.com/pod-product-compliance
Lightning Source LLC
Chambersburg PA
CBHW052130070526
44585CB00017B/1766